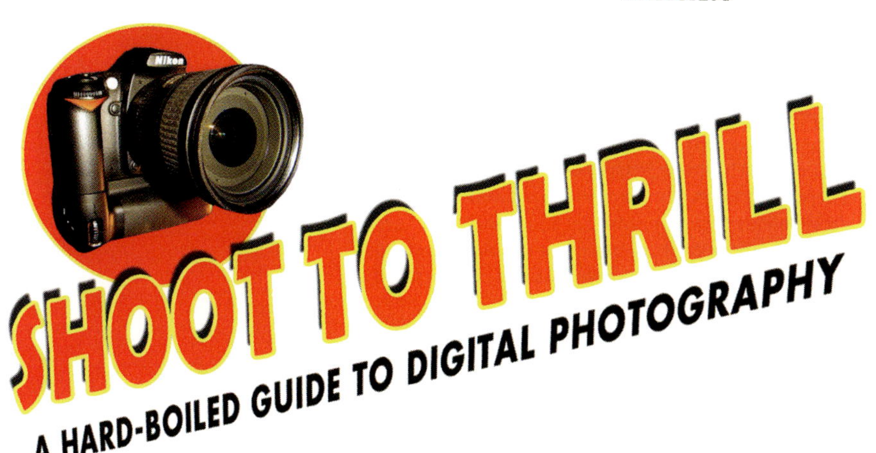

Derek Pell

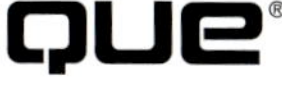

800 East 96th Street, Indianapolis, Indiana 46240 USA

Shoot to Thrill: A Hard-Boiled Guide to Digital Photography

Copyright © 2010 by Derek Pell

Cover photograph by the author.
All photographs in the book are by Derek Pell, except where otherwise indicated.

ISBN-13: 978-0-7897-4240-7
ISBN-10: 0-7897-4240-3

Library of Congress Cataloging-in-Publication Data is on file

Printed in the United States of America

First Printing: September 2009

Trademarks

All terms mentioned in this book that are known to be trademarks or service marks have been appropriately capitalized. Que Publishing cannot attest to the accuracy of this information. Use of a term in this book should not be regarded as affecting the validity of any trademark or service mark.

Warning and Disclaimer

Every effort has been made to make this book as complete and as accurate as possible, but no warranty or fitness is implied. The information provided is on an "as is" basis. The author and the publisher shall have neither liability nor responsibility to any person or entity with respect to any loss or damages arising from the information contained in this book.

Bulk Sales

Que Publishing offers excellent discounts on this book when ordered in quantity for bulk purchases or special sales. For more information, please contact

> **U.S. Corporate and Government Sales**
> **1-800-382-3419**
> **corpsales@pearsontechgroup.com**

For sales outside the United States, please contact

> **International Sales**
> **international@pearson.com**

Associate Publisher
Greg Wiegand

Acquisitions Editor
Laura Norman

Development Editor
Laura Norman

Managing Editor
Patrick Kanouse

Senior Project Editor
Tonya Simpson

Copy Editor
Karen Gill

Indexer
Ken Johnson

Technical Editor
Robyn Ness

Publishing Coordinator
Cindy Teeters

CONTENTS AT A GLANCE

Introduction: THE F STOPS HERE   3

Prologue: I COVER THE WATERGATE   7

1. **PACKIN' HEAT:** *Gear for the Gumshoe Shutterbug*   15

2. **CALL FOR BACKUP!** *Defend & Protect Your Photos*   31

3. **PRIVATE EYES:** *Look Before You Shoot*   49

4. **HAND-TO-CAM COMBAT:** *From Auto Pilot to Taking Control*   67

5. **TWINKLE, TWINKLE LITTLE NOIR:** *Ambient Light and Flash*   89

6. **A THIRST FOR BURST:** *Thrilling Action Adventures*   119

7. **FROM CHUMP TO CHAMP:** *Tampering with Photos*   139

8. **THE DEVIL IS IN THE DETAILS**   171

9. **"I'VE BEEN FRAMED!":** *Showing Off in Public*   199

10. **"PLAY IT AGAIN, CAM...."** *The Future Is DV*   215

A. **HOT LINKS, COOL LEADS**   229

B. **A HARD-BOILED LIBRARY**   239

Index   247

TABLE OF CONTENTS

INTRODUCTION: **THE F STOPS HERE** 3

PROLOGUE: **I COVER THE WATERGATE** 7

CHAPTER 1 **PACKIN' HEAT** 15

THE D-SLR 16

ASSAULT & BATTERIES 18

MEMORY CARDS 20

GEAR BAGS 22

LEGS 24

FLASH 24

CHEAP THRILLS: ODDS 'N ENDS 26

AUTHOR'S NOTE: 29

CHAPTER 2 **CALL FOR BACKUP!** 31

HOW MANY BACKUPS ARE ENOUGH? 32

IF THE MOB CAN GET ORGANIZED, SO CAN YOU 34

PHOTOSHOP, LIGHTROOM, & BRIDGE, OH MY! 35

CREATING A CUSTOM PRESET 38

THE BRIDGE 39

A VIEW FROM THE BRIDGE 41

CHAPTER 3 **PRIVATE EYES** 49

SLEEP MODE 49

METHOD ACTING: COMEDY OR TRAGEDY? 50

YOU'RE THE LEAD, NOT THE WALK-ON 51

FIND THE A.N.G.E.L. 52

ANOMALY 54

GESTURE 58

EXPRESSION 63

CHAPTER 4   HAND-TO-CAM COMBAT **67**

GET TO KNOW YOUR ISO 68

WHOSE WHITE BALANCE IS IT, ANYWAY? 70

METERING PATTERNS 75

MATRIX METERING 75

SPOT METERING 76

CENTER-WEIGHTED METERING 76

PLAY IT AGAIN, S.A.M. 77

APERTURE PRIORITY 78

SHUTTER PRIORITY (S) 82

MANUAL MODE (M) 83

PROGRAMMED-AUTO (P) 84

BUSTING THE BRACKET RACKET 84

EXPOSURE COMPENSATION (EV) 86

CHAPTER 5   TWINKLE, TWINKLE LITTLE NOIR **89**

AMBIENT LIGHT 90

IMAGINING LIGHT AND RE-CREATING IT 93

NIGHTTIME IS THE RIGHT TIME...FOR NOIR 95

PORTABLE FLASH IS YOUR BUDDY 97

AN OUNCE OF BOUNCE = FILLS & THRILLS 102

GRIDS, SNOOTS, GOBOS, & CHIZZLERS 106

A KNOCKOUT IN THE RING 108

WHAT, ME POP-UP? 111

THE BIG GUNS: STUDIO STROBES 112

COVER STORY 116

CHAPTER 6   A THIRST FOR BURST **119**

SPEED TRAPS: THE CURSE OF BURST 120

   TWIST 'N SHOOT 121

   SCREEN IDLE 121

HOCUS-POCUS, HOKUM-FOCUS 122

"YOU LOOKIN' FOR ACTION?" 125

   GOOD BURST, BAD BURST 128

   LET'S ROLL 130

   "EVERYBODY FREEZE!" 133

THERE'S MORE TO BURST THAN SPORTS 135

TAKE A BREAK FROM THE ACTION AND LOOK AROUND136

CHAPTER 7   FROM CHUMP TO CHAMP **139**

DID SOMEBODY CALL THE CROPS? 140

   THE CASE OF THE MISSING SUBJECT 142

   LESS IS MORE...MORE OR LESS 146

   STRETCHIN' THE TRUTH 148

SHARPEN ME DEADLY 152

"HAVE YOU TRIED CALLING NOISE ABATEMENT?" 156

MANIPULATIONS, GREAT AND SMALL 157

   TRICK OR TREAT? 160

ART FOR ART'S SAKE (AND FOR PETE'S SAKE, TOO) 162

THERE AIN'T NOTHIN' LIKE A DAME 165

   THE BLEMISH MASTERS 165

CHAPTER 8   THE DEVIL IS IN THE DETAILS **171**

HDRI ON THE STREETS OF SAN DIEGO 174

CHEAP THRILLS CONTEST 177

BYPASS THE BLEACHED BLONDE WITH THE LUGER 182

HIGH PASS: THE KNOCKOUT PUNCH 192

    HIGH PASS THRILLS AND CHILLS 196

CHAPTER 9   **"I'VE BEEN FRAMED!"** **199**

HANGIN' ON THE WEB 200

HANGIN' ON THE WALL 207

A ROGUE'S GALLERY MEETS MOMA 210

PRINT IT FOR POSTERITY 212

CHAPTER 10   **"PLAY IT AGAIN, CAM..."** **215**

"LIGHTS...CAMERAS...LIMITATIONS!" 216

HYBRID ON A HOT TIN ROOF 218

    DV DINNERS 219

    DEAD PANS AND ZOOM GOONS 220

    "WE DIDN'T NEED FACES. WE HAD DIALOGUE." 222

    A DV THRILL 226

THE HAPPY ENDING 226

APPENDIX A   **HOT LINKS, COOL LEADS** **229**

CAMERAS / COMPUTERS / BACKUP / PORTABLE
  DRIVES / PRINTERS 229

MEMORY CARDS 230

TRIPODS / MONOPODS / GORILLAS 230

LIGHTS / LIGHTING ACCESSORIES 230

CAMERA BAGS AND STRAPS 231

ACCESSORIES 231

FRAMES / INKJET PAPERS 232

HARD-BOILED SOFTWARE 232

    INSPIRATION 234

ONLINE PUBS, BLOGS, AND REFERENCE 236

APPENDIX B   A HARD-BOILED LIBRARY **239**

NUTS 'N BOLTS 240

ART PHOTOGRAPHY/CRITICAL WORKS 241

NOIR REFERENCE 242

FICTION 242

DV 244

INDEX **246**

ABOUT THE AUTHOR

Derek Pell is a writer, visual artist, and photographer. He's the author of more than 20 books, including *Morbid Curiosities*, *Doktor Bey's Bedside Bug Book*, *Assassination Rhapsody*, and *The Little Red Book of Adobe LiveMotion*. Novelist Robert Coover calls Pell "*...a wordplay master and a parodist of great wit and cunning.*" Larry McCaffery declared him "*the most wickedly funny writer in America.*" *The New York Times Book Review* referred to him as "*a British misanthrope-humorist*"—despite the fact he was born in New York City. He describes himself as "self-uneducated," although he attended The Art Institute of Chicago and The Goodman School of Drama.

Pell worked as a press photographer for United Press International (UPI) for several years. As a freelance photojournalist, his photographs have appeared in many newspapers and magazines, including *The New York Times Sunday Magazine*, *Rolling Stone*, *Lens Culture*, *L.A. Weekly*, *The London Times*, *New York Magazine*, *Interview*, *The Village Voice*, *American Forests*, and *Zink*.

He created the popular "hard-boiled" column *The Laptop Detective*, which appeared monthly in *PC Laptop Magazine*, and for 12 years served as editor-in-chief of the online technology review, *DingBat*.

Today, Derek lives in San Diego, California, where he edits *Zoom Street* (www.zoomstreet.org), an online magazine devoted to digital photography.

DEDICATION

In memory of my father, Bill Pell… the real photographer in the family.

ACKNOWLEDGMENTS

Thanks to Wendell Sweda for playing a hard-boiled heavy on the cover, and for making the movie version come alive; my son, Nick, for helping with the lights when he'd have rather watched videos; my agent, Neil Salkind, for loving the idea from the beginning and sticking with it through tough times; Linda and Denny, for getting me back to SD so I could soak up the noir; and, finally, my wife Sheila, for putting up with all the macho wisecracks ("Thanks, sweetheart.")

WE WANT TO HEAR FROM YOU!

As the reader of this book, *you* are our most important critic and commentator. We value your opinion and want to know what we're doing right, what we could do better, what areas you'd like to see us publish in, and any other words of wisdom you're willing to pass our way.

As an associate publisher for Que Publishing, I welcome your comments. You can email or write me directly to let me know what you did or didn't like about this book[md]as well as what we can do to make our books better.

Please note that I cannot help you with technical problems related to the topic of this book. We do have a User Services group, however, where I will forward specific technical questions related to the book.

When you write, please be sure to include this book's title and author as well as your name, email address, and phone number. I will carefully review your comments and share them with the author and editors who worked on the book.

Email: feedback@quepublishing.com

Mail: Greg Wiegand
Associate Publisher
Que Publishing
800 East 96th Street
Indianapolis, IN 46240 USA

READER SERVICES

Visit our website and register this book at informit.com/register for convenient access to any updates, downloads, or errata that might be available for this book.

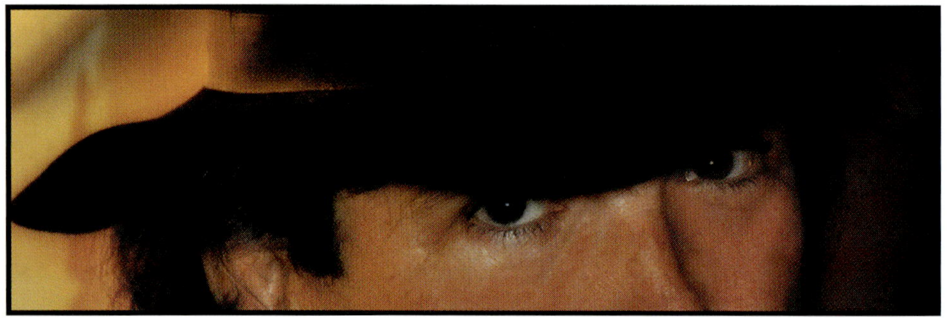

Portrait of the Author as a Hard-Boiled PI. (Photo by Wendell Sweda.)

THE F STOPS HERE

"It was his story against mine, but of course I told my story better."
–Humphrey Bogart (*In a Lonely Place*: 1950)

Nobody move—you're surrounded.

Must be a couple hundred books on digital photography starin' at you. They've all got slick covers, pretty pictures, acknowledgements stretching from here to eternity, technical data, and buzzwords like "workflow." (Whenever I hear that word, I reach for my gun.) You got books written by pro photographers, teachers, technocrats, gadget hacks, computer wizards, maybe a writer or two.

Well, you can bet the farm on this: None were authored by a fiction writer with a case of the hard-boiled, how-to blues. That's no compliment, just the facts.

There's nothin' but sunny-side-up on the subject, packed with enough smiley faces to wallpaper every dentist's office in North America. Believe me, I've read 'em all. I've even learned stuff, too, despite the cloying, *have a nice day* tone. It's enough to make me hit the bottle, but then any excuse'll do. (Truth be told, I'm self-uneducated, and everything I know I got by reading or making mistakes.) Only a few of these books deserve the tag "inspiring," like Joe McNally's *The Moment It Clicks,* David duChemin's *Within the Frame,* and Julie Blackmon's *Domestic Vacations.* The latter is just photos and an interview, but this dame's work is so spectacular it could prod a mob boss to start shootin'. Pictures, that is.

So what's up with the book you're holdin' now?

You've wandered into some strange new territory. Mean streets after hours, where jazz and noir are swirling, and mysteries drift like the smoke from a discharged 6-shot .38 special snub nose. (Thanks for the heat, Chris.) You've stepped smack in the middle of a genre without a name.

Private Eye-Fi? SLR-Noir? Shutterbug Pulp? Call it whatever you want—I'll leave the labels to critics and keep the bottle for myself. Suffice to say, I come to the table with a loaded gun, a loaded cam, and a loaded '40s attitude. And when I finish this bottle of bourbon, I'll be fully loaded.

Hell, to make it through these tough times, you need street smarts and indestructible gear; you need vision (yours, not mine) and a hard-boiled sensibility. Look at it this way—you could do a lot worse. At least this book gives you more slang for your buck.

I started out as a writer and visual artist, not a photographer. First, I wrote poetry that coulda put Ezra Pound to sleep. Then I tossed the meter and veered off that rarefied road into the untamed wilds of satire (*National Lampoon*). I soon lost my appetite for spite and retreated to the distant realm of literary fiction. When I grew bored, I turned to manual labor: collage, mixed media, book objects, and multiples.

Then came a brainstorm: a how-to book on suicide. I was sick to death of reading about *attempted* suicides. Why the hell couldn't people get it right the first time? A primer was called for, so I wrote one—a how-to to end all, literally. Alas, the book wound up killing its publisher. Now that would've stopped most writers in their tracks, but not me. I don't know the meaning of the word *quit*. I went on to write a whole series of self-help books. One, a guide for new parents,* was chosen as a "New and Noteworthy" title by *The New York Times Book Review*. (Go figure, I didn't even have kids.) Would've been a feather in my fedora had they not referred to me as "…a British misanthrope-humorist." I'd never stepped foot in the UK, although some of my best friends were brats.

Okay, so what's all this literary crap got to do with digital photography? Nothing. And everything.

Since I'm the son of a photographer, you might assume I gravitated to the camera at an early age. I didn't. In fact, I had virtually no interest in the medium when I was growin' up. It was simply what somebody

---

Doktor Bey's Book of Brats

in our house did. When the classic movie *Blow-up* came out, kids came up to me and said: "Your old man's a photographer—*cool!*"

That's not the way I saw it. My dad snapped pictures of Mr. Clean, Coke, Jaguars. Big deal. But then one day we were walking through Grand Central Station where, above the big archway, was a billboard-sized Kodak display featuring a breathtaking color shot of downhill racers. He pointed up at it and said, "That's my photograph."

Cool...

My photography came much later, purely by accident, and I reveal the sordid details in the Prologue. The question here is why I wrote this book. I wanted to write the first technical book that reads like a novel. (Go ahead, kill a guy for tryin'.) No, this book is intended—in its own peculiar way—to inspire you to take pictures you've only dreamed about—to explore your own concepts, create visual stories, and capture shots that'll thrill you and everyone around you. I want you to make art with a camera and be fearless in the process.

All of us—amateur and pro alike—take lots of shots destined for the ash heap. It goes with the territory, just as writers slam-dunk crumpled pages and painters paint over their canvases. Yet, as photographers, we strive each day to make a picture that deserves to be framed.

If you can imagine a photo you haven't shot, and the image in your mind excites you, you're halfway there.

Come inside. I've got a few stories to tell that are stranger than fiction. They just might change the way you see.

Derek Pell

San Diego, 2009

Author's Note: I shot most of the photos in this book with a Nikon D90 and refer to its nomenclature. With the exception of the camera's video capability, similar features are found on all recent D-SLRs, so non-Nikon shooters shouldn't feel excluded.

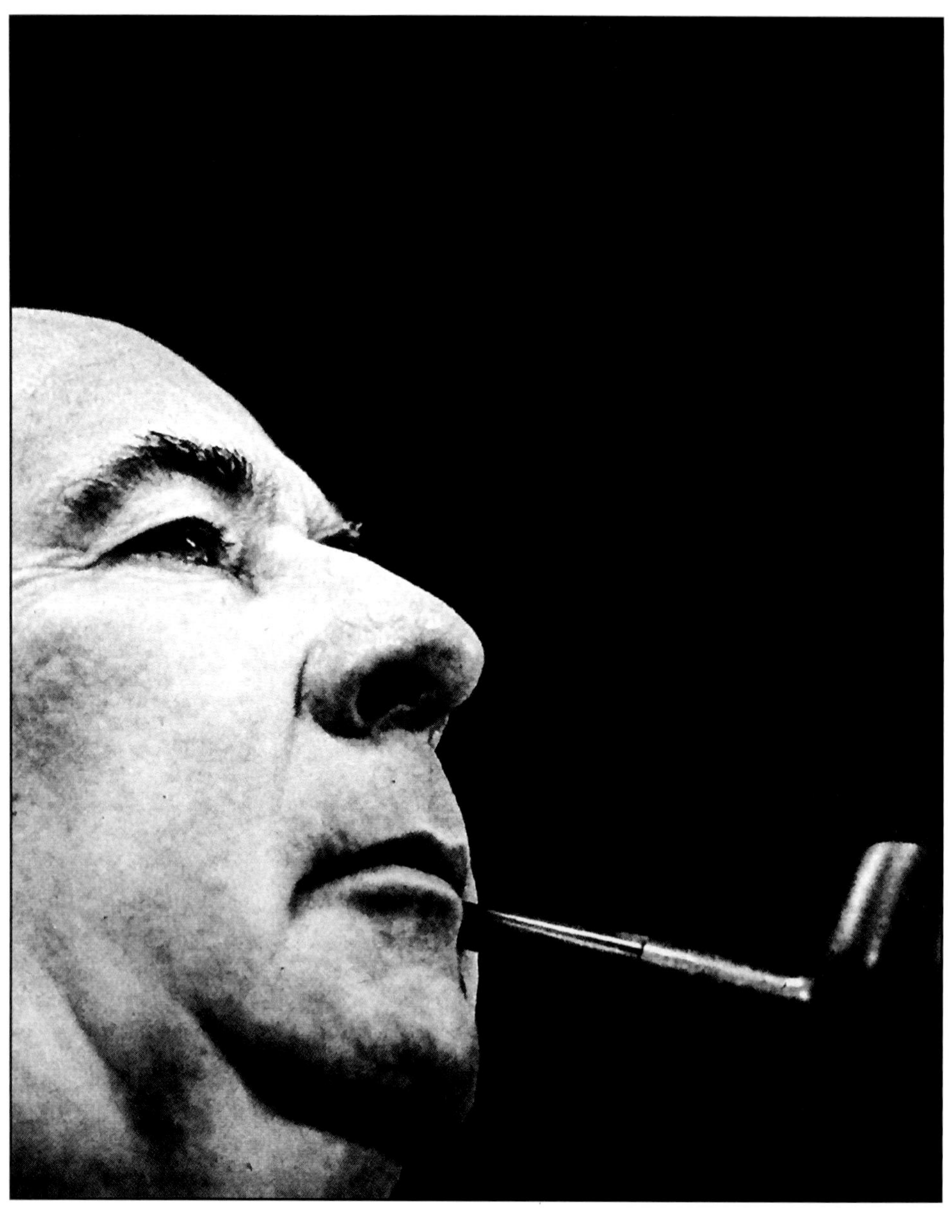

John Mitchell (1973). Photo by Derek Pell.

I COVER THE WATERGATE
From Nixon to Nikon

"He's the quiet sort, and yet you get a feeling if you step out of line you'd get your teeth kicked down your throat."—Born to Kill (1947)

I was hanging around waiting for the big cheese to show. Turns out the chief law enforcement officer in the land was on the wrong side of the law. He'd dipped his hand in some very nasty business and was front page news in every paper in the country. The attorney general of the United States, John Mitchell, was starting to look like just another crook—a common bagman in cahoots with a gang of burglars bent on heisting the U.S. Constitution.

Mitchell was a pipe-sucking thug with an impenetrable, glassy-eyed gaze. He had the smuggest mug I'd ever seen. Of course, I'd never seen him in the flesh, just in newspapers and on TV.

As the Watergate scandal raged, Mitchell's wife Martha started hitting the booze and phoning reporters in the dead of night, hinting she might spill the beans on her hubby and other higher-ups, but feared for her life. Somebody was out to get her… wanted to shut her up for good. She was dismissed by some as just "a crazy drunk" and became the butt of jokes on the late-night talk shows. Others believed she was on the verge of a mental breakdown, trapped in a nightmare because of what she knew.

As it turned out, Watergate would be a nightmare for us all.

The year was 1973, and Washington, DC was awash in paranoia. It was like the movie *Invasion of the Body Snatchers*. You never knew who might turn out to be a pod. People were scared, didn't know who to trust. Rumors swirled around the city like a San Francisco fog. The president, they whispered, had gone off the deep end… was wandering the White House corridors after hours, talking to himself. Every day the headlines grew bolder, screamed new accusations. Big names in the Nixon administration were dropping like flies. And John Mitchell was a biggie.

My job: nail the AG for posterity with a borrowed SLR and a 135mm lens duct-taped to the body.

I wasn't killing time alone in the Senate Caucus Room. The joint was packed with spectators, SRO. A pool TV crew was cooling their Klieg lights, while I stood out like a sore thumb, a tinhorn tourist in a pack of pros. The top White House Press shooters were there—legends all, like Wally McNamee of *Newsweek* and George Thames of *The New York Times*. The wires were present too, of course, AP and UPI, and me… a kid who'd never taken a picture in his life, except with a Polaroid "Swinger."

When I'd first shown up at the hearings weeks before as John Dean was being sworn in, one pro eyed the beat-up Nikon hanging around my neck and turned to another: "Who's the kid with the Mickey Mouse camera?" A burst of gruff laughter burned my ears. My face flushed red.

Good thing I ain't thin-skinned, or I'd have high-tailed it out of Dodge with my tail between my legs. Instead, I took it on the chin.

So what the hell was I doing there, you're probably asking yourself.

I was, in fact, assigned to cover the Senate Watergate Hearings as a writer, not a photographer. I was freelancing for a rag called *Crawdaddy*. Only problem was the magazine couldn't get me press credentials because they weren't considered "mainstream." Thus, I was on my own. It was kind of like landing a plum assignment to cover the Super Bowl from the parking lot. Because the Watergate scandal was one of the biggest in history, every reporter in the country (not to mention hundreds of foreign press) wanted to be in that room. Space was extremely limited, and they were operating on a rotating basis. With the exception of the major print organizations, the wire services, and TV reporters who were granted daily access, the rest of the press could only get a one- or two-day pass and that was it. So, if you worked for the *St. Louis Dispatch* or the *Bloomington Gazette*, you'd get a tiny window of opportunity without knowing who'd be testifying and that was that. Wham-bam. Next!

How I managed to finagle press credentials for the entire summer is a story punctuated by a blast of sucker's luck and mistaken identity. Having grown up in Westport, Connecticut, I knew a dame who headed an organization there called the World Affairs Center—a leftist peace group active in the antiwar movement. It was influential locally, but not a publication. I asked the lady if she'd scrawl a note saying I was covering the hearings for them. She said sure. So I hopped a train to DC, marched into the Press Office, and tossed my note to the sap in charge. He consulted a clipboard, scratched his buzzcut, then handed me a one-week pass and informed me I'd have to return each week to renew it.

I managed to constrain my reaction to a curt nod and a "Thanks, pal…" but once outside I leapt in the air and clicked my heels. Yeah, it was like a bad scene in a Broadway musical, but I was stoked.

How in the hell had *I* gained access reserved for the top echelon of journalism? To this day I haven't cracked it. My hunch is they mistook the organization for *World Affairs* magazine. Or maybe the guy just liked my fedora.

I returned to the Big Apple where I was hangin' my hat at the time, and went to see my old man to tell him the good news. He was a hotshot commercial photographer with a posh studio on Madison Avenue. At one point in our conversation he suggested I take a camera to the hearings. "Since you'll be in the room, you might as well take some shots. You can sell them."

What?

He pried open a dusty cabinet that hadn't seen daylight since the Hoover administration and pulled out an old Nikon F. He didn't use 35mm because, back then, print ads demanded large format. 35mm was the de facto standard for newspapers, but the quality was not up to par for the slicks. The old man usually shot with 4 x 5 Hassel-blads and those giant 8x10 dinosaurs with their heads shrouded with black cloth. But they got the job done. The Nikon, on the other hand, was merely a paperweight.

I took the camera and held it, looking helpless.

"I don't even know how to use it," I said.

"It's easy," he replied. "I'll show you how to load the film."

So began a 15-minute crash course in photography.

Had I known anything about the medium, I would've gotten out of Dodge in a hurry. It was sheer ignorance and an overriding desire to be part of history that gave me the chutzpah to drape that SLR around my neck.

CUT TO: Washington, DC.

Outside the building, a crowd of the curious had gathered, along with protestors waving signs reading "Crime in the Suites!" and "Impeach Tricky Dick!" The Capital was shaking, and so was I as I stood in front of the witness table, guarding my position. I turned to aim the camera at some of the senators on the committee, focus-ing on the famous faces, warming up, so to speak, but not shoot-ing. I'd already taken plenty of shots of the committee members in the preceding weeks. Besides, this was the era of film, and even though I wasn't packin' color (the Nikon was loaded with Tri-X, 36 exposures), it was expensive, and every shot had to count.

Suddenly there were murmurs in the crowd. The TV lights came on. The attorney general was entering the room, surrounded by Secret Service agents and a small band of high-priced lawyers armed with briefcases. True to form, Mitchell strutted through the entrance puffing on his trademark pipe. I don't think smoking was allowed in the building, but this guy was above the law—*literally*.

I found myself trapped in a vice between two beefy pros who elbowed and sucker-shoved me as we clustered around the witness table, jockeying for position. I felt like a high school bench-warmer thrust into an NFL huddle, only it wasn't a huddle, but more like a mugging. Motor-driven Nikons were whirring all around me, while I couldn't even fire a single shot. Just keeping my grip on the camera was tough enough as the competition muscled me out of the game.

As the shutterbugs tightened the vice, I felt my legs start to give. Bang—I was on my knees on the floor. It might all have ended then and there, but I didn't bite the dust. Instead, I aimed the camera up at Mitchell's face, focused, and fired. Click-click-click, until the roll was spent.

There was no telling what I'd captured that day. Would have to wait until the weekend when I returned to the city and handed the film to my old man to process in his darkroom.

As it turned out, I'd managed to nab some striking headshots of Mitchell—pipe in mouth, smoke drifting up into darkness thanks to a very high, unlit ceiling—looking as arrogant as ever. The portrait that was ultimately published was pure beginner's luck, of course. I had those pros to thank for knocking me down and giving me the perfect angle. The other photographers all remained standing, shoving their lenses in the subject's face. In other words, they all got the same shot, and close-ups of the guy's nostrils.

It was with this photo that my career as a photojournalist was launched. I started selling my shots on weekends to magazines and newspapers: *Rolling Stone*, *New York*, *The Village Voice*, and many others. But how could I miss? These publications couldn't get their own photographers on the scene and had to rely on the wire services. Thus, they were clamoring to get their hands on original shots they could byline. One mag actually paid me a grand just to hold three photos for a week, which they wound up not using. Talk about easy dough.

One morning walking through Grand Central Station past a newsstand, I spied two of my photos on the front page of *The Village Voice*. One was a shot of novelist Norman Mailer (see Chapter 3, Fig. 9), the other of John Lennon, both of whom had attended the hearings for a day as spectators. Below the photos was a credit with my name. *Wow*.

I wound up making a lot more moola from my photos than what *Crawdaddy* forked over for the cover story I wrote. It dawned on me that it might be wise to set aside the typewriter for a while and buy myself a camera. No Mickey Mouse job, either, but a top-of-the-line SLR, just like the big boys.

So that's what I did, and I began stringing for UPI, which was conveniently located just a few blocks from my apartment.

It was a wild way to start a career, and the lesson I learned from photographing Mitchell was the most valuable one of all.

Don't follow the pack.

Look for a unique angle, an opening, a view that nobody else has found. Or, as the Italian artist Nanucci wrote: *Always strive to find an interesting variation.*

Shoot for the pure thrill of it, and you'll wind up thrilling others. It's not about what camera you use—it's about your eyes and learning how to see, as if for the first time. Your vision, not mine, is ultimately all that matters.

The rest, like Watergate, is history.

Author's Notes: My photo of John Mitchell was scanned from the pages of *Crawdaddy Magazine.* Alas, the negative has vanished, and I possess no print of the original. The photo was used to illustrate an article by Martin Lewis titled, "John Mitchell in Prison: A Parable." The art editor intentionally cropped it very tight to emphasize Mitchell's future confinement. Otherwise, as a rule with portraits, you'd want to leave plenty of "air" on the right side where the subject is facing, rather than box him in like this. Breaking the rule here made sense.

The 1933 film, *I Cover the Waterfront,* was based on a book by Max Miller, a reporter in San Diego who covered stories on the city's docks. It must be fate because I now hang my hat in Miller's city.

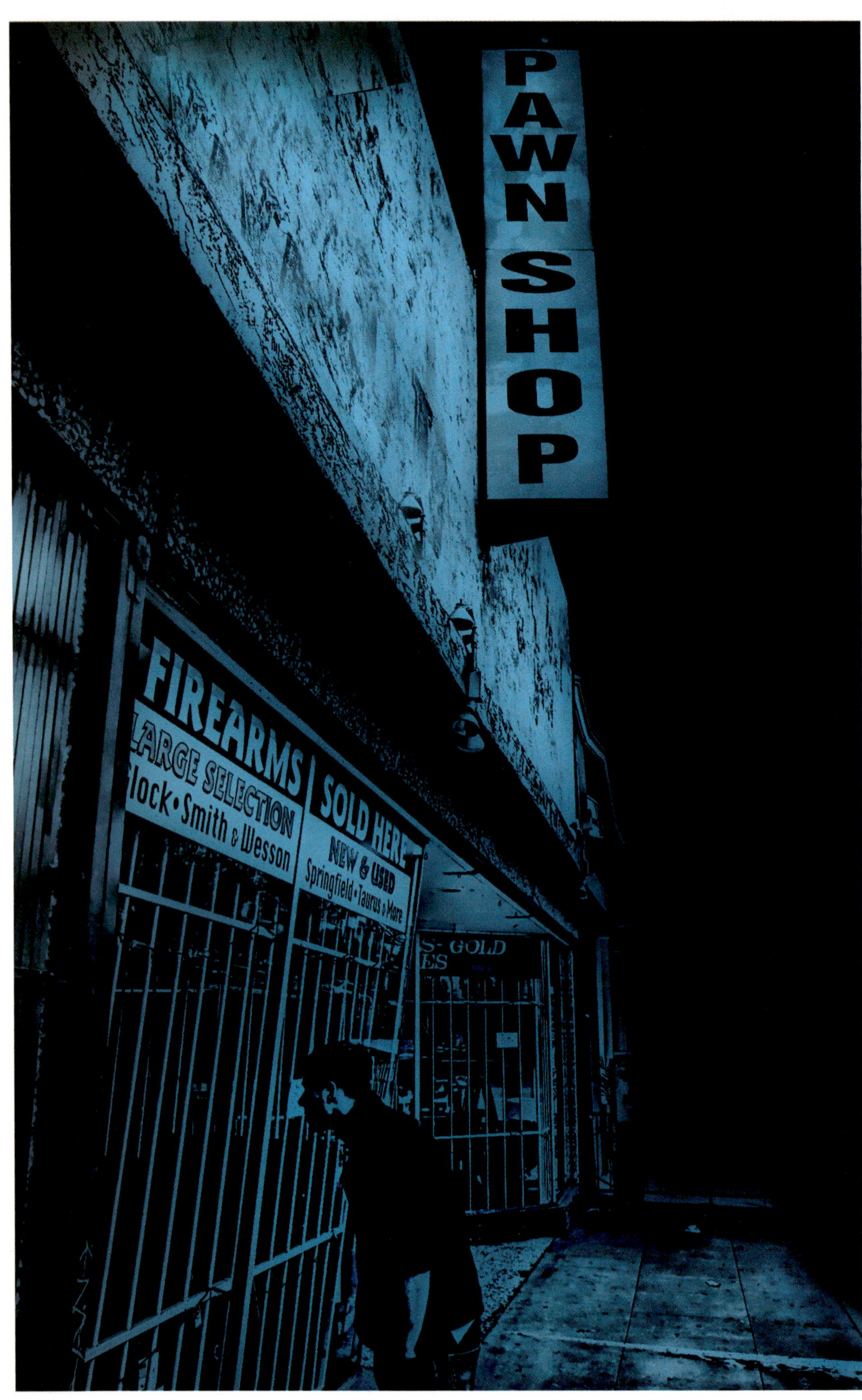

Shop Till You Drop (2009). Photo by Derek Pell.

1

PACKIN' HEAT
Gear for the Gumshoe Shutterbug

"My, my. Such a lot of guns around town and so few brains."—The Big Sleep (1946)

A helluva lot of cams, too. Seems like everybody is armed today, whether with a snub-nosed point-and-shoot, a concealed cell phone, or a full-blown digital SLR, it's a trigger-happy planet we inhabit. Yeah, we're all shutterbugs under the skin, and why not? Digicams are a dime a dozen and *"Look, Ma, no film!"* They're fully automatic and come loaded with Buck Rogers features like "face recognition," "vibration reduction," and "smile detection." *Smile detection??* Somebody please notify the DMV!

I hear the new Hasselblad comes with a wireless decoder ring.

It's almost impossible to take a blurry shot nowadays, even when you're trying. And yet there are a lot of crummy snapshots out there. You see 'em on Flicker, attached to e-mails, hanging by a magnet on the neighbor's fridge, or on the front page of your local newspaper. That's because it's not the camera or the gear that makes the photo—*it's the photographer.* It's like the pro who took an antique "box brownie" to a prize fight and landed the only shot of the knockout punch. He made all the other pros look like saps. And, sheesh, burst mode hadn't even been invented yet. All he had going for him was a an eagle's eye and great timing.

So it ain't the meat, it's the motion. That said, we all like new tools and cool gear. We may be full-grown guys and dolls, but we still like our toys. Rather than drag out everything I own, I'll give you the lowdown on the stuff I find most useful. The obvious and the not so obvious, odds and ends that just might make your day.

First, of course, comes the heat.

THE D-SLR

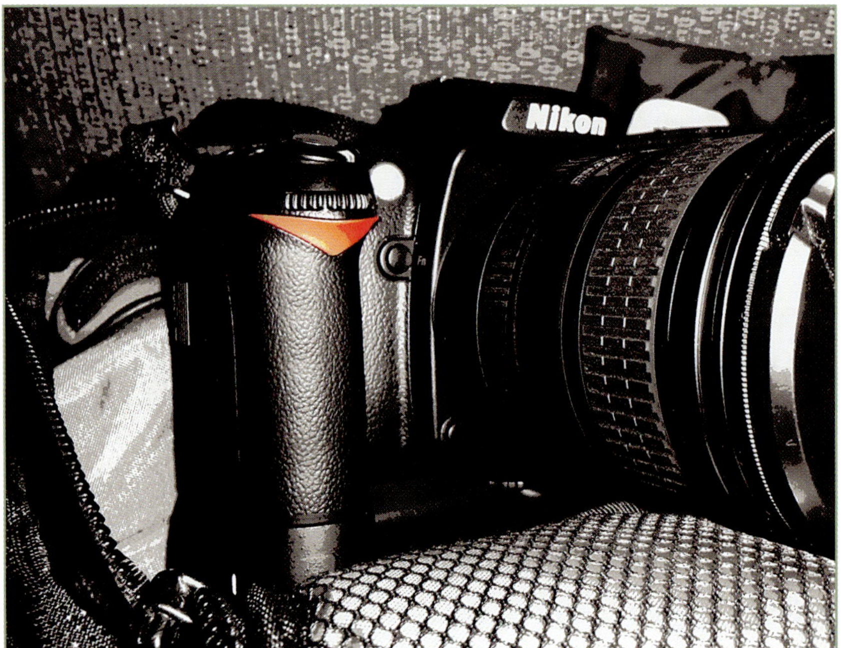

Fig. 1. Hard-Boiled Hardware: The Author's Nikon D90

I'm not gonna tell you which camera to buy since that would be like telling Sam Spade which revolver he should pack. It's a personal decision, and a lot depends on what sort of shooting you want to do. But you can't go wrong with a D-SLR from Canon or Nikon—they've cornered the pro market. That doesn't mean other brands can't cut the mustard. I've used cameras from Sigma, Fujifilm, and Casio and loved 'em. It's important that the cam has the right "feel," i.e., when you've got it in your paws, it should feel like an extension of your arm and your eye. Is it too light, too heavy, just right? Are the controls within reach? Is it responsive to the touch? The perfect camera will fit like a glove, and that's something you can't find out from the ads or reviews. You've got to head to a store and get your hands on them.

These days I shoot with a Nikon D90. I chose it for several reasons. It has the same hefty 12.3 million pixel CMOS sensor you'll find in the popular D300 but for a lot less dough. (If you tell me it's an "intermediate" model, I'll probably smack you around. It has more than enough firepower to blow the bad guys away.) It also has—according to D90 expert Simon Stafford—"improved data processing algorithms." Then there's the speed factor. No lag time and a shutter that fires 4.5 frames a second—perfect for getaways. The D90 also happens to have been the world's first D-SLR to offer high-definition video recording at 24 frames per second. (Canon came in a close second with its EOS 5D Mark II.) We'll talk about the all-important convergence of still and video in Chapter 12, "Play It Again, Cam...".

Mainly, I love Nikon glass. The lenses can't be beat. I didn't, however, buy the mediocre kit lens offered with the D90, just the body. Instead, I opted for the Nikon 18–200mm f/3.5-5.6 ED-IF AF-S VR (Vibration Reduction) DX zoom lens. Reason? It's sharp, fast, reasonably priced, and has the walk-around coverage I need. 18mm is great for wide shots, and 200mm brings you in tight on distant subjects. Remember, I'm 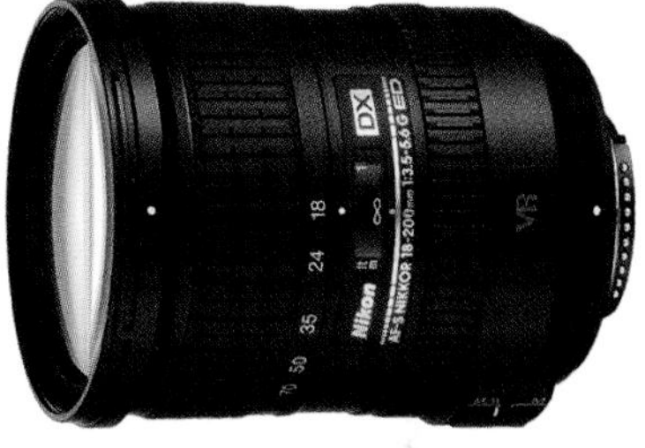 lazy and I don't like having to swap lenses in the field. My advice is to get yourself a good zoom lens and keep it on the camera—spare yourself the hassle of swapping in midstream. You travel lighter, and there's less risk of getting dust on the camera's sensor with the lens screwed on.

Back in the dinosaur era of film, telephoto lenses were inferior to stand-alones, so you had to have your glass on the side. In other words, you got much better results shooting with a 135mm lens than shooting at 135mm on an 80–200mm telephoto. Today's technology changes all that. You'll get nice results across the focal spectrum with a quality zoom lens. And speaking of lenses, when you buy one it comes with a cap and a lens shade to protect it. But what about when you're not using the shade and you're taking pictures? Forgive me for getting really basic here, but sometimes we forget the most obvious things. **Buy an ultraviolet (UV) filter for your lens.** It cuts down the atmospheric haze, but that's not the main point. Bottom line: it's cheap, and if it gets scratched or broken you can toss it and get another. If, on the other hand, you scratch your lens…well, that's the Crash of '29. Get a UV filter for your lens, period.

Packing a second camera for backup is a good strategy. It doesn't have to be a D-SLR, either. An inexpensive point-and-shoot makes a convenient sidekick for your big gun. If something goes wrong… you pull out the digicam and you still get the shot. They're also handy when you're working surveillance or on a stake-out and want to grab a shot on the sly without drawing a lot of attention to yourself. The smart pro knows there are times to "think small."

ASSAULT & BATTERIES

Who among us hasn't stumbled upon a great photo op, composed the image in the viewfinder, squeezed the shutter button, and…*oh crap*…where's the tell-tale "click"? So you kiss the perfect shot good-bye and head off to the mall in search of batteries. *Damn.*

A D-SLR is a vampire on a power trip. Fire it up, and it instantly sucks the life out of your batteries. You can ration your use of the LCD monitor, turn on every "power-saving" feature imaginable, even carry a crucifix, but ultimately it's a losing battle… there's no stopping Count D-racula.

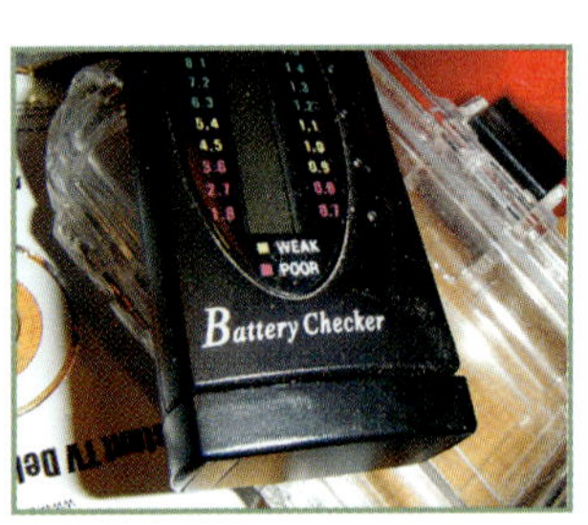

So invest in a second proprietary battery—that way you can rotate 'em and always have a charged one ready. If your camera uses AAs, keep plenty of spares within reach. Designate a pouch in your gear bag as "the morgue" just for duds…so you don't mix 'em up with the good ones.

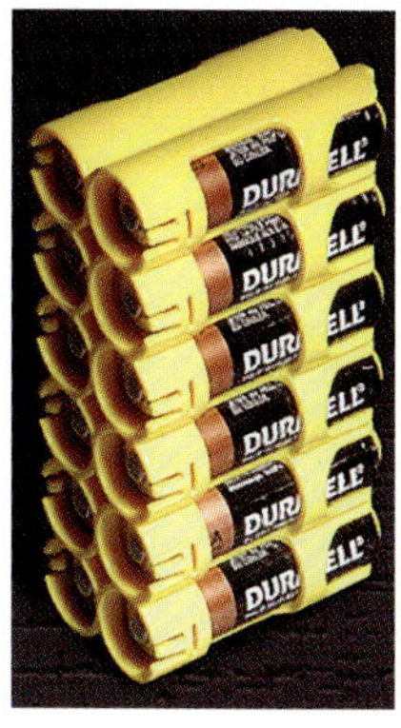

I pack a nifty little gizmo called the **Battery Checker** (available online from C. Crane) so I know if my ammo is alive and well or headed for the morgue. Rechargeables are a good idea, too, as a backup when you run out of spares. And while you're at it, grab a plastic battery organizer like the **Battery Caddy**, which keeps batteries from floating around in your camera bag.

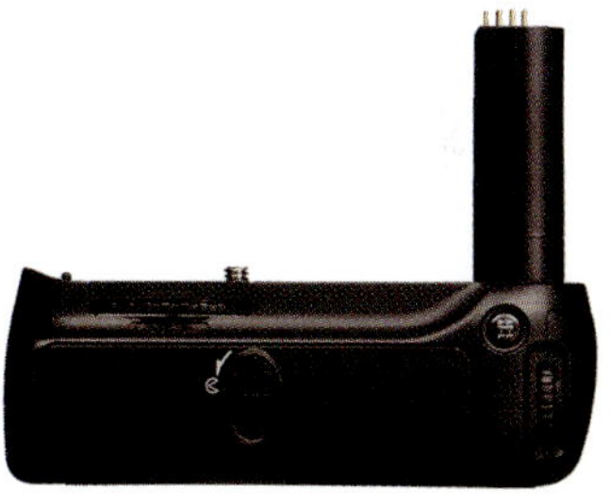

Take it a step further and buy an optional battery pack for your camera. I use a Nikon MB-D80 and never run out of juice. A battery pack will add some weight to the body, but it also provides a more balanced feel. I find gripping the camera easier with a battery pack, and it makes shooting in portrait orientation easier with its added shutter release button.

And while I'm thinking about it, your camera comes with a strap, which is fine if you like wearing the equivalent of a sandwich board saying "I'm COOL. My camera is a NIKON!!!" I hate the garish color, the unnecessary advertising…the brand is already emblazoned on the camera body, right? But the real reason I don't like the manufacturer's strap is that it slips off your shoulder when you lean or bend down. It may be fine when you're wearing the camera around your

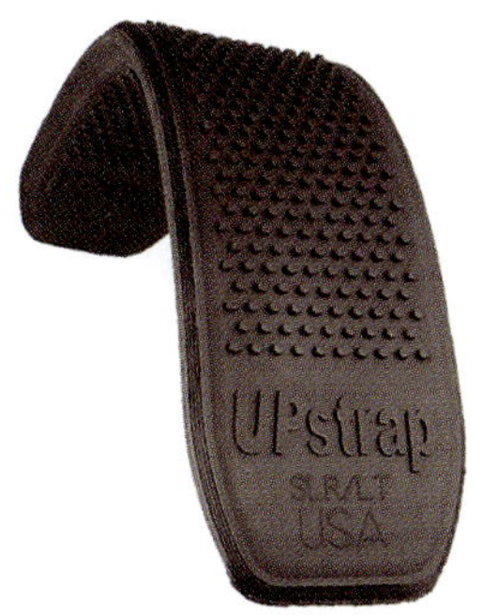

neck and shooting the Eiffel Tower, but not when you're dodging bullets with two cams dangling from your shoulders.

Well, here's a secret that'll make your day. It's called the **UpStrap,** and the damn thing doesn't slip off even when you jump up and down and flap your arms like a lunatic. (Now you know why I love it.) I've been using these babies for years, and not just on my cameras, but on my gear bags as well. They're rugged little devils and just about the last word in straps. Note, I said *just about…* because there's another fairly obscure accessory that deserves your consideration—especially if you shoot breaking news and need to be quick on the draw.

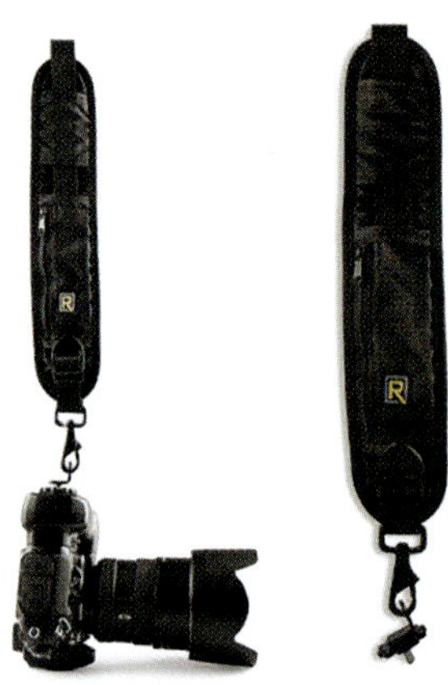

The **RapidStrap** is something both Dirty Harry and Harry Benson could appreciate. Designed by a press photographer named Ron Henry, this strap has *High Noon* written all over it. It attaches to the camera via the tripod socket. You sling the strap over your shoulder, and the camera hangs upside down at your hip. Yep, you'll feel like a gunslinger. When the action breaks, you bring the camera's view finder to eye level in a single, fluid motion and fire. When you're done shooting, you swing the camera back to your hip. Smooth and fast. NOTE: There's an online video demonstration of the RapidStrap at the following URL: www.blackrapid.com/video.

MEMORY CARDS

Hard to think of memory as an accessory. I mean, what would your brain be without it? What's a gun without bullets? A paperweight, you got it. Here's my advice: don't cut corners when it comes to memory cards. Buy only name-brand cards, no imitations. I use SDHC cards made by Kingston, Lexar, and SanDisk, and they've never failed me. Besides, prices have dropped dramatically, so it ain't worth looking for a bargain at the expense of your priceless photos. Choose the highest capacity card your budget will allow.

It seems like only yesterday when a 1MB card was the big kid on the block. Today my D90 is loaded with a Kingston 32GB SDHC card, and I've yet to fill the sucker up. I can shoot with confidence day and night without looking over my shoulder. By the way, the HC in SDHC stands for high capacity, and these cards are fast on the draw during transfers. Check the manual, and make sure your camera supports these faster cards. Most recent D-SLRs do. They're worth every penny.

A 32GB card may be overkill for you. 4GBs hold a lot of high-resolution photos. Consider using two smaller capacity cards, like two 4GB cards—that way you'll have added protection against potential card failure.

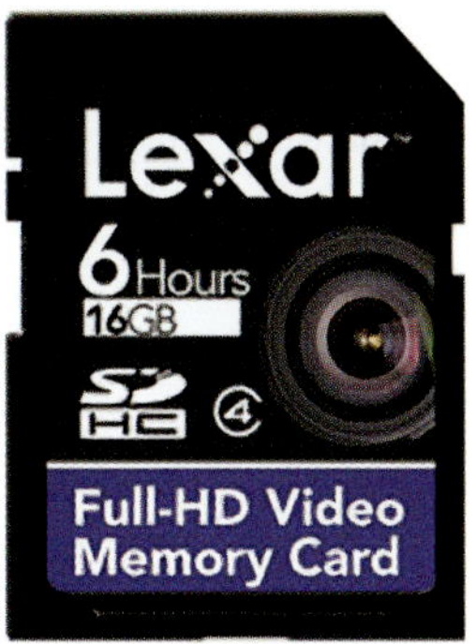

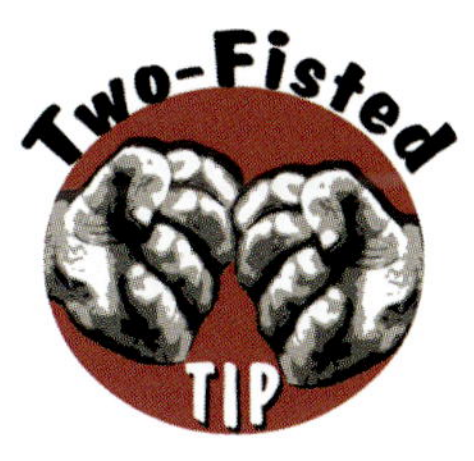

Once you've safely transferred your photos from your camera to your PC (and made extra backups), load the memory card back in the camera and *format* it. This wipes out any leftover data and debris and gives the card new life. In fact, regular formatting will *extend* the life of a memory card, so make this a habit every time you load one. Avoid subjecting the card to extreme temperatures, and keep spares stored in their original case. Also, *never* format the card using a PC because that can screw things up when it's in the camera. Dedicate a card for your D-SLR, and use the camera's format option.

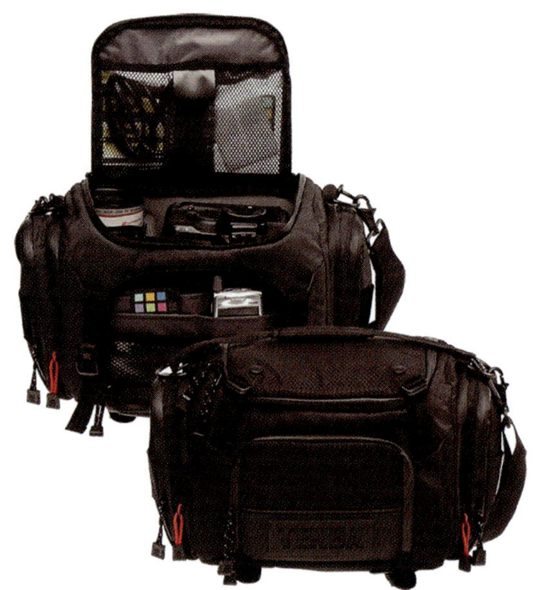

GEAR BAGS

As the editor of an online photography review (www.zoomstreet. org), I've grabbed more bags than a handler at LAX. Plenty of good ones, too—all shapes, sizes, and specs. Of course, what constitutes the perfect one depends on what you're packin', whether it's the crown jewels or the Maltese Laptop. In my case I wanted one durable bag to hold a single D-SLR, a small flash and accessories, and a larger bag to fit two cameras and assorted gear. Seems I always came close but no cigar. The bags were either too big or too small. So maybe I was too picky.

Then, one day, I got lucky.

I found the two bags I'd been looking for all my life—both made by Tenba, go figure. First, the **Shootout Medium Shoulder Bag**, which has enough room for my D90 with battery pack, an 18-200mm zoom, an SB-900 Speedlight, as well as spare batteries, portable backup drive, cell phone, gaffer's tape, and a paperback copy of *Trouble Is My Business*. The all-weather Shootout has plenty of padding and is about as rugged as yours truly. It features "Quick Access" side zippers, and when you don't have time to zip up the top flap, you can quickly close it via snap-in straps.

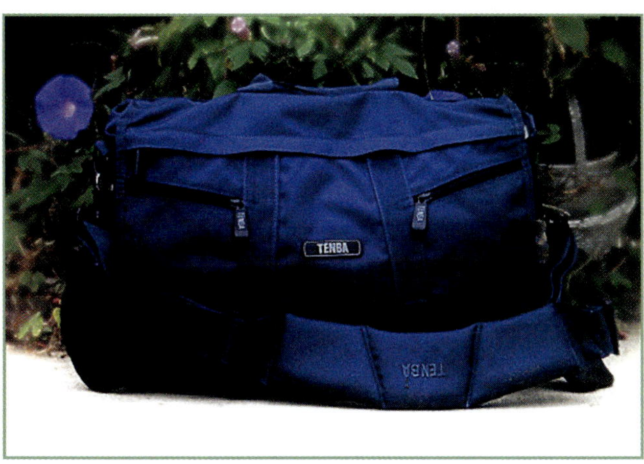

When I need to pack more, I take my blue **ProDigital Messenger Satchel** from Tenba. It's amazingly lightweight and has room for everything—even a laptop. It's a great walk-around bag without bulk and clings to your side when you're moving. It doesn't look like a camera bag, either, which is a decided advantage when I'm shooting on the mean streets of San Diego. It doesn't offer the tough protection of the Shootout, so I inserted some bubble wrap for extra padding. It's got space and grace.

Backpacks are hot with a lot of shooters today, but I prefer to have my cameras within reach. But whatever style you desire, it's out there with your name on it. Or at least the manufacturer's.

Other brands worth casing are Lowepro, Tamrac, Crumpler, and Eagle Creek.

LEGS

No, I'm not talking dames here; I just wanted to get your attention. I'm talking three-legged beasts: tripods. Now I hate lugging one around as much as the next guy, but there's no getting around it. Into night photography? Landscapes? Tornadoes? Use a tripod. Figure on spending at least $100 to get one that's sturdy enough to support a D-SLR. If you want lightweight and sturdy, expect to pay more. Want a fluid head or ballhead mount? The price zooms up.

I know a few pros who manage to get by using high ISO settings and VR technology, but if you use a tripod you'll get the sharpest shots possible. The big names in the arena are Manfrotto, Bogen, Miller…. For most jobs I use an old Vista Voyager FZ10. It's ultra-light (4.4 lbs.) and has a 3-way pan and tilt aluminum head, with a convenient bottom center post hook where I hang a sandbag on windy days, or small accessory case containing—you guessed it!—odds and ends.

If you want a solution that's more travel-friendly than a tripod, consider wielding a monopod—a one-legged stabilizer that can serve as a weapon at the drop of a dime.

Museums, for example, usually don't allow tripods, but they'll let a monopod through the door, no questions asked. The best one I've found is the Swiss-made **Monostat RS16**. It gives remarkable balance via a unique "Swivel Toe Stabilizer" that grips any surface. I've even gotten steady shots standing on ice with this baby. Use the Monostat for videos, too, and you'll get some nice smooth tilts in the bargain.

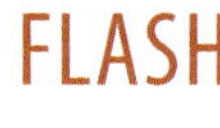

FLASH

Here's another reason why I use Nikon cameras: their Creative Lighting System (CLS). This boils down to tight integration between Nikon cameras and Nikon Speedlights—notably, the new SB-900 model. The flexibility of small strobes used either indoors or out has triggered a worldwide cult of "strobists"—inspired by Master flash guru David Hobby, whose popular blog *strobist* is dedicated to the subject.

IMHO, the SB-900 is the most versatile hot shoe flash around, and it really shines in combination with other Speedlights fired wirelessly off-camera. (Sounds like I'm telling you which camera to buy, doesn't it?)...

The obvious advantage of a small flash is its compact size. You can easily stuff several Speedlights in your kit bag. Nor is there any need for an electrical outlet since they're powered by AA batteries. They also pack a helluva lot of power for their size.

I shot the cover of this book on the street using one Nikon SB-900. (See **Chapter 5, "Twinkle, Twinkle Little Noir,"** for details.)

The downside of a small flash is less power and slower recycling times. If you do most of your shooting in a studio, you'll probably opt for the big strobes, umbrellas, softboxes, the whole kit and kaboodle. I have four monolights in my studio but no expensive portable power packs. So when I go on location, I pack a Speedlight. Later in the book I'll show you how to put your lights—large and small—to good use.

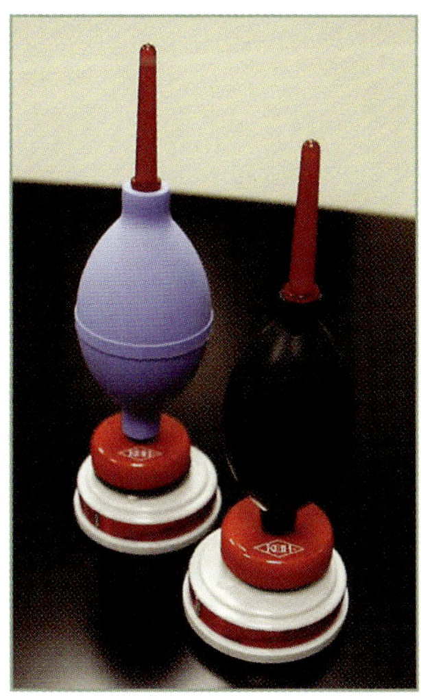

CHEAP THRILLS: ODDS 'N ENDS

As you can see from the the photo on the previous page, the emphasis is on *odds*. It could be a scene right out of *Plan 9 From Outer Space*, but those gizmos are, in reality, a clever way to keep foreign bodies—aliens and lunar dust—off your D-SLR's delicate sensor. This is the Koh **HEPA Jet Air Blower**. Give one a squeeze, and you'll discover it's no dinky dime-store puff-job like the ones

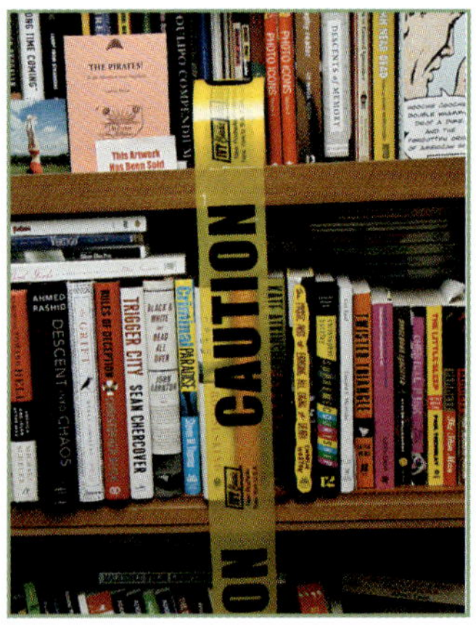

at the local camera shop. This is an industrial-strength air bulb worthy of a NASA launchpad. Unlike cheapo bulbs, which simply blow the air right back into the camera, the Jet actually *removes* the air particles via an attached HEPA air filter. I don't even wait for spots to appear on my photos—I give the cam a few shots after every session. The old *ounce of prevention* routine.

You can buy expensive DIY cleaning kits, but my advice is to avoid them. If your camera body needs real deep cleaning, it's safer to take it in to an authorized service center, as one false move and you can do some serious damage.

I keep a roll of gaffer's tape (a.k.a. electrician's tape) in my gear bag because it comes in handy on location. It's a quick fix for securing cables and backdrops, attaching a white card to a stand, or plugging an interior light leak. You can gaf cords to the floor to avoid tripping over them, or mark off spots where you want your models to stand. There are a million and one uses.

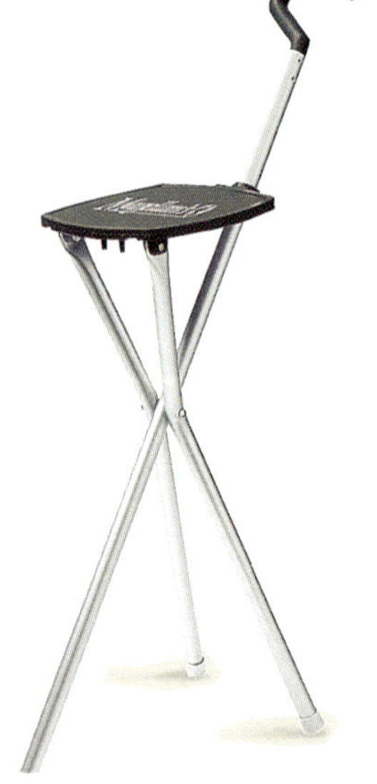

Caution tape is useful for keeping pedestrians from strolling onto the set when you're shooting, say, Paris Hilton. More to the point, it's for safety. You can "rope off" an area around potholes, wires, cords, and light stands. Nosy Parkers may gather and gawk thinking they've found a crime scene, but at least they won't wind up in the ER—or worse, the picture.

A small stepladder is a nice tool for the studio when you want to shoot from a higher angle and don't feel like jumping. I owned a 3-step model that had wheels and did double duty as a dolly. Alas, some palooka heisted it.

I'll often take a **PackSeat** on location. It's a folding 3-legged stool that fits in a pouch and clips on to my camera bag. When I'm feeling particularly lazy, I carry a **Sport Seat**. It has a handle like a walking stick and folds out into a high stool. I use it when I'm shooting landscapes with the camera on a tripod—it's just the right height. It's also handy when you have to stand in a long line at the airport. It weighs a mere 28 ounces but can support a 300 lb. shutterbug!

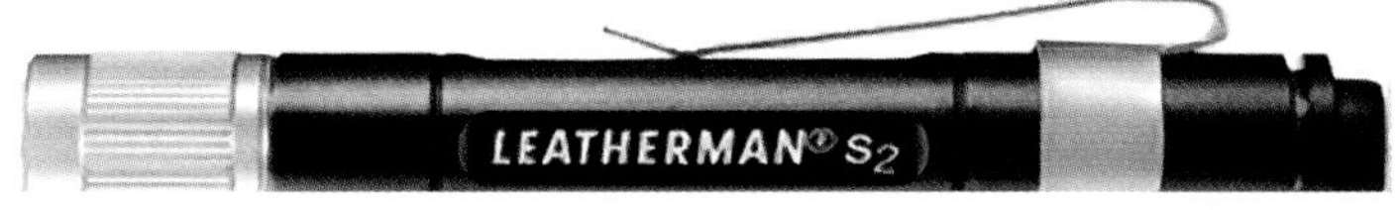

A freelance cat burglar turned me on to this pocket light. It's ideal after dusk when you need to search your gear bag or consult a manual. (Yep, I stash my camera's manual in my bag since I didn't come with a photographic memory.) I swear by my **Serac S2** LED Flashlight from Leatherman. (I've been known to curse around my camera, too.) It's just a shade over 3 inches long and weighs about an ounce. You can clip it to the brim of a hat and keep both hands free. I've used mine while biking around Coronado Island scouting locations at night. It has dual brightness settings—discreet low and mighty high, and set to the latter it gives as powerful a beam as those barbell-sized flashlights the flatfoots carry.

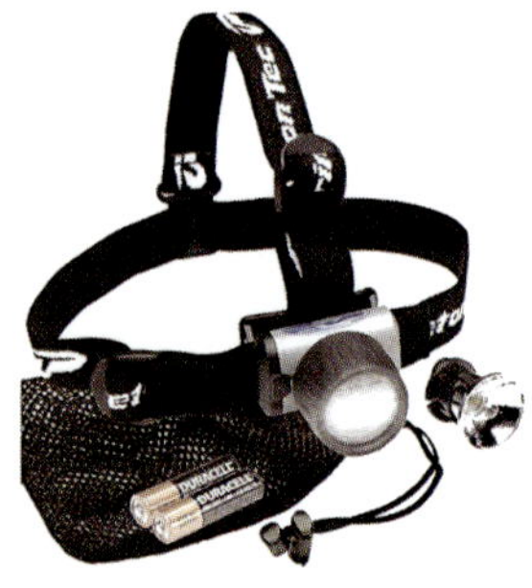

If you don't mind leaving your fedora at home, consider this bit of alternative headgear from Princeton Tec: **Matrix 2**, a AA alkaline-powered headlamp. It's not exactly stylish if worn at the local speakeasy, but it's comfortable on the head. When you need some light, simply twist the LED.

And while we're on the subject of *haute couture*... they don't call me the best dressed photographer for nothing. (Hell, nobody calls me that, but this is *my* book.) Indeed, when I'm shooting outdoors on chilly nights, I don a pair of gloves. No bulky mittens or formal whites, mind you, I ain't a sissy, but rather the **370 Atlas Nitrile Glove**. The 370 was obviously designed with the photographer in mind as there's absolutely no bulk—like slipping on a second skin. These gloves keep your hands warm, and you can actually use your D-SLR's controls. Pretty cool.

Here's something you probably haven't seen, and it's particularly popular with private eyes—a mirror angle scope for D-SLRs and camcorders. Looks like a telephoto, only it has a hole cut in the side. It screws on to your lens via a custom thread. Now you can aim your camera at an imaginary subject and actually be shooting at a 90-degree angle to the right or left. It's ideal for capturing suspicious characters without them knowing it. I use the **Opteka HD2 High Definition Conversion Lens**, and it works as advertised with minimum distortion. It doesn't interfere with the camera's auto-focus system or other functions— just attach it and shoot. You can even attach filters.

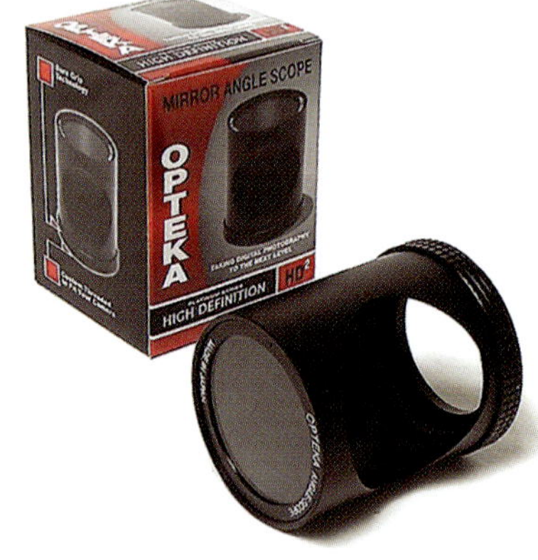

I'll end this chapter with a practical pair of footwear for the traveling photographer. If you're in and out of airports, schlepping around in the rain, whatever, snag a pair of waterproof **Slip-Ons** from Magellan's. They're the most comfortable damn shoes I've ever worn; they're easy to slip off and on and look spiffy even when I don't. (They carry a similar style for dames, too.) The shoes fold up and can fit in a spare pouch, and they have great traction for walking wet streets with your gear. I swear your feet'll thank me for this tip.

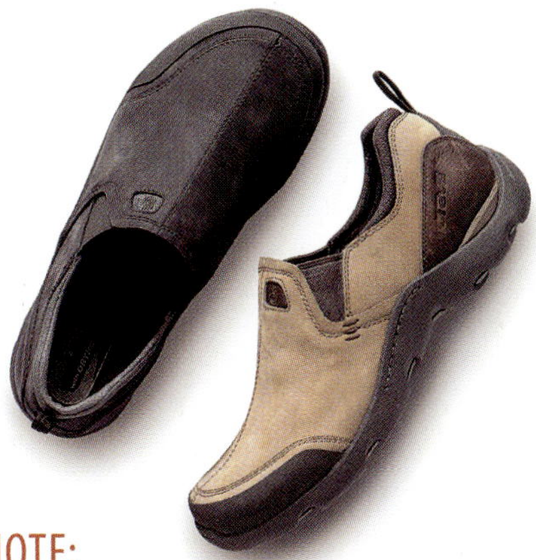

AUTHOR'S NOTE:

I forgot to include one last accessory that I use when I need a light. After weighing the pros and cons, however, I decided it wasn't all that practical...but here's a photo.

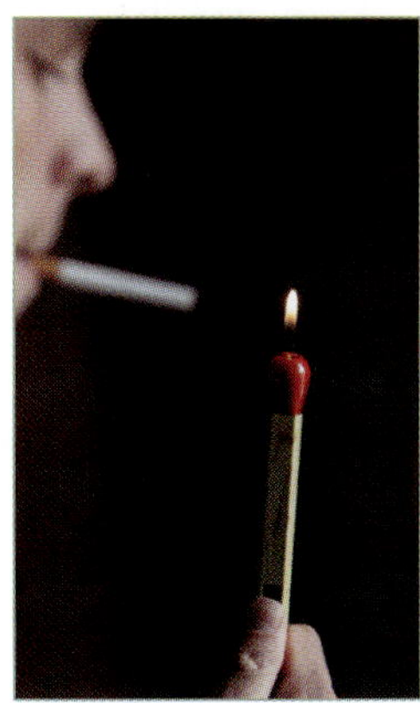

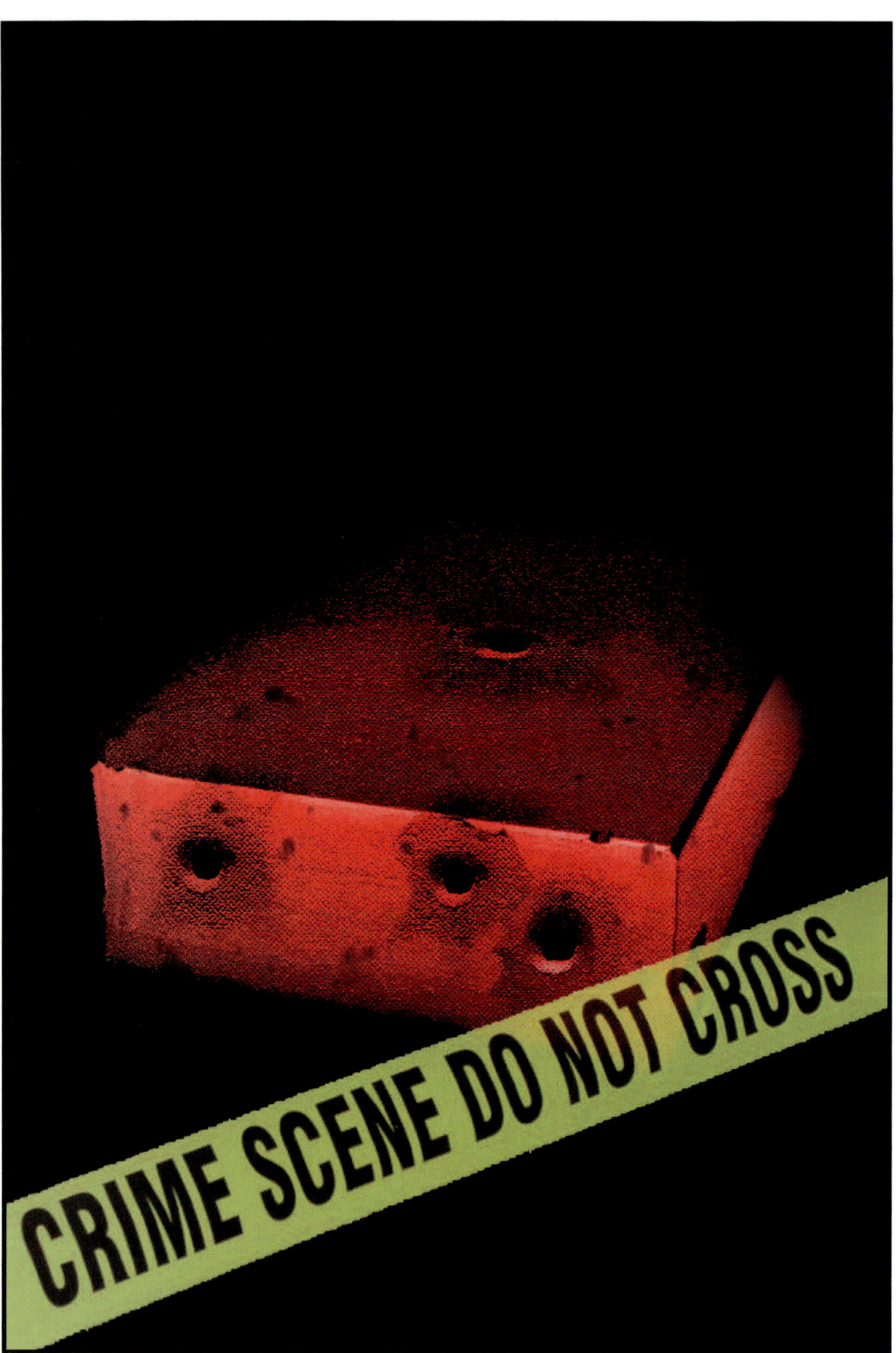

Illustration by Derek Pell.

2
CALL FOR BACKUP!
Defend & Protect Your Photos

"It's better to be a live coward than a dead hero." —from Key Largo (1948)

Call me paranoid, but if you've ever watched an external drive with thousands of your photos go up in smoke, you'll understand. It happened to me once after wrapping up a big case (24 cans). Wipe that smirk off your face—it'll happen to you some day, too. Sad fact of life, but if you've made multiple backups it's not the end of your career, just the end of some expendable hardware. I know, I know, backing up is like the weather… everybody talks about it but nobody does anything about it. It ain't fun and it sure ain't sexy—unless you're a geek—but it's mission critical if you live and die by your photos.

That's why you need a redundant backup routine that fits your photoflow. (I swore to myself I wouldn't say the word *workflow*.) A failsafe system, a grand strategy, a security blanket—call it whatever you like. It doesn't matter how it works as long as it *works*.

Like those guys at Nike say, *just do it.*

It's easier said than done, yeah, but remember this: everything fails. You fail, I fail, and technology fails 24/7. That's why a single backup doesn't cut it. A PC konks out, a laptop gets hijacked, a memory card becomes corrupted, an external drive goes south on vacation, the CD gets clawed by a cat named Cairo, and the online storage company suddenly declares bankruptcy.

"Hey, I'm cool, I've got all my photos on a DVD."

Sure thing, Joe… and one day you'll pop that sucker into the tray to retrieve your favorite sunset snap and up'll jump an **Error Message** telling you the computer can't read the disc. WTF?!!!

Call for backup!

"Thanks for the copies, boys, you saved the day."

Multiple copies are an insurance policy that'll pay off in the long run.

HOW MANY BACKUPS ARE ENOUGH?

Between you, me, and the bedpost, I make *seven*. But if danger ain't your business, three should be sufficient. Three, by the way, is no arbitrary number I pulled out of my fedora. The Pentagon uses a triage defense strategy, right? (Okay, so maybe they're paranoid, too.)

Here's the lowdown on my hard-boiled backup scheme. Feel free to adapt it to suit your zoot. Dismiss it outright at your own peril.

First, I start by loading the camera with a high-capacity memory card (8GB or more), which I'm not likely to fill up in a single session— unless, of course, I'm shooting in Burst mode. (See **Chapter 6, "A Thirst for Burst."**) I also arm myself with the handheld, battery-powered storage device shown below (Fig. 1).

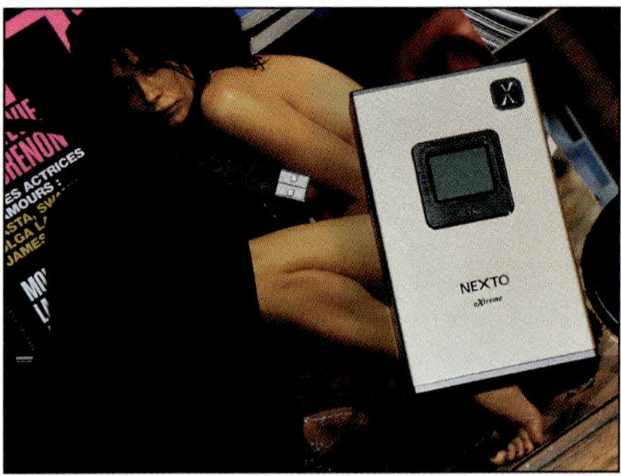

Fig. 1. Nexto eXtreme portable backup drive.

You can get a flashy **Epson P-4000 Multimedia Storage Viewer**, which costs as much as a Buick, but I use a no-frills 150 GB **Nexto eXtreme**. It doesn't give me previews of my photos on its teeny LCD (my camera does that), but it monitors file transfers, and even says "Bye!" when I shut it off. The device has only one button; a short press copies images from the card, a long press moves them. Raise your glass—here's a toast to simplicity.

When I take a break from shooting, I remove the memory card from the camera, plug it in to the Nexto and *copy* (never move) the photos to the drive. That way, if the memory card goes belly up, I'm covered.

Back at my desk I plug the Nexto in to the PC's USB port, which automatically launches Adobe Lightroom. I import all the photos and store them on an external drive. **(BACKUP SET #1)** While importing, Lightroom simultaneously adds my customized metadata (copyright, contact info, etc.) to each photo—a real time-saver. (See page 38 to learn how to create a custom metadata preset.)

OK, so far, so good. But hold on—I'm not finished.

I review thumbnails of all the images from the shoot in Lightroom's Preview area. The deadbeats are terminated with extreme prejudice, which is to say I select the clunkers and press the Delete key. I apply a 5-star rating to the best of the keepers and color-code photos that require editing.

Outside Lightroom, I navigate to the folder where the images are stored and drag and copy it to a second external backup drive. **(BACKUP SET #2)** That backup gets automatically copied to yet another handheld drive, a Seagate FreeAgent. **(BACKUP SET #3)** The FreeAgent comes with built-in sync software, so when I plug it in to my laptop it transfers all the new files. **(BACKUP SET #4)** If you're starting to get dizzy, step outside for some air.

Next, I burn all the photos to a DVD. **(BACKUP SET #5)**

Later, after I've had time to edit the keepers, I burn two DVD copies of the final photos (**BACKUP SET #s 6 & 7**) and post one to a friend in a state not subject to earthquakes. Thus, if my office turns to rubble (and some say it already has), I haven't lost my work.

Go ahead, call me paranoid, but my photos never go missing and will probably outlive us all. To reiterate, you don't have to go to the extreme of making seven copies, but less than three… well, let's just say that's risky.

When I'm all backed up and done patting myself on the back, I wipe all the photos from the memory card by formatting it in the camera. As mentioned in the previous chapter, never delete the photos from the card—format the card instead.

It might seem natural to keep your photos stored on the computer's hard drive, but why do that when external drives are dirt cheap and have huge capacities? You should keep your hard drive as spacious as possible so the operating system, RAM, and software have plenty of air to function smoothly.

Get this straight: There's no excuse for not backing up your files. Your time is limited? Get auto backup DVDs that require "no user intervention." Insert 'em and go walk the dog—they find and copy all your media files for you—*bingo!* There are even portable drives that do the same thing, like the **clickfree** from Storage Appliance.

Believe it or not, I'm not drowning in a sea of images. Half of all my photos never get backed up. How come? Because they go directly to the Recycle Bin where they belong. I'm my own toughest critic.

IF THE MOB CAN GET ORGANIZED, SO CAN YOU

We're getting dangerously close to that buzzword again… you know, the one with "work" and "flow" joined at the hip. Instead, think of an assembly line running smoothly or, in my case, an absurd, Rube Goldberg operation that manages to function, despite looking chaotic. Looks count only if you're a fashion model. If you're a photographer, organization is what counts, big time.

For the digital photographer, that boils down to being able to find a specific photo at the drop of a hat.

How do you pluck the one image your client is desperate for out of a million bits of drifting space debris? The answer is software from Adobe Systems; namely, the aforementioned Adobe Photoshop Lightroom, and Adobe Bridge (an app included in Creative Suite CS4). I use both daily. In fact, when I'm not out taking pictures or skulking around Starbucks (Fig. 2), I *live* inside them.

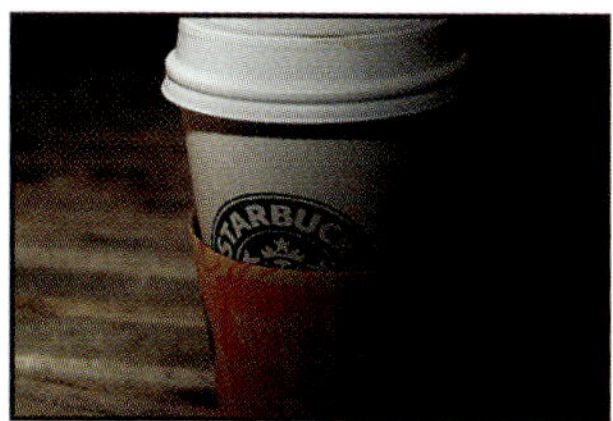

Fig. 2. This might look like product placement, but Starbucks won't pay me a dime.

PHOTOSHOP, LIGHTROOM, & BRIDGE, OH MY!

Lightroom is aimed directly at photographers who don't need all the features Photoshop has to offer, not to mention its steep learning curve. I've been using Photoshop since the Windows version first hit the crime scene in 1992. I still use it religiously, although for quick enhancements Lightroom is fine and dandy. Rumors have circulated that Lightroom will eventually replace the big cheese, but I'm doubtful. If you stuck all Photoshop's features in Lightroom it would cease to be a tool for shutterbugs. My one gripe with Adobe is that it named the application *Photoshop Lightroom*. Talk about muddying the waters, sheesh.

Which should you use, Photoshop or Lightroom? That's easy. *Both.*

If, like me, you want to tamper with evidence and do intense image manipulation, Photoshop is the only game in town.

You can't make mischief like the doctored photo in Fig. 3 on the next page with Lightroom. If you want to cook up a collage; marinade a montage; work with layers, painting tools, masks and selections, text, 3D, etc., grab Photoshop, pure and simple.

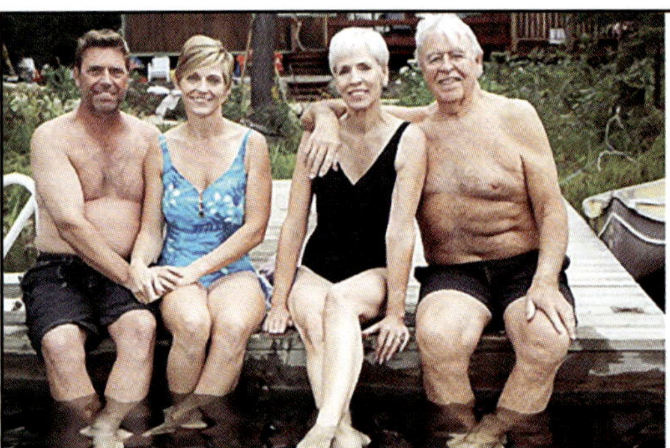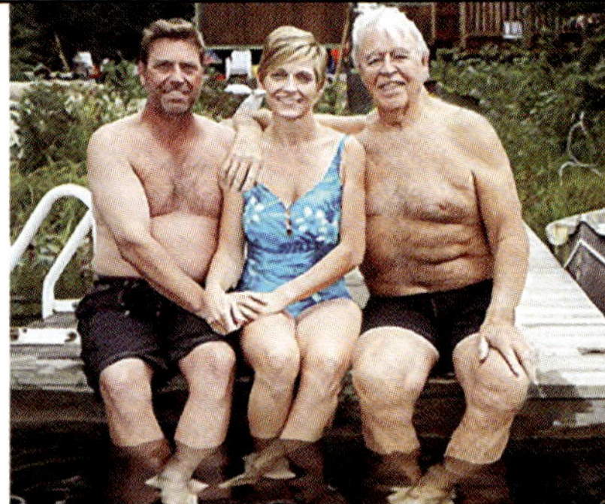

Fig. 3. Three's Company. (Stock photo courtesy of Masterfile.)

A NOTE ON FIGURE 3: A DOCTORED PHOTO

The original photo appears on the left and the doctored version on the right. Removing grandma was no cakewalk, trust me. It took about two hours (not counting cigarette breaks) and required nerves of steel, a steady mouse, and Photoshop's selection tools and Clone Stamp.

Look closely, and you'll see I took some liberties with the house in the background; otherwise, the job might've taken all day.

In addition to manipulations like this, Photoshop excels at "arty" transformations like collage. You can combine multiple photos and concoct an entirely new image. Add text, paint over or tint, toss in some line illustrations, or filter the image till the cows come home. Herein lies the beauty of Photoshop: anything and everything is possible. This one-stop digital darkroom rivals a Hollywood special effects department. (Hell, Hollywood uses it, too.) Virtually every photograph you see in print has gone through "the shop" for a minor touch-up or a total makeover, and usually it's impossible to tell which.

Who's the sap who said photographs don't lie?

Lightroom, on the other hand, is a gem when it comes to importing photos directly from a memory card or drive, adding metadata, making quick image enhancements, creating web galleries and slide shows, and (in combination with Adobe Bridge) organizing your photos.

Here's Lightroom's Import window (Fig. 4) showing shots of a classic 1940 Buick Eight I discovered near Zoom Street. You can play editor and select which photos to import via the convenient check box next to each thumbnail preview. You can also choose where the imported files (as well as a backup set) should go; whether to organize the photos by date (the default); what filename and sequence numbering should be applied; and which metadata preset, if any, should be included. You can even type in keywords before you import—very handy.

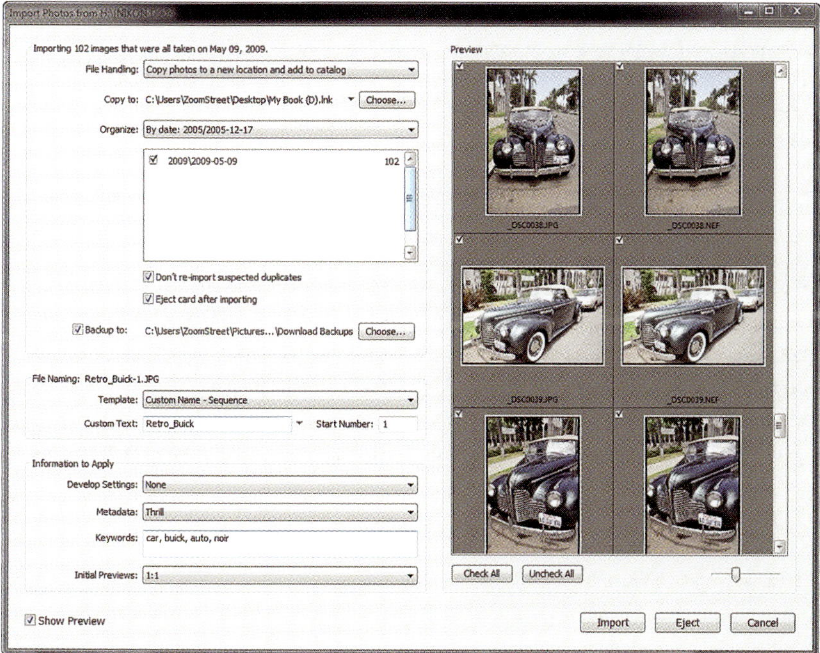

Fig. 4. The Lightroom Import window.

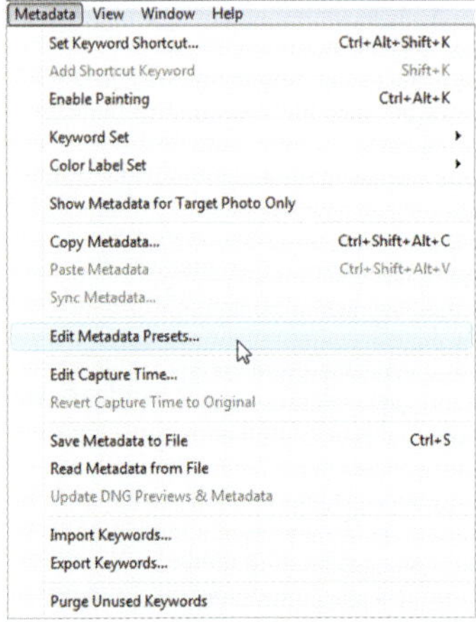

Fig. 5. The Metadata menu, yum.

I mentioned earlier that I use a custom metadata preset for adding my copyright and contact info. I want that data to be part of all my photos. That way any potential clients can track me down for jobs. It also alerts thieves and bandits to steer clear if they're thinking of heisting a photo.

CREATING A CUSTOM PRESET

Here's how to customize your own preset in Lightroom. Click the Metadata button and from the drop-down menu (Fig. 5) choose Metadata > Edit Metadata Presets.

In the Custom Presets pop-up (Fig. 6), check the boxes for IPTC Copyright and IPTC Creator and fill in your copyright information. In the Creator section, type your contact info. If you have time, enter some keywords. Click Done and the New Preset window in Fig. 7 appears.

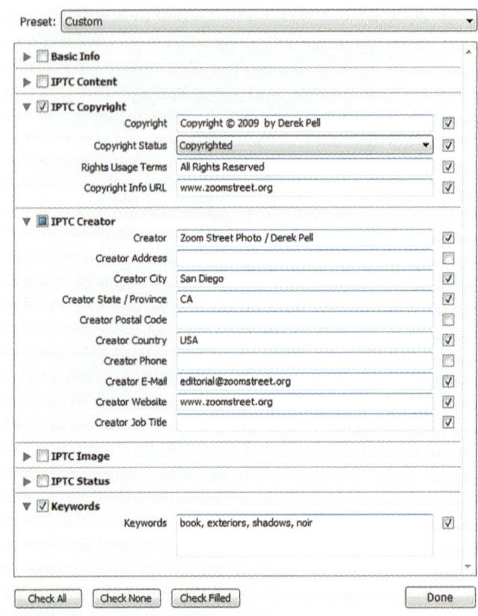

Fig. 6. The Custom Preset panel.

Type a name for the preset. You can have as many presets as you like. Click the Create button. The next time you import photos, simply select your custom preset from the list and *hello, Easy Street!* By the way, Easy Street intersects with Avenue of the Organized.

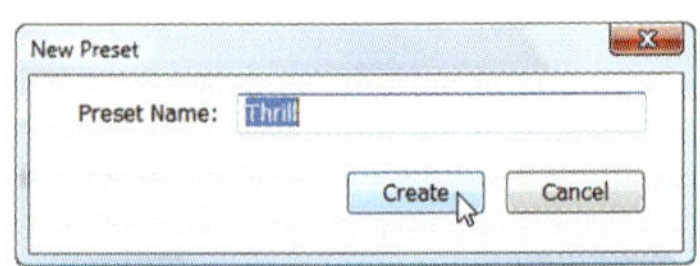

Fig. 7. Give the preset a thrilling name.

Used in combination, Adobe Photoshop, Lightroom, and Bridge make for a very powerful, crime-busting combo. Think Sam Spade, Phil Marlowe, and me.

THE BRIDGE

For overall image management, Bridge is a multimedia management app you can really sink your teeth into. You can sort, search, compare, organize, stack, rename, edit metadata, and batch process—not to mention print contact sheets, run slide shows, and create Flash-based web galleries. You can open and edit RAW files right within Bridge or launch Photoshop with a single mouse click. The integration with Photoshop is about as tight as it gets. You can even drag image thumbnails into other applications to open the files.

If you work with video or Flash animations, Bridge handles these files as well—and they can be previewed directly inside the app.

Let's take a closer look at Bridge.

Fig. 8 shows the Bridge CS4 interface and some thumbnails of images that appear in this book. There are three areas of interest here: (1) the panel on the left is devoted to navigating to and viewing the contents of image folders. The section just below is where you create keywords, make collections, and filter your searches. (2) The center is reserved for thumbnails, the size of which can be quickly changed via the slider bar below. (You can switch to a Details view that—in addition to a thumbnail—includes text info such as date created, file size, exposure, etc.) (3) The panel on the right provides a large preview of the selected thumbnail(s) and can include a column featuring complete metadata. The interface can also be customized; all three areas can be resized and additional panels added and subtracted.

Fig. 9 shows the Bridge custom keyword panel with keywords I created for the chapters in this book.

To create a keyword, you simply press the large plus button (circled here in red) in the lower-right corner and type it in. The button

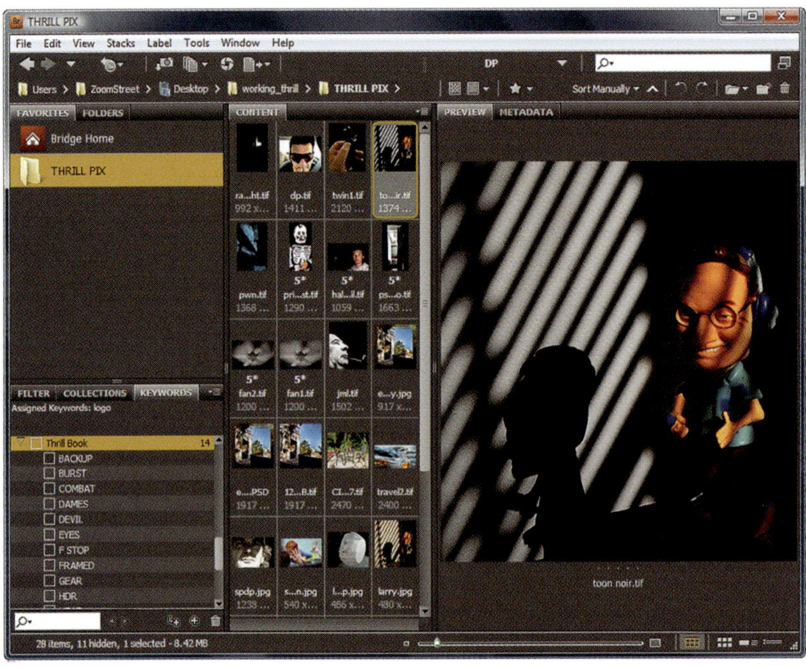

Fig. 8. The Adobe Bridge CS4 interface.

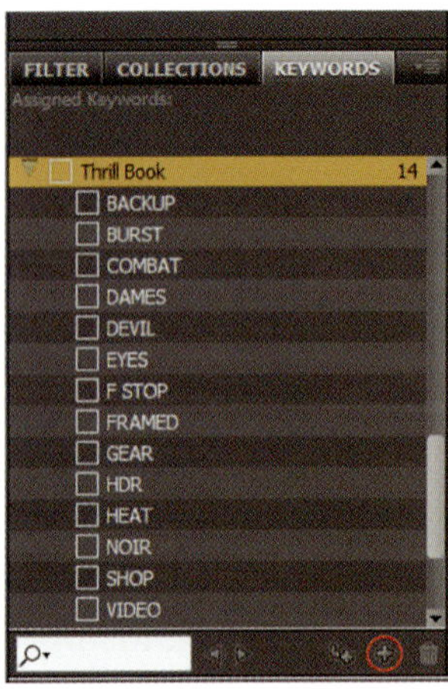

Fig. 9. Custom keywords panel.

to the left with the tiny plus sign is for creating a subcategory keyword. For example, if you had a main category for "Architecture," you might want to make subcategory keywords such as "Deco," "Tudor," etc.

Assigning a keyword to photos is just as easy. Select a thumbnail photo with the mouse and check the box next to the keyword. Even better, select multiple thumbnails by holding down the Ctrl key (for contiguous files hold down the Shift key) and highlight them; then click the box next to one or more keywords to apply to all the selected photos in one fell swoop.

Smart shutterbugs always assign multiple keywords to their images because it narrows searches and makes finding photos a lot faster. For example, say I'm looking for a certain suspicious character I photographed in a bar in Brooklyn years ago. All I remember is that he was fat, had a moustache, and wore a fez. If I just searched by the keywords "Brooklyn" or "bar," I could wind up with a thousand shots. But if I also assigned the keywords "fat," "moustache," and "fez," I'd nail the sucker in a nanosecond.

Taking the time to keyword your photos as you acquire them is the best advice I can give. Do it for yourself, and then buy me a drink.

> **NOTE:** If you assign keywords using Lightroom, they'll appear in Bridge's Metadata panel.

A VIEW FROM THE BRIDGE

There's a lot more to Adobe Bridge than its capability to deftly juggle keywords. It's loaded with features designed to help you efficiently manage your archives.

For example, I like being able to select a bunch of related photos and *stack* the thumbnails in a pile (Fig. 10). Notice the little number 4 in the corner. That tells me I've got four photos in the stack (You can stack as many as you want.) To view them all, I click on the number and the images expand into view; click again, and they're back in the stack. Neat trick.

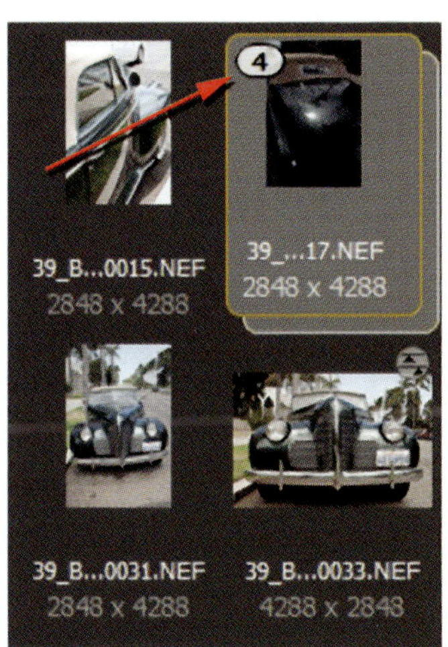

Fig. 10. A nice, neat little stack.

One essential file management chore is renaming images that get labelled in the camera with cute tags like _DSC010.JPG or worse. If we had to rename each photo one at a time, it'd be worse than banging out license plates at Alcatraz. That's why some enlightened geek who happened to like photographers invented Batch Renaming. It's a very straightforward operation in Bridge. Select the thumbnails and go up to the Tools menu and choose Batch Rename (Fig. 11). The Batch Rename window (Fig. 12) will appear miraculously before your eyes.

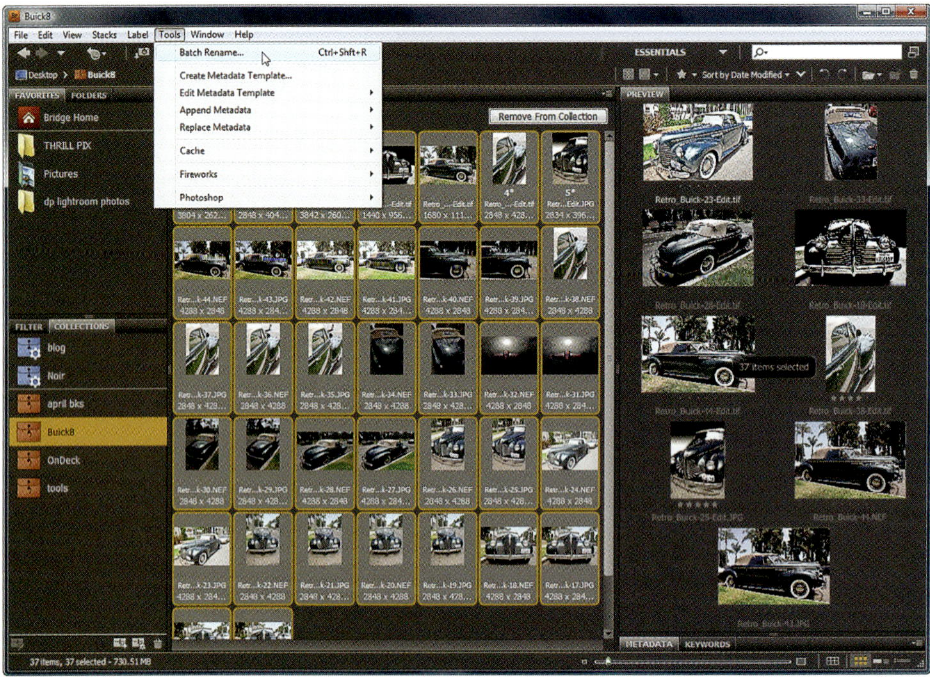

Fig. 11. Batch renaming photos is a tropical breeze.

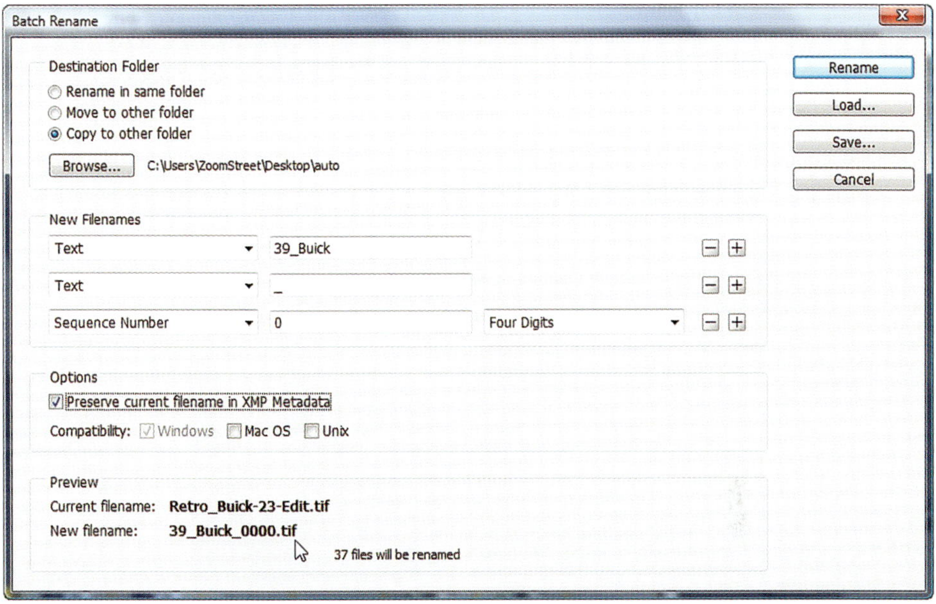

Fig. 12. The Batch Rename window.

First, tell Bridge where you want the folder with your renamed photos copied or moved. You can opt to keep them in the same folder as the originals, but it's best to create a nice fresh folder for the newborns.

Type a descriptive filename and numbering sequence. (The name can be as elaborate as you wish and can include location, subject, creation date, project number, client code, etc.)

If you want to keep a record of the original gibberish, check the box next to Preserve Current Filename in XMP Metadata. This could be useful if you accidentally deleted the renamed file but kept a copy of the original.

A tip of the hat goes to Adobe for including a preview of the current and new filenames. If you make a typo you'll probably spot it here, or you may decide to choose a different name altogether.

When you're done, press the Rename button and—presto!—all the photos have a spanking new moniker!

Nothing beats being able to make side-by-side comparisons of photos (Fig. 13). You can zoom in and out and keep the magnification levels identical in both previews. If you click on an area of the image, a loupe pops up so you can magnify a tiny portion to inspect the detail and check sharpness.

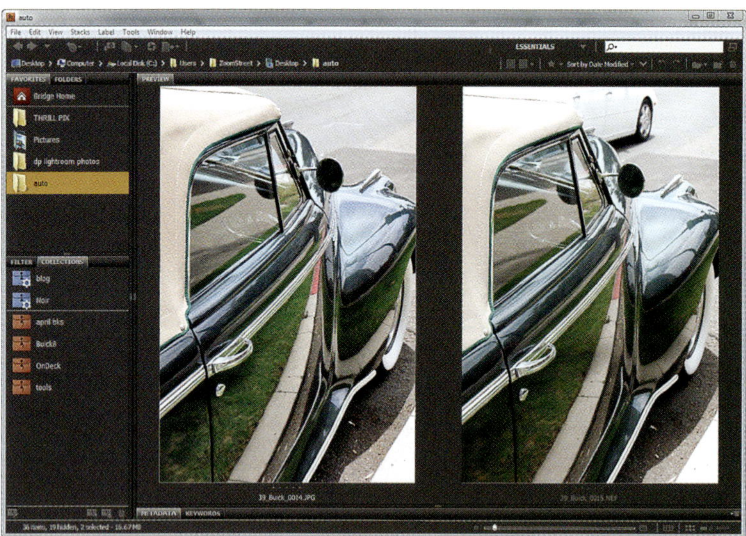

Fig. 13. Comparison view.

If you press the spacebar on your keyboard, you'll get a full-screen preview of the selected photo.

You can preview an entire folder of photos as a slideshow, or go for some eye candy and choose Review Mode (Fig. 14) from the View menu and treat yourself to a 3D merry-go-round style view. Cool it is, but I've yet to discover its usefulness. Then again, it might impress a client and land you a million-dollar dream assignment.

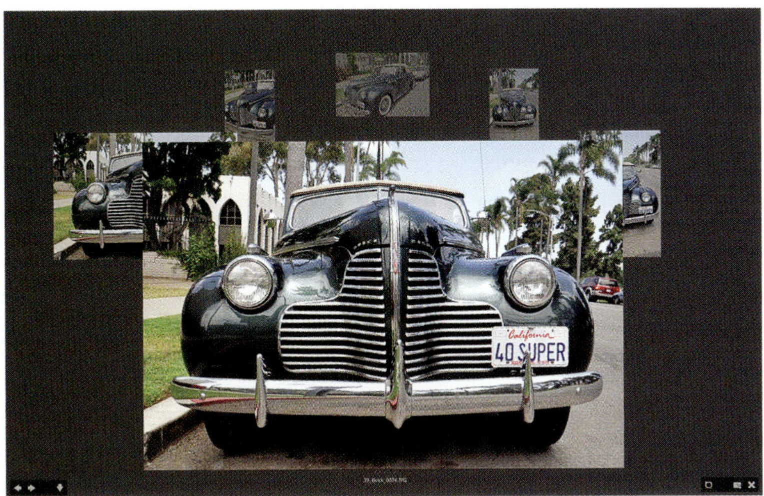

Fig. 14. Review Mode—hang on to your hats.

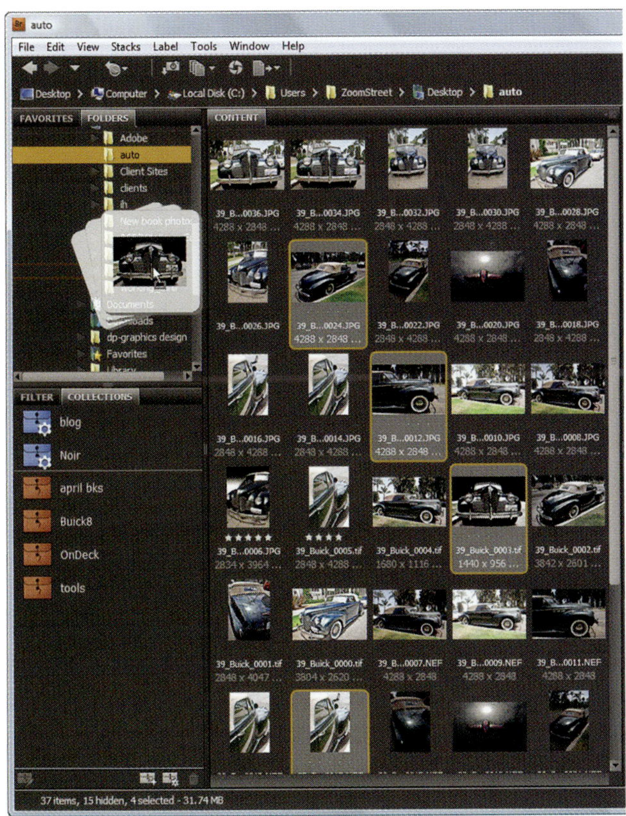

Fig. 15. Drag and drop a fistful of thumbnails for easy file management.

I've always been a sucker for drag-and-drop operations, so naturally I love the fact that I can select a whole batch of thumbnails and copy or move them by dragging them directly to a folder. As soon as you've selected several thumbnails and pressed the left mouse button, a fanned-out representation of the files appears beneath your cursor (Fig. 15), which gives the illusion you're clutching the photos in your hand and physically moving them. Hell, it's little touches like this that make me wish I hadn't been born a cynic.

To the Truly Useful category, add the ability to right-click a RAW file's thumbnail and choose Open in Camera Raw. This instantly launches the window in Fig. 16. Now you can get your hands dirty and do some serious color correction and image enhancement without launching Photoshop.

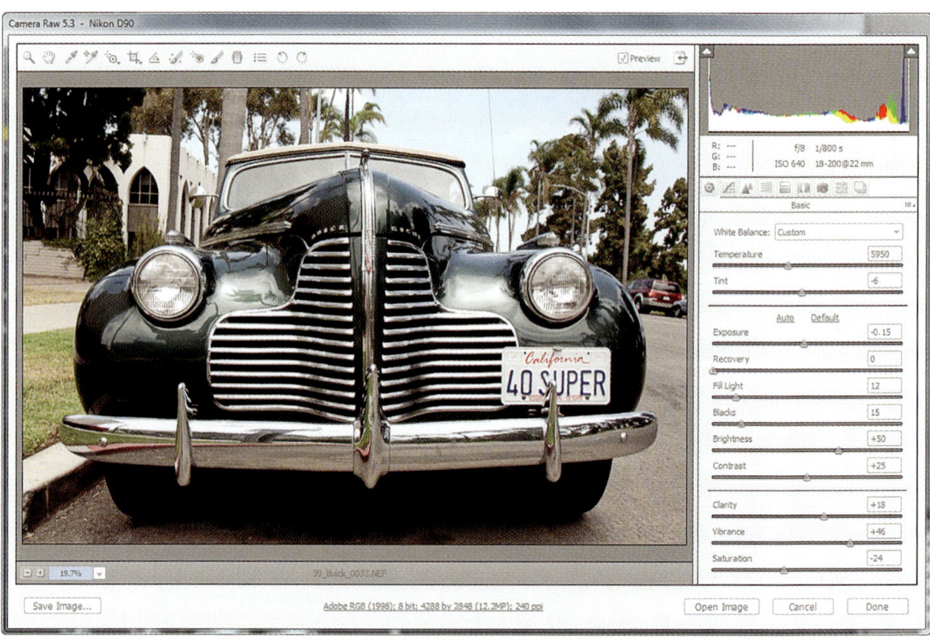

Fig. 16. Adobe Camera Raw within Bridge.

You can make some really radical adjustments right here in Bridge. You can alter a photo's white balance, change the temperature, add a tint, alter the exposure, add fill light, heighten the blacks, the brightness, the contrast, increase clarity and vibrance, boost the saturation (or desaturate)... in short, transform an okay chump into a museum-quality champ. (We'll perform some thrilling enhancement tricks in **Chapter 7, "From Chump to Champ."**)

So we've moved seamlessly from backing up and managing photos to standing at the digital darkroom's door. It's early still, so before you knock three times and say "Sam sent me," let's take a long hard look at how we "see." That, ultimately, determines how good our photos will be.

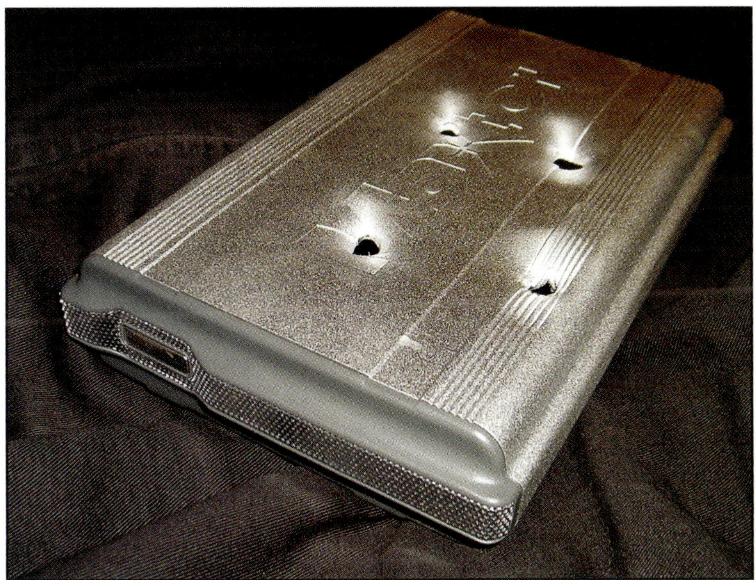

The author's bullet-riddled backup drive. (Photo and bullets courtesy of Chris Councill.)

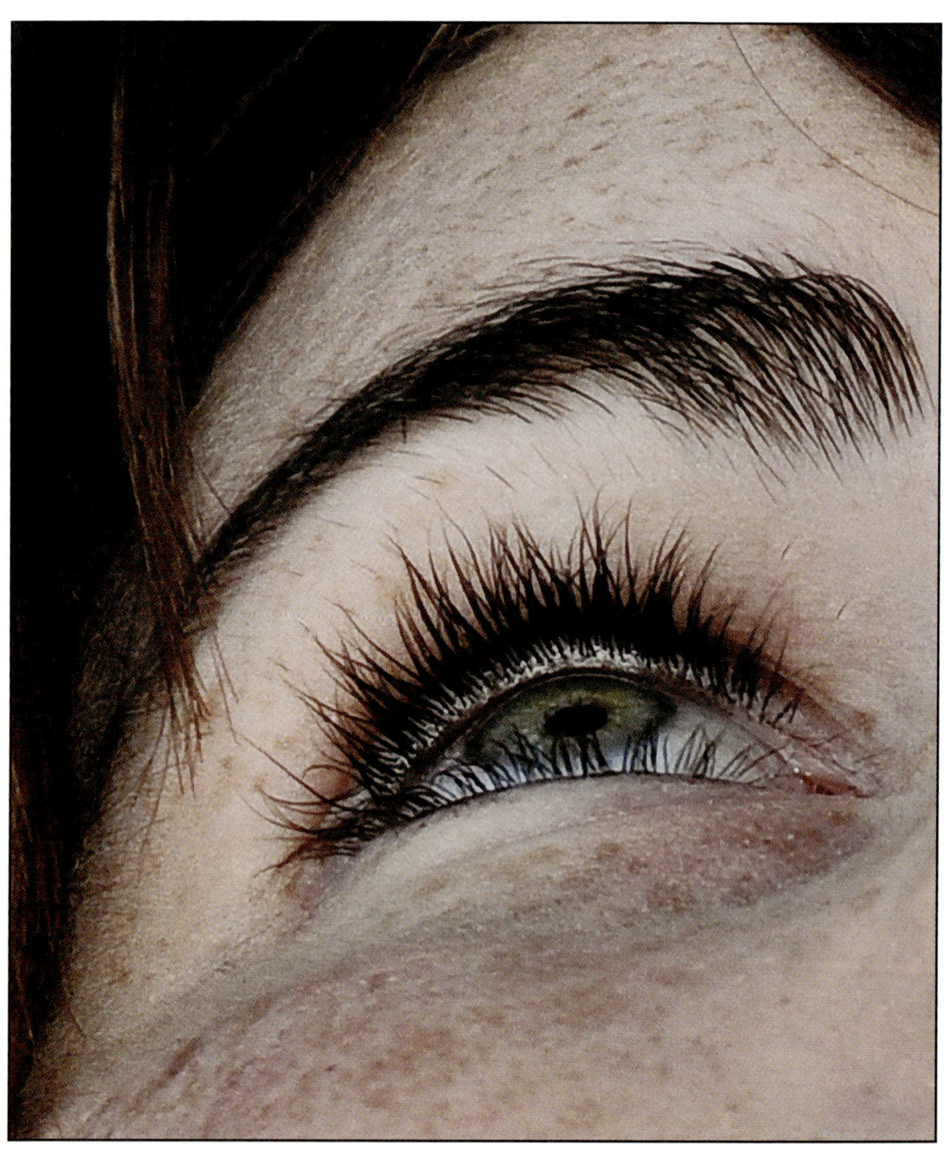

Photo by Derek Pell.

3
PRIVATE EYES
Look Before You Shoot

"You ain't seen nothing yet." —Al Jolson

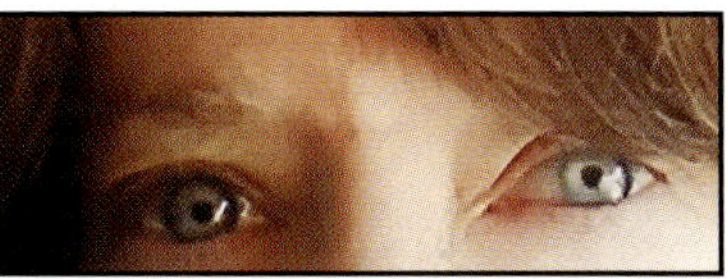

If this were a mystery novel (and I'm doing the best I can), this would be the chapter where I plant the clues. Only difference here is—I want you to solve the mystery before you reach The End. I want you to experience a lightbulb moment. I want you to see a colorful cluster of thought balloons rising up like an air show over the desert. I want you to dream about this chapter tonight and wake up in the morning with a fresh pair of eyes and a burning desire in your gut.

OK, even Raymond Chandler couldn't pull that off, but I'm gonna try just the same. Nothing to lose but a few tired trees.

SLEEP MODE

Here's a combo to avoid: a loaded D-SLR and an empty head.

We've all been there, done that—taken pictures with our brains in Sleep mode. We've gone through the motions of photography like camera-toting zombies... aimed the lens at a subject, squeezed the shutter, shuffled off to a new location, and repeated the routine. Later, on our computer screen, we had evidence of activity—an alibi... time-stamped, no less, and a folder filled with the fruits of our labor: digital photographs! All accurately exposed, sharp, nice colors. So what?

When I was kid I discovered the book *Henry Miller on Writing*. It had a big impact on me, and I'm still thinking about it today. A lot of the hard-boiled advice Miller dished out is applicable not just to writers, but to photographers as well.

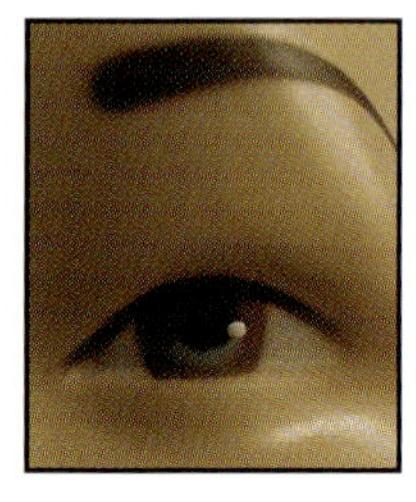

Miller taught me to fill my head with ideas of all stripes, to devour books on every imaginable topic, not just those of immediate interest. He advised novelists to avoid fiction and read everything else, instead. That way, he reasoned, you'd have a wealth of material to draw on when you sat down to write: history, places, psychology, themes, the whole damn universe.

I'm not going to tell you to stop reading books on photography or studying photos in magazines. That's a process that begins the day you finish school and ends at the boneyard. What I'm driving at is this: develop an *approach* to making photographs that's rooted in *ideas* that fire your imagination.

Once you've nailed a creative approach that's concept-driven, you'll rediscover the thrill you felt when you took your first shot.

Bye-bye, Burnout.

METHOD ACTING: COMEDY OR TRAGEDY?

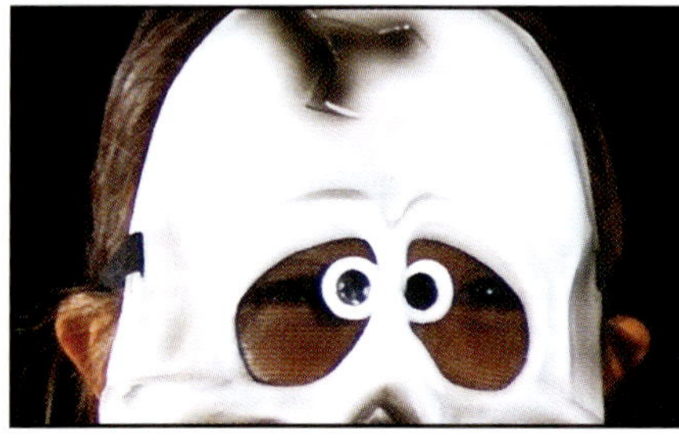

My approach to photography is akin to method acting. I can't spell Stanislavski to save my life (so let's hear it for the copy editor!), but I know what he was getting at. Using his technique, an actor attempts to embody the thoughts and emotions of the character to create a *believable* performance. By drawing on sense memories, personal experiences, and emotions, the actor digs deeper into the role.

I bring my passions and obsessions to photography. I want to *make* pictures, not simply *take* them. The role must be active, not passive or mechanical. Thus, I try to imagine the image I want to capture before I've even picked up the camera. Frame that vision in a rectangle. Then, when you shoot, move in close and crop like a cop ("Just the facts, ma'am…"). A common mistake the novice makes is ignoring composition, not bothering to crop in the camera before squeezing the shutter. That's what I call a "crop out." Get active, and put yourself *in* the scene, not just *on* it. Move in close to the subject; it won't bite. (If the subject is a pit bull, ignore my advice.) Don't think a zoom lens is a license to stand back; in fact, stop zooming and start moving… use your feet and get as close to your subject as possible. You'll get a better shot and spend less time cropping in post. (More on this in **Chapter 8, "The Devil Is in the Details."**)

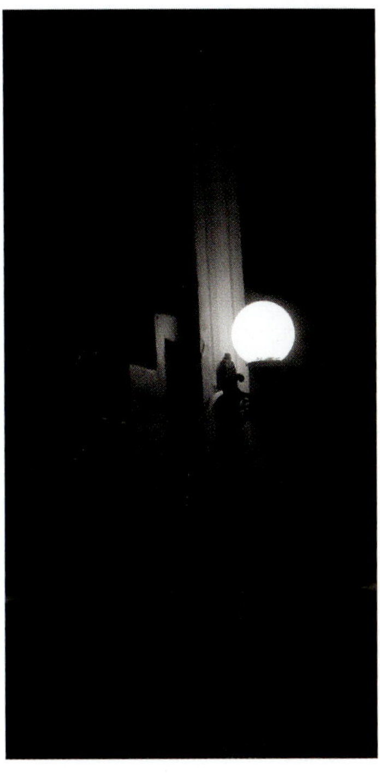

YOU'RE THE LEAD, NOT THE WALK-ON

For the past year, I've been working on a book-length series of photographs called *San Diego Noir.* When scouting for locations, I become a private dick like Sam Spade. I see my city the way he sees his—San Francisco—or through the eyes of Philip Marlowe as he drives around L.A.

Both PIs would feel right at home at my office in a fading, two-story Deco overlooking Balboa Park. You can trace the cracks in the stucco like a map with no destination. Each day the building gets hot-washed by the desert sun, the light thick and glimmering in the corners, carving statues out of sharp-edged shadows. At night, the statues begin to breathe. The street lamp below the front window throws black shards through the slatted blinds, while year-round Christmas lights in the courtyard add a tint of dried blood to the sweeping palm fronds gesturing across the walls. Their jittery movements seem menacing… orchestrated by the blades of the ceiling fan above my desk. I lean back in the swivel chair and take a swig of the aura like it's the last shot of tequila.

That's where my head is when I'm taking pictures or scouting locations. Acting is believing, and so is *making* pictures.

First, ask yourself the classic method actor's question: *What's my motivation?*

Want to change the world? Document poverty, political corruption, the savaging of our environment? Or maybe commemorate a free meal you had at some fleabag in Palookaville (next page).

Want to capture someone's soul in a portrait? Record unforgettable moments in sports? Explore objects with macro-intensity?

Think storytelling. A visual sequence that rivets an audience. A still image that *moves*, transports the viewer to another place. Provokes a visible reaction from inanimate critics.

It's all possible, and that's what makes photography so seductive. Everyone *owns* a camera, but not everyone *uses* it.

Like an actor in a repertory company, my role changes, shifts with the assignment, the subject in front of my lens, or whatever obsesses me, yet the underlying spirit that compels me to take pictures remains.

FIND THE A.N.G.E.L.

When people hear the word *muse* (and let's face it, most never do), they conjure up a goddess inspiring a poet or painter. Well, I'm here to report that we photographers have our muses, too.

The great Alfred Stieglitz had Georgia O'Keeffe for inspiration and—who knows?—maybe he was her muse, although it's hard to

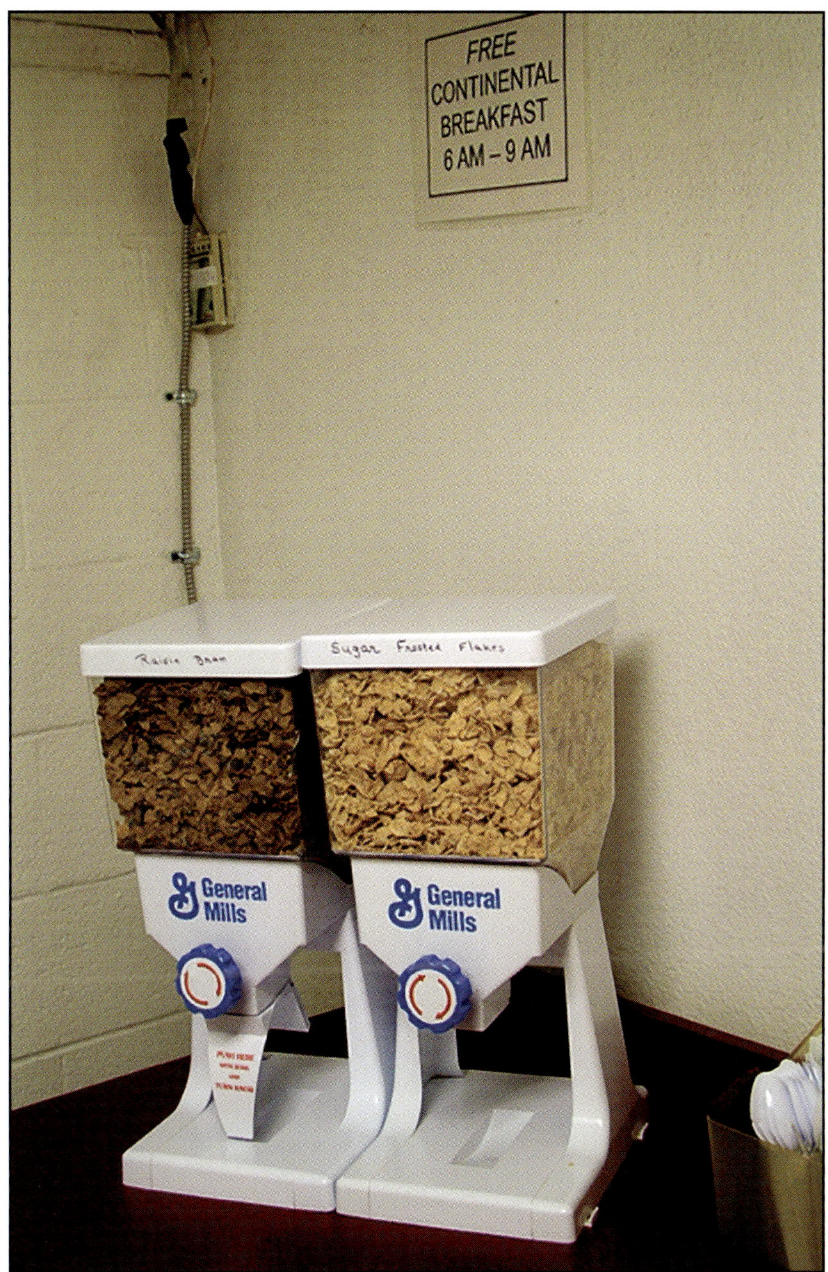

Continental Breakfast. I grabbed this shot at the crack of dawn when confronted with the absurdity of a "free" breakfast (B.Y.O.M.—bring your own milk). The ambiance, complete with exposed wiring, made me feel right at home.

imagine Stieglitz in goddess getup. Then, of course, there was Ron Galella (where else but here would you find Steiglitz and Galella in the same paragraph?), the king of the paparazzi, who made a career out of stalking his muse, Jackie Onassis.

Because I'm not a household name (not even in my own household), you'd never guess I have a muse of my own. Rather, an angel. An *acronymph* you might call her, because she defines the things I look for when I'm walking the shutterbug beat. She doesn't encompass everything, mind you, but the critical stuff that keeps me on my toes.

Anomaly

Nuance

Gesture

Expression

Light

I'll focus on three here: anomaly, gesture, and expression. We'll save nuance and light for Chapter 5, "Twinkle, Twinkle Little Noir."

ANOMALY

Who among us doesn't appreciate a visual quirk? It momentarily erases the drudgery of existence and reminds us how things aren't always what they seem.

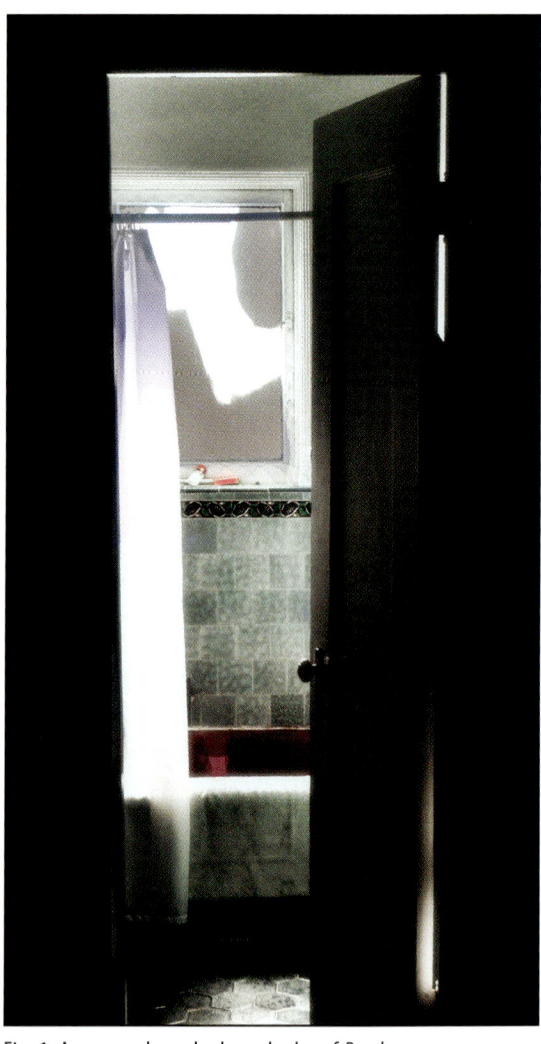

Fig. 1. An anomolous shadow, shades of *Psycho*.

I keep my eye peeled for the anomaly. It might be a strange shadow like the one I spotted on a bathroom window that made me think of Hitchcock's *Psycho* (Fig. 1). Or it could be a neon sign like the one I discovered at 3:00am while searching for a motel in the Arizona desert. (Fig. 2). Maybe it's a person, like the guy sitting in Balboa Park last night playing bagpipes, or the dandy strolling down 6th Avenue at noon in an oriental silk robe over his pj's, embroidered slippers on his feet, and a fez on his head with a long red tassle. (Nope, it wasn't Halloween, just my neighborhood.) Ain't it a shamus, the camera wasn't handy.

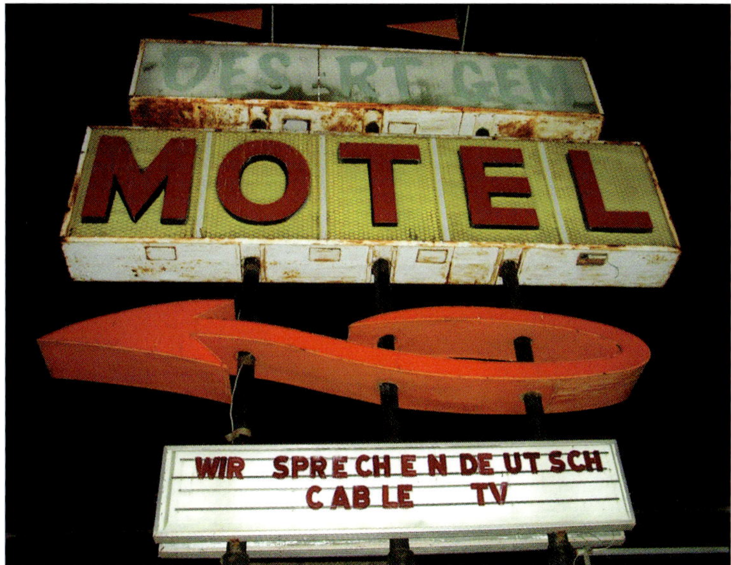

Fig. 2. Desert Gem (2004). Photo by Derek Pell.
I stumbled upon this sign in the middle of the night while lost in the Arizona desert. I used a digicam and its pop-up flash—too tired to lift the D-SLR. Where have all the Germans go ne since the Gem went bust?

You can find eccentricity in nature and landcsapes. There are architectural anomalies galore—especially here in Southern California. You just have to be tuned to the right frequency. That means take a second look at everything. At first glance a lot of oddities go unnoticed.

When living on the island of Coronado, I decided to take a morning walk. I stepped outside the front door, camera in hand, and was slipping the strap over my shoulder when directly across the street I was confronted by the scene in Fig. 3 below.

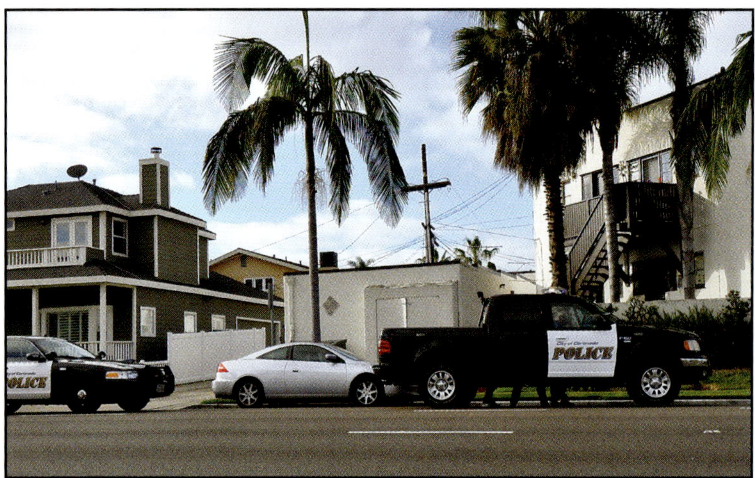

Fig. 3. Common traffic incident. No anomaly in sight, right?

To a photojournalist, a pair of cop cars on duty is steak and eggs—a signal to *"Play ball!"*—so I started shooting, natch, even though it looked like a routine traffic bust on the surface. You never know. Could be a perp on the lam. He suddenly draws a gat and starts squirtin' metal. Shoot first, delete later... that's my motto.

I grabbed some wide shots (Fig. 3) to cover the scene (what they call an "establishing" shot in Hollywood). I zoomed in close on the window of the van. Not much going on, except one cop apparently writing up a ticket (Fig. 4). When I zoomed out, I spied an anomaly relative to the three figures in the frame (Fig. 5). Might've been a one-legged perp, but it still looked oddball to me. I knew the pics wouldn't win me a Pulitzer or rake in a lot of jack, but they fell into the category known in the biz as "human interest," which newspapers crave. (NOTE: About 60% of the photos I sold to UPI were in this vein.) In this case, the photo editor would probably run the first shot alongside a cropped version of Fig. 5 (Fig. 6) and slap on a clever tagline. *Voila*—instant filler!

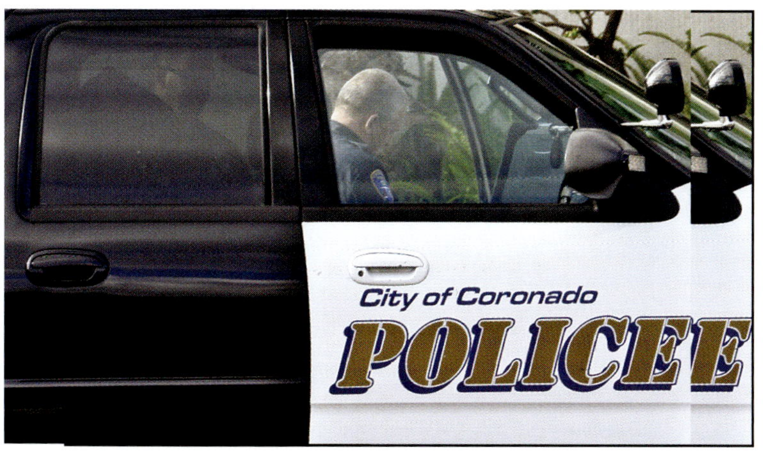

Fig. 4. A zoomed-in view.

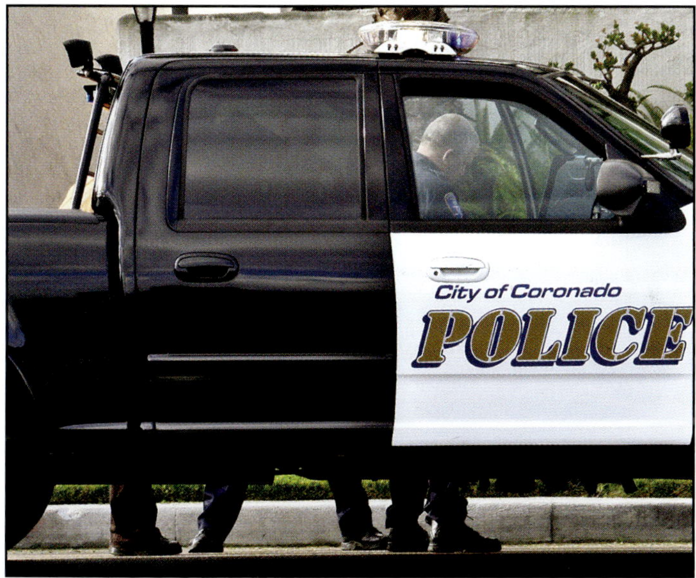

Fig. 5. A visual anomaly: three palookas, two flat-foots, yet only five feet.

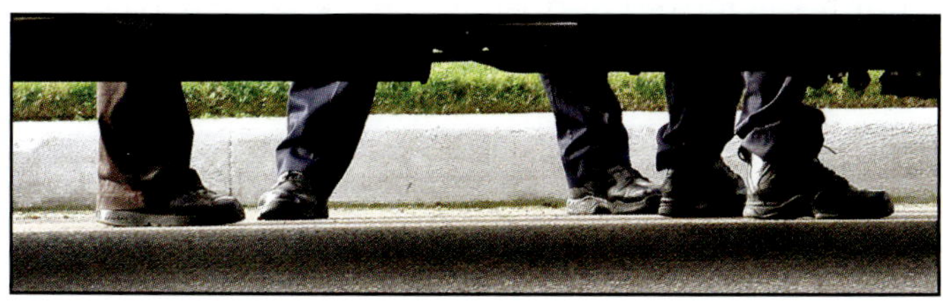

Fig. 6. If the shoe fits...

GESTURE

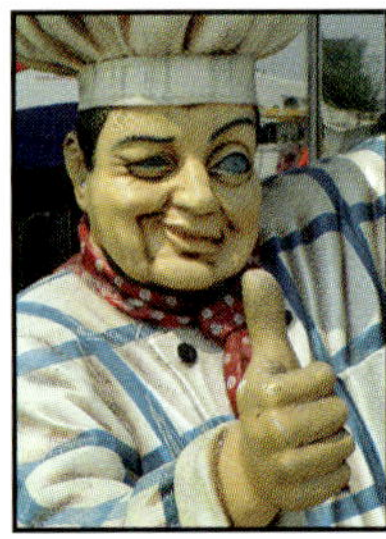

If you've ever had to photograph someone yapping at a podium, you know how hard it is to get a shot that stands out from the crowd (no pun intended). More than likely, the crowd stands out. Worst-case scenario: a boring topic and a stone-faced speaker who doesn't use his/her hands. Hell, without gestures and expression, what've you got? Nothing but a bronze bust in a dimly lit museum. Grab a ladder and go for an aerial shot.

When photographing people, watch for gesture and expression. Glom how someone moves, stands, reacts, shrugs, uses his hands, and you'll find the clue to a good shot. Don't hold out for some "grand gesture" destined to be seen around the world, like that classic of Winston Churchill flashing the victory sign. But look for a telling movement, and it just might wind up the subject of the photo. A good example is a shot I took of a hack in New York whose cab got rear-ended by a truck (Fig. 7).

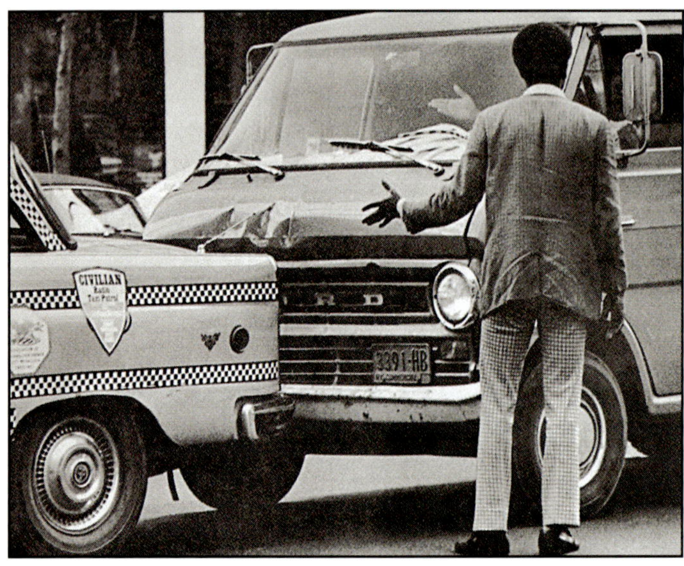

Fig. 7. Crash. Photo by Derek Pell.
The hands make this photo a winner. Two gestures for the price of one!

The key to capturing a defining gesture is simple: total focus and concentration. Keep your eye glued to the viewfinder and your finger on the trigger. Look away for a second, and you miss it. Your camera's Burst Mode (see **Chapter 6, "A Thirst for Burst"**) can aid and abet the killer shot, especially if you can anticipate it like in a tie game, bases loaded, bottom of the ninth. Who's gonna go to the powder room then?

When Mo Dean (wife of star Watergate witness John Dean) showed up at the hearings, all hell broke loose among the photographers. They hovered around her like she was the queen bee. She wasn't there to testify, just support hubby. She wasn't news, but one look at her and you see why she got all the attention, my own included. She was a shy, photogenic beauty. Hard to miss with a subject this pretty, but what makes the shot in Fig. 8 good is that one small unguarded gesture.

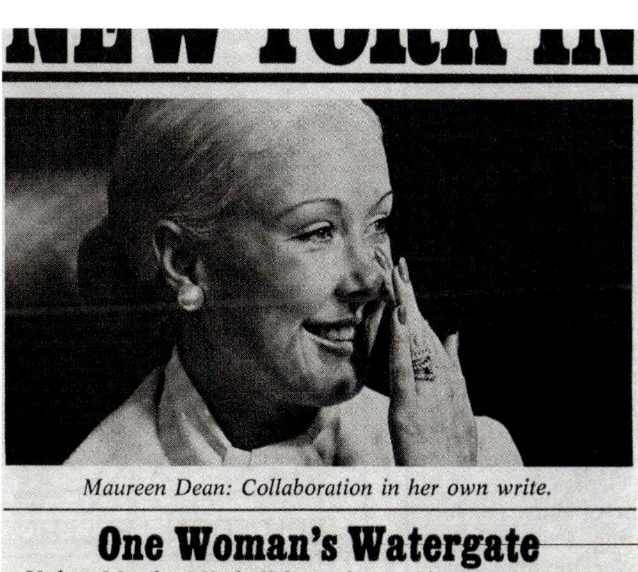

Maureen Dean: Collaboration in her own write.

One Woman's Watergate

Unless Martha Mitchell beats her to the punch, Maureen Dean will probably be the first Watergate wife to bring out a book about it all. A proposal for her personal story

Fig. 8. Maureen Dean at the Watergate Hearings. Photo by Derek Pell.

Back in the 1970s, when people actually read novels, writers were treated like rock stars. In the world of Lit, nobody had a bigger ego than novelist Norman Mailer. He thought of himself as the heavyweight champ of literature and was always looking for a fight—or a metaphor for one. He'd been photographed more times than Paris Hilton. In other words, he wasn't camera shy or unaware of his celebrity status. So capturing him when he was focused on something other than himself was a challenge. I had about 30 minutes to study him and when the opportunity arose I was ready (Fig. 9).

The photo wound up on the front page of the *Village Voice*. The day the paper hit the stands, the editor rang me up. "I've been informed by sources that Norman Mailer liked your photo of him and wants a glossy 8x10 print. Can you drop it on my desk this afternoon?" Hmm, maybe he did pose for the photo.

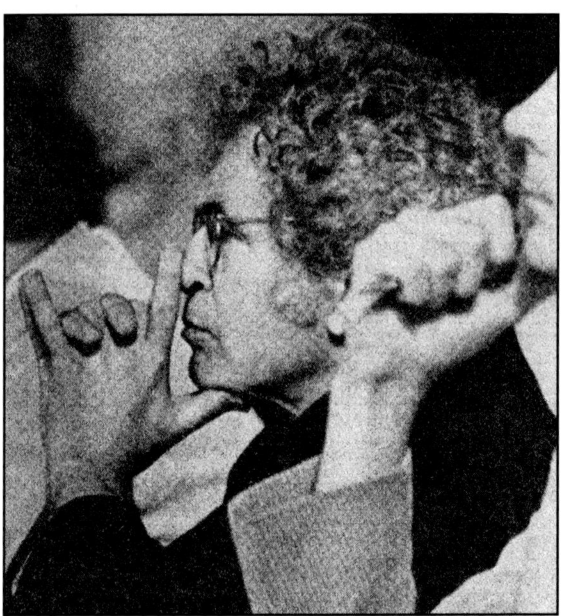

Fig. 9. Norman Mailer. Photo by Derek Pell.

In Fig. 10 you'll see the quintessential gesture of the pol: the hand-shake. It's the most common gesture of all, so what makes this one interesting? For one, it's being offered by former New York Governor Hugh Carey at a rally in midtown Manhattan. The composition is dead on, running from the top-right corner to the subject (Carey's hand). There's also some dramatic edginess to the photo thanks to the distortion provided by a Nikon Fisheye lens.

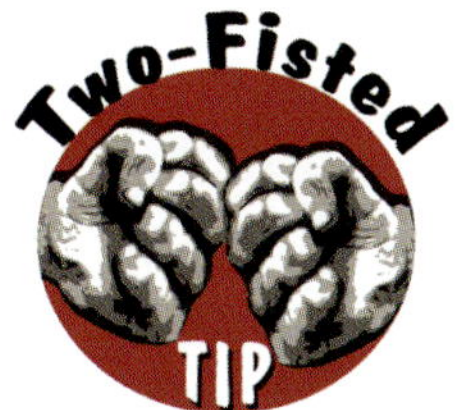

I was standing on the platform about a foot from Mayor Ed Koch (the guy in the foreground looking pissed), yet I was able to reel in all the usual suspects: the buildings in the background—even another press photographer wishing he was standing where I was. Never could have pulled this off with a 135mm lens.

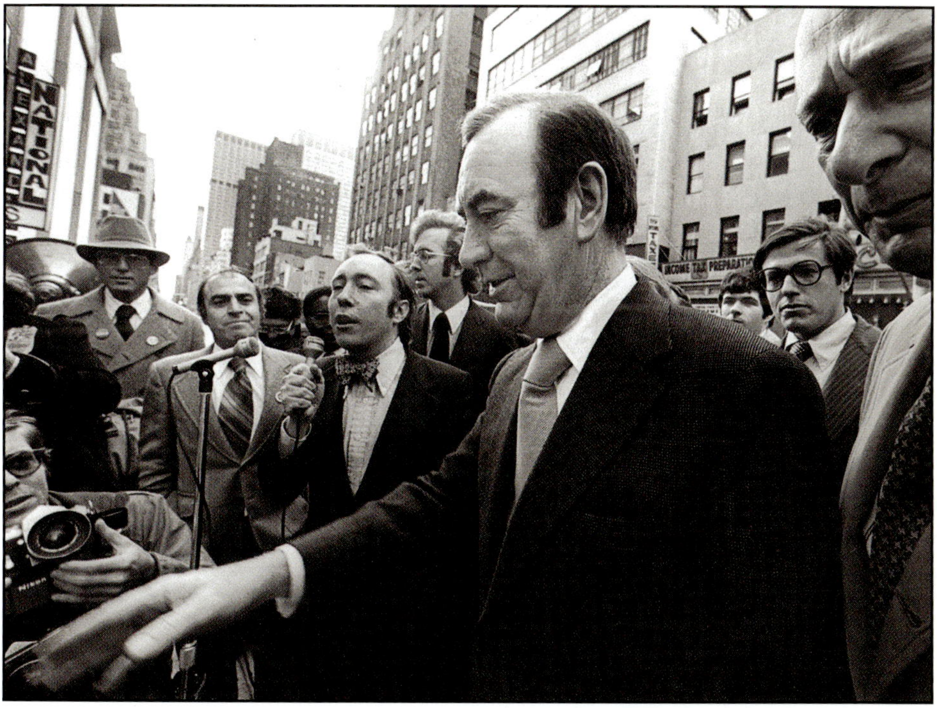

Fig. 10. Political Rally. Photo by Derek Pell. NY Gov. Hugh Carey extends a hand in the classic gesture of the politician. At his left, Mayor Ed Koch.

If you're covering a political rally, arrive *early* and case the joint. Find the best position and claim squatter's rights. Use a telephoto lens with plenty of range (18–200mm or better). Get as close to the subject as humanly possible, and make yourself invisible; i.e., don't step on anyone's toes. Not easy when your eye's on the viewfinder.

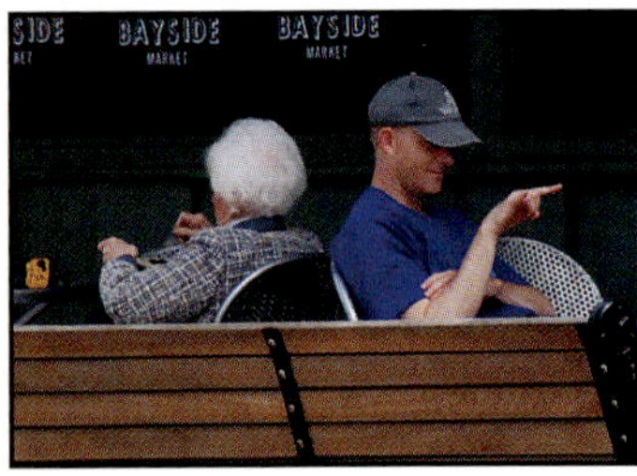

Fig. 11. A pot-luck street gesture.

It should go without saying that you don't need a hot assignment or some bigshot celebrity subject to practice what I'm preaching. Hone your skills in your own neighborhood, and train your eye to watch for gestures. Capture them in your personal work, family outings, and weekend shoots, for the sheer hell of it. Trust me, your people pix will really stand out.

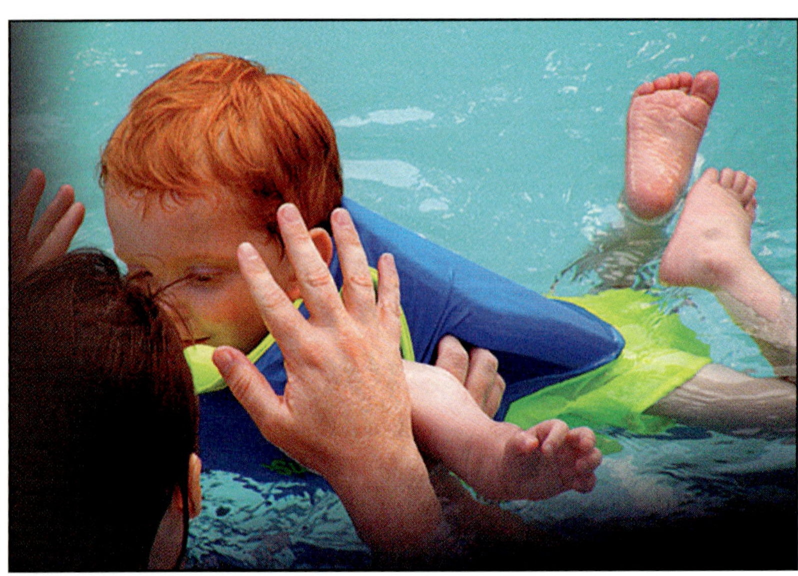

Fig. 12. Mom reacts to the kid's first swim lesson. (Kid looks pretty proud of himself, too.)

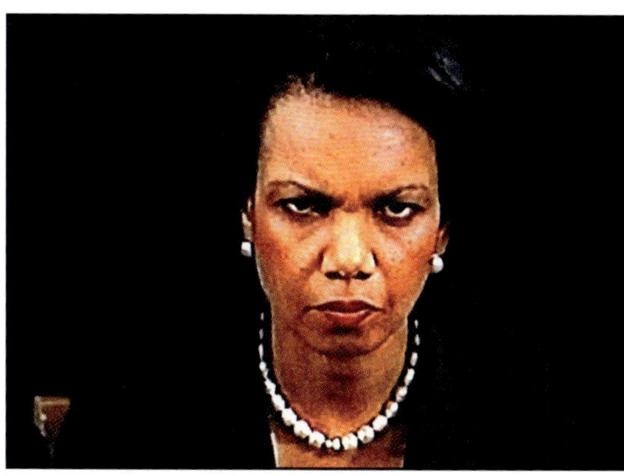

Fig. 13. Condi the Zombie.

EXPRESSION

Pardon my pun (or at least commute this sentence), but gesture and expression can go hand in hand. When they do it's like Happy Hour or 2-for-1 at your favorite hash house.

And while we're on the subject of happy hour, the shot of Condi Rice looking like a zombie (Fig. 13) is about as far from a smiley face as I want to travel. I nabbed it off a TV screen with a digicam during one of George W's State of the Union speeches. (Snapping shots off a TV is a great way to improve your timing for capturing expressions, not to mention sports action.) After the speech, MSNBC commentator Chris Matthews asked a colleague incredulously, "God, did you see that look on Condi's face?"

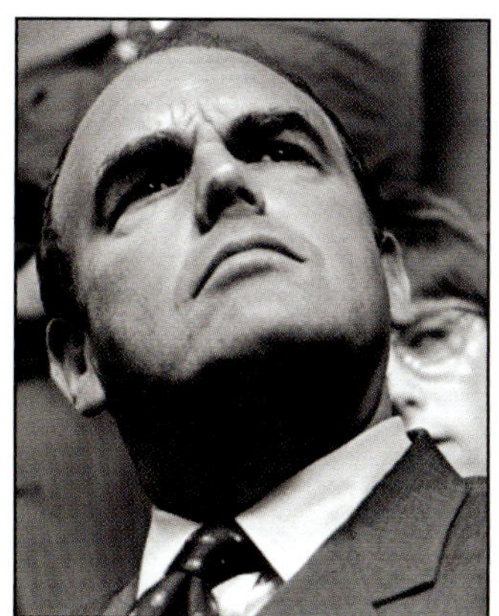

Fig. 14. John Ehrlichman, man of a thousand faces. Photo by Derek Pell.

I wound up using the photo in a short video about the war in Iraq called *Plan 9B from Outer Space.* But Condi's expression paled in comparison to those I witnesssed during the Watergate scandal. Aside from Nixon, John Ehrlichman (Fig. 14) had more weird facial expressions than actress Linda Blair in the movie *The Exorcist.* Ehrlichman was a portrait photographer's dream come true.

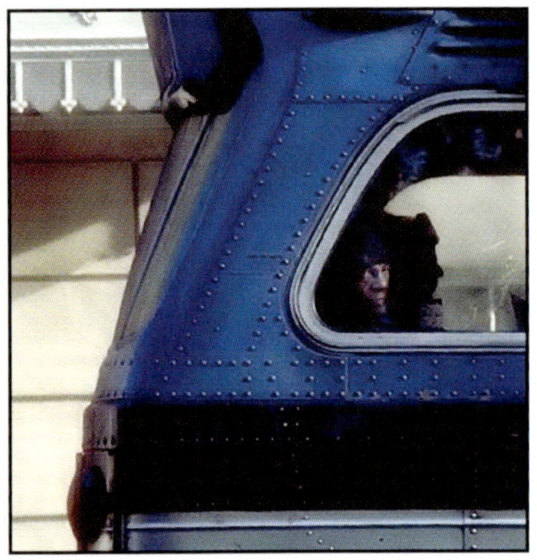

Fig. 15. Bus Stop. Photo by Derek Pell.

The photo in Fig. 15 was shot long after the Civil Rights era had ended and was not intended as a comment on race relations. What grabbed my attention was the guy's expression and how the sunlight caught his eye, in contrast to the silhouette of the man in the background. The bus made a stop, and I had only a few seconds to capture it.

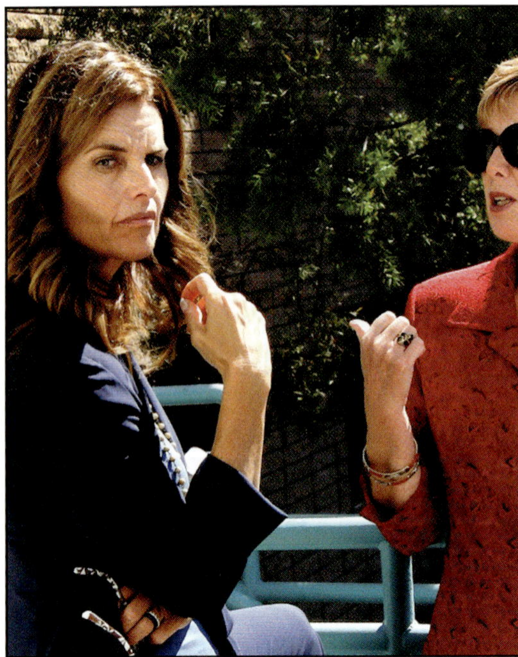

Fig. 16. Maria Shriver. Photo by Derek Pell.

Fig.16 is a recent photo of Maria Shriver. I was following California's First Lady around for a few hours as she toured a senior daycare facility in San Diego. I got some flattering photos of her, but they weren't particularly interesting. This shot (Fig. 16) had some drama, peppered by the other dame's *let's split* gesture. Although it appears Maria's dirty look is aimed smack-dab at yours truly, it wasn't. Heck, she even smiled when I tipped my fedora and cracked, "Welcome to SD, sweetheart."

OK, so maybe I never pitched that line, but she smiled.

Unlike a formal portrait shot in some swank studio where the photographer controls everything—the background, the lighting, the pose—street shooting is a lot riskier but, for my money, more of a kick.

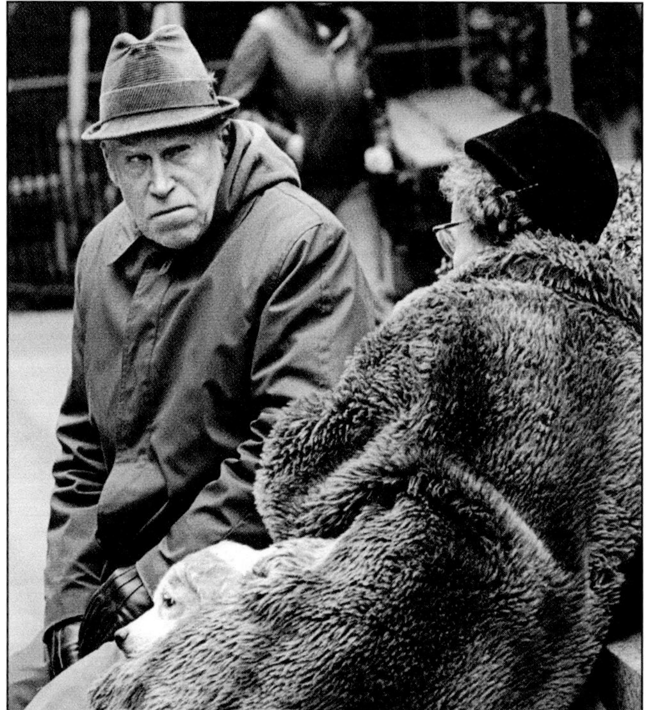

Fig. 17. Trio. Photo by Derek Pell.

Nuance and light underscore anomaly, gesture, and expression and give definition to a photograph. Examples are the dog's head in Fig. 17 above; the glint of sunlight in Fig. 15; the balance of hands and feet in Fig. 12; and the random shadow in Fig. 1.

Study the ambient light. Find the subtle balance between shadow and light that make a picture worth capturing. (In the next chapter we'll tackle both ambient and artificial light.)

You have to think fast, adapt to circumstances beyond your control, and remain in a state of readiness. The antenna is extended, the eyes in full scan, the body mobile, the brain fired up… anticipating, calculating, improvising. This holds true even when you think you know the score and can sense your prey. What you were looking for may turn out to be something you hadn't counted on. A grifter behind the wheel of a speeding heap, roscoe in hand aimed right at you. The unexpected is always there, just around the corner.

An angel.

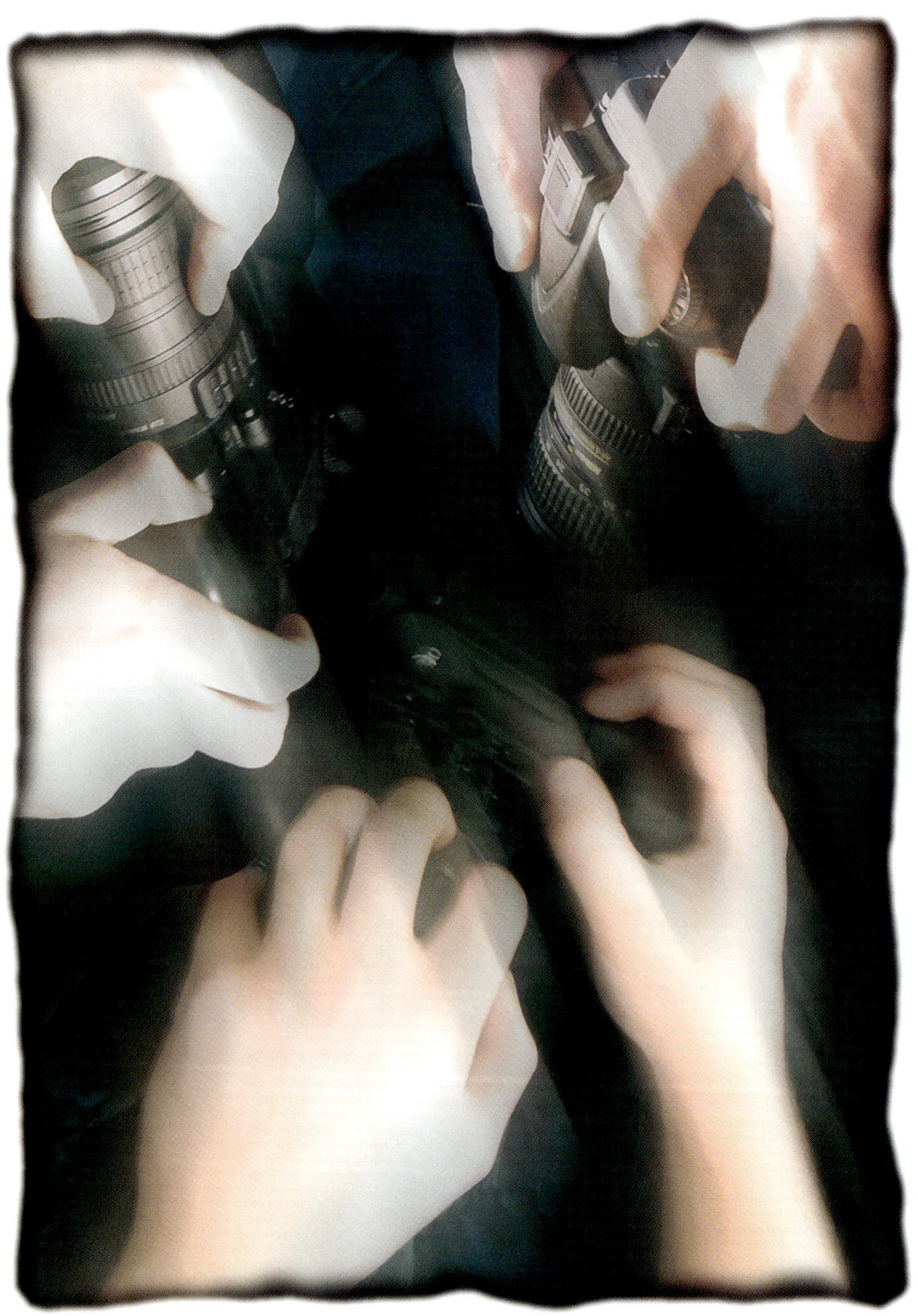

Photo by Derek Pell

4
HAND-TO-CAM COMBAT
From Auto Pilot to Taking Control

"Shoots me with my own gun, that's what gets me." –The Big Combo *(1955)*

Scene mode is for sissies. Sound cruel? Well, that's what you're paying me for, not to whistle Dixie and whitewash some cute little icons. You know the ones I mean: the smiley sun for cloudless days, the outhouse moon for night shots, the skier for sports. Hell, if you set the dial on *tsunami* you'll get a pretty decent shot of one, even if you never live to see it. Ain't technology great?

Here's my beef with Easy Street: *who's the photographer?* You, or that expensive contraption you're holding?

If you want to leave the camera in charge, be my guest. I'll make a clean sneak out of town and write a potboiler.

I confess, temptation is hovering...just like I might be tempted if a grifter offered to sell me software that would finish writing this book. (If you hear of any, let me know.)

It ain't just dimestore point-and-shoots that feature no-sweat scene modes; D-SLRs do, too. My advice: Save your soul and ignore the temptation. Instead, find the manual that came with your camera and read it cover to cover. Then read it again and *memorize it*. Right down to the exciting, action-packed trademark disclaimer.

Know your weapon like a PI knows his. Wrestle away the controls from the camera and go take a thousand test shots using manual settings. The power trip's on me. Remember, you're not paying for film.

AUTO is fine until the moment you decide to *make* a photo rather than snap one. For example, you want your subject to stand out against an out-of-focus background. Auto won't do that, but *Aperture Priority* will.

Now, I can't tell you how to use your particular camera's controls, but I can sure show you what to look for.

GET TO KNOW YOUR ISO

Back in the Dumb Ages, I loaded my SLR with Kodachrome film—the equivalent of armor-piercing bullets—the be-all end-all for rich, gorgeous, saturated color. Yet there came times when I'd have, say, 12 exposures left on a roll of 36 and the light got lousy, late afternoon low, with no tripod handy. So what did I do?

I called it a day. The speed of Kodachrome was too slow for a decent shot, and I wasn't about to blow those 12 exposures and load a roll of high-speed, black-and-white Tri-X.

Well, that's the past, and good riddance.

Digital cameras don't sweat film speed; they eat it for breakfast. That is, they've got ISO settings (you don't need to know what ISO stands for, but since you insist it's International Standards Organization. Happy now?), which amounts to the same thing with one big advantage—you can change the ISO speed on every shot!

Here's a common scenario. You're outside the Big House snappin' a perp walk in broad daylight. You've got a nice low ISO profile set to 200. Then you step indoors, where it's dimly lit and the cops are allergic to flash. No problem; you just twist the dial to maybe ISO 600 and everything's jake. Makes one glad to be living in the future.

Today's ISO range is so wide it could make a palm tree tango. My Nikon D90 accelerates from 200 to—stand back—3200. I can adjust it even further at either end of the spectrum in small increments, so I wind up with an effective range of 100–4000!

Bring on the darkness, baby!

Like everything else, however, there's a downside to high ISO speeds. It comes in the form of **noise**, and I'm not talking Glenn Miller's orchestra—I'm talking grungy dots and garbage in the photo. Color shifts, too, that look like a postcard from the 1940s.

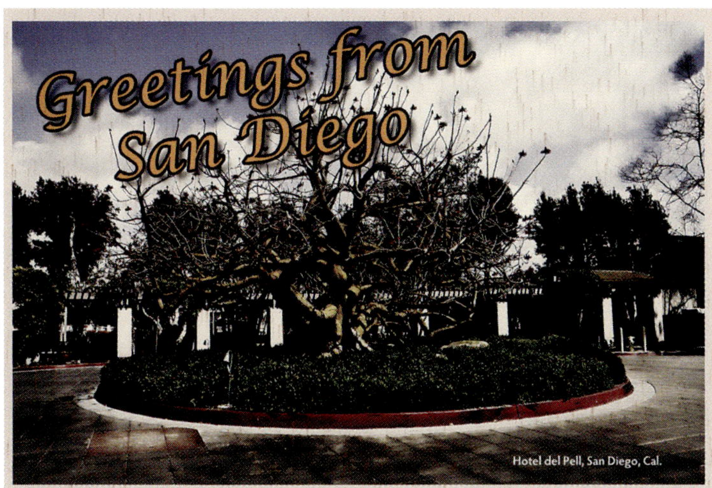

Photo by Derek Pell

Now all digital images have noise, but look at a properly exposed image shot at a low ISO setting, and you won't see any unless you blow it up to billboard size and stand on a ladder. Shoot at ISO 4000, on the other hand, and it'll look like you were out in a blizzard. (If you *were* out in a blizzard, you need a long vacation.)

Lucky for us, mysterious geeks who never take vacations are working on the noise problem even as we speak. Quality is on the rise. The Nikon D90 has a rep for keeping the noise down to a minimum at high settings. I've shot at ISO 800+, and you'd swear it was 200.

Still, noise is an eyesore to beware of.

There are post-production fixes for noise, third-party plug-in filters for Photoshop such as **Noiseware Professional** and **Noise Ninja**. Both are good joes that scrub away artifacts while preserving sharpness. But less time spent in post production means more time taking pictures.

Then again, you can always choose to make noise your style, push the ISO to the max, and revel in the retro film effect.

If you set the camera to Auto ISO, it'll make the decision for you, so set it yourself and go with the cam's lowest setting. That way you'll get the highest-quality results.

WHOSE WHITE BALANCE IS IT, ANYWAY?

What you see ain't always what you get… colorwise. The job of a digital camera's white balance is to take the temperature of the light with an invisible thermometer and neutralize it so you don't get sci-fi color casts. It renders colors accurately so the scene reflects what your eye sees. In daylight with a clear sky, the temperature is around 5500k. (The "k" stands for Kelvin, a temperature scale, but don't drop the name at a cocktail party.) Indoor shooting under tungsten lamps, and the temp will be lower—around 3200K. Those are the extremes, and the camera measures the light to reproduce it.

The camera can do this automatically, or you can set the balance manually. My D-SLR's Auto White Balance is usually right on the nose, so here's one area where I'm usually content to hop in the backseat. But if the lighting is contrasty and temperamental, I go manual. If you're unhappy with the way your Auto White Balance performs, consult the cam's user guide and set it yourself. Basically you turn a dial, point the camera at a white wall or piece of paper (making sure you're in tight so it fills the viewfinder), and press the shutter. That locks in the right white and the rest of the rainbow tags along.

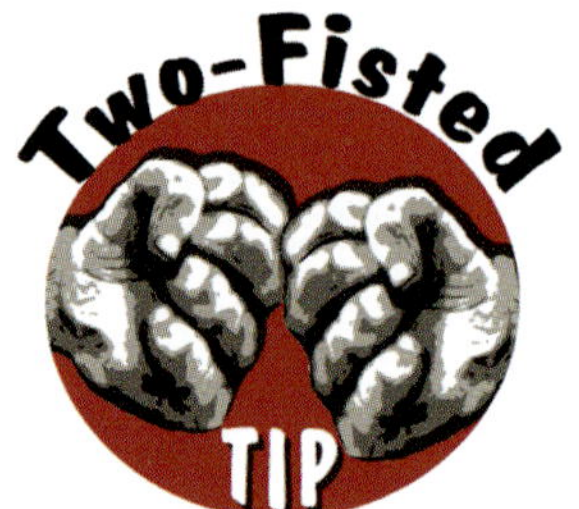

If you set your own White Balance and then move to a new location (or if the lighting conditions change), remember to switch to Auto White Balance, or take another manual WB reading. Otherwise, you'll wind up with screwy color.

There are gizmos you can buy that improve White Balance accuracy. There's one I use called the **Lally Cap** (Fig. 1). It's like a mini shower cap that fits over the lens. Yeah, I know, it doesn't go with my macho image, but it's easy to slip off and on when nobody's looking. Sometimes the results are noticeably improved, other times indistinguishable from Auto. When I use the cap I play it safe.

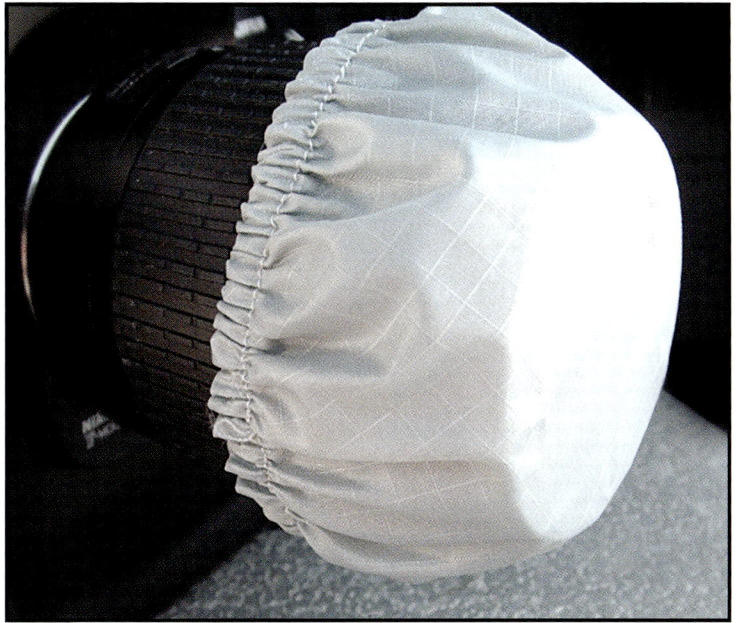

Fig. 1. The Lally Cap.

D-SLRs also come with their own generic White Balance presets, which usually include Cloudy, Shade, Incandescent, Fluorescent, and Direct Sunlight. I'm still waitin' for L.A. Smog; are you listening, Nikon? The presets can be handy in a pinch when you're pressed for time. The D90 even lets you customize its presets via a color grid, but that's a road I'll leave to more daring detectives.

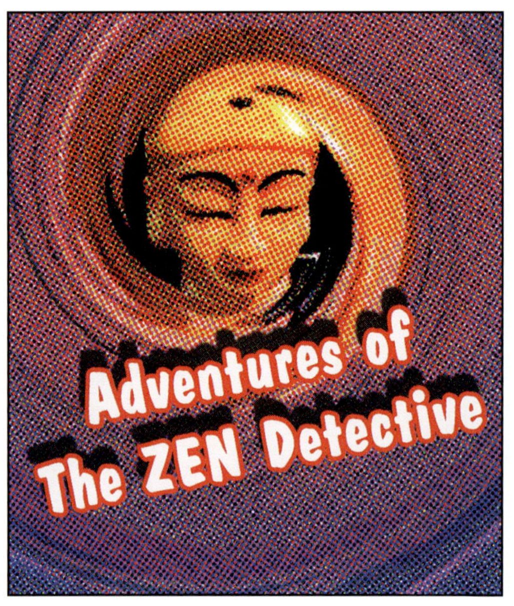

I once got tagged the "Zen Detective" because I cracked a case with an ice cream koan. *(OK, so I ain't Charlie Chan.)* Remember when I suggested you shoot in RAW format? Well, let me bang a conundrum: Shoot in RAW+JPEG. RAW gives you options. It's like digital reincarnation: you get to return to the scene of the crime and do it over again. So if the White Balance goes south, it ain't the end of the world. You can edit the image in Adobe Camera Raw and fix it. Anyone still bemoaning the demise of film should see a shrink.

Extreme case: In Fig. 2 on the opposite page I intentionally shot my partner (Zenny the Laptop Buddha) with the camera's preset White Balance set to Fluorescent. "A big bowl of wrong," to quote a Hollywood agent I know. Notice the arrow I added pointing to the words "As Shot" to drive home the error. The photo looks like it had a bad "Day For Night" filter applied to it. To correct the color cast, I selected Auto from the drop-down menu in Adobe Camera Raw. Presto! The natural color returned (Fig. 3), and those old White Balance blues disappeared.

When the White Balance is off by only a hair, try adjusting the Temperature and Tint sliders to correct it.

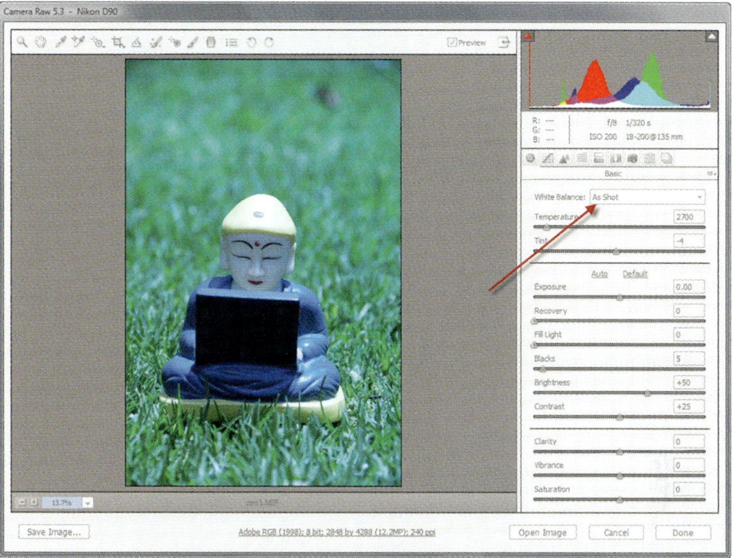

Fig. 2. Camera Raw panel showing photo "as shot," with a blue color cast caused by the camera's fluorescent White Balance setting.

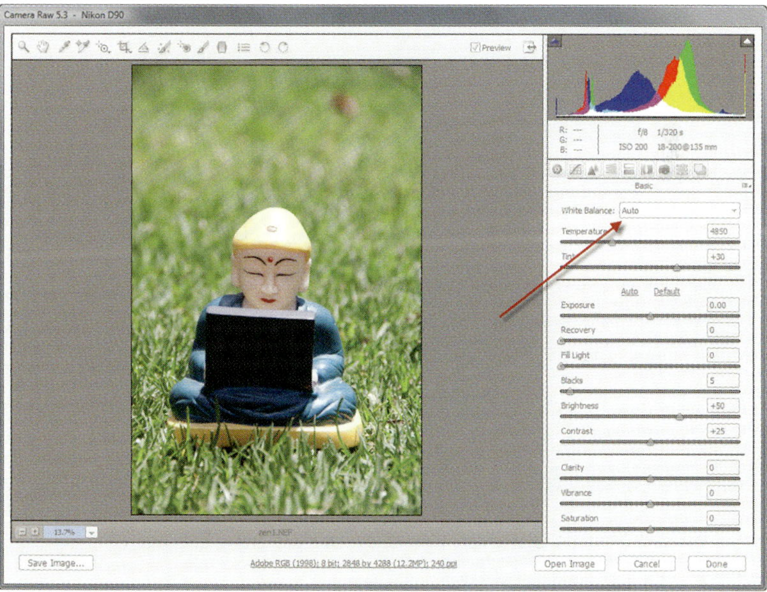

Fig. 3. White Balance changed to Auto.

Another choice in Camera RAW is Daylight, which, in the example in Fig. 4, added some saturation but also slightly overexposed the image. The exposure can be changed via the Exposure slider. Dragging left decreases exposure; dragging right bumps it up. In Fig. 5, I customized the array settings to suit my taste. My taste runs to tequila on ice and saturated color. Some folks like wine and desaturated hues; there's room for all kinds on this planet. No rules here—it's whatever grabs you.

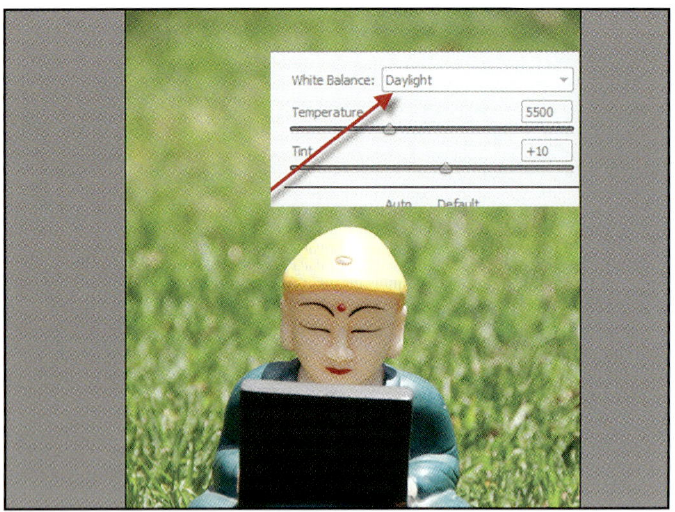

Fig. 4. Daylight White Balance setting.

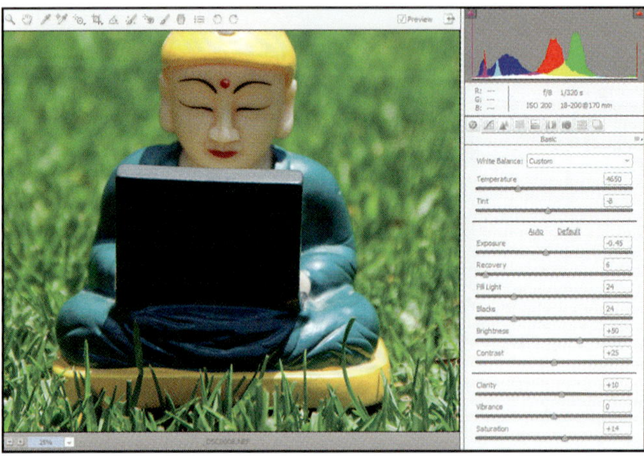

Fig. 5. Customized White Balance with my "macho" saturation applied.

METERING PATTERNS

Dedicated Nikonians such as myself have long enjoyed three main TTL (Through the Lens) metering patterns dating back to when film ruled the world:

Matrix, Spot, Center-Weighted

That holy trio pretty much covers the territory when the territory being covered is what you see in the viewfinder. The big picture on the little screen, so to speak.

Take a gander at 'em and see what they can do for you.

NOTE TO CANON (AND OTHER BRAND) SHOOTERS: I can't cover every camera because they're all different and I don't own 'em. With the exception of video capability, however, many of the D90's features are found on other D-SLRs, only they have weird names. (Just kiddin.') All have multiple metering modes. For example, Canon's equivalents are *Evaluative*, *Partial*, and *Center-Weighted*. So non-Nikon shooters consult your manual. Better yet (if you've done what I suggested at the start of this chapter), recall from memory.

MATRIX METERING

Matrix metering struts its stuff in evenly lit situations. It reads the overall frame. Light reflected from the subject strikes the lens and gets chopped up into cells like a stool pigeon, where the brightness ratios and focal distance (depending on the lens in use) get measured. My brain is no match for the camera's (I flunked math at Private Eye school)… it makes mathematical calculations faster than a bullet whizzing by. Throw in today's sophisticated Scene Recognition technology, and you've got astoundingly accurate AF (AutoFocus) light readings that make a handheld meter look like a divining rod. Okay, divining rods are cool, too, but when was the last time you actually saw somebody use one?

SPOT METERING

Use Spot metering when you want to hit a bull's eye, like a person's eyes or a small part of an object. I used Spot metering for this test shot of a wireless flash trigger (Fig. 6).

The Spot pattern covers only about 2% of the total frame, so the aim here is about as narrow as an undertaker's tie.

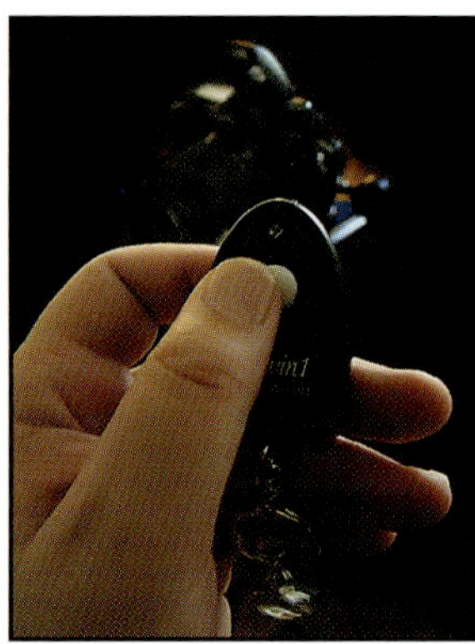

Fig. 6. Spot-metered subject in foreground.

Put Spot to good use when you don't want the background light butting in and influencing the metered light on the subject. Say, for example, you're shooting a mug shot and don't want to wind up dead-weighted in the East River. A portrait of a racketeer from Hoboken, and he's standing in front of a wall that's draped in black crepe (so maybe it's his high school reunion, who knows?). If you have the camera set on Matrix, the guy will be overexposed, and what racketeer wants that?

CENTER-WEIGHTED METERING

Like its name suggests, this pattern concentrates on the center of the frame, reading roughly about 75% of the center area and 25% of the outside. The difference between this and Matrix is that Center-Weighted takes into consideration all the zones of the frame while leaning in favor of the middle. This is a good choice when the background area is brighter than the foreground. In that situation Matrix might go a little nuts and overexpose the foreground.

For walkaround grab shots, you're pretty safe with the camera set to Matrix. When the light gets tricky and there's a lot of contrast, apply the brakes and pick the pattern best suited to the conditions.

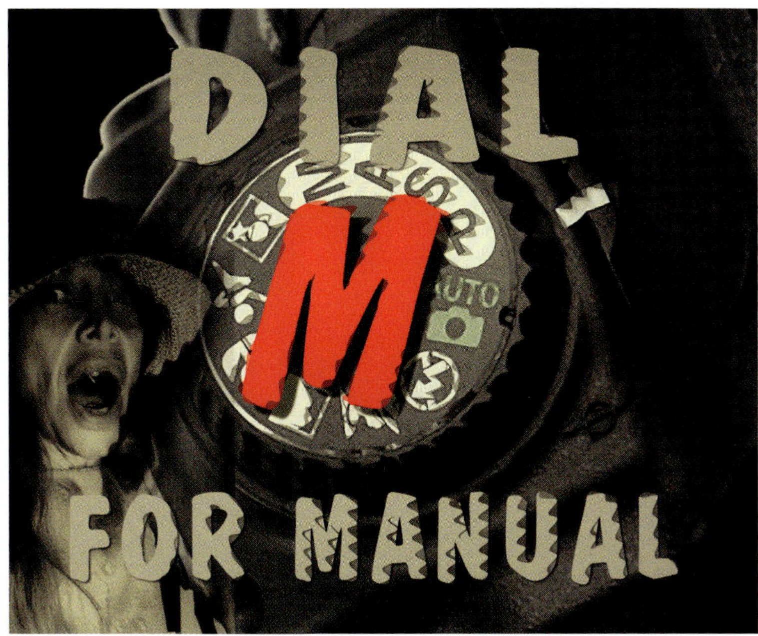

Ladies and gentlemen, may I present the main attraction: **Advanced Exposure Modes**. Time to take the bull by the horns (or, in this case, the mode dial) and give it a twist. Hell, you might just pick a winner and clean out the casino.

PLAY IT AGAIN, S.A.M.

I'm going to focus on three settings here: **S** for Shutter Priority, **A** for Aperture Priority, and **M** for full-tilt Manual. With either S or A modes selected, you and the camera become bosom buddies collaborating on a case, solving the mystery of the missing exposure.

Most pros I know tend to favor either Aperture or Shutter Priority, depending on the nature of their photography, but you'll use both.

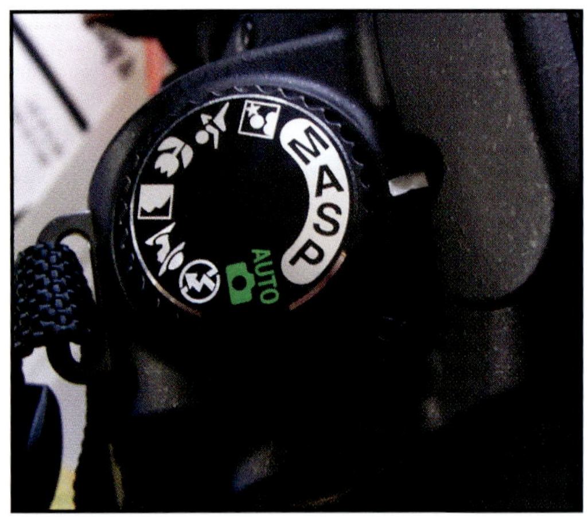

APERTURE PRIORITY

Aperture Priority means what it says, and it don't mess around. Choose an aperture value (f-stop), and the camera automatically selects the apropriate shutter speed for a good exposure. (Caveat: If you set the aperture to, say, f/11 when there's not enough light, you'll get a warning in your viewfinder—maybe even a blinking light on a cop's cruiser—telling you to "open up" the lens to compensate, or bump up the ISO.

The primary reason to shoot in Aperture Priority is to control a photo's *depth of field* (DOF). It's all about control. That's why you're packin' a D-SLR and not a pea shooter, right?—*be creative.* For instance, when shooting outdoor portraits, you'll want to put a lid on distracting details in the background that could steal the scene. Or maybe you're after an artsy look... a single flower isolated against a soft swash of color (Fig. 7). See, even this hard-boiled dick has a sentimental side.

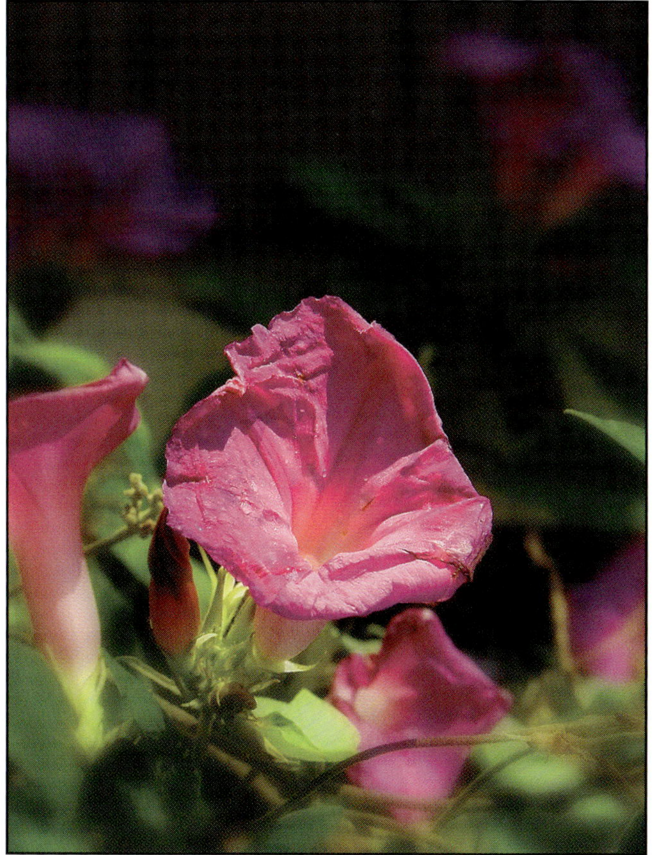

Fig. 7. A wide aperture of f/4.3 (1/400 sec., ISO 100. 24mm) softened the background and made the flower stand out.

Your D-SLR has a depth of field preview button so you can check the effect of your aperture setting. Try it.

You can also produce a nice blurred background by using a tele-photo or a long focal length on a zoom lens. The longer the lens, the shallower the depth of field. If you shoot with a zoom set to 170mm you'll get an effect similar to Fig. 8. Plenty of sunlight enabled me to stop down to f/11 and get razor-sharp detail in the petals. I also set the EV (Exposure Compensation) to underexpose by −1/3 a stop, which added a dash of saturation.

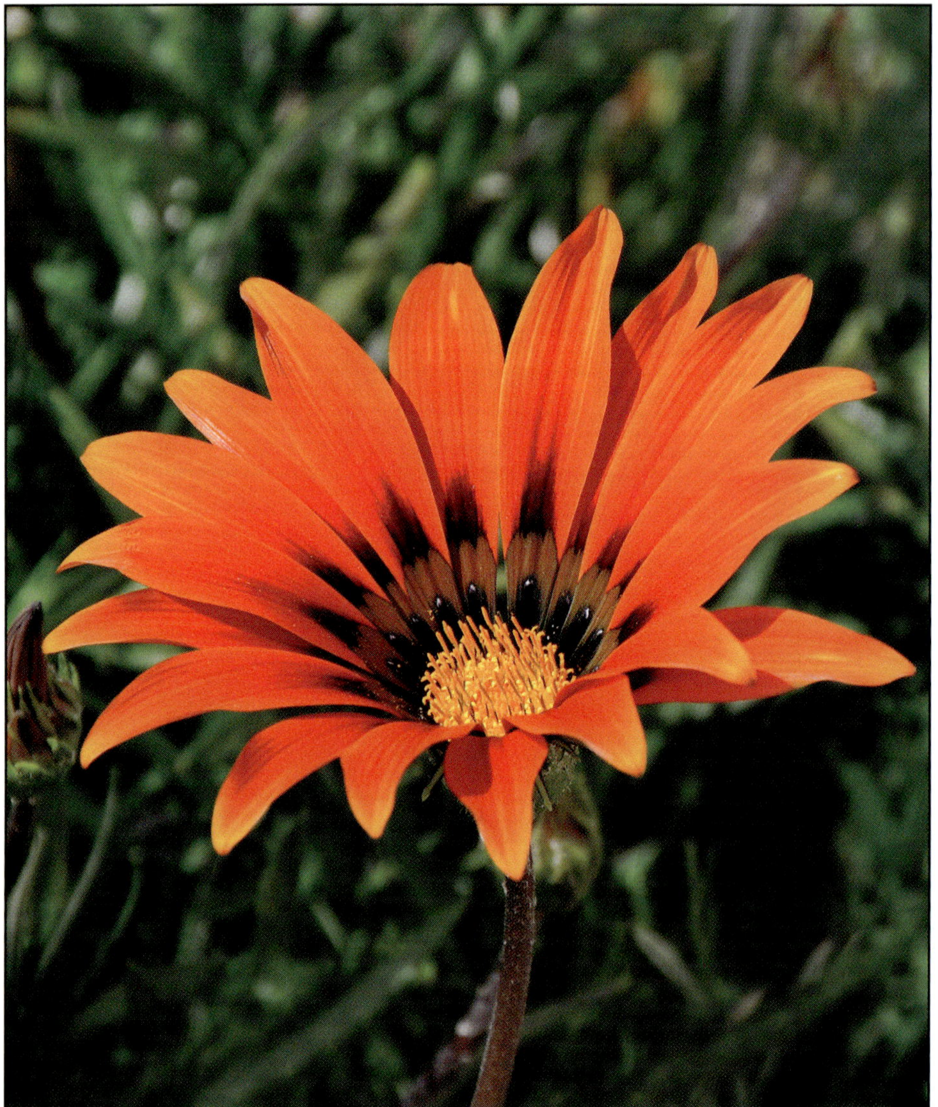

Fig. 8. A long focal length of 170mm gave this photo a shallow depth of field. (1/250 sec. at f/11; -1/3 EV; ISO 200) Photo by Derek Pell.

A good exposure is like a wedding night. The groom is the Shutter Speed, and Aperture's the bride. When this couple "clicks," they make beautiful music together while you get a top-notch shot. You can't have one without the other, so remember to keep 'em both in mind. For example, if you stop the lens way down to f/18, the camera may select a shutter speed that's too slow for you to handhold. (Sadly, there's a limit to how much shake, rattle, and roll you can get away with—even using a lens with vibration reduction.) So if the camera wants to shoot at, say, 1/4 sec., you'd better whip out a tripod or open up the lens and shoot faster.

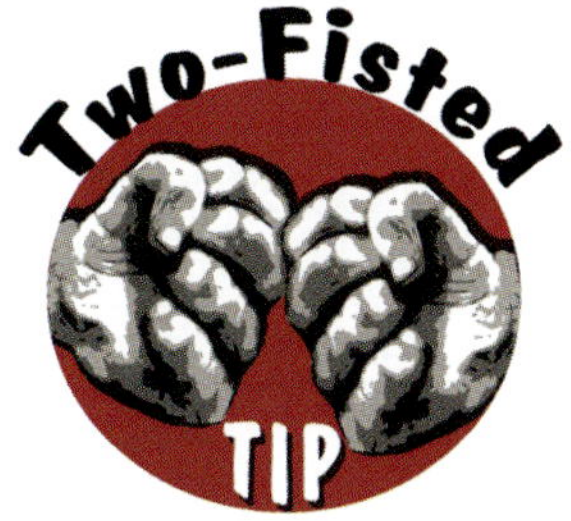

SLOW ZONE SPEED TRAP: I didn't have a tripod the night I eyed the fountain scene in Fig. 9. I tried to handhold the camera at 1/5 of a second and got a bad case of the blurs. No time to crank up the ISO; the kids got bored and moved on. Would've made a nice shot. LESSON: If you want to take terrific night shots, *pack a tripod.*

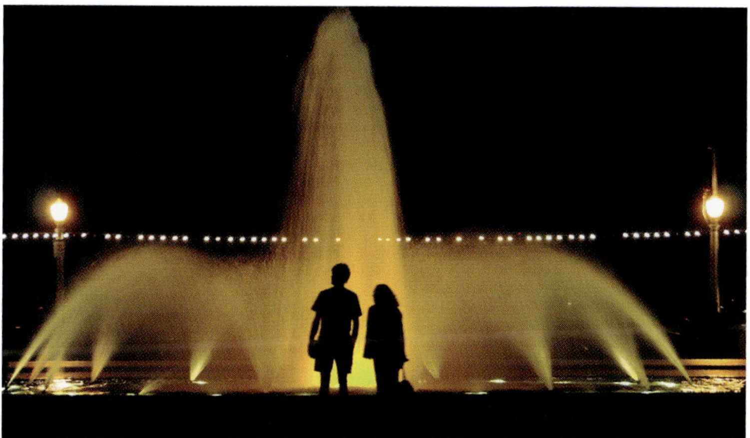

Fig 9. Missed opportunity for a nice not shot, thanks to handholding the camera when I should've used a tripod.

With Aperture Priority, you can direct the viewer's gaze to the chosen subject rather than letting their eyes wander around aimlessly searching for one. It's like those boring wide-angle landscape shots with nothing in the foreground for scale and everything equally sharp. Average Joe can't find a subject because the photographer didn't bother to make a creative decision.

SHUTTER PRIORITY (S)

With S Mode you can stomp on the gas and let the camera control aperture. News photographers and sports shooters favor Shutter Priority because they're out to capture action—to freeze fleeting movements like a bank heist, the Indy 500, a slam dunk, a grand slam, a comet streaking across the sky. 1/500 and up is the ballpark.

The Nikon D90 offers speeds ranging from a snail-on-a-bad-day 30 seconds to a sound-barrier bustin' 1/4000. (If it takes 1/4000 of a second to freeze the subject, you probably can't see it with the naked eye.)

A shutter speed of 1/500 of a second was fast enough to freeze this runner (Fig. 10), but it wouldn't be enough to nab a speeding Ferrari.

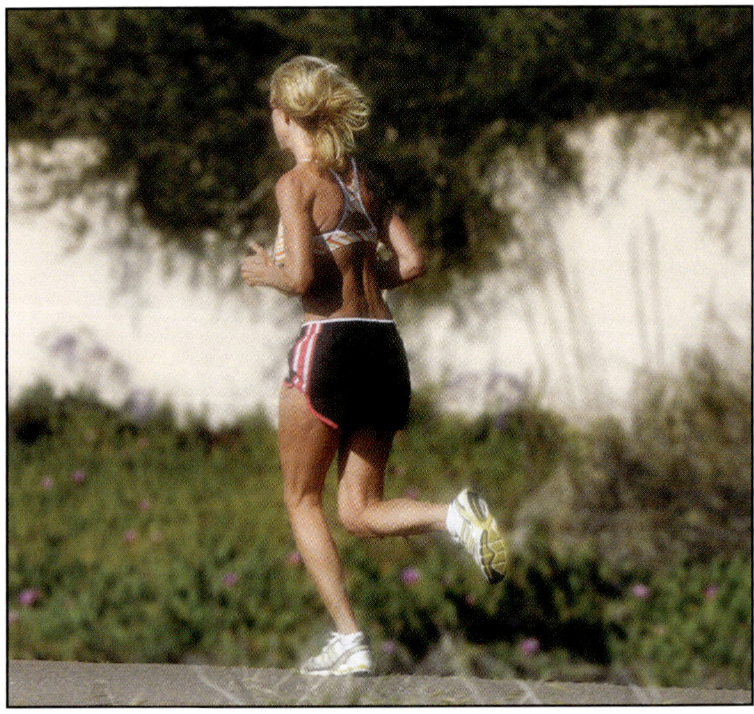

Fig. 10. A shutter speed of 1/500 freezes this runner in mid-stride..

When shooting fast-moving subjects, you'll want to take advantage of your camera's Continuous Shooting mode. It enables you to fire in bursts like a machine gun. (See **Chapter 6, "A Thirst for Burst,"** for the lowdown on Burst mode.)

What shutter speed you choose will depend on the speed of the subject. If you photograph a stationary object at 1/125 and the camera moves a fraction, it might not affect the shot; but if the *subject* moves you'll get blur. Better to hit the accelerator when shooting moving targets. If depth of field (DOF) is a concern, keep your eye on the aperture value. High aperture = greater DOF.

MANUAL MODE (M)

Dialing M is like calling a pal in the DA's office and saying, "I can crack this case wide open if you keep the flatfoots outta my hair."

In Manual mode you're flying solo with all the controls at your fingertips. You get the credit (or the blame) by determining both the aperture value and shutter speed.

Look in the viewfinder, and you'll be able to tell whether the exposure you've chosen is on the money. For example, the Nikon D90 displays a little scale with indent marks and a zero point in the middle. If the scale indicates you're left of the zero, you're underexposed; to the right you're overboard. Shoot for a week with your camera set on Manual, and you'll have yourself a crash course in the mechanics of exposure. There's no better way to understand the relationship between aperture and shutter than by shooting full-tilt Manual.

Once you've got M under your belt, you rule the world. Me, I prefer makin' fewer decisions. I switch between A and S modes, but you'll usually find me ridin' the A train. Besides, I'm daft about DOF.

When you find which letter thrills ya—take control and go with it.

PROGRAMMED-AUTO (P)

Why am I bringing up this mode when it takes away the control from you and sets both aperture and shutter speed? Because, unlike the fully point-and-shoot AUTO Mode (which henceforth shall forever remain nameless), highlighted in alien green on the Nikon D90, Programmed-Auto mode lets you override its selections and change them.

This can be handy if you're out walking and stumble upon some breaking news. If the camera is set to Programmed-Auto, you're guaranteed to quickly capture the action, and you can then tweak the auto settings if there's time.

It's also helpful if you're shooting in a dimly lit church or a burlesque house, where a flash is as frowned upon as a tux at a nudist colony. Set on P, the camera's built-in flash will not automatically pop up and fire (like it would if you had the camera set to that, uh, "nameless" mode I mentioned earlier). Simply put, P just might save your A and spare you the bum's rush out of there.

BUSTING THE BRACKET RACKET

Back in the days of film, I was given a tip by a crusty old pro. He had a fat Cuban cigar dangling from his lips as he polished his beat-up old Nikons with a rag. "I've got one word of advice for you, kid..." he grumbled, and blew a smoke ring the size of a hula hoop. "...*bracket*."

I didn't know what the hell the word meant, so I went home and looked it up. Sure enough, the old coot had passed along some valuable wisdom. Bracketing meant making three different exposures of the same shot: the meter's suggested exposure, plus 1 stop over and 1 stop under. One of the three was almost guaranteed to be good.

It made a lot of sense, especially because you never knew what you'd captured until the film came back from the lab. Hard to imagine life without an instant preview on the LCD screen, ain't it? But just because today we can review our photos in a slideshow right inside the camera doesn't mean we shouldn't bracket. For one thing, previewing shots on the LCD sucks the juice out of batteries like a vampire on a binge. That's also the reason I've never bothered to crop, edit, or filter my photos in the camera. Strikes me as a dumb gimmick the boys in marketing dreamed up. Besides, that's what the digital darkroom is for. (If I'm on a tight deadline, I'll haul my laptop on location and edit the photos on that.) Bracketing with a D-SLR is a no-brainer. It's automatic and fast. Choose the bracketing options you want (for example, the number of frames and the amount of shift between them) and snap three shots. Bracketing means you can hand the client a well-exposed photo instead of an excuse. Here's a bracketed series I shot today near Zoom Street. (Figs. 11–13). I used a wide angle, 18mm. The ISO: 200.

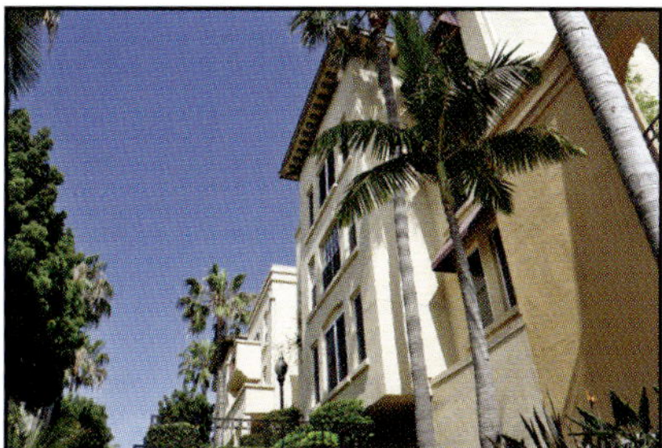

Fig. 11. First exposure: 1/250 sec. at f/10, 0EV.

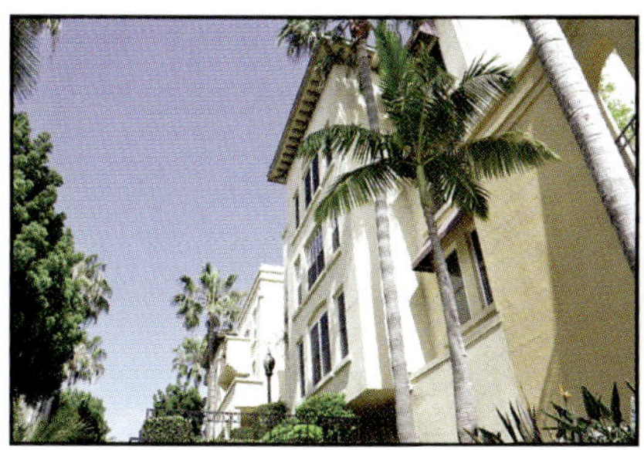

Fig. 12. 1/250 sec. at f/10, 1EV.

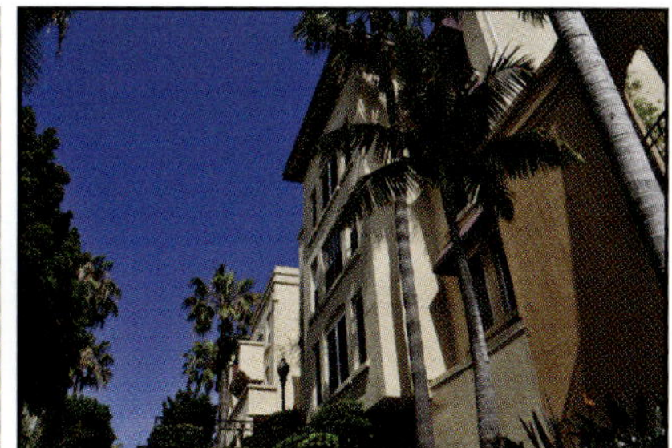

Fig. 13. 1/250 sec. at f/10, -1EV.

EXPOSURE COMPENSATION (EV)

I've got an itchy finger when it comes to the Exposure Compensation button. It's a control I gravitate to like a gambler to the slots. Although I haven't kept score, I'd lay you odds I use it on a third of all my shots.

The EV dial (or button, as the case may be) is where you go when you're shooting under extreme or tricky lighting situations that'll throw the meter off balance. Like when you're standing in snow. Take a shot with the best metering system on earth, and the photo will be overexposed. Conversely, if you're shooting a dark, hairy beast like King Kong, the reading is likely to be underexposed. EV to the rescue. It lets you compensate by adjusting the exposure value, up or down, in increments. The Nikon D90, for example, can dial in values between -5 Ev and +5 Ev, in increments of 1/3 or 1/2 of a stop.

NOTE: EV is disabled when shooting in Manual (M) mode; it works only with A, S, and P modes.

Since I don't hang my hat in the Arctic or shoot for the San Diego Zoo, you might wonder why I use EV so much. The reason is twofold. First, I confess to having a fetish for saturated colors that leap off the page and get in your face. A small dose of underexposure adds some nice snap to the colors, like the flower in Fig. 8, which I shot with the EV dialed down to −1/3.

My photo of a lonely guy standing on the jetty in Fig. 14 was shot on film (no metadata available). I underexposed by two full stops to cut down on the glare coming off the Atlantic and to intensify the mood.

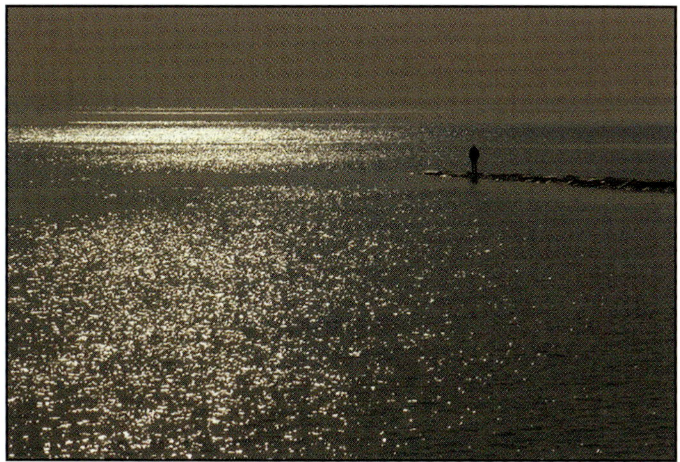

Fig. 14. Underexposing can heighten the impact of a photo.

Lucky break the guy wandered out and stood there, looking like Philip Marlowe trying to get over a dame.

Remove the figure in Photoshop and what would you have? Nothing but the fading echo of a yawn.

The other reason I lean toward underexposure is you can boost it in post if you go too far, whereas if you overexpose and blow out the highlights, you're up the creek without a paddle.

Even Marlowe couldn't bring a white shroud back to life.

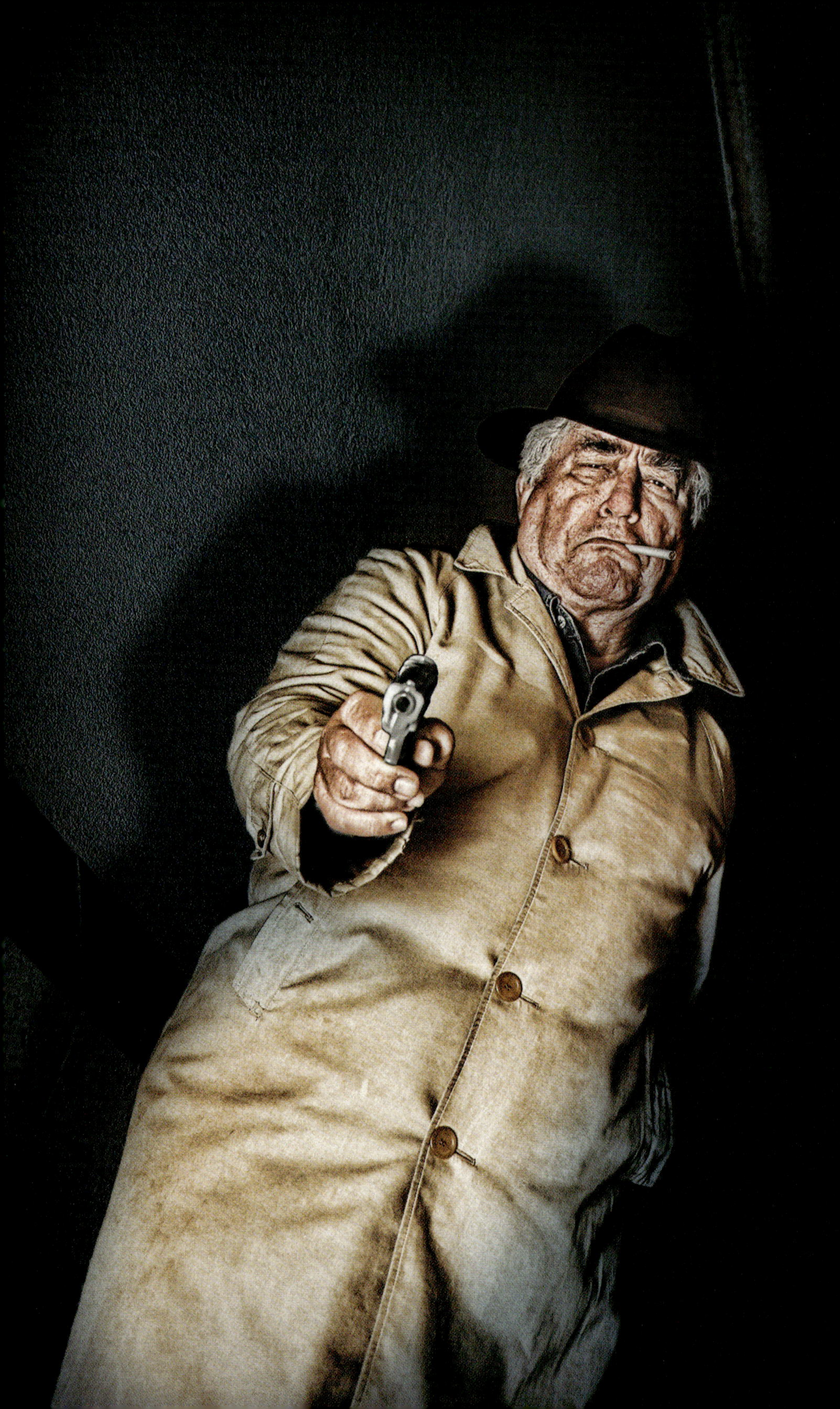

5
TWINKLE, TWINKLE LITTLE NOIR
Ambient Light and Flash

*"A moon half gone from the full glowed through a ring
of mist among the branches of the eucalyptus trees..."* —The Big Sleep

Shadow and light. What else is there in this crazy game called life? It's the Big Mystery, best as I can tell. Solve it and the game's over; you win. As for photography, crack the riddle of light and you've got it made in the shade, no pun intended.

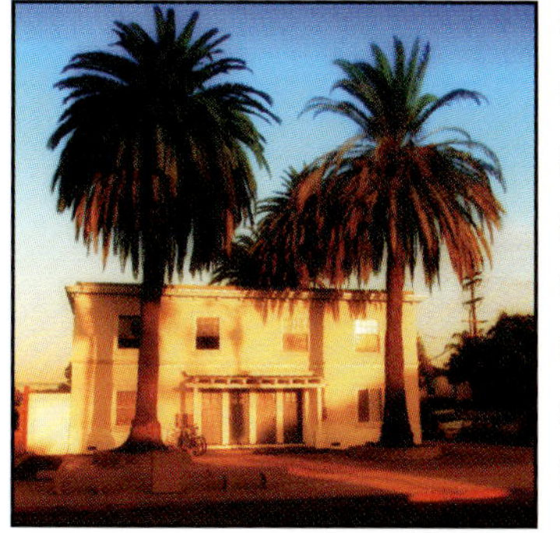

What first attracted me to San Diego was the quality of the light. Sometimes alien and surreal, other times biblical, as garish as a Hollywood epic. I'm transfixed by the contrast between harsh desert sun and murky pools of shadow. Stalactite shapes, stark and edgy, or painterly, lantern-like, ambient light.

Lawrence Durrell's book *Spirit of Place* is about capturing the essence of a location. I'm trying to capture visuals that define a city's core. It's hard to get a handle on, and difficult to explain in textbook fashion. A poem would get you closer to what I mean. It's a subjective enigma, an "eye of the beholder" thing. It's what drives me to keep squeezing the shutter.

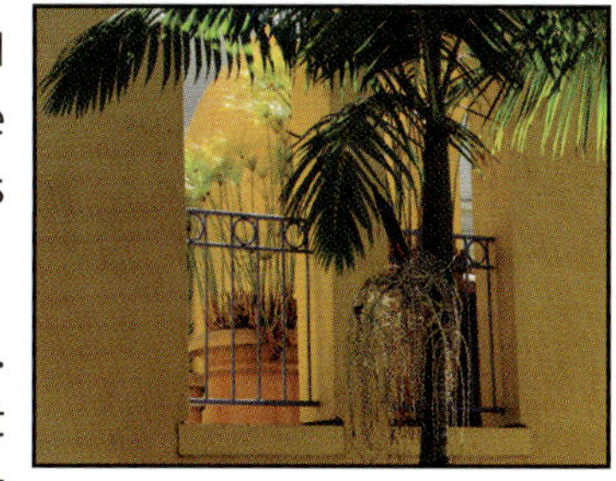

I'm not always successful in my quest. Sometimes the light is perfect but there's no subject in sight. Or that perfect light fades before I've even taken out the camera. Light can be as elusive as a pickpocket on the 4th of July.

AMBIENT LIGHT

While walking around my neighborhood one overcast day—
perfect weather for making pictures—a Mediterranean archway presented itself. The soft light accentuated the texture of
the facade, and a bird of paradise intruded like a blood-stained
talisman (Fig. 1). Taking the photo felt like writing the first chapter
of a novel without words. The digital frame I added gives the effect
of a doorway into the picture. The viewer enters and follows the
thread.

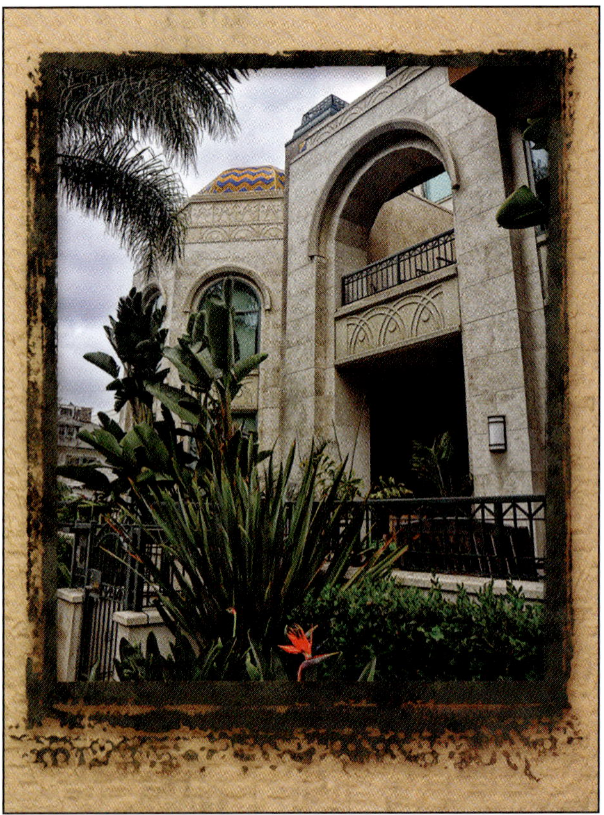

Fig.1. Omen (2009). Photo by Derek Pell.

Be careful when applying a digital frame. Make sure it complements the photo instead of hogging all the attention. I discuss
both virtual and real frames in **Chapter 9, "I've Been Framed!"**

Fig. 1 is more interesting to me than the pretty sunset in Fig. 2 because it tells a story, or at least prods the viewer to imagine one. There's no story in the sunset photo. It's a cliché that can't match the majesty of the scene when you're standing there.

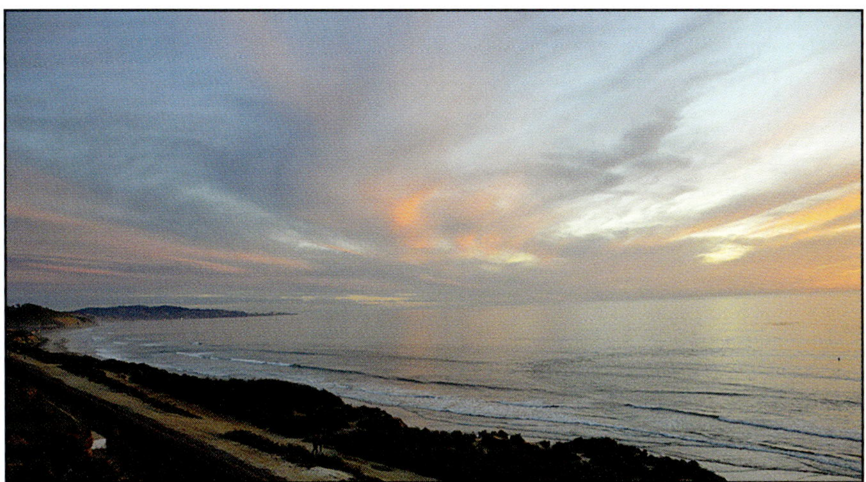

Fig. 2. La Jolla (2009). Photo by Derek Pell.

Don't get me wrong; I'm not saying you shouldn't shoot sunsets. What I'm getting at is this: Nice ambient light, in and of itself, doesn't make an interesting photo. The right light on the right subject does. So when you think about light, keep that in mind.

When I'm out to score some noir, shadows rise to the surface like shark fins. The fire escape in Fig. 3 is a case in point. The shadows are sharp as knives and convey a sense of drama with their Dutch angularity. (AUTHOR'S NOTE: A "Dutch angle" is a film noir technique where the camera is tilted to the side so that the shot is composed with the horizon at an angle to the bottom of the frame. It makes the audience uneasy.) Stare at the photo for a minute, and it's easy to imagine the shadow of some shapely gams rushing down the stairs pursued by a figure with a gun.

When taking a shot like this, exercise caution. It's easy to overexpose and blow out the highlights. Try underexposing 1/2 stop or so to preserve texture and retain detail in the shadow areas (Fig. 4).

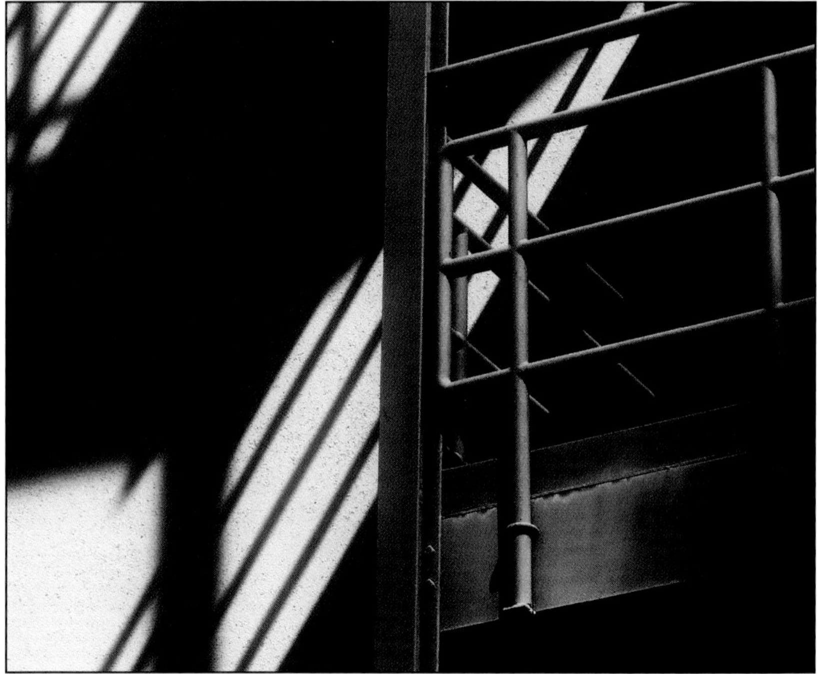

Fig. 3. Dramatic natural light provides texture and knife-like noir shadows.

The photo was taken at high noon, with a brazen sun making trouble: mondo contrast. The exposure was 1/640 at f/10, ISO 200, zoomed to 27mm.

I converted the original from color to black and white in Photoshop to emphasize the noir feeling. But, usually, my brand of neo-noir likes a little color to bleed through.

In general, noir lighting is kick-in-the-pants high contrast and black shadows. It's the opposite of the soft, diffused light found in portraits. For fashion, well, the rules are always being broken by talented photographers and—right now—hard, flat lighting is hot. (I discuss ring flash later in this chapter.)

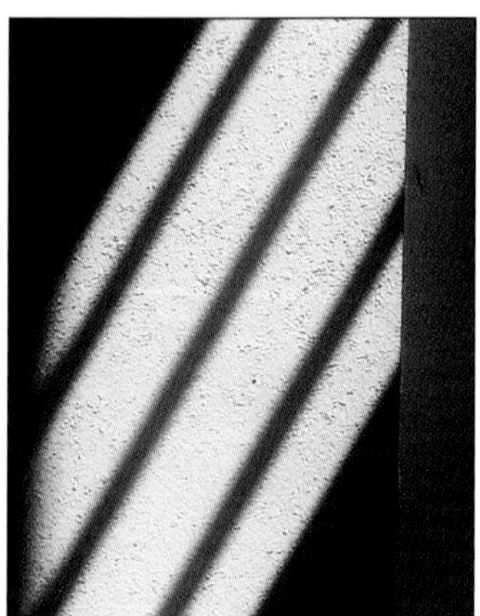

Fig. 4. Cropped detail showing the texture of the wall and detail in the shadows.

IMAGINING LIGHT AND RE-CREATING IT

There might be times when you'll stumble on a location that whispers, "Go ahead, shoot me." But there's nothing there. You take a long, hard look and begin to sense something—the light's not great, but there's a potential image here. Then, slowly, it starts developing in your mind. You take a few shots and move on, but the excitement is growing and suddenly you can't wait to get to the PC and make the picture that wasn't there. Here's an example.

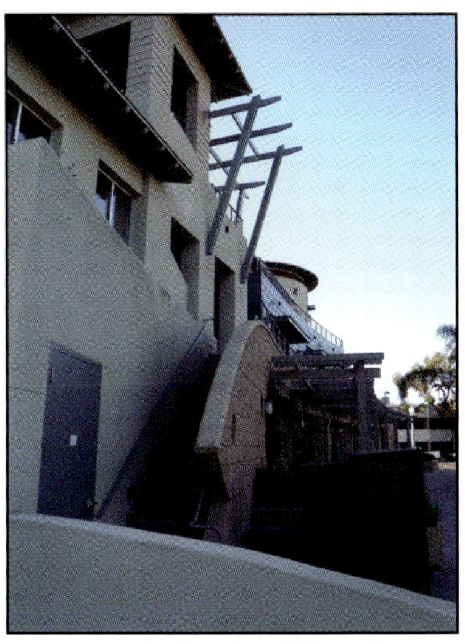

Fig. 5. Before (dull daylight snap).

Fig. 5 shows an office building on Coronado Island that whispered to me. There's nothing special about it; the architecture is mildly interesting but the photo is basically a dud destined for delete. So what's going on here?

Something about the stairs and that isolated door told me it could make a slice of noir. If only it were night...

Here's what I did to get the photo I saw in my mind (Fig. 6). I opened the image in Photoshop and selected the sky using the Quick Selection Tool. With the sky selected (and some distracting trees in the background), I pressed the Delete key. Bye-bye daylight. Using the Color Picker, I chose a dark shade of blue as my foreground color and made the background color white. Inside the selection, I dragged the Gradient tool from top to bottom, creating a gradated night sky with a faint glow on the horizon (Fig. 6). The area to the right of the stairs was a distracting mess so, with Burn tool in hand, I made the area a solid shadow.

I made the entire building into a selection and used the Contrast slider to darken it. For the final touch I took the Dodge tool and lightened areas around the door and the stairs so they appeared to be lit by an unseen source. Now the forbidding door became the focus of the photo. *Presto!*—twinkle, twinkle little noir.

The lesson: Take the time to *imagine* a photograph. Find the potential image in a photo that seemingly missed the boat. Available light doesn't always cooperate, so consider manufacturing your own.

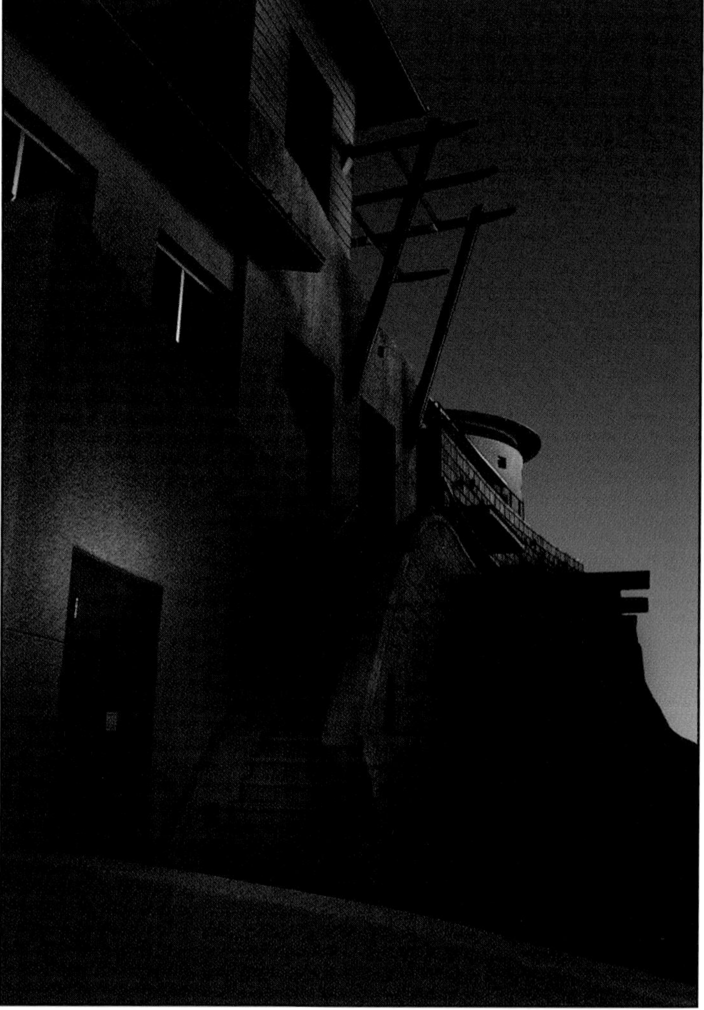

Fig. 6. After (cool noir night).

NIGHTTIME IS THE RIGHT TIME...FOR NOIR

Although he's not my favorite painter, Edward Hopper knew a thing or two about light which—if you could bottle it—I'd stand in line to buy. You might even describe some of his works as "noirish." However, when I shot the photo in Fig. 7, Hopper wasn't on my radar, but just underneath. What I saw was almost an abstract. Like the barristas, most of the ambient light had gone home for the night, so this was a job for a portable flash. Only I didn't have one with me. And—*uh-oh*— no tripod, either. It was one of those bite-the-bullet moments when you say to yourself, "WTF, give it a shot...might get an interesting blur."

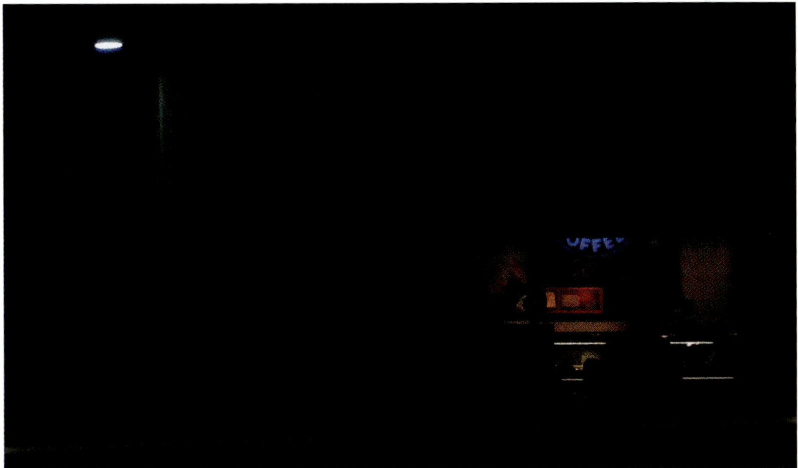

Fig. 7. Hopper's Cafe (2009). Photo by Derek Pell.

I tried to Zen myself as I braced the camera against a trash can, repeating the mantra, "I am a tripod, I am a tripod..." until I became rigid as a corpse, held my breath, and squeezed the shutter. 1/8 sec at f/5.6; ISO 200. (I could've bumped up the ISO setting but, in this case, I wanted maximum clarity, minimum noise.) Only when I looked at the photo in Lightroom did I see a connection to Hopper's classic, *Nighthawks.* I liked what I initially saw: the glow of the neon coffee sign, the street lamp, the shadows. The composition draws the eye from upper left to lower right. In the black void between, you expect to see a figure in a trench coat emerge... maybe a dame with a cigarette and heels. This was a still image that begged to be a movie, so I eventually used it as the background in a Flash animation. I added audio and the one visual aspect that seemed to be missing: swirling fog. You can check it out at www.zoomstreet.org/thrill/flash1.htm.

I find a lot of shutterbugs are afraid of the dark. Maybe it's the long exposures that make 'em nervous, the sheer hit-or-miss quality of night. Or they're just too lazy to lug a tripod around. Big mistake. Put the camera to bed after sundown and you're missing out on a world of photographic opportunities. Night is when things start to get interesting. A whole new cast of characters takes the stage. Buildings reveal secret identities. Trees perform shadow plays. Cats, like extras, ham it up in alleys. Windows wink like flirtatious eyes.

With the sun turned off you've got a smorgasbord of illumination: moonlight, street lamps, headlights, and neon. Different light, different subjects, *different photos*. Fewer distractions, too. No flash? Up the ISO setting. No tripod? Rest the camera on a Fed-Ex drop box or the roof of a car. Hold your breath and try a hand-held (Fig. 8), or use blur for effect, like in Fig. 9.

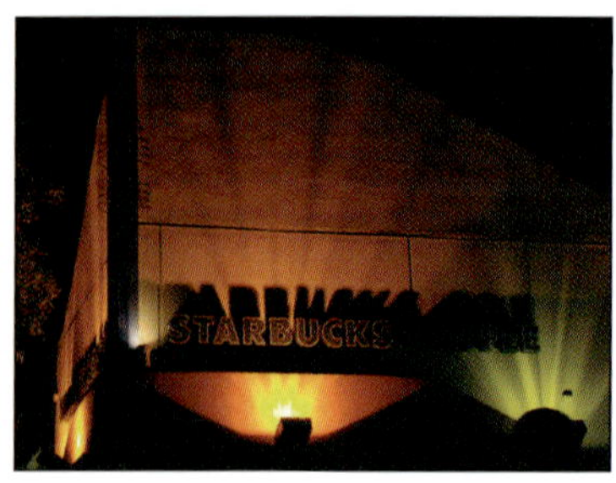

Fig. 8. This noirish facade was shot hand-holding the camera, without flash. Auto White Balance accurately captured the color of the scene.

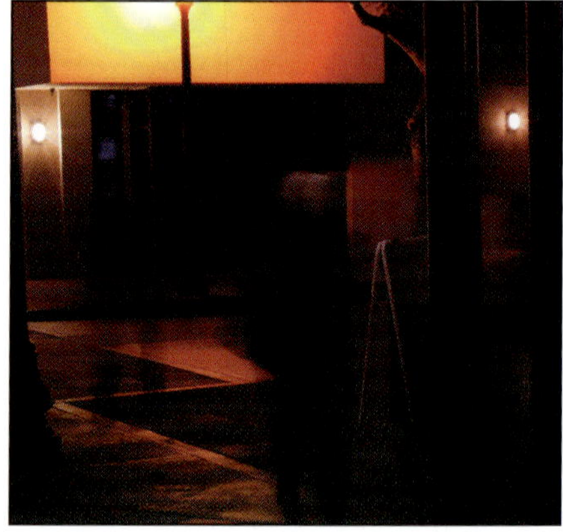

Fig. 9. Using a slow shutter speed produces the ghost-like blur of two pedestrians (1.0 sec at f/8.3).

PORTABLE FLASH IS YOUR BUDDY

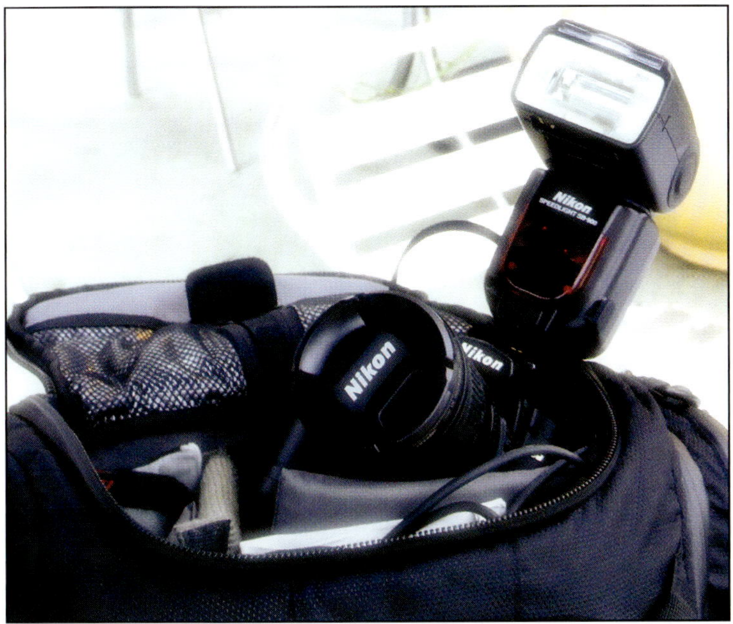

Flash was no pal of mine when I began shooting. It didn't fit my M.O. It was available light or nothing. Flash photos looked like flash photos, so forget it and, believe me, I forgot it. When digicams finally rolled around, they had their own little built-in pop-up flashes that were impossible to escape. Light too low?— *pop!*— you were flashing whether you liked it or not, and there wasn't much to like. Subjects looked like the proverbial deer caught in the headlights, or rats with rabid "red-eye." Not to mention those ugly shadows and solid black backgrounds...what the hell's *that* all about?

No subtlety, no style. Portable strobes were for crime scene photographers and the paparazzi mob. Even when I knew better (i.e., I saw how good flash could look when I used big studio strobes) I still avoided wireless portables. *Why?* Guess I didn't want to do the math, calculate the distance to subject, etc. If I had any talent for math I'd be an accountant.

When I finally got my hands on a review unit of the Nikon Speedlight SB-900, all that changed. It was like a barn door being thrown open in my brain. Flash was actually doable, flexible, powerful, *portable*. No math required, no cords to trip over. I could trial and error my shots and learn from experience.

I made a classic mistake the first time I tried to test-fire the strobe off the hot shoe in "Remote" mode. Everything looked fine, appeared to be working, the SB-900's ready light was on, but when I pressed the shutter nothing happened. I called photographer Drew Wyeth and grumbled, "Must be a defective unit, huh?" He chuckled and asked, "Did you remember to pop up the camera's built-in flash?"

Uh, no. (Doh!)

When you're using a Speedlight untethered, as a wireless remote, *something* has to trigger the unit, and that's where the camera's built-in flash comes in. If you don't put that little flash up, the Speedlight goes to Vegas.

I was on my own now, a tourist without a map . . . didn't know Joe McNally from Rand; had never heard of legendary shooter David Hobby and his maniacal cult of Strobists. All I knew was that flash provided those double O's that are the lifeblood of creativity: *options* and *opportunities*.

My first true test of the speedlight came on assignment for *Zoom Street Magazine* to shoot photos for a special "Noir Issue." I was hanging my hat on Coronado at the time and scoped a retro coffee shop that looked like a promising location. I paid a visit to the cops and arranged permission for a sidewalk night shot. (It was quiet and out of season, so no "event insurance" was required.) The magazine's DV editor (and former actor), Wendell Sweda, agreed to play the heavy. He drove down from Santa Monica armed with a fedora and a hard-boiled attitude. Alas, he forgot his trench coat, and there was no time for rentals. (Always pack a spare TC.)

We arrived on location late, leaving only about 15 minutes for the shoot. It was dark, the atmosphere dead-on, and no pedestrians were in sight, so there was no need to block off the area with crime scene tape. (Actually, yellow "caution tape"—a handy accessory available at any hardware store.) One minor flaw I hadn't noticed while casing the joint during daylight: although it was late January, the coffee shop still had its Christmas lights up, strung along the facade's Alamo-style roof. Oh well. I could clone out the holiday spirit in Photoshop.

Pressed for time, there was no elaborate setup...I had the speed-light mounted on the hot shoe of a Fujifilm S3 Pro. I rotated the flash head and bounced the light off a gold reflector clamped to a C-stand. I hand-held the camera and shot wide at 18mm (1/125 sec at f/5.6; ISO 100).

As you can see in Fig. 10, the strobe knocked out the puny illumination of the holiday lights, leaving just the scraggly cord. The Speed-light was so powerful, in fact, that its spill illuminated the interior ceiling. Feisty sucker.

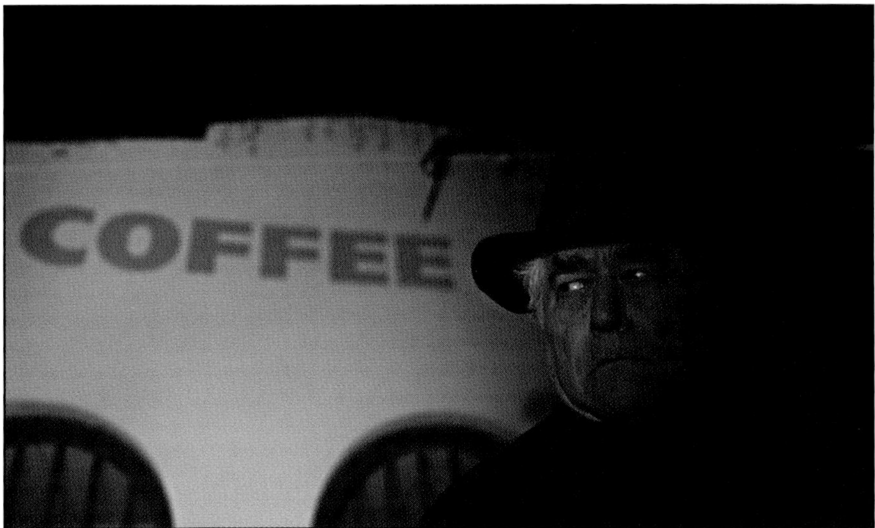

Fig.10. My first shot using the Nikon SB-900 Speedlight.

Those dual spotlights above the lettering might've been distracting, but they actually worked within the composition because they echoed the subject's eyes. Credit, of course, must go to the model, whose range of menacing expressions would've made Orson Welles proud. In my experience, actors make the best models, but rarely vice versa.

For me the killer shot was Fig. 11.

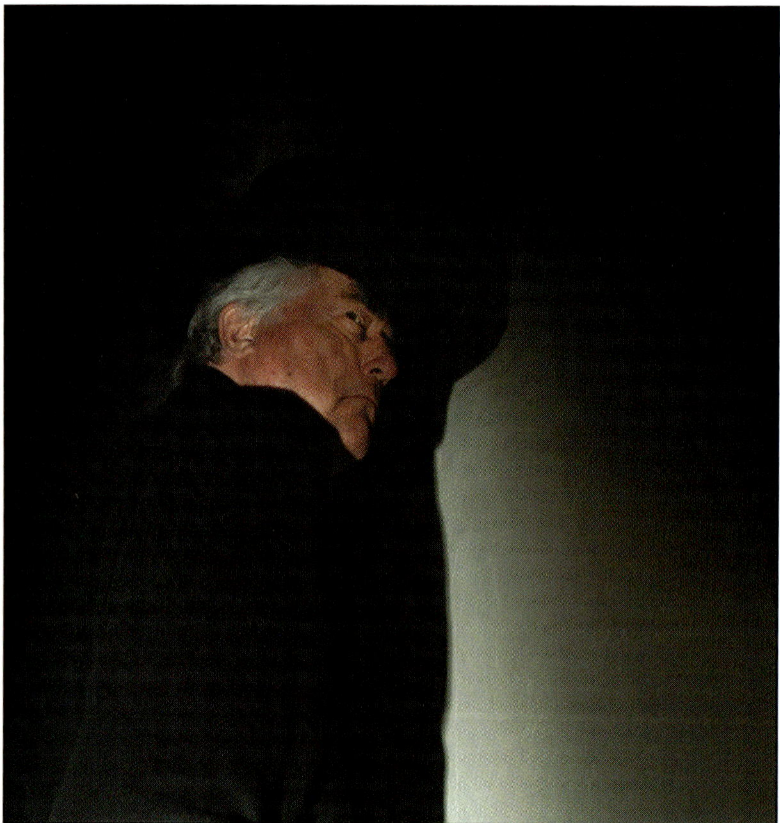

Fig. 11. One portable strobe produced this killer shot.

I dialed the SB-900 down to −1.16 and again bounced the light off a gold reflector that was positioned at left just outside the frame. The light caught the subject's eye, threw a dramatic shadow, and revealed the stucco wall's texture. An incremental step up the power ladder would have overexposed the face and blown out the highlights.

But before you go calling me a genius, I gotta confess I didn't nail the perfect exposure off the top of my head or with a tape measure. It was the old T & E (trial and error). That's the beauty of the SB-900; you can quickly adjust the output via either a button or a dial. I fired a shot, checked the result in the LCD, adjusted the exposure, shot again—lather, rinse, repeat—until I had the light I wanted.

The SB-900 is packed with cool features. You can use it as a commander to trigger an entire army of Speedlights. (Talk about a power trip!) I like to keep things simple on location—one strobe and some reflectors. I leave it to guys like Joe McNally to conduct an orchestra of Speedlights and make a symphony out of light.

The SB-900's flexible flash head is a bouncer's delight; you can rotate it horizontally 180 degrees to each side and 90 degrees vertically. A lot of coverage!

Let's slip outside for a second while there's still light and grab some tests to illustrate adjusting the output setting.

In Fig. 12, the strobe is too bright and overpowers the ambient light.

Fig. 13 shows what happens when you dial down the setting one stop to –1.0. The mix of ambient/flash appears more natural.

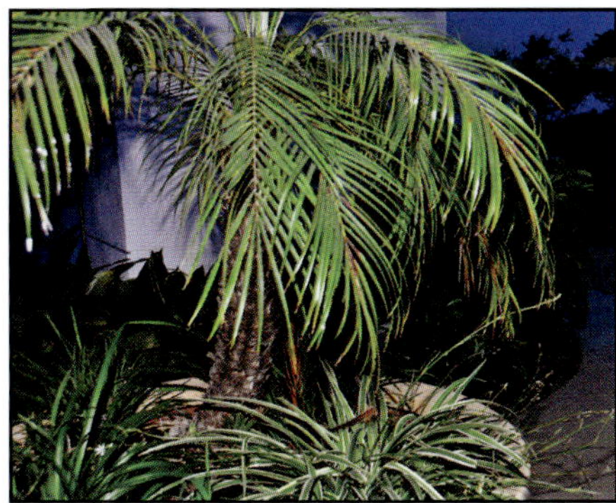

Fig. 12. Too much flash power squashes the ambient light.

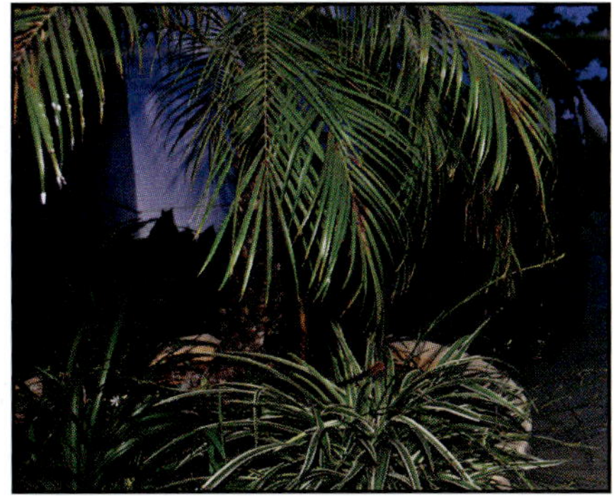

Fig. 13. Dial down the flash power until you get a blend.

Fig. 14 is a montage I made using a photo from the noir cover series and a shot of the moon, which I blurred in Photoshop. I wanted a grainy film effect, so I treated it to a heavy dose of the Add Noise filter, and then converted it to black and white. The most interesting part of the photo is that double shadow. I'd love to be able to tell you I intentionally lit the scene to achieve it but, truth be told, it was a gift from the Flash gods.

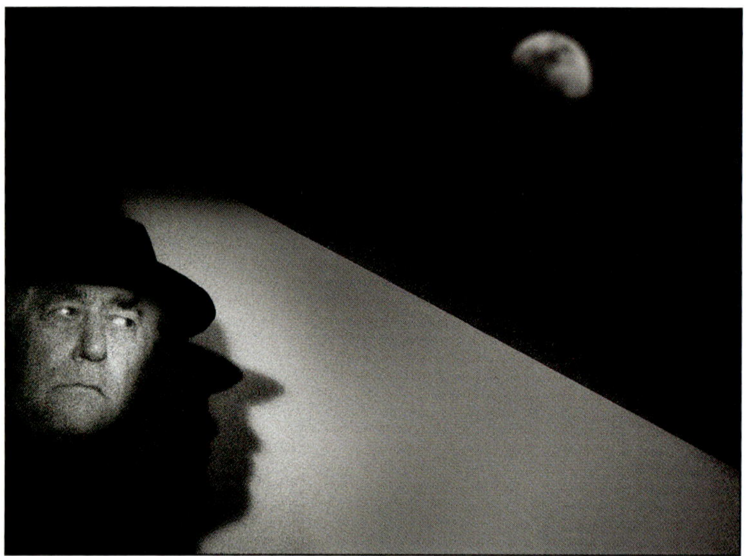

Fig. 14. Double Indemnity, anyone?

Nope, I can't explain it. Might have been the way the reflector was positioned, or maybe I inadvertently jerked the camera and wound up with a Buy One Get One Free. *Double Indemnity.*

AN OUNCE OF BOUNCE = FILLS & THRILLS

Accidents happen; I just wish I could plan on 'em. What I *do* plan on when shooting exteriors is no roof overhead to bounce light off. That's why I carry reflectors, and so should you. I keep a Photoflex mini in a pouch attached to my gear bag that opens out to about 12 inches. I can hold it easily in one hand and the camera in the other, or—when shooting close-ups—give it to the model to hold at chest

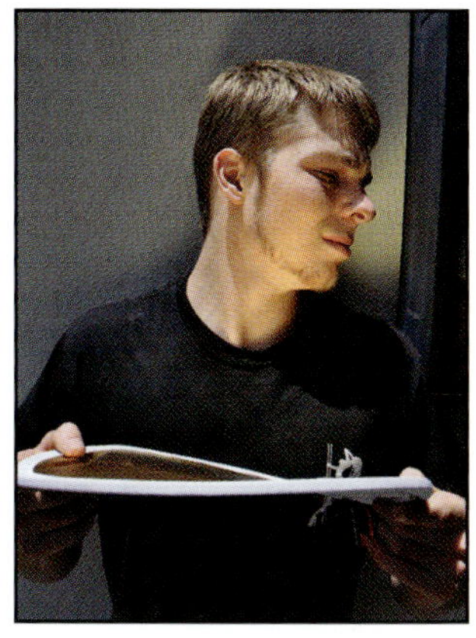
Fig. 15. Model with mini reflector.

level for fill light (Fig. 15). It's double-sided, white and gold. Gold is great for enhancing skin tones and adding warmth to a heartless desert sun.

The mini is made by **Photoflex**, which also sells a **MultiDisc Kit** (Fig. 16) that includes a circular 42" frame, 5 reflectors (gold, soft gold, silver, white, and translucent), a holder, and a stand. You get a big bounce and lots of flexibility, and you can put the reflectors wherever you want 'em. The holder has removable clamps and swivels into position.

I also use the **Photoflex Lite Panel Kit** (Fig. 17) for full-length portraits because it provides a rectangular swash of light. It comes with its own stand and doesn't weigh you down. I hate lugging a lot of gear around and am always trying to pack smarter and lighter. A good reflector is as essential as a tripod and a toothbrush.

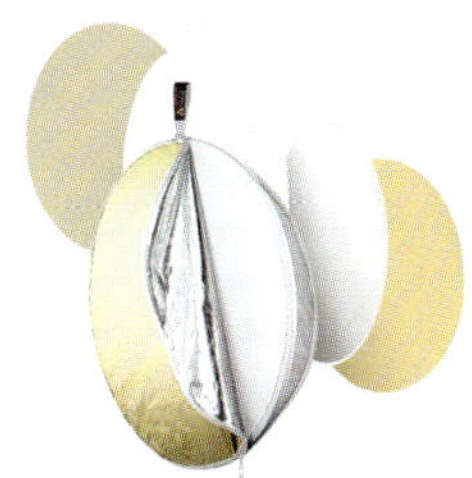
Fig. 16. MultiDisc Kit.

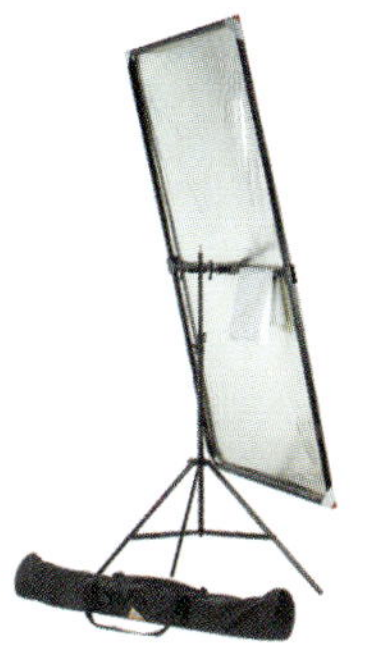
Fig. 17. Lite Panel Kit.

You can make do with white cards, sheets, shirts, foam board, aluminum foil. Haven't tried my underwear, but you never know.

I don't own stock in Photoflex. I'm plugging their products here because I've been using them successfully for years—they're reliable, well-made, durable, and the best bargain around. There are plenty of other good companies out there if you search, but if you're on a tight budget, go Photoflex. Trust me; it could be the start of a beautiful friendship.

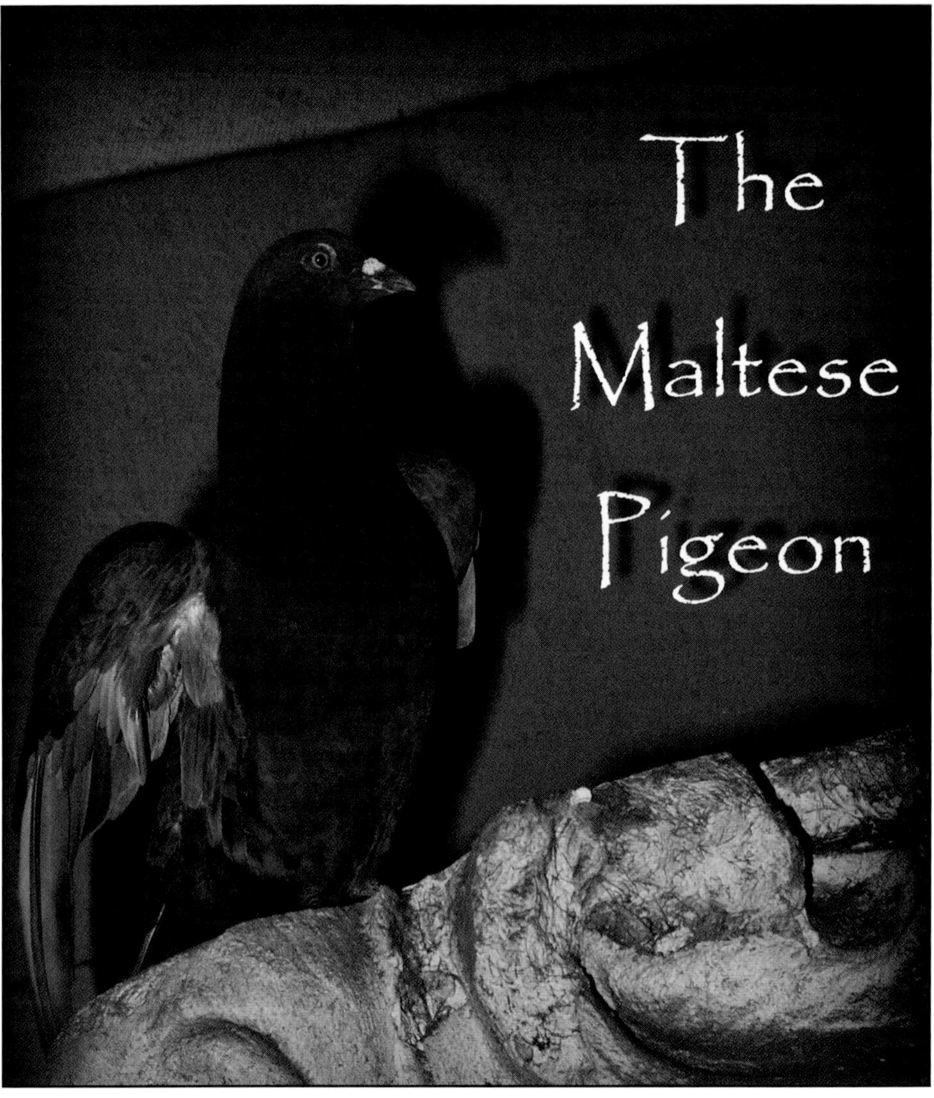

Since I was born smack in the middle of Manhattan, you probably wouldn't expect this New Yawker to get excited about a pigeon... unless my revolver was in hand. Those "doity stinkin boids" are a dime a dozen and a pain in the butt. Well, maybe I'm gettin' soft in my old age. Here's the story. The other day I was lying around the office watching Bogart do his cool in *The Maltese Falcon*. It's one

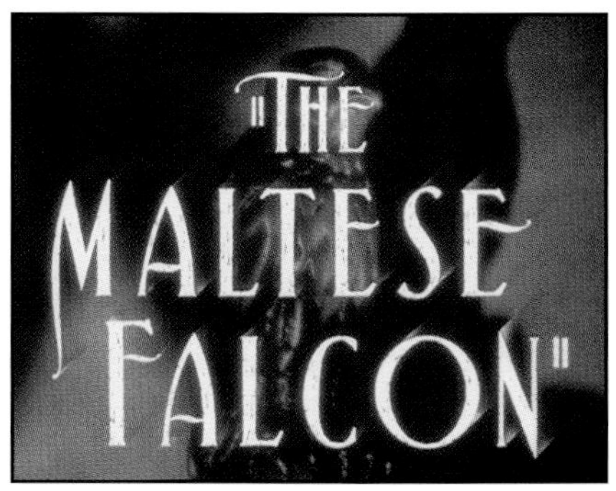

of my favorite motion pictures. I should have been working on this book, but I wrote it off as "reference" and gave my secretary (Effie Perine) the day off.

Later that night I was on a case in Balboa Park, nosing around the museums, when I spied the specimen on the facing page. It was framed beneath a Spanish archway, perched on a pedestal, posing like it had been waitin' for me all its life—an omen. I glanced over my shoulder, half expecting to see Sam Spade standing with a cigarette and a smile on his lips. The bird gave me a look like it was about to blow town, so I had to act fast. The ambient light was murky, but I had an SB-900 mounted on the hot shoe. I dialed it down to –1 1/3 EV (to try to preserve the texture and drama), spot-metered the eye, and fired at 1/60 sec at f/10 (ISO 200; 90mm).

A moment later it was gone, but I had the evidence on a memory card. For a hard-boiled dick, it's the shot that dreams are made of. No digital retouching necessary. I added a "Dutch Angle" crop for good measure and poured myself a drink.

This red-eyed beauty had Silver Screen written all over it but didn't leave a calling card (thankfully). So I tagged it "The Maltese Pigeon" and gave it a perch in this book.

Not bad for a boid.

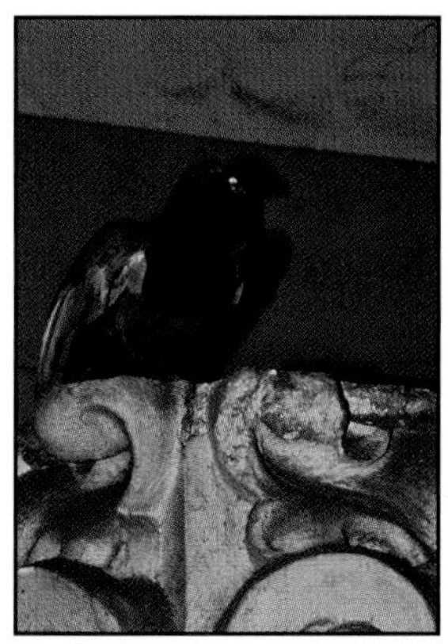

GRIDS, SNOOTS, GOBOS, & CHIZZLERS

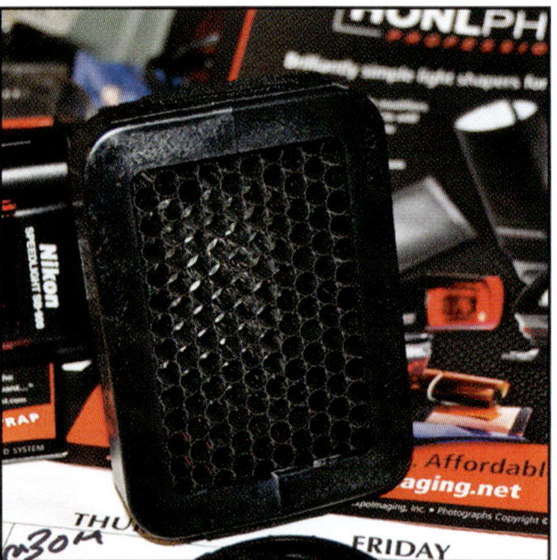

Fig. 18. Honl 1/4" Speed Grid.

They might sound like thug words, but they're 100% pure shutterbug slang for light-shaping tools. Except *chizzler*...I coined that to describe when I hold my hand in front of a strobe to deflect the light. I call that "chizzling," get it? It also happens to be the cheapest accessory I own. In fact, I own two of 'em.

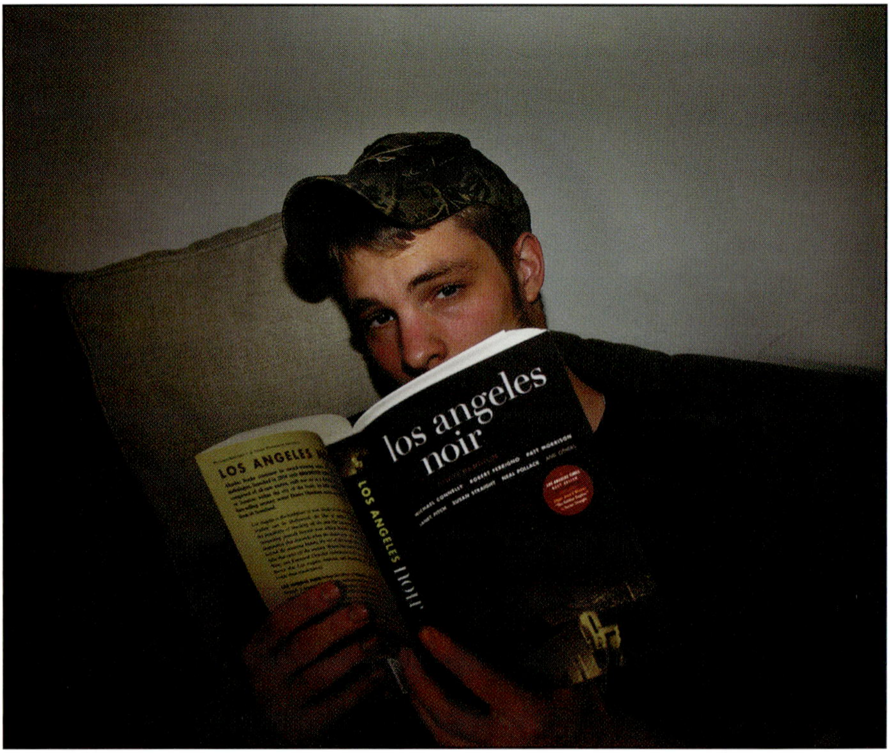

Fig. 19. A 1/4" Honl Speed Grid attached to my strobe head gave this shot some dramatic light.

So I gabbed about reflectors in the previous section, but in addition to bouncing light there are times when you want to *shape* it. You got to roll up your sleeves like a sculptor and start kneading away...molding the light... smoothing and shifting it into patterns and shapes. Throwing light on a subject to see it is one thing, but it's more fun to use light creatively in collaboration with the subject.

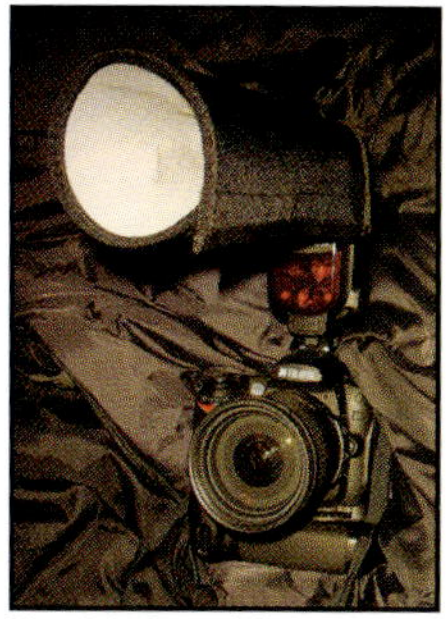
Fig. 20. Speed Snoot.

Honl Photo makes a bunch of great, dirt-cheap, light-shaping tools. I've been using the 1/4-inch **Speed Grid** a lot lately (Fig. 18). It attaches to your strobe via a Velcro **Speed Strap** that wraps around the head and forms the basis of the Honl System—a quick and easy way to swap accessories. The Speed Grid features a honeycomb pattern that produces a gritty oval of light around the subject (Fig. 19). It's quieter than a rusty barn door, too.

Another tool to investigate is the Honl 8″ **Speed Snoot** (Fig. 20), which can be folded funnel-like to direct a spot of light where you want it. Use it to add a cinematic touch to a shot. Use it repeatedly, and you'll have to don a zoot snoot. Fig. 21 is a plain flash shot. Figs. 22 and 23 show the effect of the snoot, which can be modified with a twist or a squeeze.

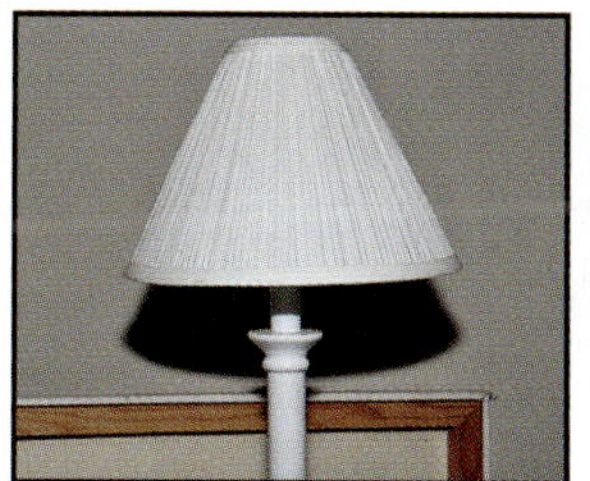
Fig. 21. No snoot.

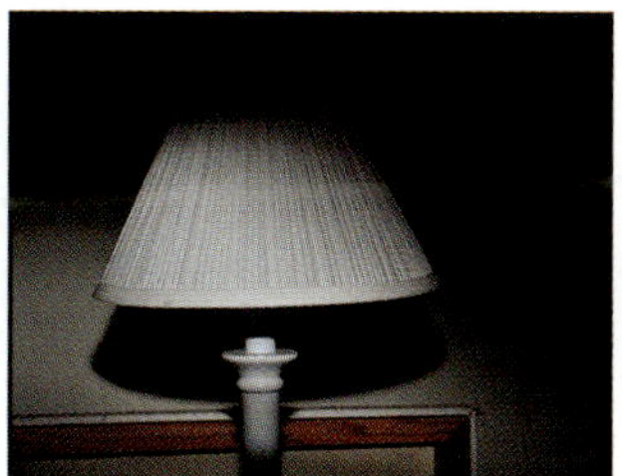
Fig. 22. Snoot shot #1.

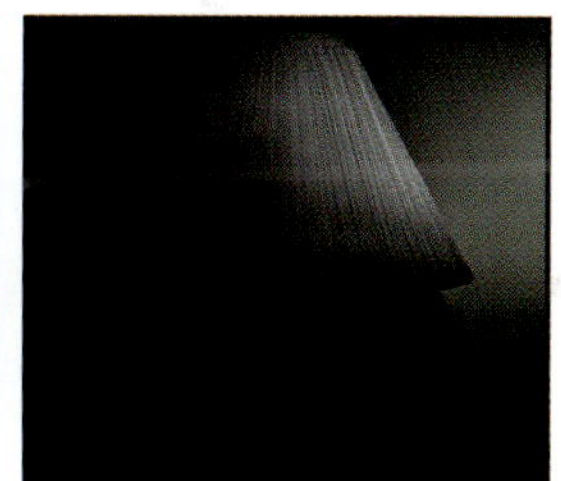
Fig. 23. Snoot shot #2.

A **gobo** (a.k.a. a flag) is short for go-between, and it's anything you can find to stick between the strobe and the subject to modify the way the light hits. It could be a slab of stained glass, corkboard, chicken wire, black card stock, whatever. If the light doesn't cut it, cut the light with a gobo.

A KNOCKOUT IN THE RING

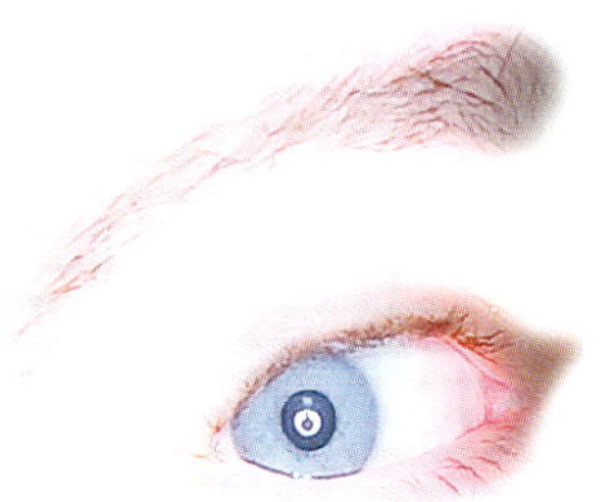

The big thing right now in fashion photography—ring flash—is actually as old as the hills. Developed in the 1950s for dental photography—*smile!*—it's aptly named because it's a circular strobe. You can always tell a photog has used it by a distinctive highlight in the model's iris. A pal of mine calls it "the alien look," and some folks hate it. Not, however, the ad agencies and clients screaming, *"Gimme that ring flash look!"* That "look" boils down to a flat, hard, *in-your-face* light that softens shadows, erases wrinkles, and creates a slight glow around the edge of the subject so it pops out from the background. Ring lighting is hip, hard-boiled, and something a guy like me can really sink his teeth into, pardon the pun.

If you shoot fashion or portraits, you'll want to consider adding a ring flash to your bag of tricks. The only drawback is cost; it ain't cheap. But wipe that frown off your face because there's an affordable alternative that turns your portable strobe into a ring flash. It's called **Ray Flash: The Ring Flash Adapter** (Fig. 24). Fit one over the strobe head, and you'll get the magic look. Because the Ray Flash isn't a light source, it weighs a lot less than an actual ring.

There's also no need for an external power source, so it's a no-brainer for location use. Even sweeter, it doesn't alter the color temperature of your

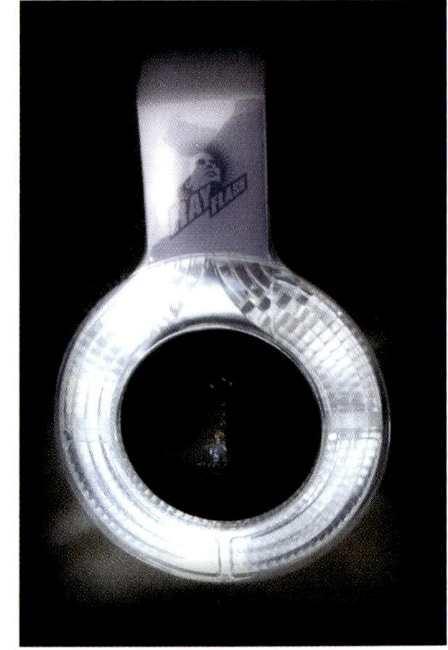

Fig. 24. The Ray Flash.

flash, so you don't have to stop and compensate. Fig. 25 shows a close-up taken with the Ray Flash. Notice the edge around the subject's face. Good separation from the background, too. In Fig. 26, I used the Ray Flash as fill light, and it did a nice job softening shadows on the model's neck.

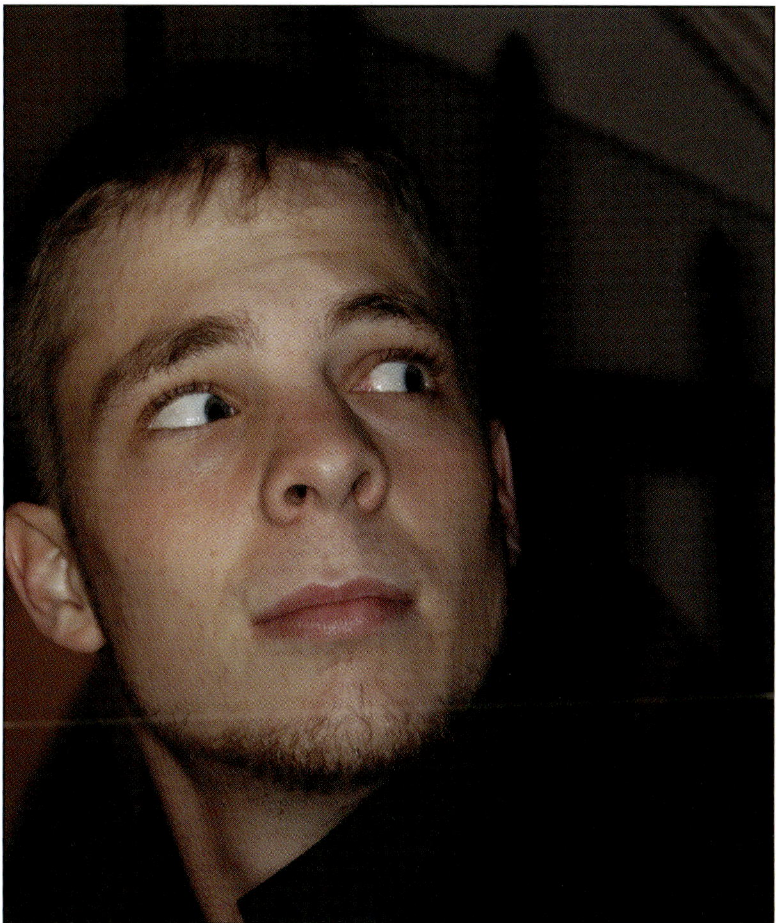

Fig. 25. The Ray Flash in action.

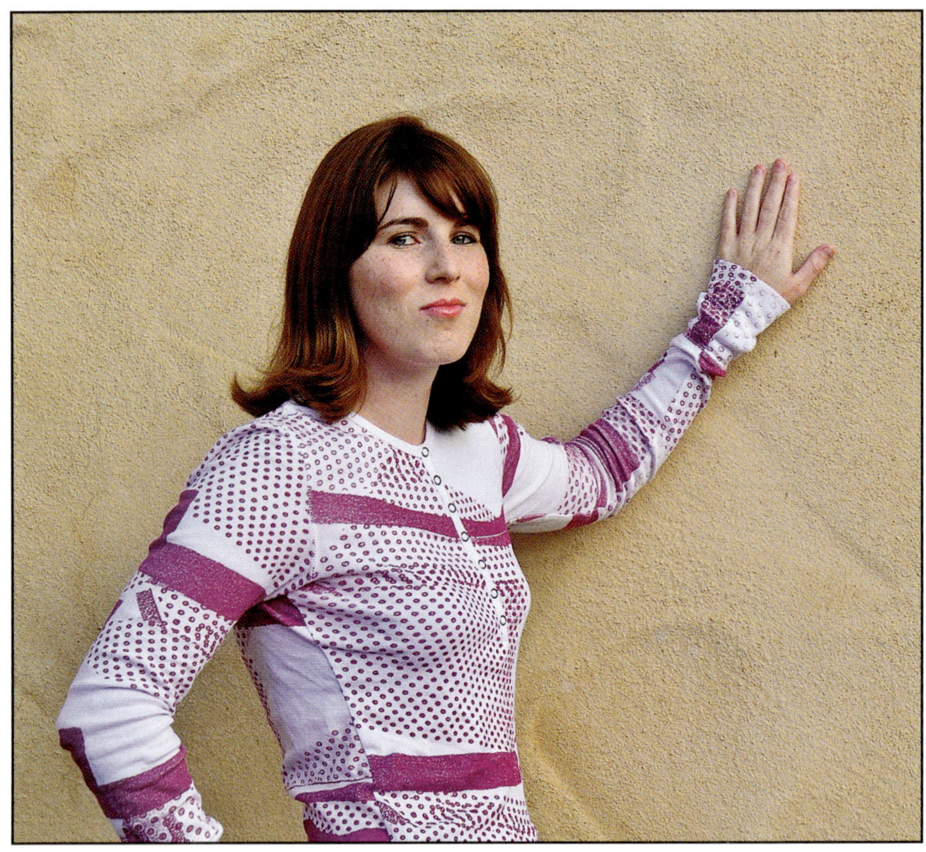

Fig. 26. I used the Ray Flash as a fill light in late afternoon. It softened the shadows on the model's neck and produced smooth skin tones.

If you've been intimidated by flash in the past or didn't see the need for it in your own work, here's what I hope you'll take away from this section. Portable strobes are fun. Hell, I'm no wizard juggling a dozen Speedlights—I've only begun exploring the damn things—but I'm learning new stuff every day. Even with limited experience, I've managed to take a few good shots for this book. That, in itself, should inspire you to test the waters. If a hard-boiled palooka like me can do it, just imagine what you can do.

WHAT, ME POP-UP?

My D-SLR has an internal pop-up flash just like the ones found on cheapo point-and-shoots. Kinda cute, like a jack-in-the-box or a hood ornament. As I've already mentioned, the pop-up serves a purpose; i.e., it triggers the SB-900 off camera. Other than that, it doesn't get used much around here. I was actually feeling sorry for the damn thing, so I used it to take the night shot in Fig. 27. Did a good job freezing the swirling smoke from my cigarette. You might find the pop-up handy in a pinch when your portable flash ain't around. So be kind. Just don't make it a habit.

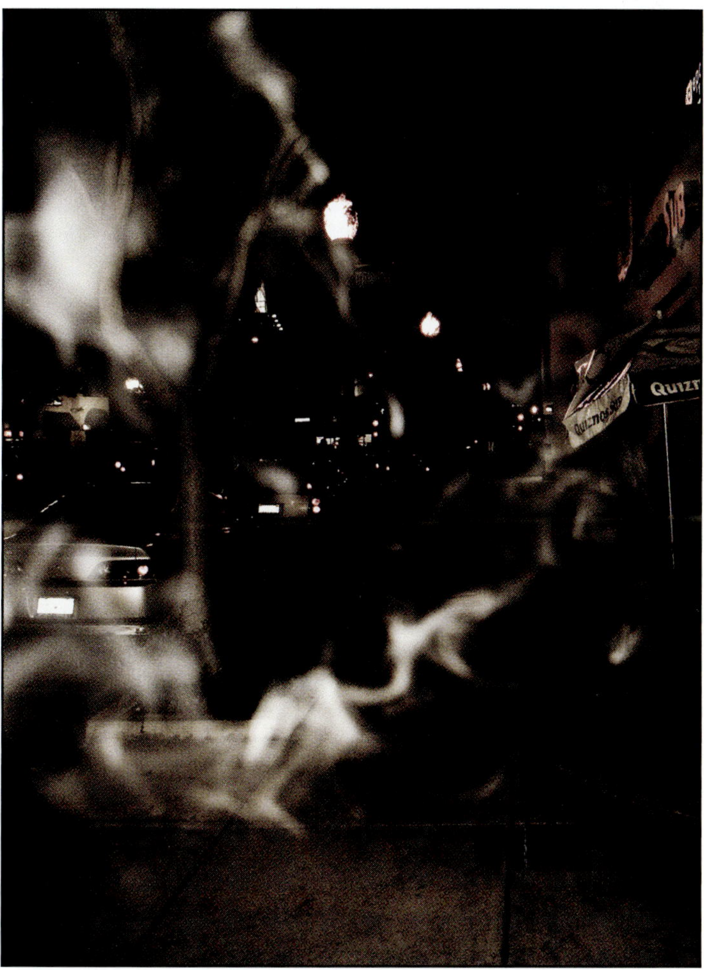

Fig. 27. Shot with a Nikon D90 using the camera's built-in pop-up flash.

THE BIG GUNS: STUDIO STROBES

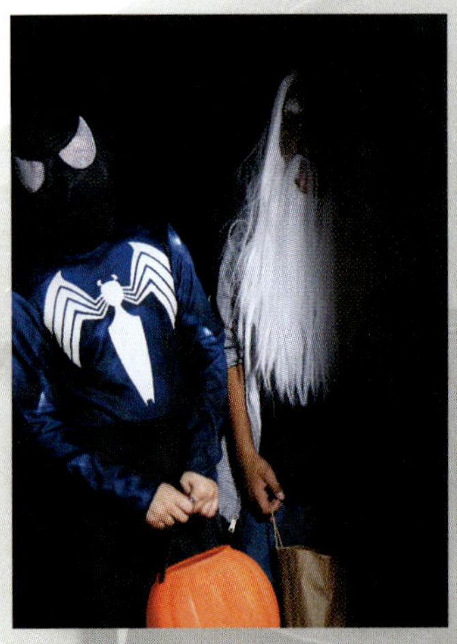

If you're thinking of lighting a blimp or a fleet of shiny new Buicks, you can pack that Speedlight away. You'll want to haul out some big guns—monoblocks, bazookas, Sherman tanks. It's all about power and how much light you want to blow on the subject. You're not gonna get 1,200 watts off a hot shoe.

I don't spend much time in the studio nowadays, but when I'm there, I use dinky 200-watt strobes. I've whittled my equipment down to the basics since I started using small flash. My entire set-up consists of just four strobes with umbrellas, a couple of softboxes, stands, and boom arm or two. I sold all my hot lights a few years ago. They're the ones that don't flash, just jack up the electric bill. As long as I can light a subject front, side, and back, I'm as happy as a clam in Okeechobee.

Last Halloween I decided to steal some shots of the neighborhood demons. I set a Fujifilm S3 Pro on a tripod in the living room and plugged in a strobe with an umbrella. I placed the light off to the side of the front door and hid another one outside in the bushes for side light. The door was kept wide open, and when the ghouls hit the welcome mat I fired. I was only able to take one shot per group because the brats were in the throes of sugar-shock and I was too scared to ask 'em to pose. My favorites in the series are Figs. 28 and 29. In the former, the strobe froze the hand in a surreal gesture. The light goes behind the masks to illuminate the eyes. The side lighting gives definition and sets the black costume apart from the dark background.

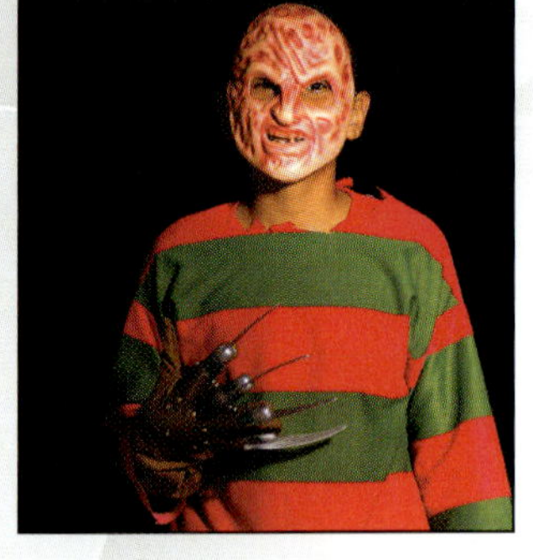

When October 31st rolls around this year, I'll be armed with a Speedlight and we'll see how the shots compare. My guess is they'll be pretty good.

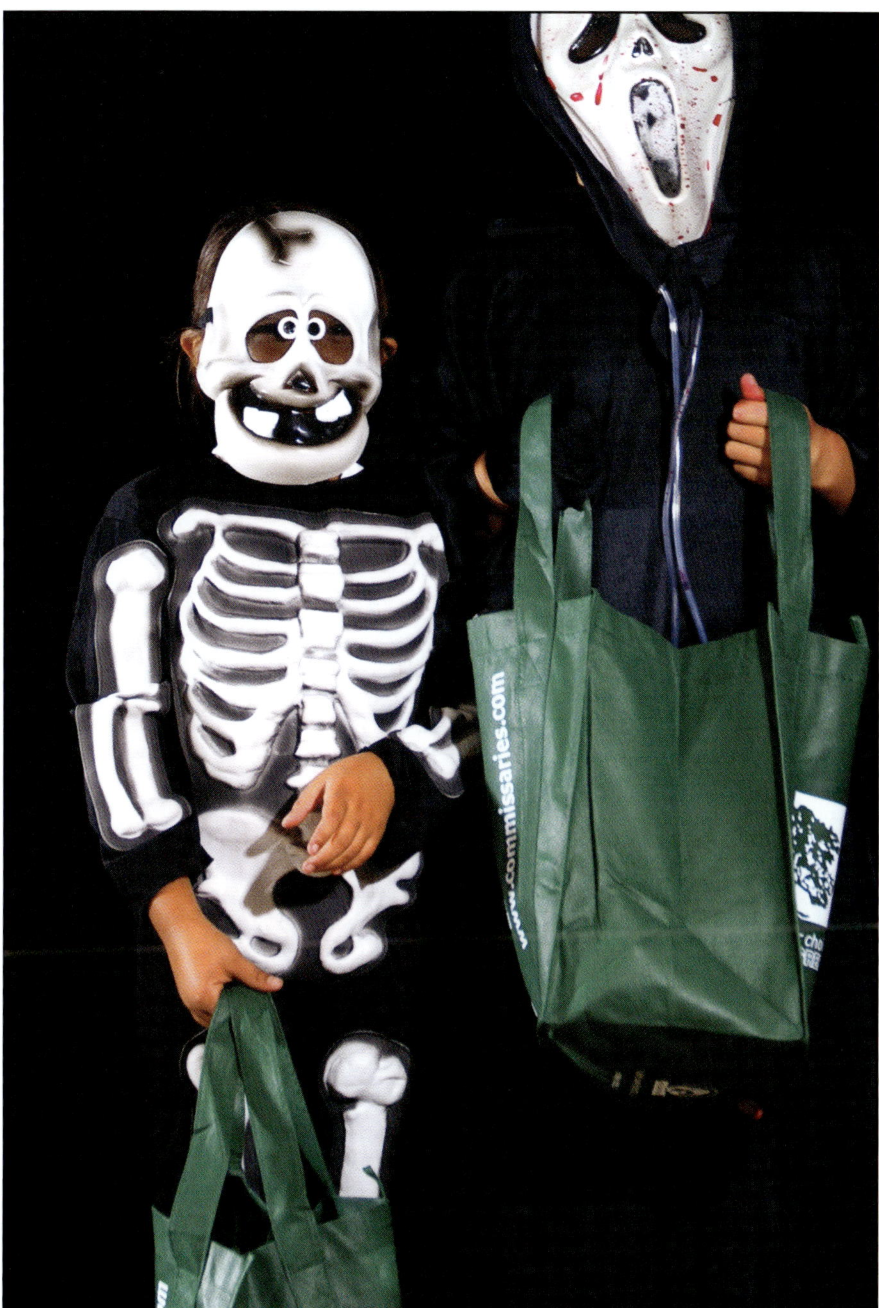

Fig. 28. Trick or Treat (2008). Photo by Derek Pell.

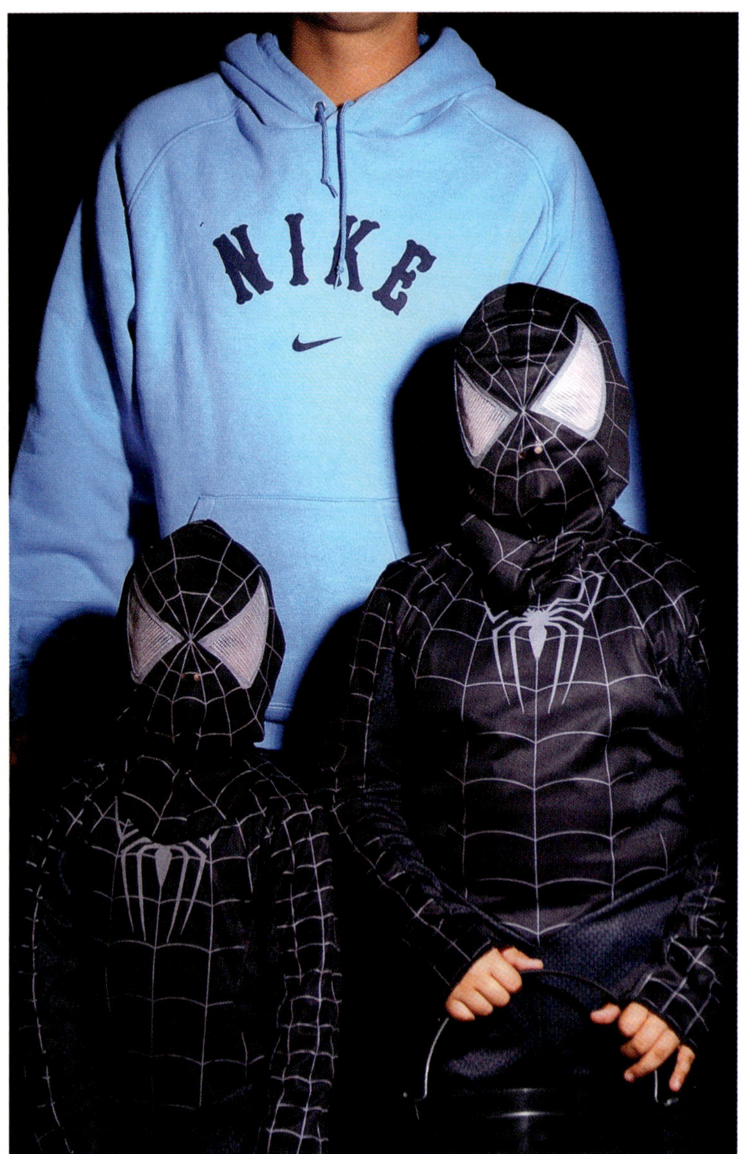

Fig. 29. Photo by Derek Pell.

The Halloween series (about 15 shots in all) were made at 1/125 sec at f/4.2 (ISO 100; 75mm). I varied the power on the strobes, between −3 and −5 stops. There's a lot of light flying around here, and I didn't want to blind the little buggers or make 'em look like Casper the Friendly Ghost.

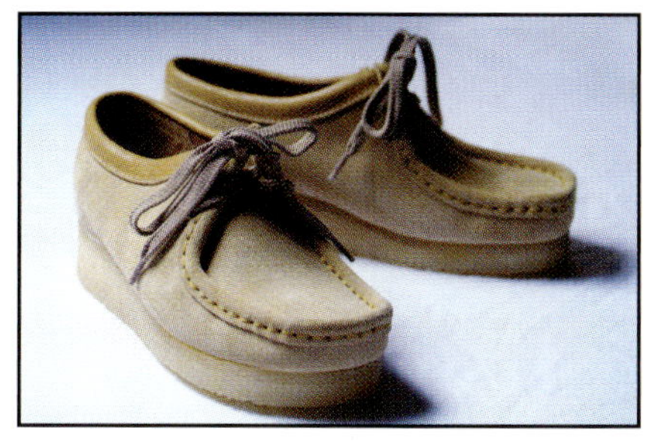

Big strobes are used to light everything from small tabletop products to full-length fashion spreads. They have a distinct advantage over continuous lights when, for example, doing food photography. Hot lights can quickly turn a plate of gourmet cuisine into a pile of mush even a dog wouldn't touch.

Instead of spending your arm and a leg on hot lights, think about getting an inexpensive strobe kit, like one I use made by Smith-Victor: the **FlashLite FL110K Kit** (Fig. 30). It includes two FL110i monolights, two sync cords, two 60-watt quartz modeling lamps, two Raven RS6 6-foot black aluminum light stands, two 32-inch black-backed white umbrellas, and a spy-style attaché case to transport it all. I love these babies because they're ultra light and compact. They're also a snap to use and perfect for portraits. The monolights have 60-degree beam spread with variable power selection, full or 1/2, and they recycle in about two seconds. You can probably pick up the kit on the street for around $300.

If you outfit yourself with a couple of speedlights and a small studio kit like this, you've got indoors and exteriors covered, and you can carry everything in your bare hands. As Charlie Chan might say: Walk softly, but carry big light in small case.

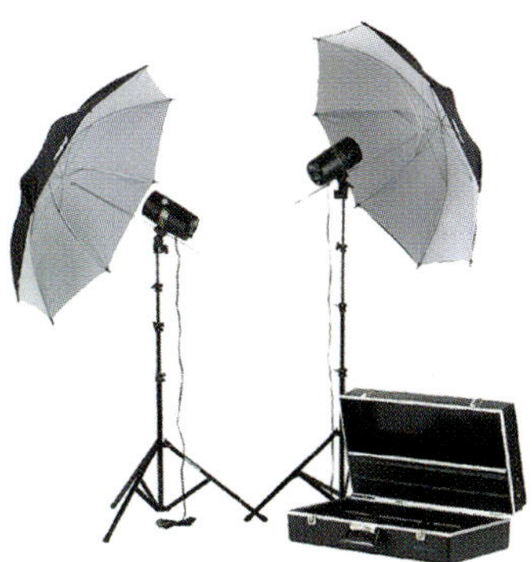

Fig. 30. Smith-Victor FlashLite Kit.

COVER STORY

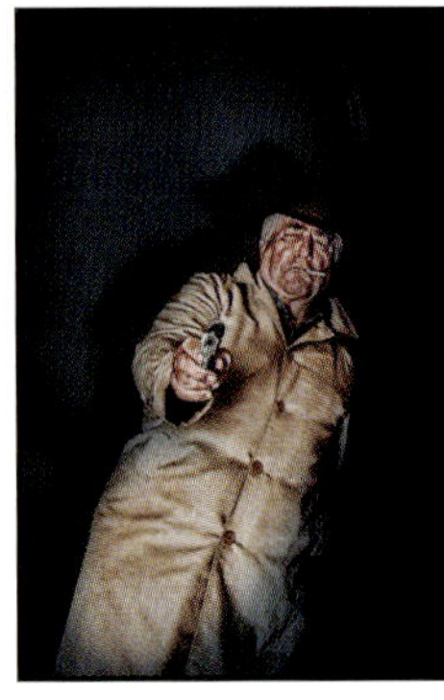

DATELINE—San Diego, CA. (July 3, 2009) Wendell Sweda made a return trip to this city from his hideout in Santa Monica. It was to be a grueling shootout for the cover of this book. This time, however, he remembered to bring his trench coat, while I supplied the heat—a Chinese-made Saturday Night Special. Unfortunately, it was Friday night and the gun fell apart after only 10 minutes. No sweat; I had backups.

I came prepared, seven guns in all. I bought 'em the day before in a value pack at CVS—five bucks, marked down from $9.99. I couldn't believe my luck. 4th of July weekend you'd expect 'em to jack up the price on squirt guns. It was a real steal, even if it wasn't real steel.

I reached into my bag and selected an orange-colored blaster to replace the dud but—lo and behold—during the break, Sweda managed to patch up the weapon. Don't ask me how; he must've been packin' Epoxy, which doesn't surprise me. The guy is always ready for the unexpected, especially when he's around me.

Our first location was under a mammoth Moreton Bay fig tree in Balboa Park, where I set up a 39 x 72-inch aluminum **Photoflex Lite-Panel**—a snap to set up, even in the dark. Unfortunately, I should've packed a sandbag, because a stiff breeze blew in just as we started shooting. This had the two of us shouting, lurching, grabbing, and hand-holding. (No, not that kind of hand-holding.)

I used one studio strobe that was powered by a **Tronix Explorer XT**. Powerpacks can cost well over $1,000, but this beaut (made by Inno-vatronix in the Philippines) goes for less than $400! I didn't need the strobe's umbrella because I was using the LitePanel for bounce. Wait a minute—I take that back—I sure could've used the umbrella when the park's sprinkler system kicked in and put an abrupt end to the session. (Personal best: Fastest Set Break-Down.) We retreated to my car parked across the street in front of a church. As I was loading gear into the trunk, I looked up at the building. Spanish Revival; red clay mission-tiled roof, whitewashed stucco walls, two side staircases lit by lanterns casting a noirish glow.

I mounted a speedlight on the camera's hot shoe and had Sweda take a position on the staircase, gun in hand. He stuck an unlit cigarette in his mouth and I lay on the ground. I told him to point the gun right at me as I skewed the camera angle. In the viewfinder I saw a mob hit man. I was about to take my last shot on this earth. Didn't matter that the gun he held was green, I knew what color my blood would be. I told him to fire, then squeezed the shutter... [1/60 sec at f/4.0, ISO 400. Post-production: High Dynamic Range.]

Later, I put the flash away and shot the shadow in Fig. 31. Pure ambient light from a lantern provided a rich orange tone. I was gonna crop out the green barrel of the water pistol but decided to leave it in. Why be gunshy?

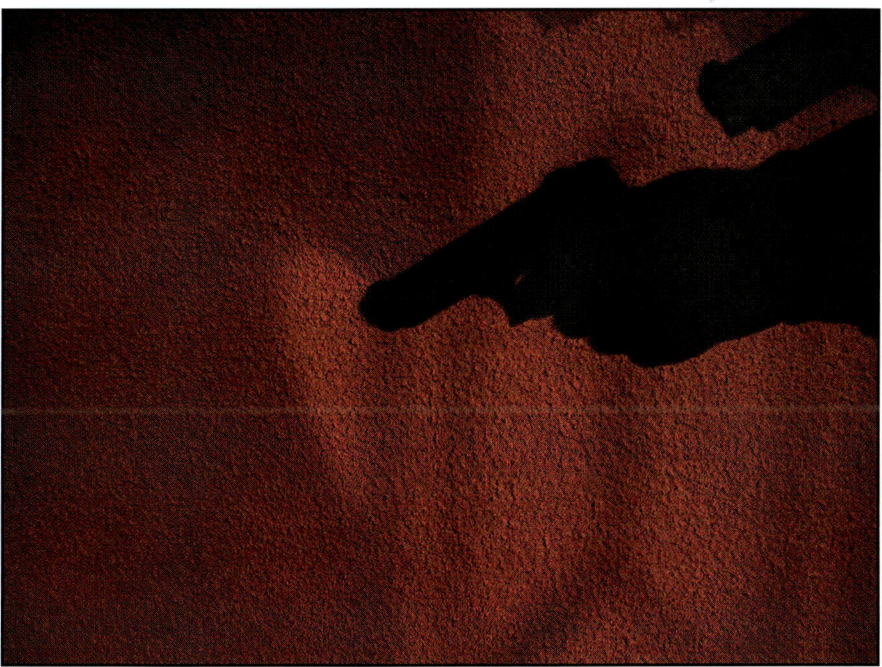

Fig. 31. A lantern's orange glow helped make this an effective shot.

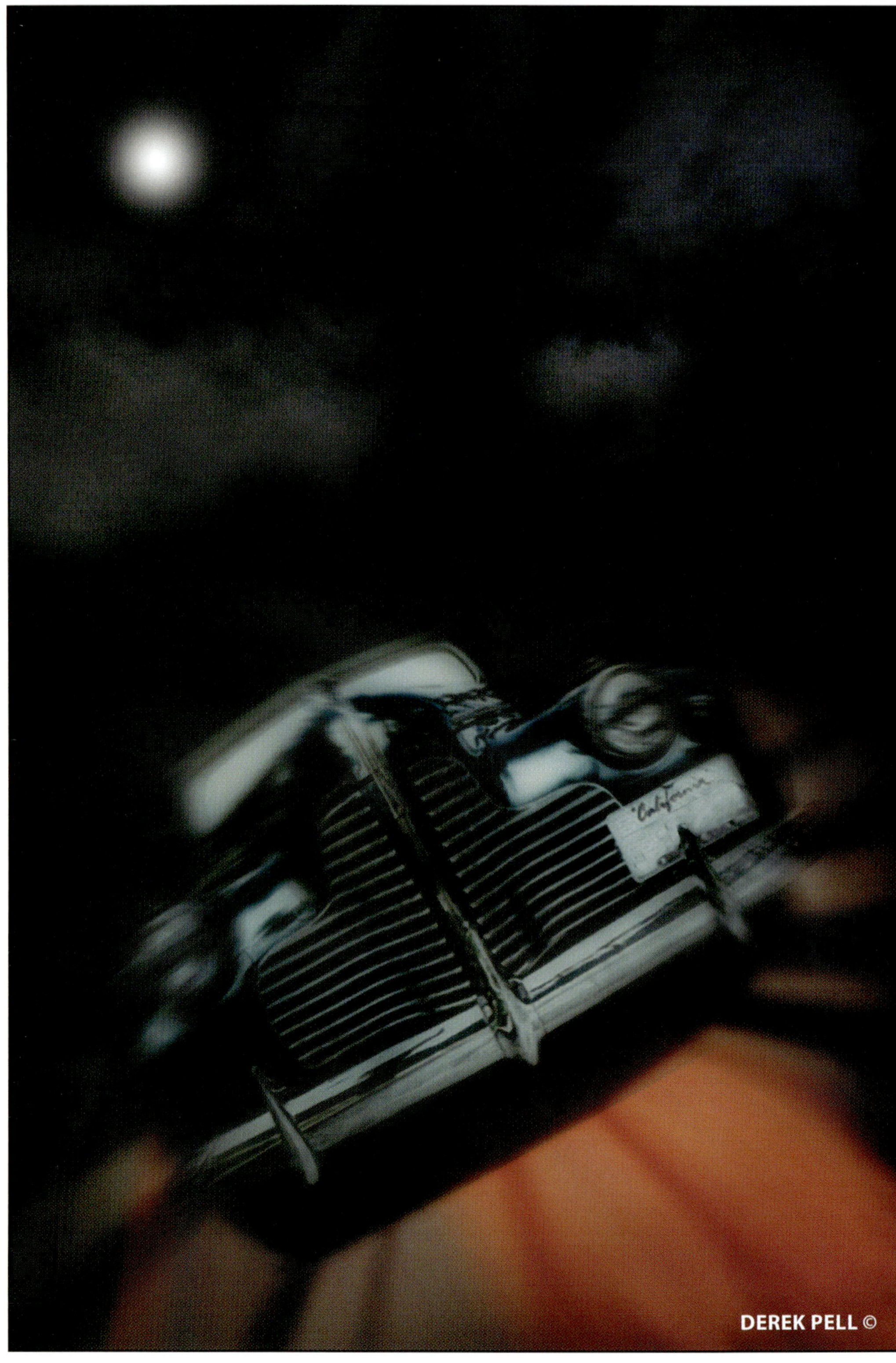

California

CHAPTER

6
A THIRST FOR BURST
Thrilling Action Adventures

"In this world you turn the other cheek and you get hit with a lug wrench."
—Impact (1949)

I've never been on safari in Africa—hell, I've never been to Africa. The wildest beasts I ever shot were behind bars at the San Diego Zoo, or behind the wheel on the Ventura freeway. I don't shoot sports for a living, and I don't chase fire trucks for kicks. So if you were expecting that kind of action, you're in for the Big Sleep. But before you skip town and grab *National Geographic,* hear me out. I've shot my share of *bang-bang* bursts, and I know a few things about "freezing the mo." In fact, I've fired the fastest still camera in the world right now—60 frames per second. Miss a shot with that sucker and you can toss your shingle in the pond.

Everybody knows that shooting movement requires a fast shutter speed. That is, unless you want to slow down for effect and catch some blur. Don't slur the blur—it can be the cat's pajamas.

How fast is fast enough? It depends on the speed of the subject. To freeze, say, a Bugatti Veyron rippin' by at 250 mph, 1/1000 of a second or faster will do it. For general sports action, a good ballpark minimum (no pun intended) is 1/500. Remember, I talked about Shutter Priority mode in **Chapter 4, "Hand-to-Cam Combat"**? Well, now's a good time to use it. (Mind you, that's not a licence to ignore your Aperture setting.)

All point-and-shoot cameras have burst modes, so everyone and their uncle is in the game. With a big telephoto lens mounted on a D-SLR, however, you're ahead of the pack... playin' in the big leagues. Too bad I don't own one of those million-dollar 800mm canons requiring muscles like my Governator and their own monopod.

My zoom lens limit is 200mm, so I have to get as close to the target as possible, but this ain't a bad thing. Like they say in the video biz, *get off your seat and zoom with your feet*. When the action rolls around you want be part of it, not a spectator with a bag of Fritos in your lap. Amateurs stand back in the crowd and snap. Pros march boldly forward even when the bullets are flyin'. They get the picture or, maybe, a purple heart. As for me...(Which way to the restroom?)

SPEED TRAPS: THE CURSE OF BURST

My D90 gives me two burst modes. (By the way, Nikon refuses to use the word "burst"—too crude for them—it's "Continuous" mode.) There's Continuous High and Continuous Low. At the high end, you get 4.5 frames per second (fps) which, in most states, will get you arrested for speeding. More expensive models shoot faster. For example, the Nikon D300 shoots up to 8 fps. So I drive an Alfa Romeo Spider, and other PIs drive Ferraris—I still move at a good clip and get where I'm going.

Photo by Derek Pell.

TWIST 'N SHOOT

As with all D-SLRs, the frame rate you actually get in a burst is determined by other camera settings. If you shoot at a slow shutter speed, like 1/15, you're not gonna get the maximum fps. Another thing that can drag down the frame rate is the camera's AutoFocus system. If you're out to break the speed limit, you can switch to manual focus and twist the focusing ring on the lens. This comes naturally to old-timers reared on film, but it seems bizarre to brainy digitalectuals. With practice, however, you can fast-focus with your eye to the viewfinder.

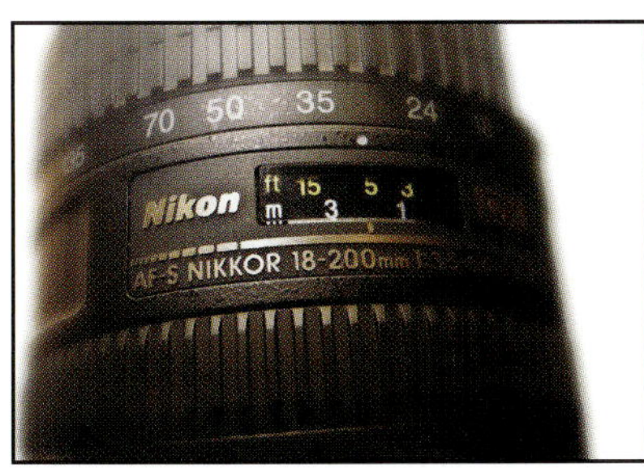

Fig. 1. Today's digital distance scale ain't what it used to be.

When I began shooting film, I taught myself to gauge distance with my eye. Sitting around my apartment, I'd look at an object— say, a lamp—and guess the distance: *Hmm, that's about ten feet.* Then I'd set the ring on the camera to 10 feet and check my focus in the viewfinder. I did this every day for an hour, and after about a month I got really good at it. Out on the street I could look at a subject and set the focus with the camera at my chest. Today, AutoFocus and the iffy accuracy of the distance scale on digital lenses make the whole point moot. Keep the cam eye level when you twist 'n shoot.

SCREEN IDLE

The LCD screen may be GGDC (God's Gift to Digital Cameras), but there are times to live without it. Like right now while shooting action. Just turn off the camera's LCD auto preview function and think about it for a minute. When you're burstin' your butt off, you're not pausing in mid action to check the quickie preview, right? So keep the damn thing off. You'll also conserve battery power and won't have to stop and swap. When you're finished rapid-firing, you can press your camera's Preview button and still see what you got.

HOCUS-POCUS, HOKUM-FOCUS

The D-SLR is a marvel of technology, blah-blah-blah, and Auto-Focus is jake with me, but you have so many choices that you really have to STOP and THINK and make decisions; spin dials, drill down deep through a maze of menus and, suddenly, the photo op has passed.

Great as it is, a digital camera is a guesser, yessir. That's to say, it generates guesstimates from its little brain (admittedly a lot bigger than mine), and it often get things right. But what happens when it's wrong? The trick is knowing when it'll make the right guess and when it'll fly off to Siberia. The Nikon D90 has a feature called 3D Tracking (based on its Dynamic Area autofocus mode), designed to capture moving subjects. What's happening here is that you select a focus point in the viewfinder, press the shutter halfway down to lock it in, and then—when the subject moves—the camera maintains focus as you recompose the shot. Kinda like magic, only this bit of *slight of cam* is performed by analyzing the colors in a subject positioned at the focus point in the viewfinder.

And that's the rub. Let's say you're shootin' a Roman Catholic cardinal who's romping in a rose bed, surrounded by jubilant dwarves wearing red blazers and matching bandanas. The camera suddenly says, *Aha! The subject is the third dwarf on the left in the foreground!* So you click-click-click and catch the motion, only the cardinal is out of focus. In a case like this, set the focus manually.

A parade is always a good opportunity to focus on moving subjects. Fig. 2 was shot AF (AutoFocus), 1/320 sec. at f/5.6 (ISO 200). Nice sharp shot of the fireman's hand—problem is, the subject was the little girl who's slightly out of focus. I accidentally spot-metered the guy's hand. I was shooting from a balcony, zoomed in full to 200mm. The shallow depth of field (DOF) left little wiggle room. A close shot, wide angle, no problem. Focusing manually would've nailed the shot, as it did in Fig. 3 (1/320 sec. at f/6.3 (ISO 200).

Since a parade travels at a nice slow pace, a shutter speed of 1/320 was sufficient (no bursts necessary). If the light changes or you switch from a 200mm lens to a 300- or 400mm lens, adjustments will be necessary.

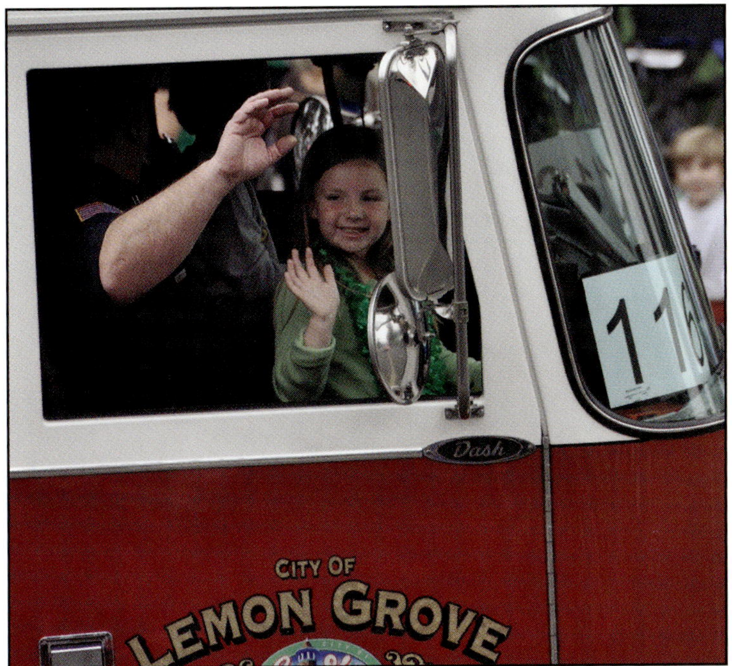

Fig. 2. Bad news: The subject is out of focus.

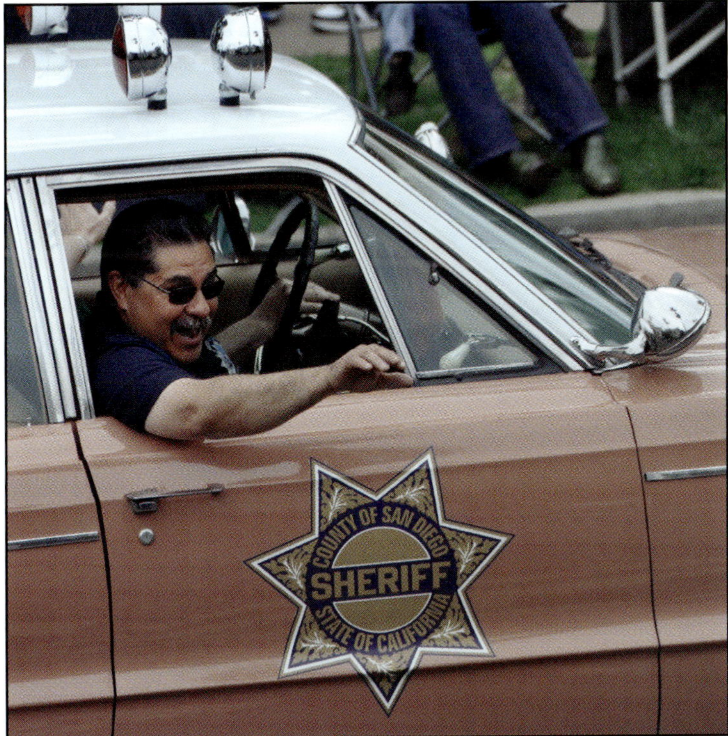

Fig. 3. Good news: I shot the sheriff. Manual focus pays off.

This parade shot packs pathos (Fig. 4). The kid's expression tells us a story—his hand pressed to the glass, worn out from wavin' to the crowd. An Irish prince in a paddy wagon. Maybe he feels incarcerated, or maybe he is. The two dames in the background are right out of the stands at Wimbledon. What's their relationship to the kid? Mother and Queen Mum or distant relations? The disassociation powers the imagination.

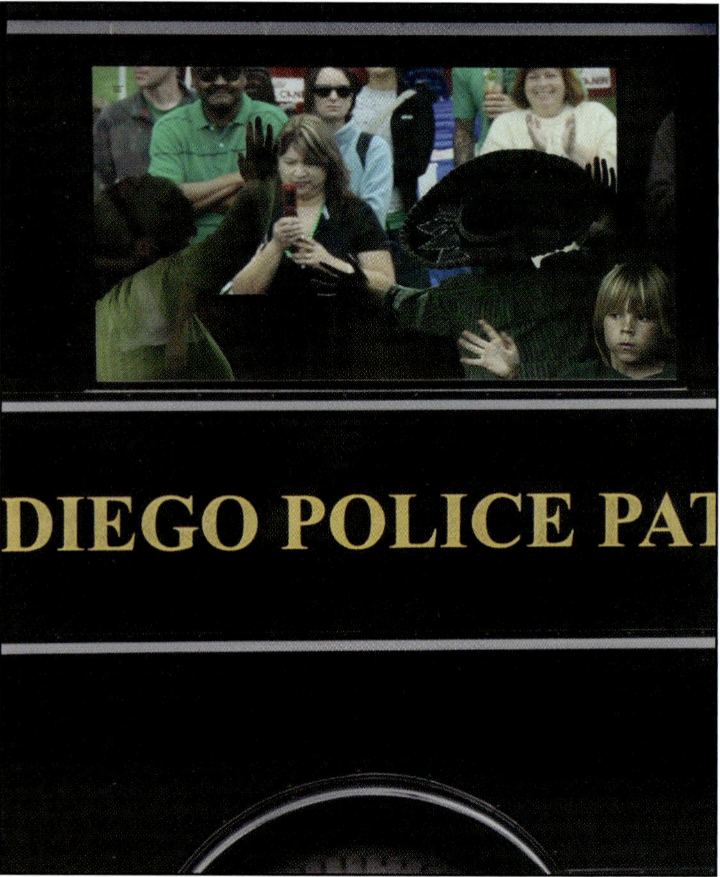

Fig. 4. This shot captures a story in mid-motion. 1/320 sec. at f/5.0 (ISO 200)

We'll revisit this image in **Chapter 7, "From Chump to Champ,"** and I'll show you how I improved upon the original.

"YOU LOOKIN' FOR ACTION?"

That's what the dame said as I turned the corner at Washington Street. I was minding my own business, although I'm technically unemployed. "Yeah," I said, "as a matter of fact I am…for a book I'm writing." She gave me a smirk. "I'm dyin' to read it." She told me to keep walkin' until I reached the freeway overpass. "It's under there," she said mysteriously. "Mind tellin' me what I'm lookin for?" The corner of her lips started to smile, but she had second thoughts. "A yappin' yellow bird," she said. She turned on her stilettos and clacked off.

I headed down the mean street, even though I knew only a sucker roams around under the freeway carrying a Nikon. But it was broad daylight and, besides, my editor was buggin' me for this chapter. I told her I hadn't seen any action since Guadalcanal, and she thought I was joking.

I found the bird, and it was long past its yap time, if you catch my drift. The scene was weird, and I mean that in the best sense of the word. Washington Street Skate Park not only had photogenic fetish objects hanging from a fence, but it was packed with a bunch of tal-ented skateboarders and their tattooed groupies. (What, you think groupies don't have talent?) There was a DJ alfresco spinnin' rap with lyrics the publisher deleted. (They made me swear I'd never try to sneak 'em into an educational book as long as I live. Of course, I didn't say I wouldn't put 'em on my website.) Ignoring sus-

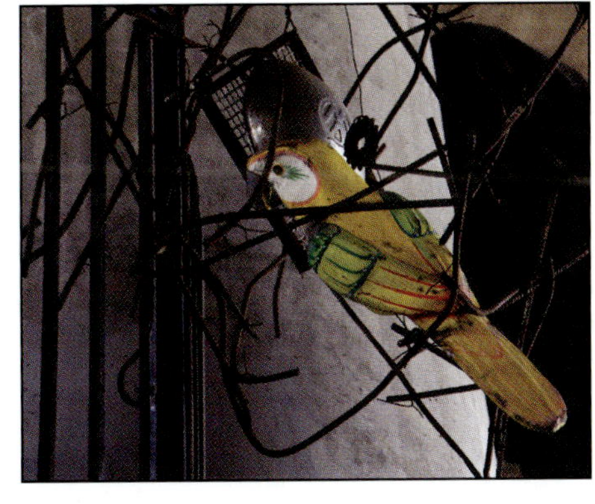

picious looks, I threaded my way *carefully* through a line of snarling athletes awaiting their turn. I emphasize the word "carefully" because there was no spectator seating—I had to maneuver along a slippery path as narrow as a skateboard that meandered around the circumfer-ence of the steep cement pit.

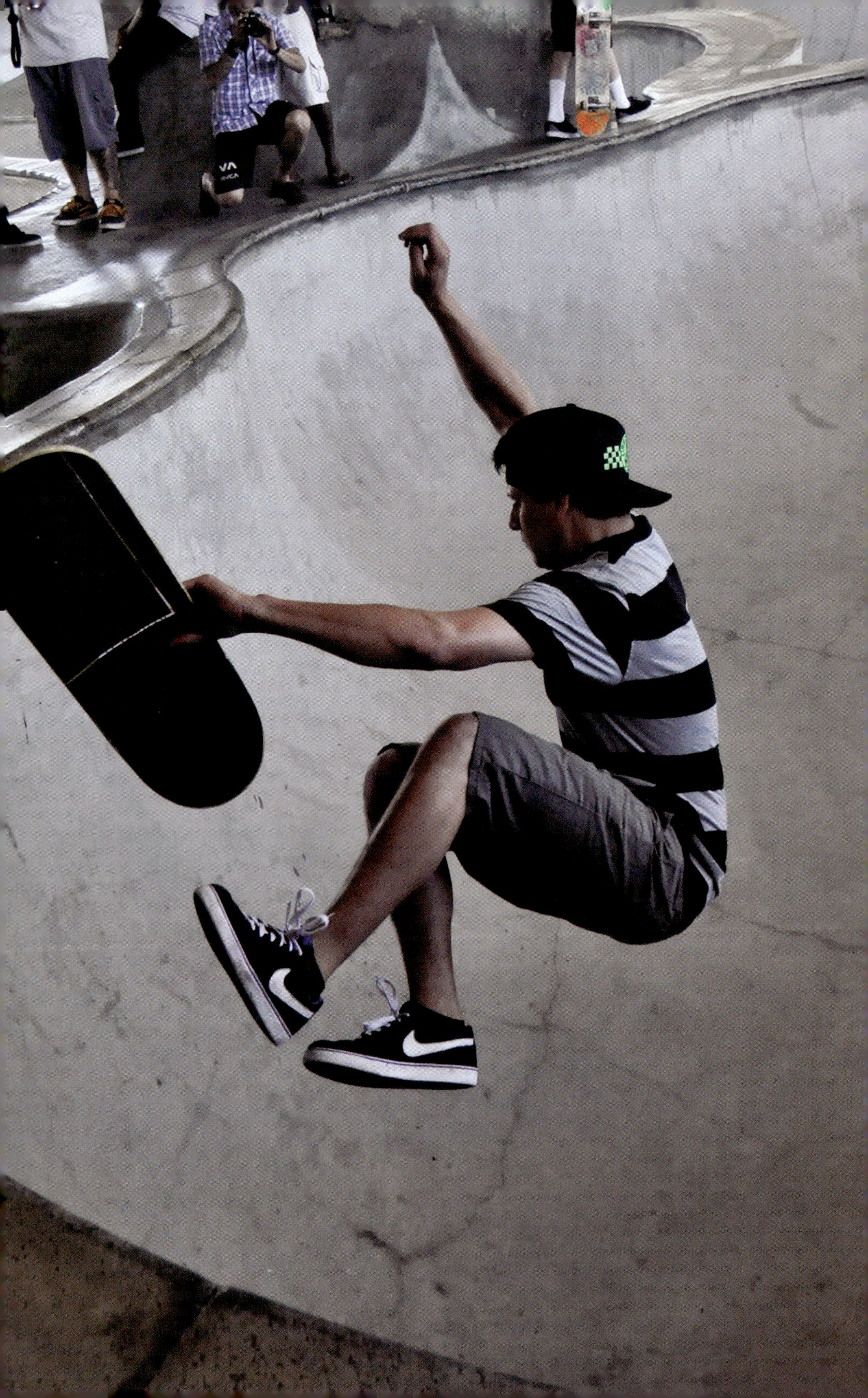

I set the camera to Continuous and cranked up the ISO because most of the park was in shade. One bank, however, was in direct sunlight, so I had to adjust when shooting there. For a few shots, like Fig. 5, I used a speedlight mounted on the hot shoe. These guys fly by like bats outta hell, so my shutter speeds averaged between 1/640 and 1/1000.

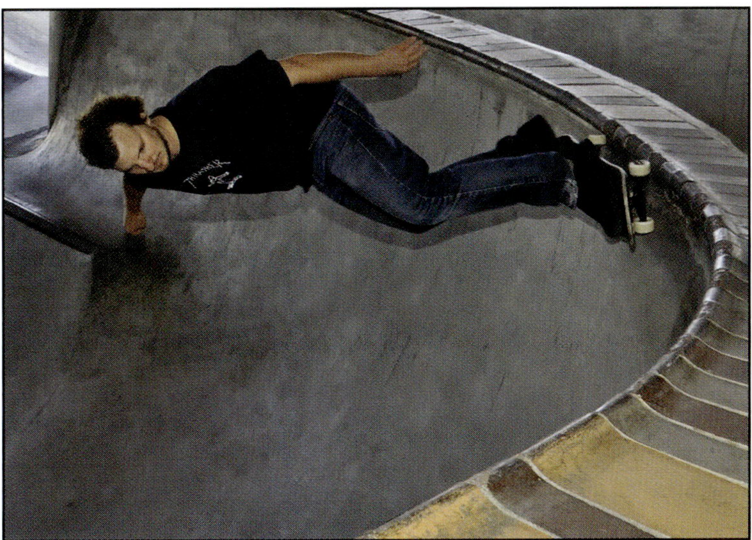

Fig. 5. A speedlight provided fill for this shot as the guy whipped by me.

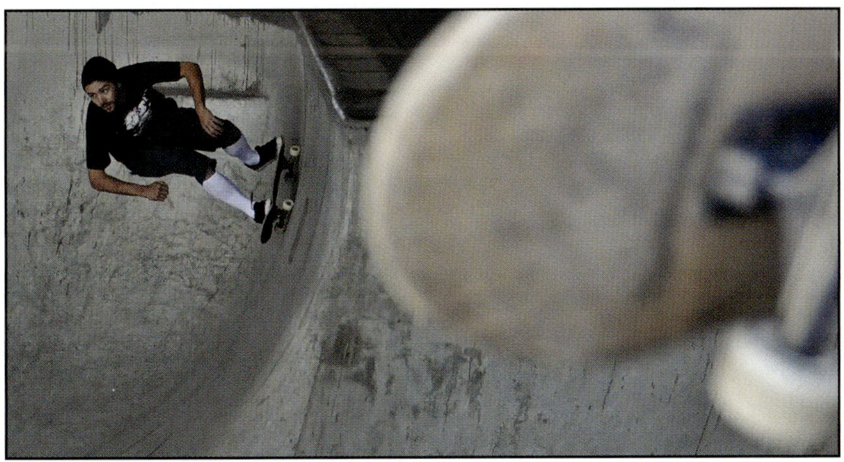

A wide aperture provided shallow depth of field, making this an effective composition. (1/500 at f/4.8; ISO 1000)

GOOD BURST, BAD BURST

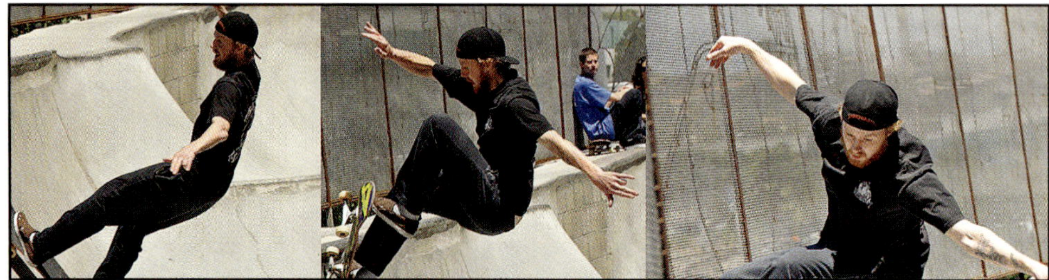

Fig. 6. BAD BURST. Zoomed in too tight. First and third image cut off the subject's arms and legs.

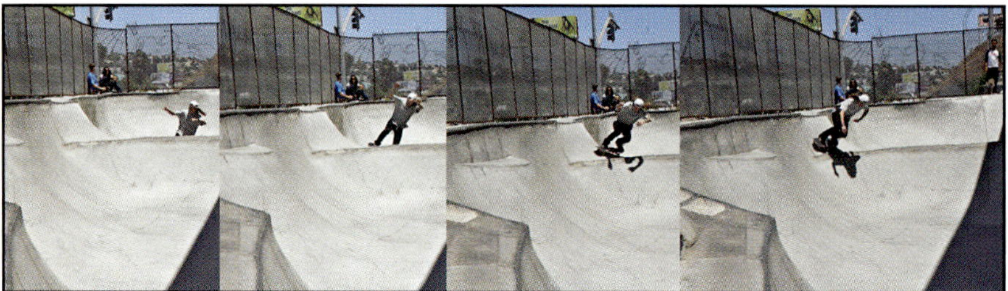

Fig. 7. BETTER BURST. We see the skateboarder in continuous motion, with room on the right to follow his path.

When shooting motion, stay ahead of the curve; that is, always leave space in the frame where the subject is headed, or it's gone in a blink and you've got nothin' but empty background (maybe a passerby if you're lucky). This way you can pan with the motion and capture it all.

If you're shooting with a zoom lens, be careful not to zoom in too tight. In the overlapping burst sequence shown in Fig. 6, I was zoomed in too close. The middle frame is okay, but the other two mercilessly cut off the poor guy's arms and legs. (Ouch). In Fig. 7, we see the complete motion of the skateboarder coming over the mound and can shoot a second burst to follow his progress as he sweeps to the right. I don't want to be too literal here. There are times when you'll opt for close-ups to focus on a person's expression, or perhaps the shadow they cast (Fig. 8).

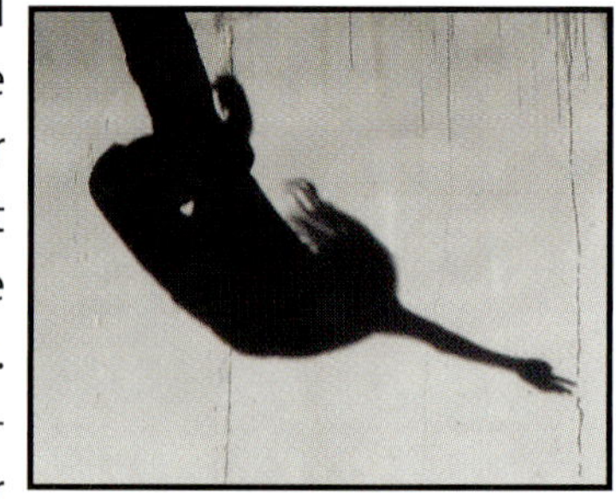

Fig. 8. A frozen shadow.

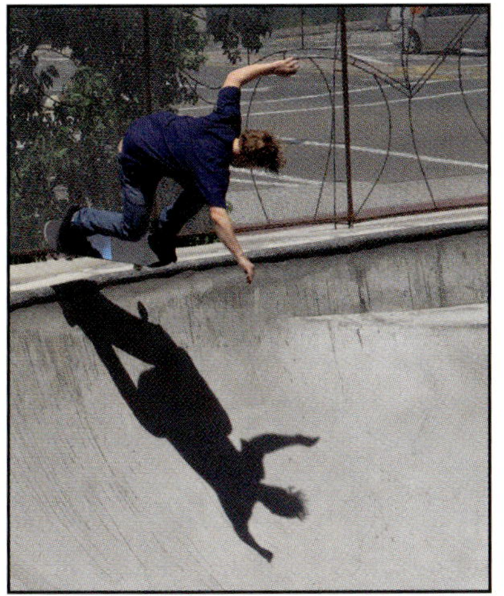

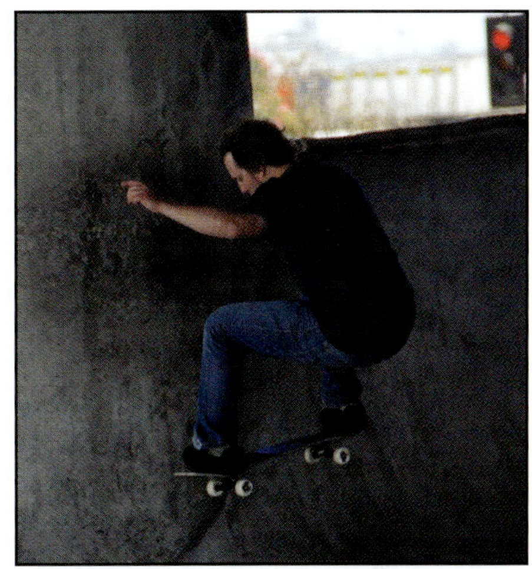

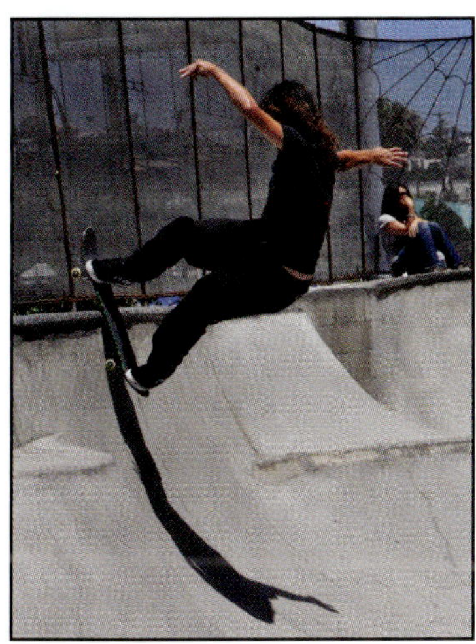

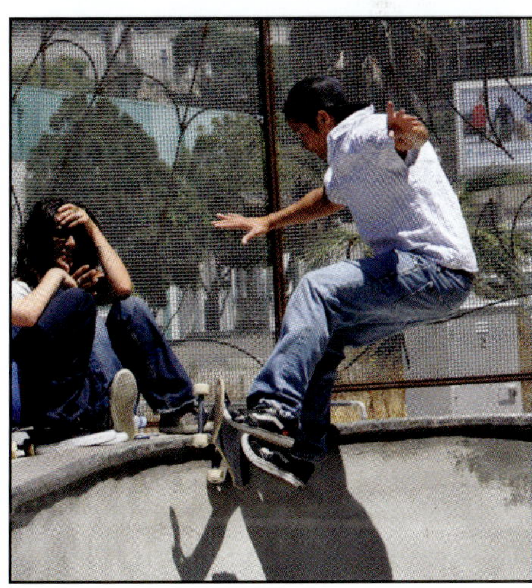

While I was taking these shots, a shutterbug with a Nikon came up and asked me if I had a spare memory card. He was shooting bursts and his 1GB memory card was full. He also asked if I had a spare battery. The only thing he didn't ask for was a smoke and a lens cap. I spent about 90 minutes shooting and took 1,433 high-resolution images, plus three 1-minute videos, all on a single 32GB memory card, and I had room for more. As I suggested at the outset of this book, always pack spare memory cards or have a portable drive to transfer to—especially if you're shooting rapid fire. The same can be said for carrying a spare battery.

LET'S ROLL

Other fancy photography guides give you shots of a ball leavin' the pitcher's hand, a flying tackle, a slam dunk, a hang-glide over a precipice. How thrilling is that?

Okay, so maybe it's thrilling, but here's something you won't find in those sissy books...*roller derby* (Fig. 9).

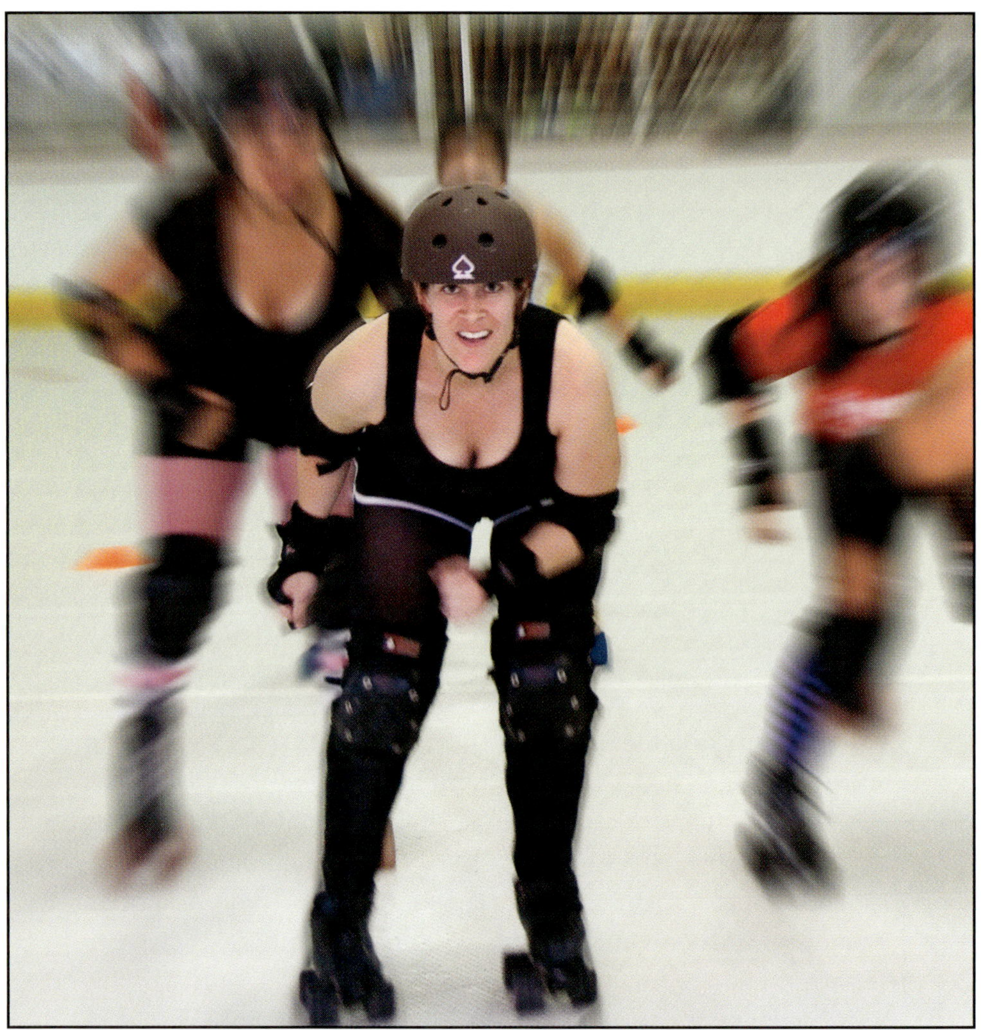

Fig. 9. Renegade Rollergirls racin' right at me—*look out!*

I traveled to National City, where the notorious *Scallyhags* hang out. (I risk everything for my readers.) Only problem was the season hadn't started, and they were just practicing at Skate San Diego. Still, these tattooed dames are tough—in or out of the rink. They have names that could make a Navy Seal sweat: *Rita Rangerface, Porn Scar, Bo Hemia* ("the hippie with anger management issues").

Since rules, like bones, were made to be broken, I shot a sport I know zilch about. When you understand a game inside-out, you know what to look for and when to look for it. You can anticipate a winning shot, know where to focus. Here, I was flyin' blind like a flatfoot on a ballet bar. I knew enough to anticipate lousy lighting, so I was packin' a speedlight. The only thing I forgot was a face mask and Valium. Whoever labeled dames "the weaker sex" ought to be tossed into the rink with some pissed-off rollergirls. But, again, it was only a warm-up, so nobody got slugged, mugged, or maimed.

I opted to shoot real slow (1/30, 1/60) to emphasize the effect of motion. There was no nasty elbowin' or grimaces to freeze, so I decided to go with the blur (Figs. 10 and 11) and escape with my fedora intact.

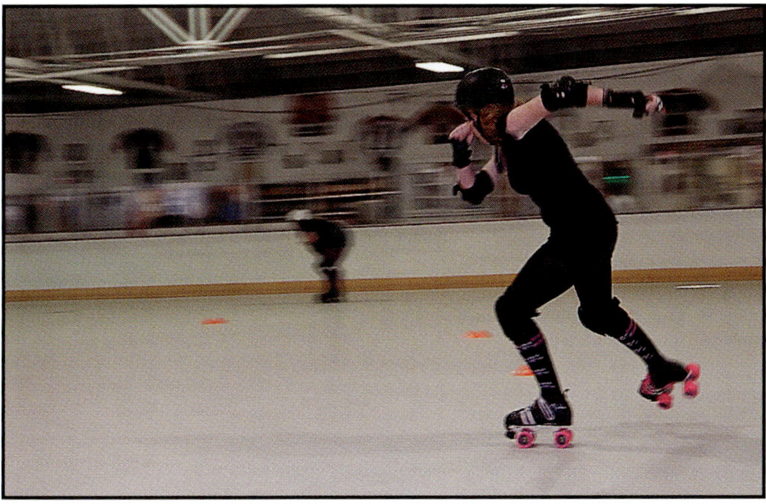

Fig. 10. The telltale blur of pink skates…

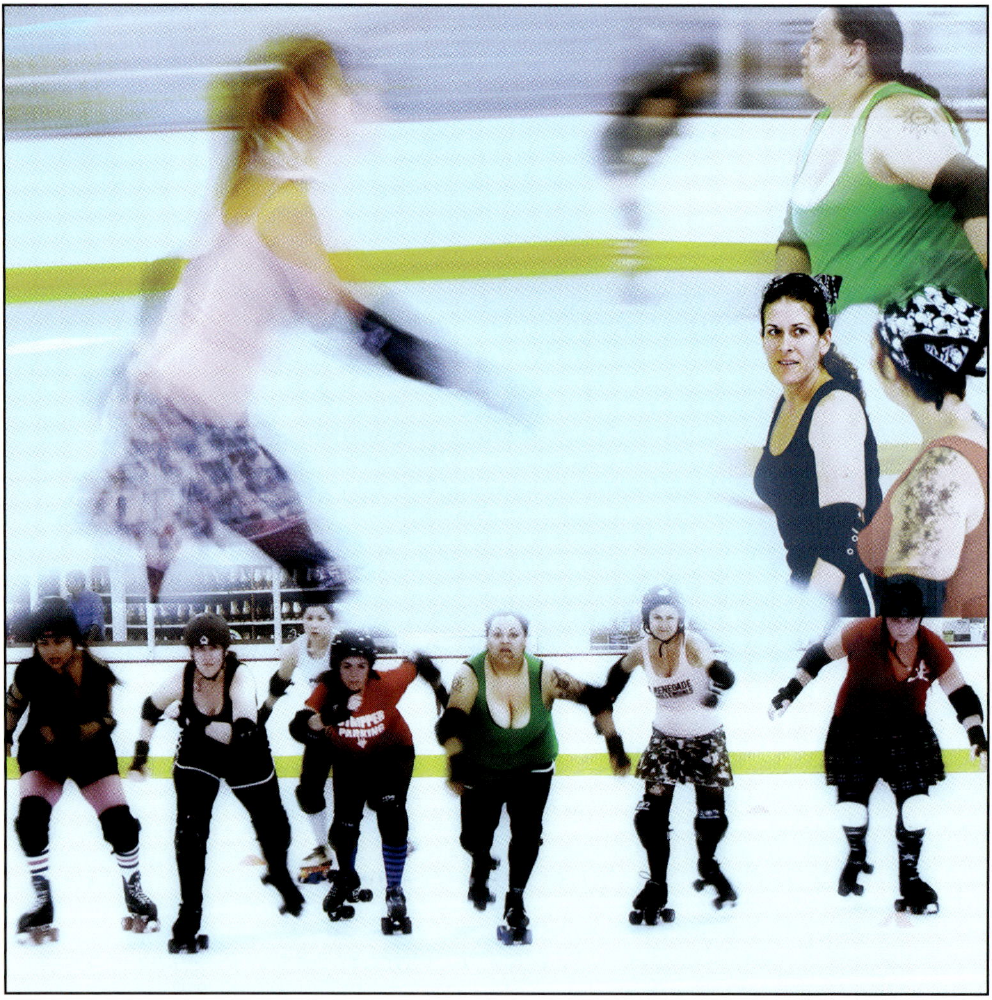

Fig. 11. A montage of Renegade Rollergirls.

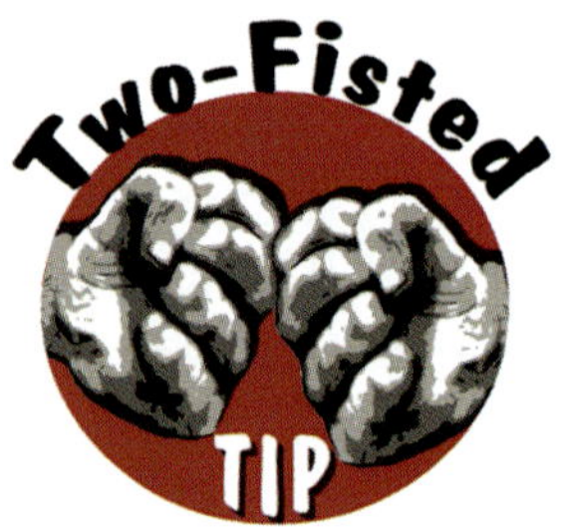

If you try to shoot action with a D-SLR's built-in flash, you're locked in to a slow shutter speed, like 1/60 of a second. Indy 500 on a rainy day? Goodbye, good luck, and good night. If you use a speedlight, you can toss off the shackles and push the envelope. For example , the combo of a D90 and an SB-900 external flash allows shutter speeds up to a whoppin' 1/4000!

"EVERYBODY FREEZE!"

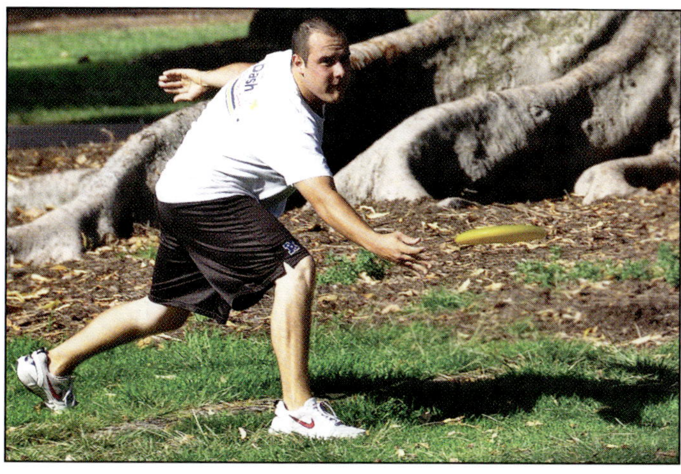

Fig. 12. The decisive moment. 1/500 sec. at f/5.6 (170mm)

I didn't have to travel far to capture some Frisbee action…a bunch of guys were flipping 'em pro style, fast as bullets, in the park across from Zoom Street. I didn't want any blur effect here; I wanted to nab the decisive moment when the plastic leaves the flesh (Fig. 12).

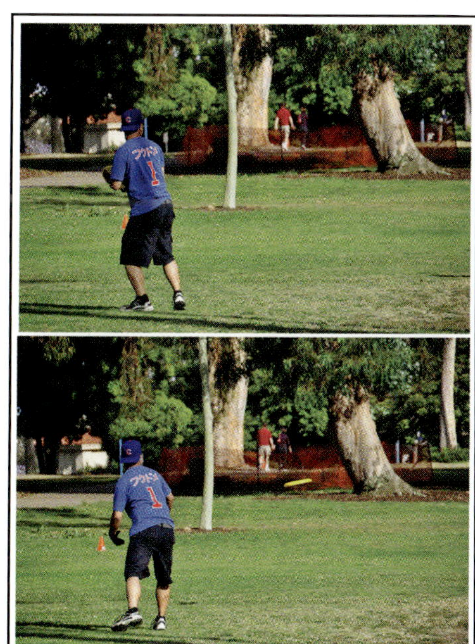

Fig. 13. Start to burst before the toss.

I set my shutter speed to 1/500 and fired off bursts at the first sign of a toss. When the guy in Fig. 13 tucked in his right shoulder, I squeezed the shutter. Wait a fraction of a second longer, and the Frisbee is out of the frame. Sayonara.

You'll never be known as "the fastest cam in the west" shootin' in single-shot mode. Burst'll make you first. Of course, you'll still miss shots from time to time, like when a player fakes a toss. Then you've got three or four clunkers to chuck, but so what? Keep the camera aimed, and fire off another round.

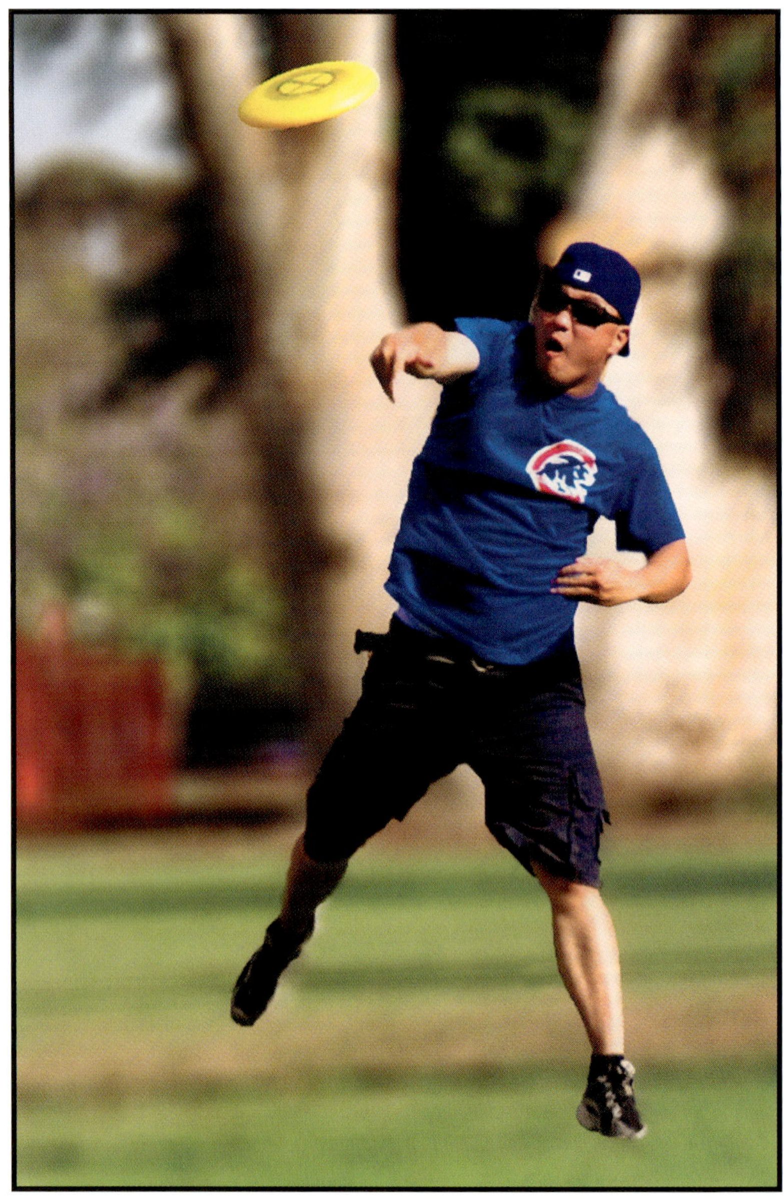

A shutter speed of 1/800 froze this powerful overhand toss mid air.

Frisbee players are everywhere, so capturing them is a great way to hone your timing while waiting to shoot the World Series or Super Bowl.

THERE'S MORE TO BURST THAN SPORTS

Phew, all that nonstop shooting has made me thirsty. I need a little R&R at the local bar, not to mention a vacation in Hawaii. Time to lick my wounds, cry in my beer, recharge all the batteries, and return to single-shot life again.

But wait—burst ain't just for sports or insanely fast action—it's good for capturing incremental movements and passing fancies. I call it Flow-Mo. An eagle soaring overhead, a hummingbird, the neighbor's cat swatting at a pup's butt. Or a couple of stool pigeons jumpin' a guy outside the New York Public Library (Fig. 14).

Rapid fire is useful when the motion ain't all that rapid but is tricky to nab. When you know there's gonna be some interesting movement, but aren't exactly sure when, set the camera to Continuous or Burst or Multiple (whatever) and be ready. Maybe you'll wind up shooting 12 shots to get the one you want, but so what? It ain't film.

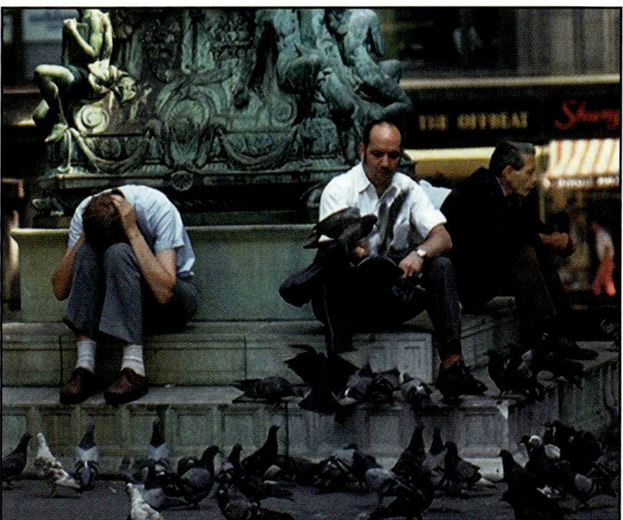

Fig. 14. This was captured with a burst from a Nikon F2 and motor drive.

TAKE A BREAK FROM THE ACTION AND LOOK AROUND

In the heat of shooting motion, it's easy to miss some gems not in the spotlight—for example, the fans or bystanders. Reaction shots tell a story, too. During a break in the action, look for interesting visuals apart from the main arena. In Fig. 15, the abandoned helmets surrounding the figure make a nice composition and convey a sense of the grunt work involved in practice.

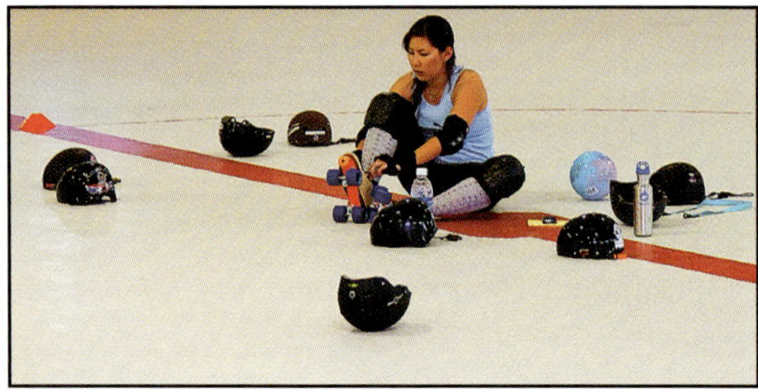

Fig. 15. Keep your eye peeled for good shots outside the action.

I discovered some unique photo opportunities under the freeway overpass on Washington Street in San Diego (Figs. 16–19). Adding a few stills will complement your motion shots.

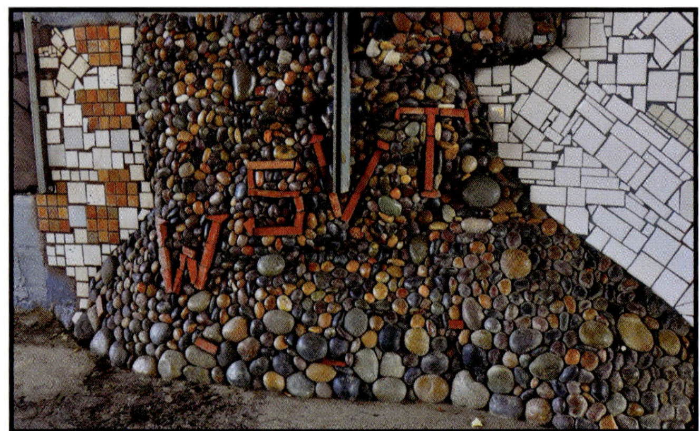

Fig. 16. A handmade tribute to an urban shrine.

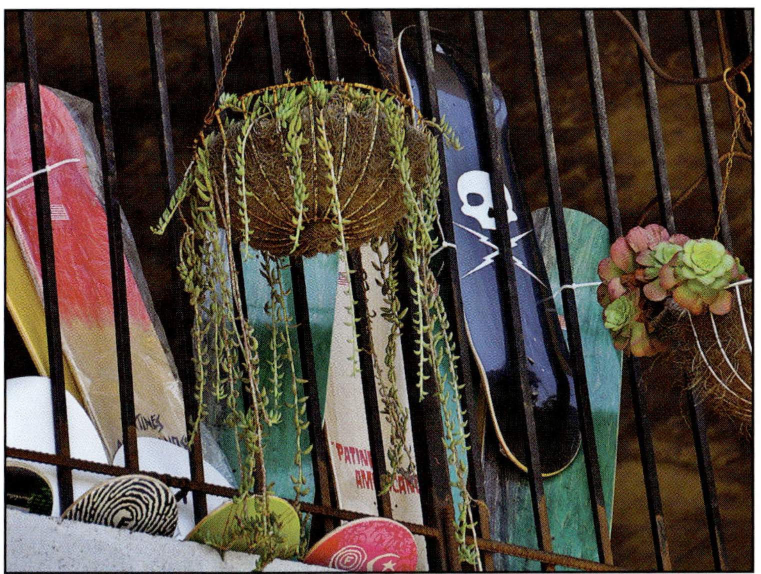

Fig. 17. California colors with a splash of noir.

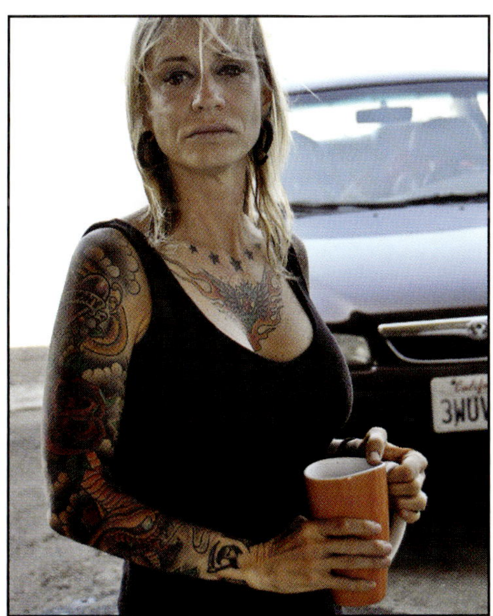

Fig. 18. A skateboard fan with a show of her own.

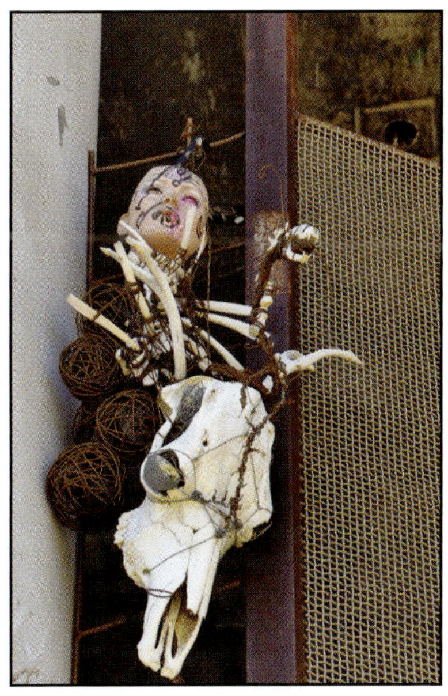

Fig. 19. It's a Hans Bellmer, dude.

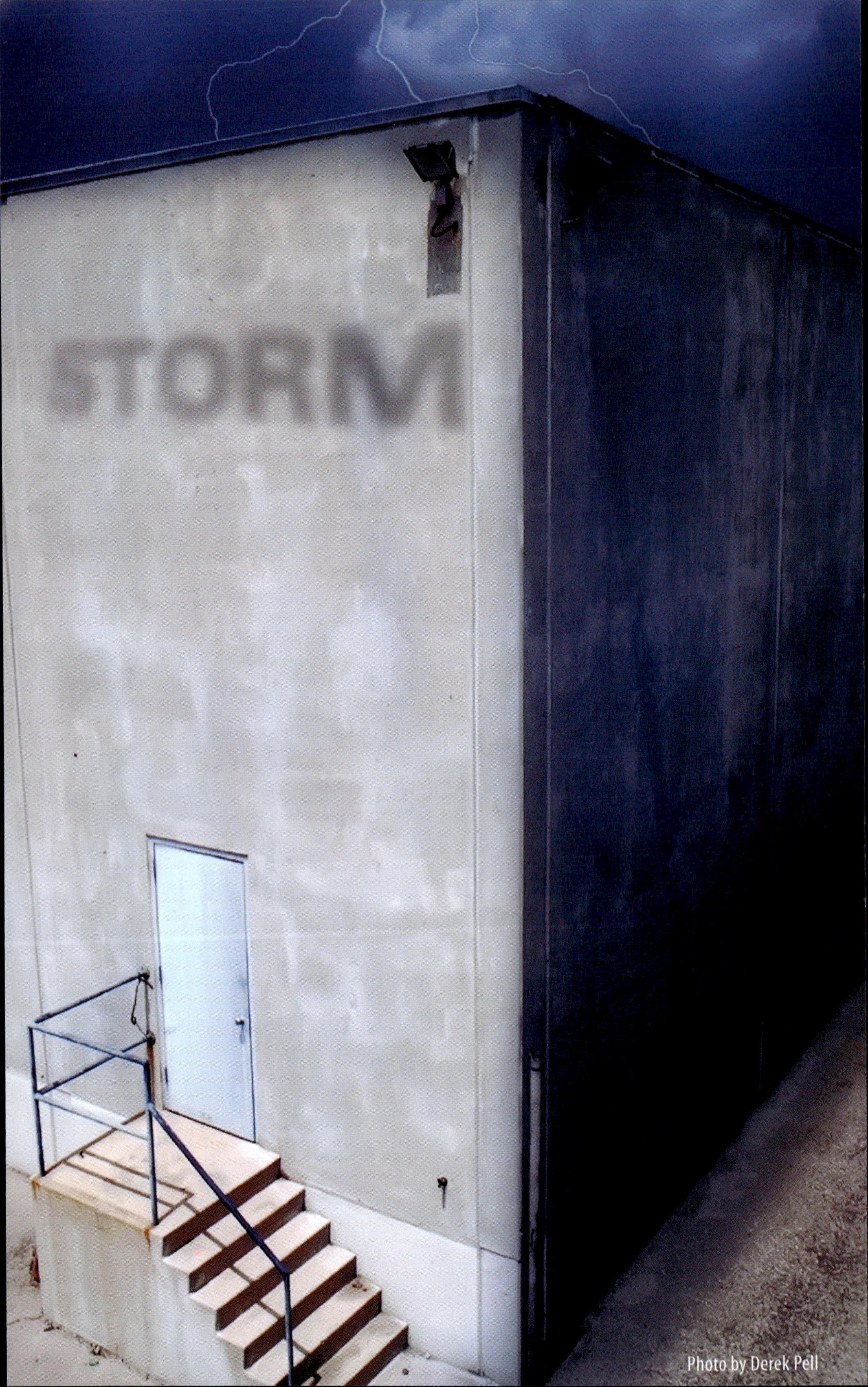

Photo by Derek Pell

7
FROM CHUMP TO CHAMP
Tampering with Photos

*"It was a blonde. A blonde to make a bishop kick a hole
in a stained-glass window."* —Raymond Chandler
Farewell, My Lovely (1940)

When I'm mindin' my own business and a thug draws a
snub-nose .38 on me, my goal is simple: Shoot the goon
before he shoots me. Nail him with a steady hand right
between the eyes—sharp, precise, no noise (TIP: Use a silencer)—
then walk away like it's a Sunday stroll. Never let 'em see you sweat.

It's not unlike shootin' a portrait: compose it in the viewfinder; aim
for the eyes; keep a low ISO to minimize noise. *Bang!* Walk away, and
pass right by the darkroom door.

Great goal. Too bad I rarely reach it. The "perfect shot" in the camera world is as rare as the perfect crime or a sober New Year's Eve.
Psst—don't breathe a word of this...*every photo you see in print has
been tampered with.*

That's what I call it. Others prefer the highfalutin' word "enhanced"
because it sounds arty. Fact is, all digital photos can benefit from
cropping, sharpening, noise reduction, spot removal, a color boost,
dodging, burning—or all of the above. Go a step further and we're
talkin' outright manipulation: taking somebody out of the picture
or stickin' somebody in (see **Chapter 2, "Call for Backup!"** for an
example of this), adding special effects, making a photomontage,
or turning an original into wallpaper noir (Fig. 1). That's tampering
in the first degree.

Subtle as it may be—like the hint of a dame's perfume in a crowded
gin mill—it's still there. Whether a quick fix using Photoshop's
unsharp mask (and will somebody please rub out the sap who

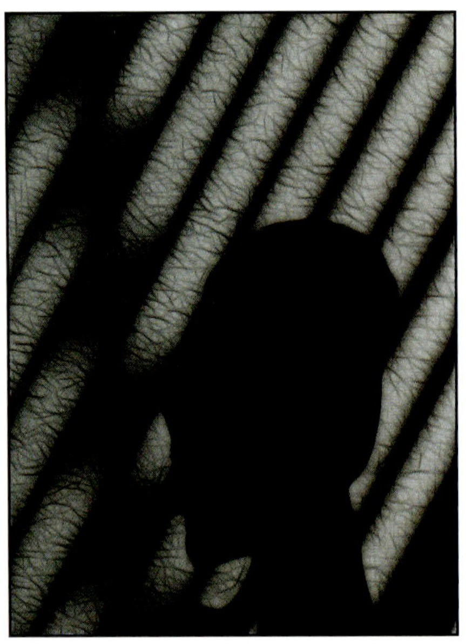

Fig. 1. Wallpaper noir.

coined that term) or just retouching a speck of dust, it's tampering, and it's a fact of digital life.

Work in the darkroom can be as grueling as a 9-to-5 job with a jackhammer. It can also be a ball. Pull the blinds, dim the lights, pop the plug-ins, and paint the town red. I can't tell you how many lost weekends began at the toolbar in Photoshop. But, like puffin' away in an opium den, tweakin' snaps can be dangerously habit-forming. One day you wake up and realize you haven't taken a shot in six months. See ya in rehab.

DID SOMEBODY CALL THE CROPS?

Yeah, I did. My photos live and die by the crop, and so should yours. Every image-editing program has a crop tool, and don't tell me you're too busy to use it...that's a crop-out.

Cropping has the potential to transport a photo from the fridge to a museum. If that smacks of hyperbole, consider this: How we frame the photo defines the subject within the composition.

If that ain't the meat and marrow of a photograph, I don't know what is. Remove the frame, and you'd see everything beyond the camera's eye and that, of course, amounts to nothing.

If a guy tried to sell me a satellite photo as art, I'd punch his lights out. Gimme the real deal, *a point of view*. "I'll have a BLT... Brassaï, Lange, and Tenneson on rye, with a side of Friedlander and a bottle of Adams."

What we choose to include in that rectangle is what turns a 19th-century mechanical process into art. So we compose a picture in the viewfinder but later, in the darkroom, discover distracting little details that yank the eye away from the subject. Or maybe we decide to rotate the image a few degrees, crop in tighter to add more punch. Can't leave decisions like these up to a photo editor today—they're our responsibility. When I worked for UPI, I had no say in the matter. I dropped off the film, saluted, and left—they did all the grunt work. In the digital age, the job is yours. Can't pass the buck to the lab.

Lately I've been cropping my shots in Lightroom because it has a feature that beats the pants off Photoshop—Crop Overlay. It superimposes a *rule of thirds* grid on the picture, and you can crop and straighten simultaneously. To cap it off, Lightroom doesn't ditch the portion you crop away, but saves the entire image. Open the photo a year later in the Develop module, click the Crop Overlay icon (circled in red in Fig. 2), and there's your original—complete with the crop area highlighted. You can tweak the crop or start from scratch.

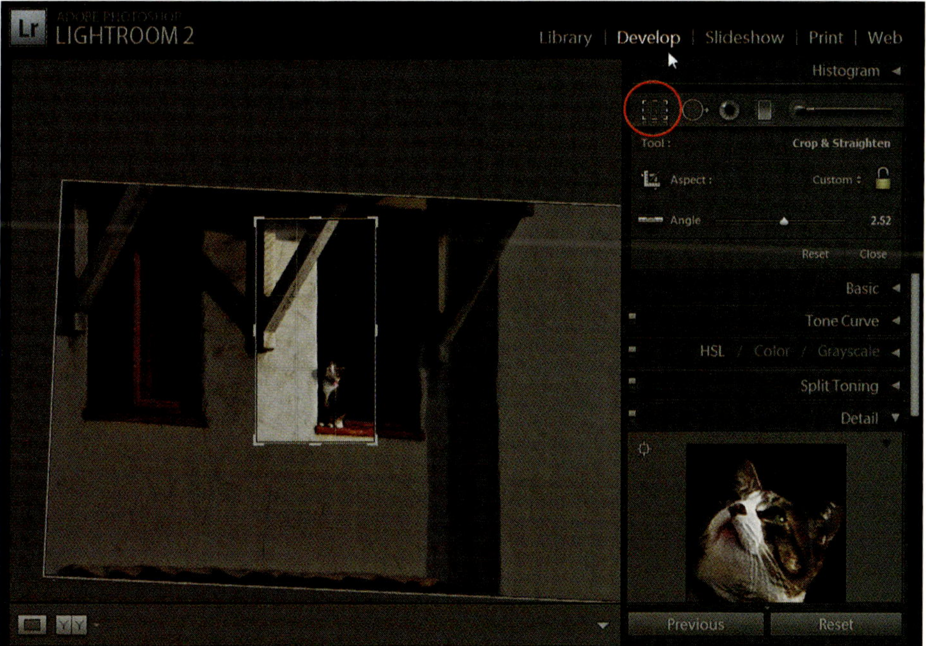

Fig. 2. You can crop till you drop in Lightroom's Develop module.

THE CASE OF THE MISSING SUBJECT

Fig. 3 shows the untouched original of a photo that appears in **Chapter 6, "A Thirst for Burst."** It was taken with a zoom lens at 65mm. (If I'd zoomed in closer I could've saved myself some work, but then I'd have nothin' to show you.) There's a good photo lurking in here; it's just hard to spot amid all the distracting elements. (HINT: Look inside the paddy wagon.)

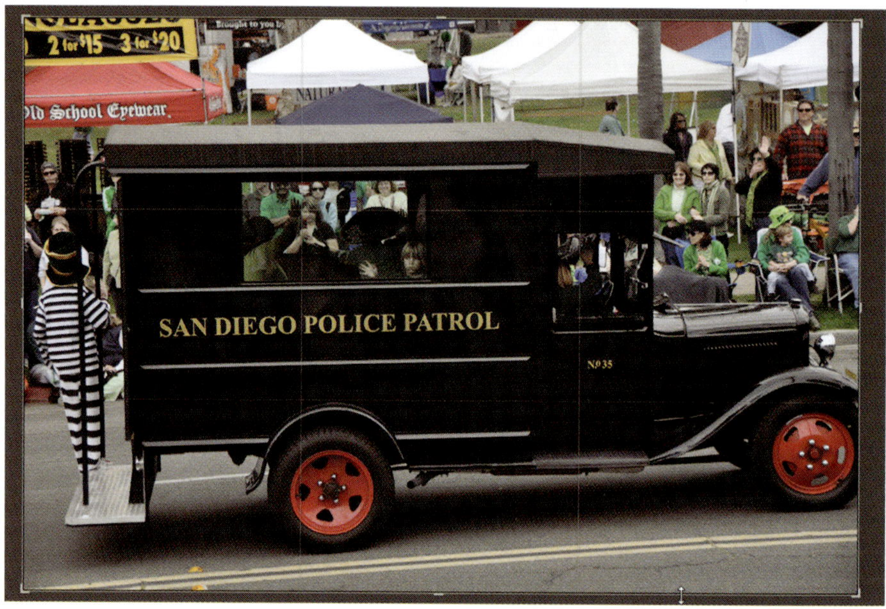

Fig. 3. The Case of the Missing Subject.

The kid is too small, and I'm gonna fix that. Since the wagon itself ain't the subject, I cropped out the cab (Fig. 4). Looks better already.

The photo is at an angle and needs to be straightened. Moving the mouse just outside the corners of the crop box (Fig. 5) enables me to click and rotate the image while using the grid for alignment.

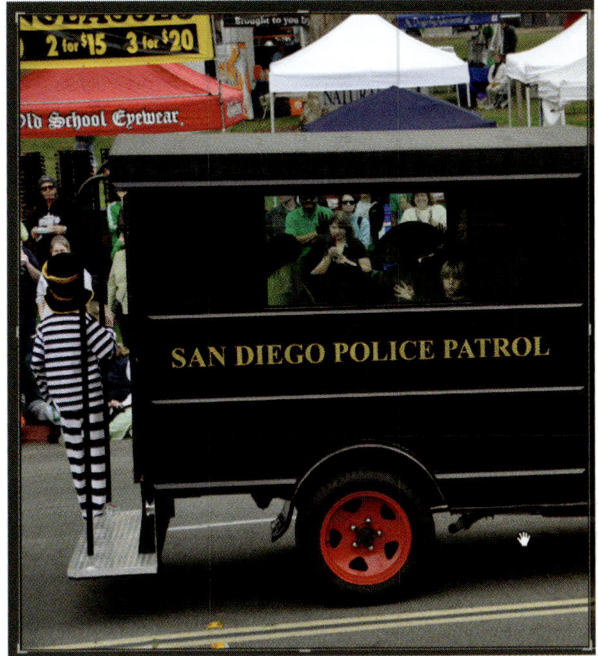

Fig. 4. Better, but still no cigar.

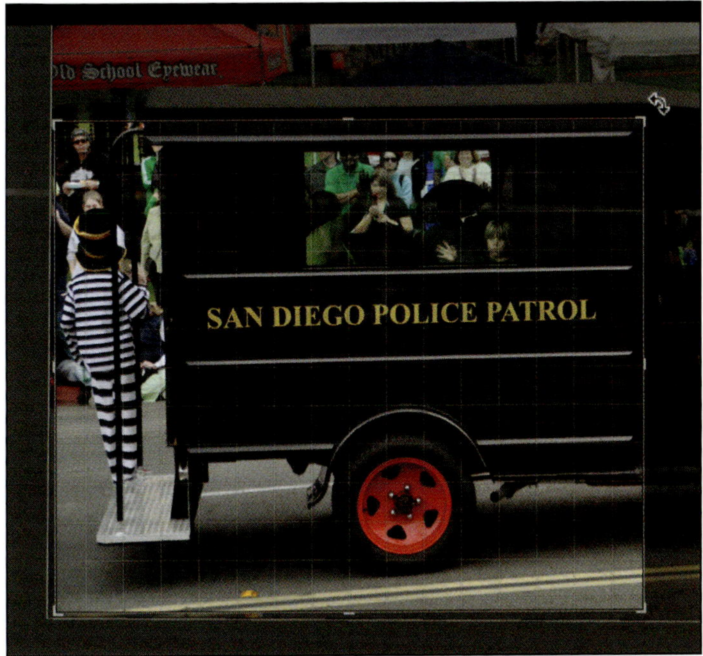

Fig. 5. Straightening the image.

With the wagon straightened out (Fig. 6), I take another hard look. I like the clown in the prison stripes but, alas, he has to disappear because he dilutes the power of the kid's expression. William Faulkner's advice to writers applies here as well: "Kill your darlings." So I killed the clown (Fig. 7).

Stop me before I crop again!

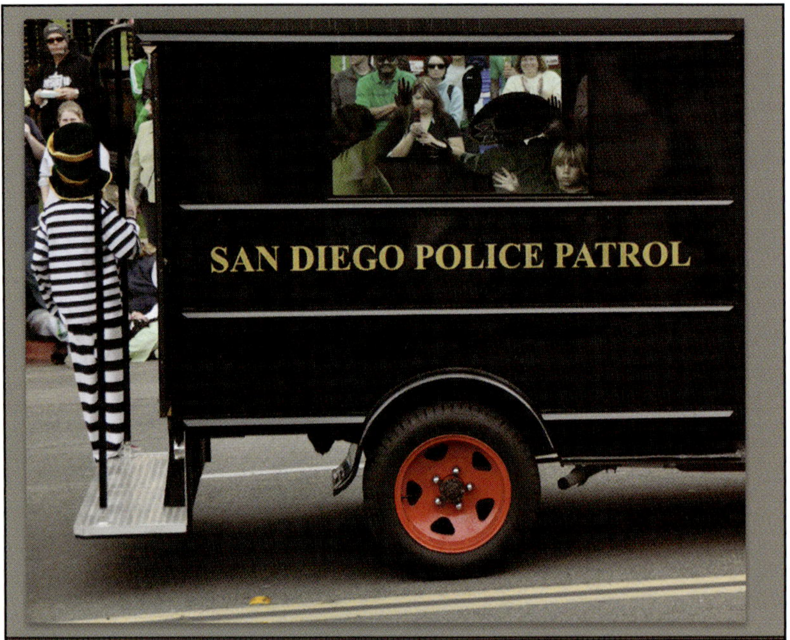

Fig. 6. The image goes straight.

But wait, the image still ain't right. Now the red rim of the tire is what first grabs the eye (boo, hiss!) so, because I wasn't on assignment for Goodyear, that had to go. And while we're at it, is the full logo "San Diego Police Patrol" essential to the picture? Adios, amigo.

Finally, the photo is finished (Fig. 8). I left in a portion of the tire so the viewer would see that the kid's in a vehicle. Also, the curve of the fender improves the overall composition. Bottom line: Be merciless when cropping, and lop off as much as you can.

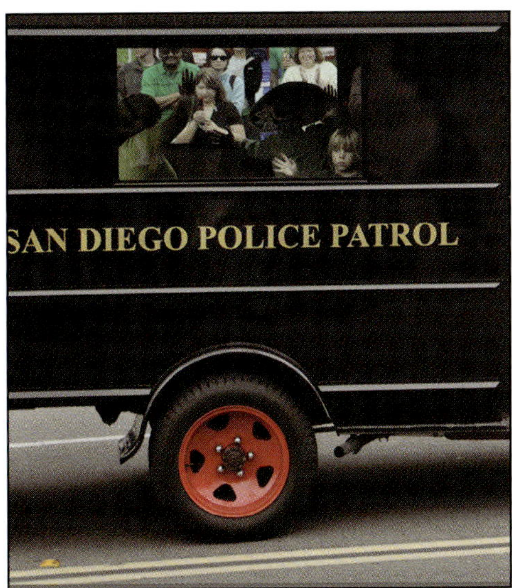

Fig. 7. The clown vanishes.

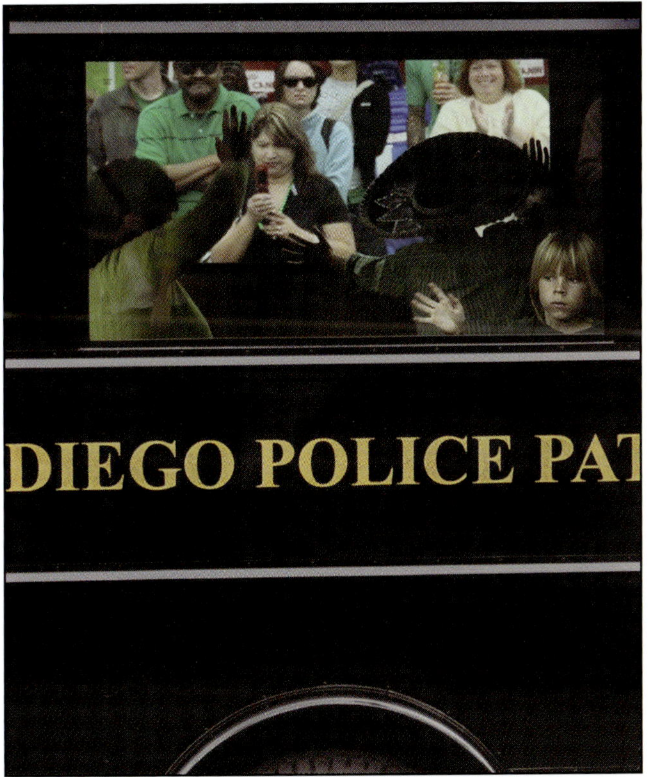

Fig. 8. The champ.

LESS IS MORE...MORE OR LESS

Sometimes it's better to focus on a few details in a photo and crop out the rest. Take this historic Victorian abode in San Diego (Fig. 9). After cropping, the emphasis becomes the Ionic columns—the texture, lines, and woodwork—as opposed to the structure as a whole, framed by fence, shrubs and sky (Fig. 10)—not to mention the intruding roof from the adjoining building. The cropped version has fewer competing colors, which makes the hues even richer. A bite-sized slice of history.

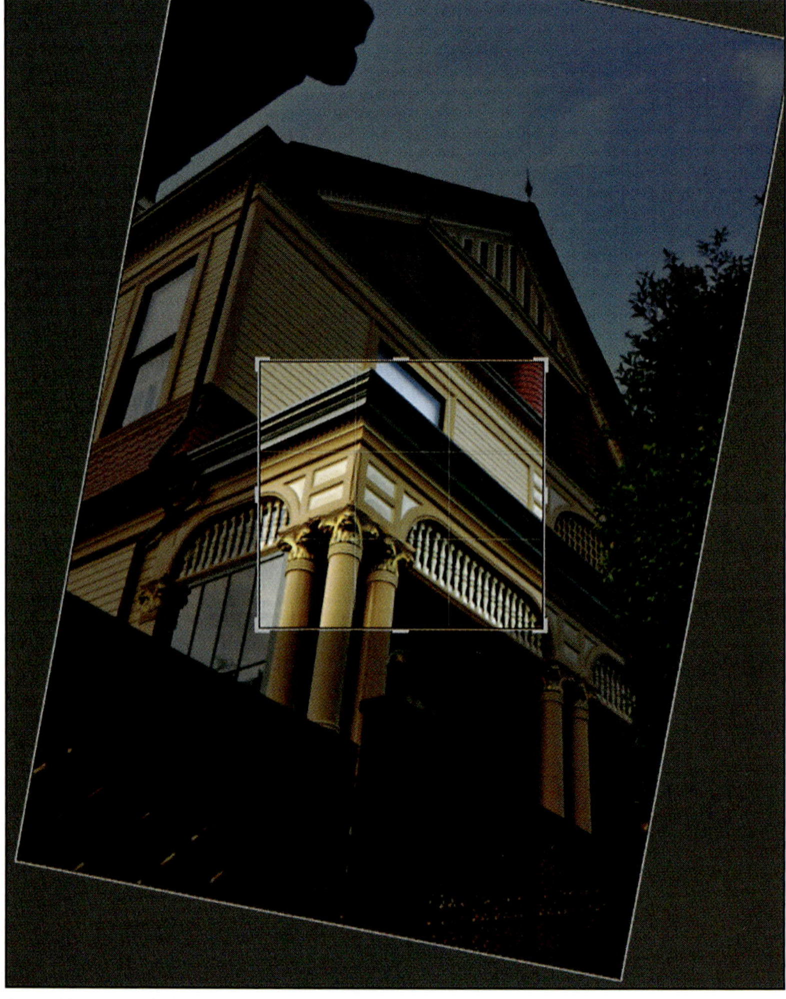

Fig. 9. The original photo in Lightroom's Develop module.

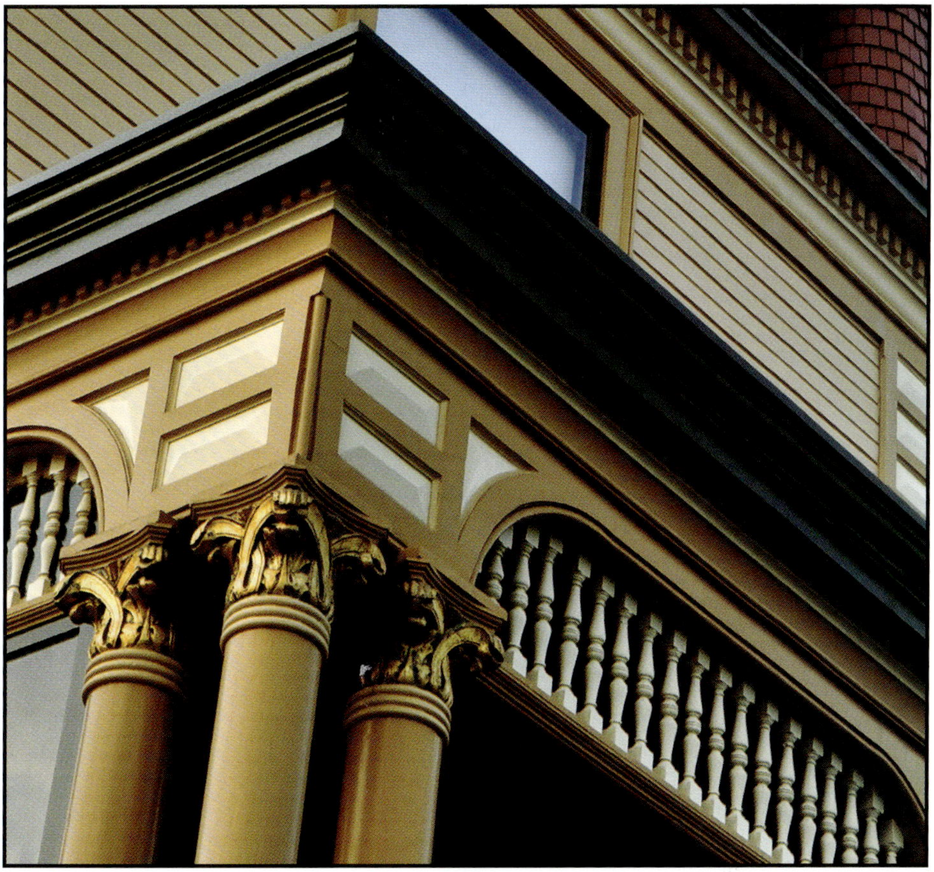

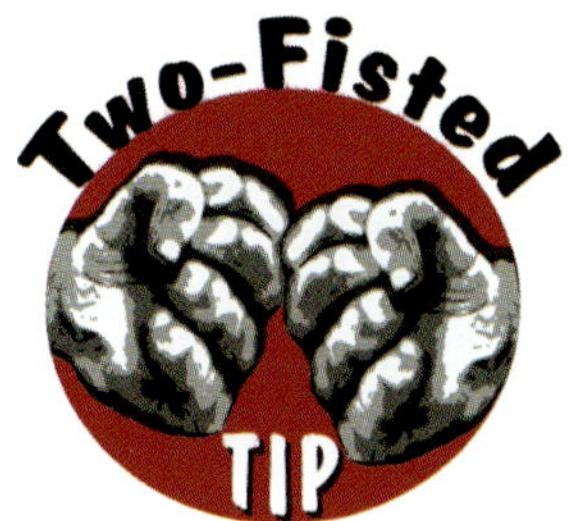

Fig. 10. The H. H. Timken House (1887). Photo by Derek Pell.

To make an extreme crop like I did back in Fig. 8 (about 1/10 of the original photo) and Fig. 10 here, make sure your original was shot at your camera's highest quality setting. Try that much cropping with a low-resolution pic, and it'll disintegrate before your eyes.

STRETCHIN' THE TRUTH

Photographs don't lie...they just stretch the truth.

Embroider that on your pillow or make it into a bumper sticker. For the benefit of the Doubting Thomas out there, I'll prove it with some evidence: a microscopic bit of tampering, courtesy of Photoshop CS4's **Content-Aware Scale**. If this feature don't break the law of physics, it sure comes close—a misdemeanor at the very least.

I had a photo of mine I needed to use on the cover of *Zoom Street* (Fig. 11). It shows a derelict movie theater that has haunted Coronado for years, and why nobody renovated the dump is a mystery even this dick can't solve. Problem was, *Zoom*'s cover shots have a fixed format in landscape orientation. The photo was shot in portrait.

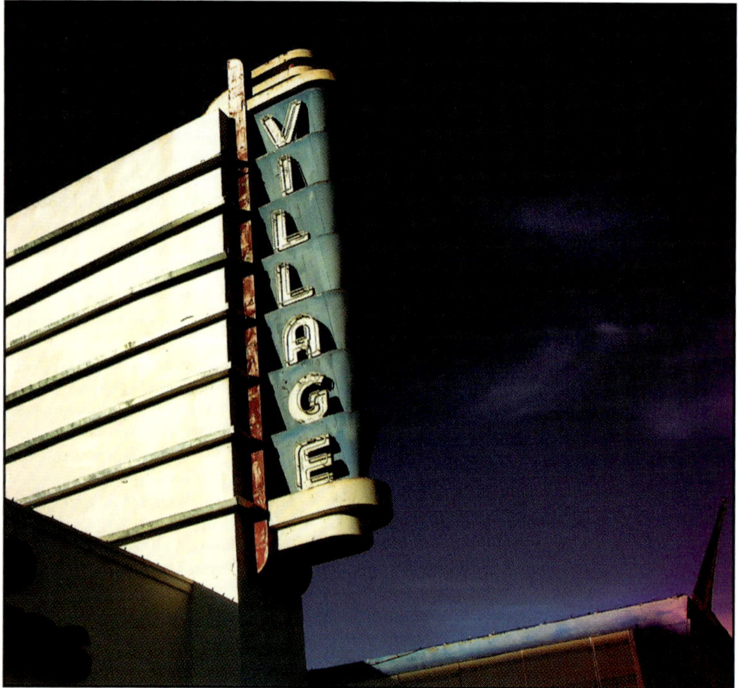

Fig. 11. A landmark movie house gone bust.

Before CS4, the only options would've been: (a) reshoot the photo, (b) spend hours in the digital darkroom trying to doctor it, or (c) use a different picture.

Here's the quick and painless solution.

With the image open in Photoshop, I clicked and dragged the Crop tool from the upper-left corner of the photo to the lower right, which put a bounding box around the image. I clicked on the middle handle on the right side and dragged to extend the canvas to the size I wanted the final image to be (Fig. 12).

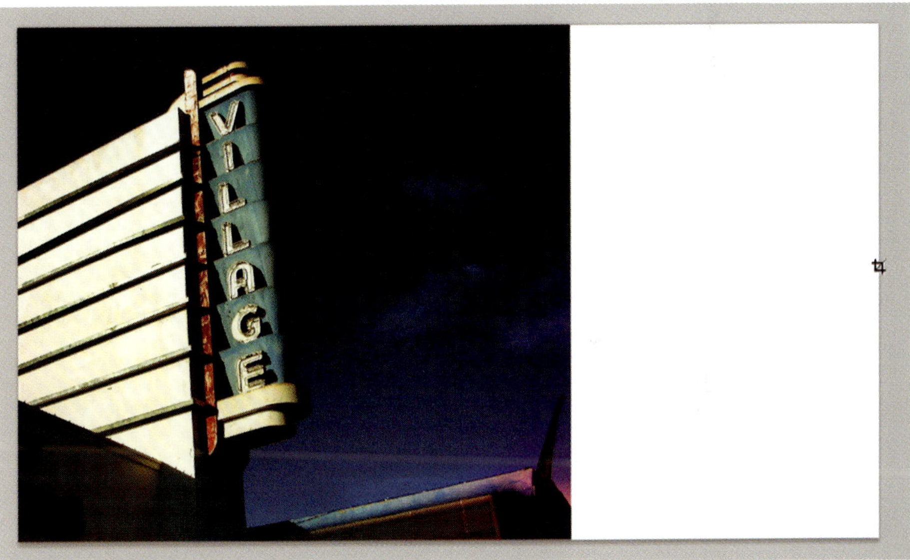

Fig. 12. Enlarged canvas after using Photoshop's Crop Tool.

Using the Rectangular Marquee tool, I dragged a selection around the border of the photo. Then came the fun part. From the Edit menu, I chose Content-Aware Scale (Fig. 13)—I bet only Scott Kelby knows the shortcut key for this (Alt+Shift+Ctrl+C).

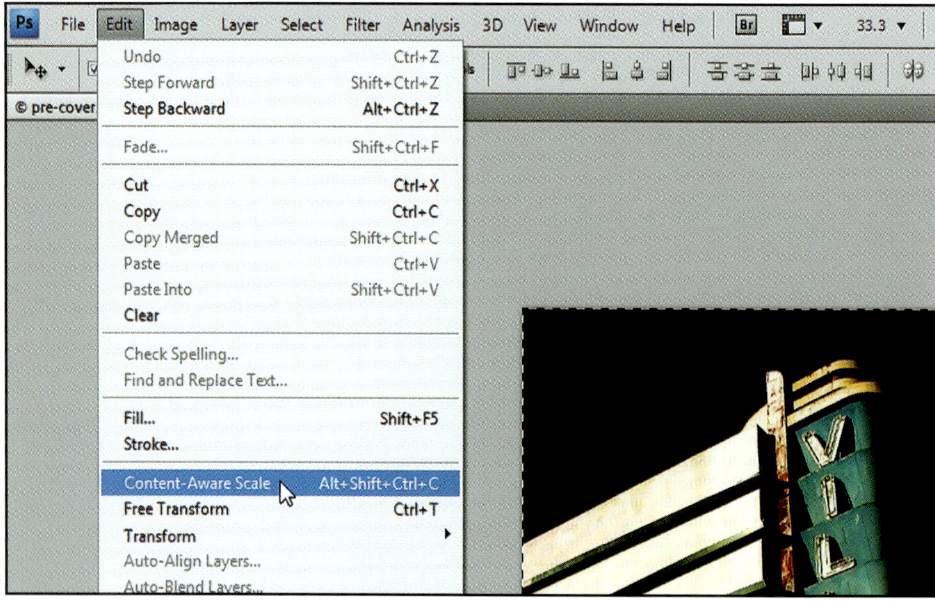

Fig. 13. The Content-Aware Scale command.

A new bounding box appeared (Fig. 14), and I dragged the middle handle on the right—the cursor changes to a double arrow (indicated in the screen shot by a red arrow)—to miraculously extend the image beyond its natural-born boundary. I say "miraculously" because there's no distortion in the image (Fig. 15).

This trick works in reverse as well—that is, you can turn a landscape-oriented photo into a proportionally perfect portrait.

If that seems like small potatoes, try writing the code to make this happen. This is the cutting edge of digital imaging—a seemingly impossible task reduced to a quick drag of the mouse. (It only seems long when it's written out like this. Try it, and you'll be amazed.)

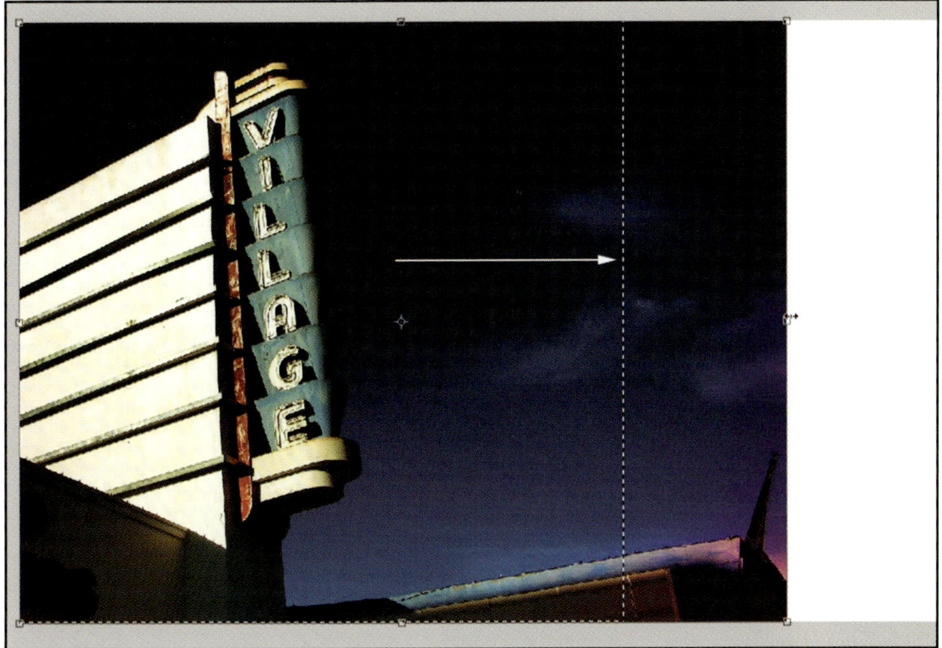

Fig. 14. The Content-Aware Scale in action. The dotted line marks the original's dimensions.

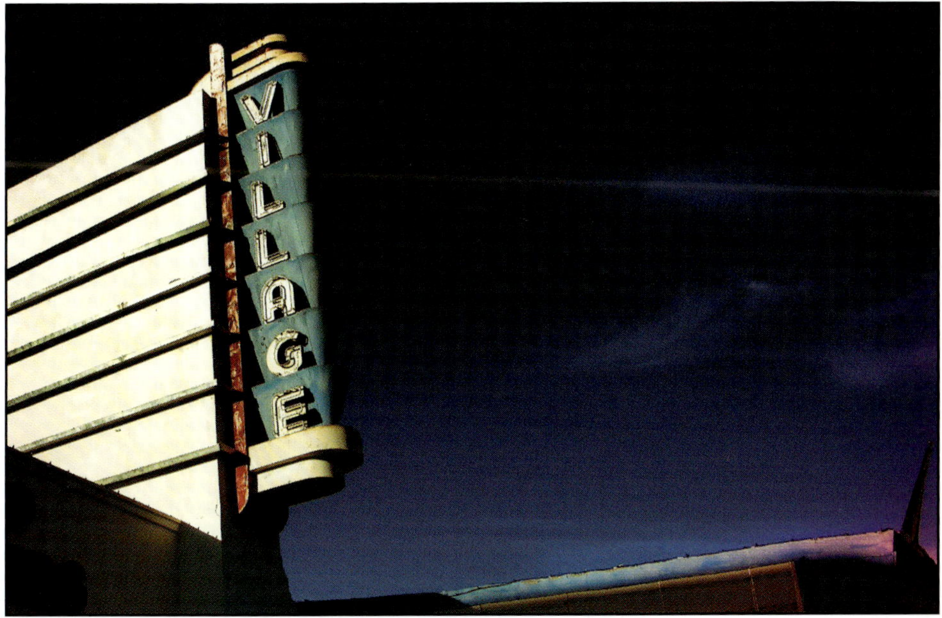

Fig. 15. The final cover image as it appeared on *Zoom Street*.

SHARPEN ME DEADLY

Nothin' beats good glass for "tack-sharp" results. Good glass, good camera, good exposure...you're off to the circus, right? Wrong. Most digital pics can use a dose of sharpening before you send 'em off into the world. (If massive doses are called for, the photo is probably a goner.) That's especially true if you're tampering via filters. Think of it this way: Sharpening is the last exit before the toll. If you sharpen an image and then make, say, a curve or vibrance adjustment, the picture loses some of its edge. To avoid this, always apply sharpening after you're finished tampering. Your mantra should be this: *sharpen, save, and store away.*

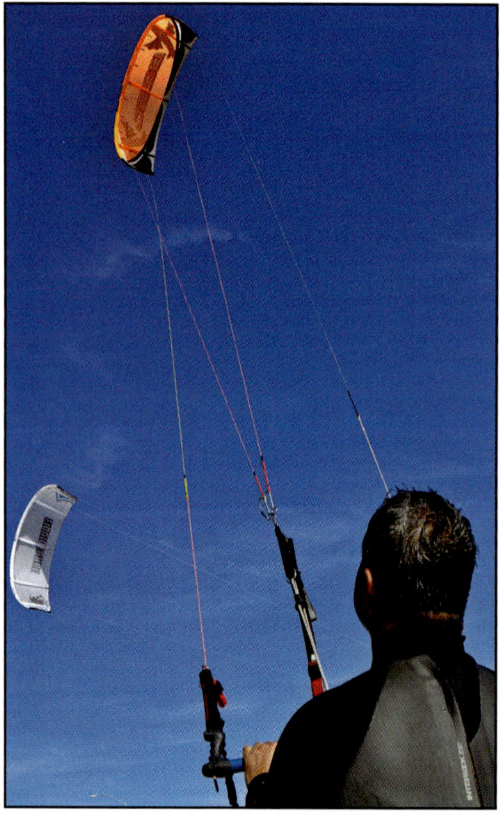

Fig. 16. Pretty sharp, but is it sharp enough?

Now, folks have written whole books on the subject of sharpening, so I have to be careful not to ruffle any feathers here. Be my guest: Pull a job using masks and layers and explore complex sharpening routines until your eyes go blurry. Or go the other direction and just slap on Photoshop's Unsharp Mask for a quick fix. Me? I turn to a plug-in that's available for both Photoshop and Lightroom: **Sharpener Pro** from Nik Software. Like many of Nik's plug-ins, Sharpener Pro uses its patented U Point control points, which let you selectively apply sharpening to areas that need it. (For a detailed look at how these control points work, see the section on Viveza in **Chapter 8, "The Devil Is in the Details."**)

When I studied my photo of the guy kiteboarding in Fig.16, it looked pretty sharp but—like every good detective knows—looks can be deceiving. From within Lightroom I launched Sharpener Pro and used a split-screen view to inspect the guy's hair. The default settings revealed softness on the left and a crisper version on the right. Then it was just a matter of tweaking the sliders to suit my taste. It's a subjective decision, no rules

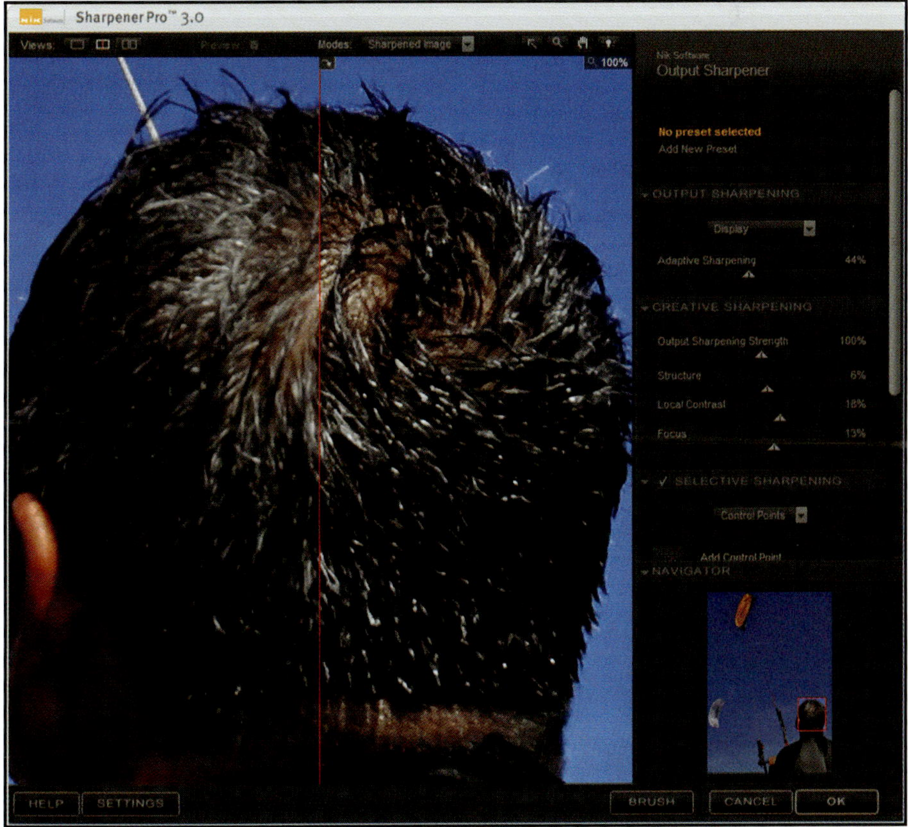

Fig. 17. Sharpener Pro's split-screen view lets you preview the effect of sharpening.

here. The only thing to beware of is oversharpening. This apples to whatever tool you use to do the job. If you're sharpening the entire image, as opposed to selected areas, inspect the photo top to bottom. Too much sharpening creates an ugly pixelated fringe around the edges of subjects and accentuates noise. Here's an extreme example (Fig. 18), showing a blown-up view of a flower petal that's too sharp for its own good.

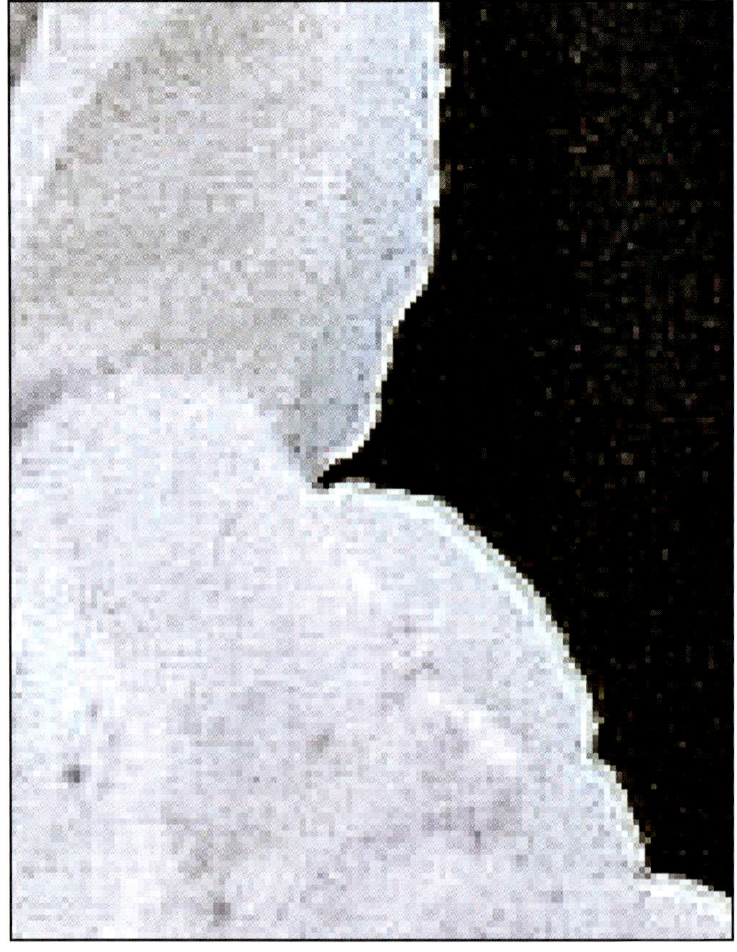

Fig. 18. Signs of deadly sharpening: fringe along edge of flower and pixelated noise.

Another important factor to consider is how you intend to use your final image. For example, the orginal photo in Fig. 16 was sharp enough for viewing on the web, where resolution is in the basement at 72 dpi. However, if I tried to make a print on my inkjet at 150–200 dpi, the image's softness would grab all the attention.

Sharpener Pro offers a varierty of output options, including Display (aimed at monitors and projectors), Continuous Tone (for labs using dye-sublimation printers), Inkjet (your printer and mine), and more. There's also a feature called RAW Presharpener, which is a two-step process that yields better results on some RAW images. Underscore "some," because the benefit escapes this PI when I'm not packin' a microscope.

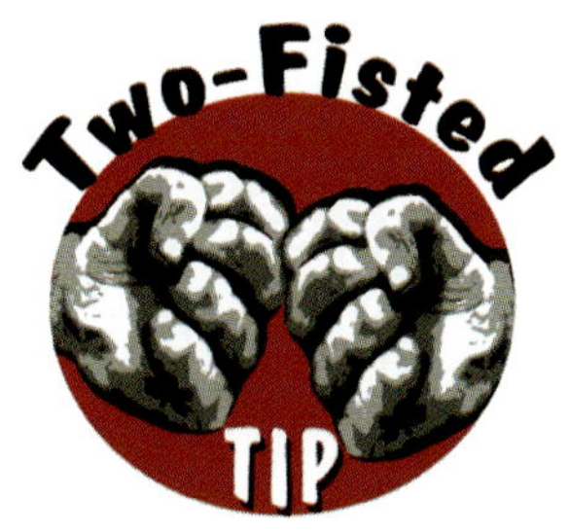

D-SLRs have picture controls for in-camera sharpening, like Nikon's Vivid setting. If you know what's good for you, don't be tempted. The camera thinks it's smarter than you and decides how much sharpening is required. Then it applies it to the whole photo, even if only one portion needs it. Remember also, if you plan on doing any tampering in post, sharpening should be the last process before you hit the sack—another reason to steer clear of in-camera sharpening.

Zenny Bruce, my wisecracking, transcendental sidekick (who's been all over the bitmap), adds this advice: "Don't be a stiff, just tamper with TIFFs."

Translation: If you shoot only JPEGs, convert 'em to the TIFF format (and/or Photoshop's native PSD format). Every time you make a change to the highly compressed JPEG and save it, the image degrades a little. Make enough changes, and your photo will look like a discarded target at a firing range. Not so with TIFF and PSD files.

"HAVE YOU TRIED CALLING NOISE ABATEMENT?"

That's what the dame said when I rang the mayor's office to complain about hardhats drillin' in the dead of night.

"Let me speak to the mayor. I got a complaint."

"The mayor's not in," she said, sounding surprised.

I stuck the phone out the window so she'd hear for herself and realize I wasn't just another nut.

"Didja hear that?—*How the hell am I supposed to sleep through that?*"

There was a long pause. "The mayor isn't responsible for noise. Have you tried calling Noise Abatement?"

That's why I split the Big Apple. The nonstop noise: horns honking, subways screetching, sirens wailing, and demonstrators shouting. (I lived a few blocks from the UN.) It was so noisy, in fact, I couldn't hear myself drink. Then, when the clowns at City Hall banned smoking at my favorite Greek coffee shop on Third Ave., well... I called it quits. I packed my cigarettes and headed west for a breath of fresh air. (Har, har.)

There's hardly any noise here in sunny San Diego, and most of it's in my photos. But at least I know how to get rid of it: Noiseware Professional, one of my top 10 favorite plug-ins.

Fig. 19 shows the Noiseware interface with a night shot I took with the ISO pushed up to 3200. The horizontal preview screens show a zoomed-in view of the clouds, the orginal on top. The bottom screen shows the power of the plug-in.

Like all quality professional-grade plug-ins, Noiseware gives you more controls for fine-tuning than you'll get around to using. There are several you'll learn to rely on, like choosing the amount of detail to protect when the filter is applied. There are also 14 presets, such as Landscape, Night Scene, Portrait, and so on, which are usually close to the mark but can also be tweaked. Of course, you can create and save your own presets, too, and then zap a whole series of shots taken under the same conditions. For photos less noisy than the one in this screen shot, the main Noise Level sliders will quickly do the trick.

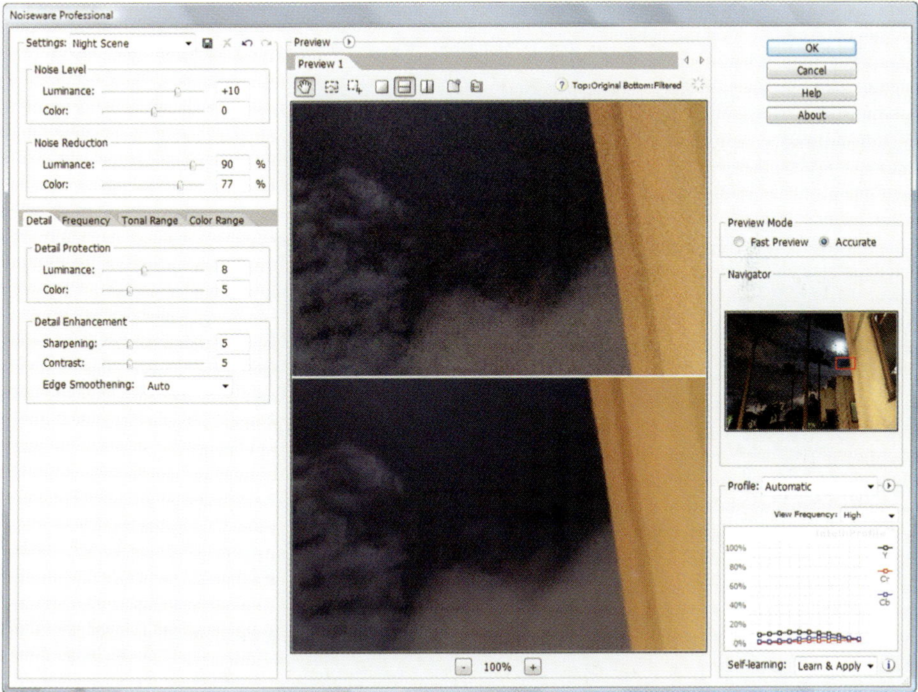

Fig. 19. Before and after views of a noisy sky treated with Noiseware Professional.

MANIPULATIONS, GREAT AND SMALL

When you turn the page you'll run smack into a big hacienda on a two-page spread that I shot a few blocks from my apartment. I processed the image for High Dynamic Range (HDR), a technique decribed in **Chapter 8, "The Devil Is in the Details."** It's a form of tampering that brings an amazing amount of image detail to the surface—it can really grab eyeballs.

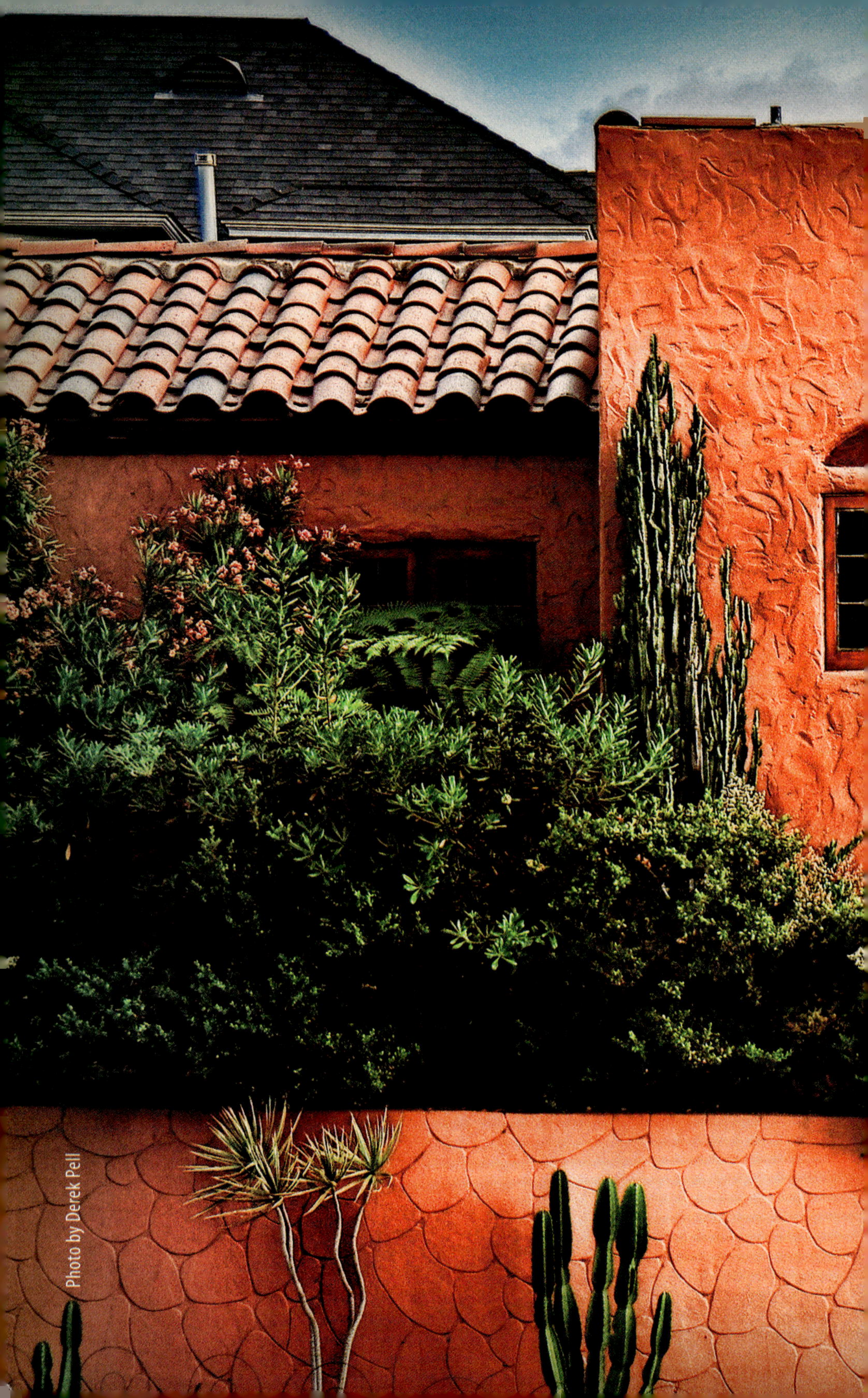
Photo by Derek Pell

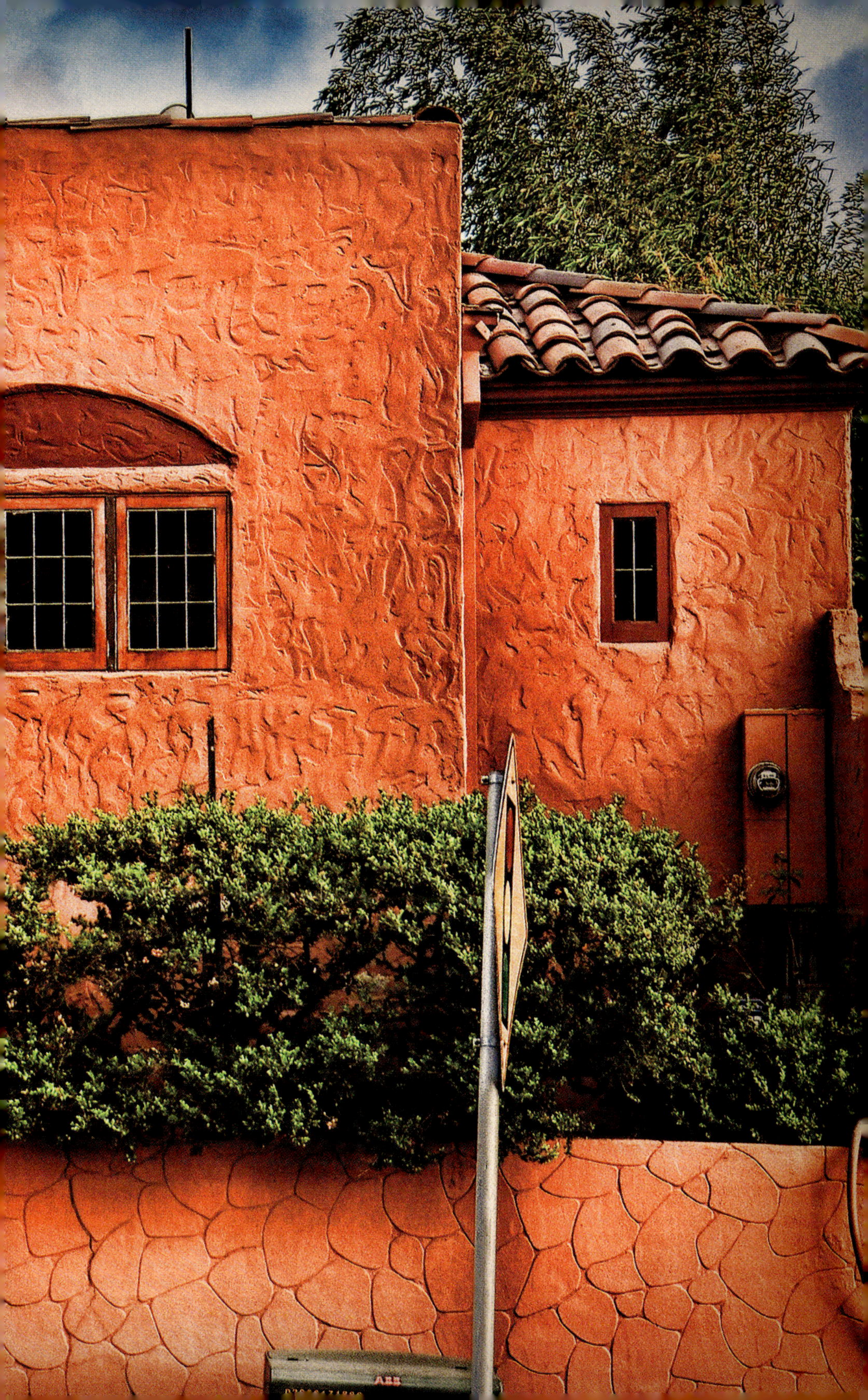

TRICK OR TREAT?

Here's an example of tampering that raises some interesting ethical issues. One night in October 2008, a few days before Halloween, the election looming like a giant bat, I took a stroll with my camera and came upon the scene in Fig. 20.

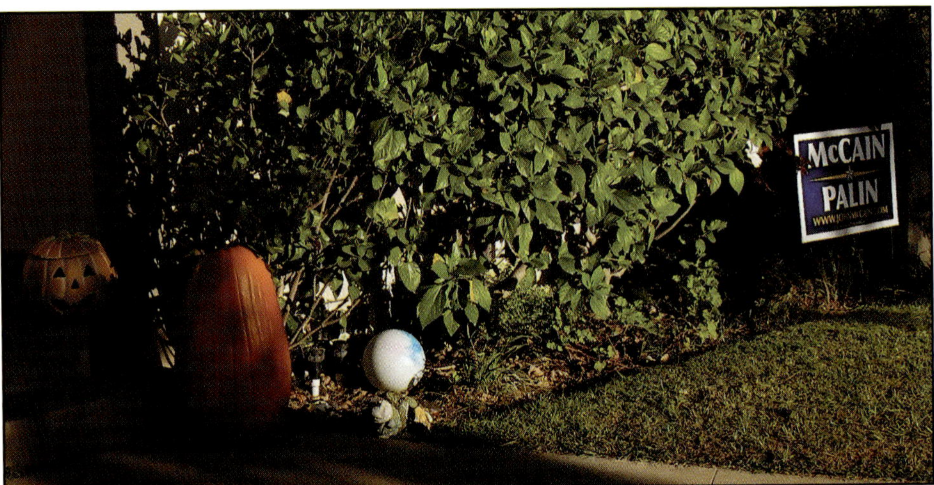

Fig. 20. The scene of the crime.

The irony bit me like a pit bull. Instant political humor.

Back at the computer, I opened the image in Photoshop and rolled up my sleeves. First off, the sign was too far from the pumpkins, so I grabbed the Lasso tool, made a rough selection around the sign, and dragged it closer (Fig. 21). Not too close, mind you, because that would kill the unintentional nature of the joke. Had to preserve reality. I used the Rubber Stamp tool to blend the sign in with the hedge, and then cropped the image tighter.

Next came the ball. It didn't belong in the shot. It served no purpose and actually interfered—being the lightest object in the scene, it was the first thing the viewer would notice. I cloned it away with the Rubber Stamp. Now the photo had some real punch (Fig. 22).

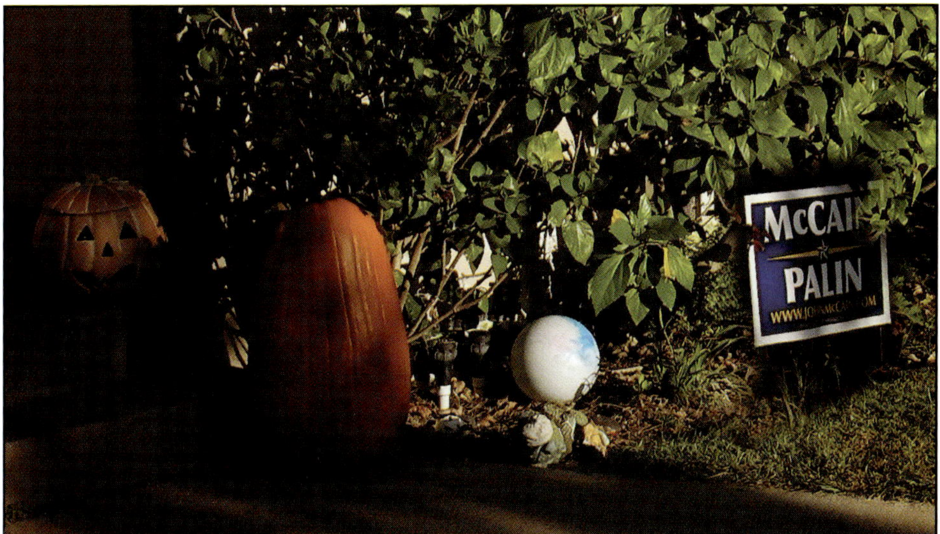

Fig. 21. The sign moved into the new position.

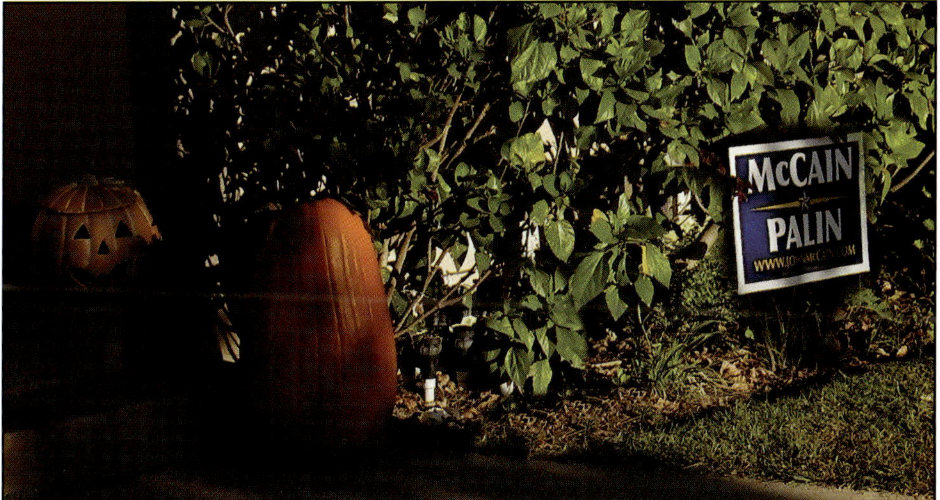

Fig. 22. Mission accomplished.

So here's the ethical issue. Let's say I submit the photo to a news-paper but don't mention the tampering. Is that cool? And say the paper runs it with a cute caption like "Trick or Treat," and a credit: "Photo by..." Would that be unethical? I could argue that the essence of what I saw was unchanged by the tampering. I merely *improved* on the truth. Hell, what if I'd kicked the ball across the street and out of the frame? Or physically moved the sign 15 feet? (Tresspassing, right.) What if I took a photo of the ball and swapped it with the actual ball? (We're not in Kansas anymore.)

Hypothetical: What if I used a special effects lens that made the sign appear next to the pumpkin? Truth or lie?

On the other hand, if I told the newspaper how I'd altered the image, and they decided to run it with a credit such as "Photo illustration by..." or "Montage by....", then everyone's off the hook—the photo becoming the equivalent of a political cartoon or commentary and not presented as "news" or **reality**.

This sort of nitpicking goes on all the time in the editorial rooms of rags and mags. Sure, the media manipulates images—only today they're a lot more cautious, with their ethics having been tarnished in recent years.

Absurd as it can get, in the digital age shutterbugs are obligated to ponder questions like these since we're publishin' our work...if only to spare ourselves from having to shake hands with ambulance-chasers.

ART FOR ART'S SAKE (AND FOR PETE'S SAKE, TOO)

When I was five, we spent the summer in Chicago, where my old man had a photo gig. Air conditioning was a novelty back then so, during a heat wave, people couldn't sleep and flocked to the lake to keep cool. Pretty thrilling for a kid to be up at midnight on a crowded beach under a full moon. That memory stuck and compelled me to create the montage in Fig. 23. I shot the beach in Nag's Head, NC during daylight and altered the color. I added the huge moon and tampered with the ocean to make it impossibly deep at the shoreline. What I call TBT (Tampering Big Time) produced an evocative, surreal scene that matches my memory.

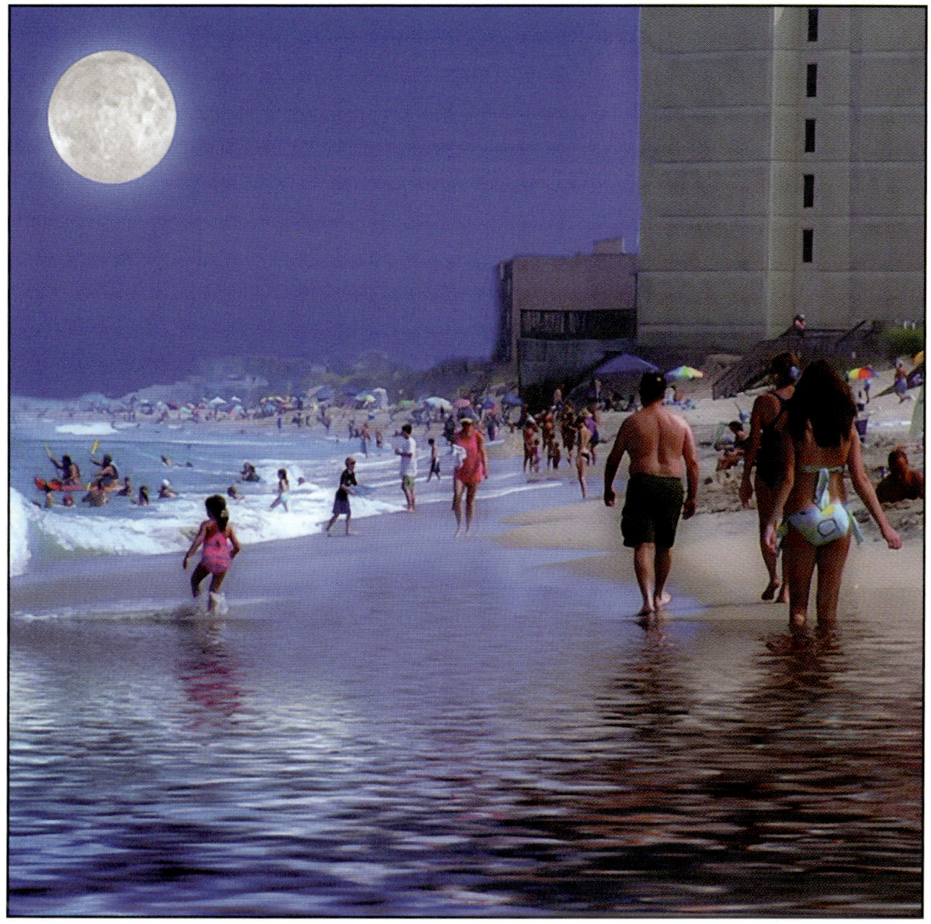

Fig. 23. Night Swim. Photomontage by Derek Pell.

Fig. 25 shows evidence of a tamper tantrum. The shapely gam was added to the original image in Photoshop. Colors were saturated to give a sultry, lush, erotic feel. Looks like it could be the Big Easy or Savannah, but was just my patio in Coronado. Photoshop's basic Hue and Saturation controls can take you places you've never been.

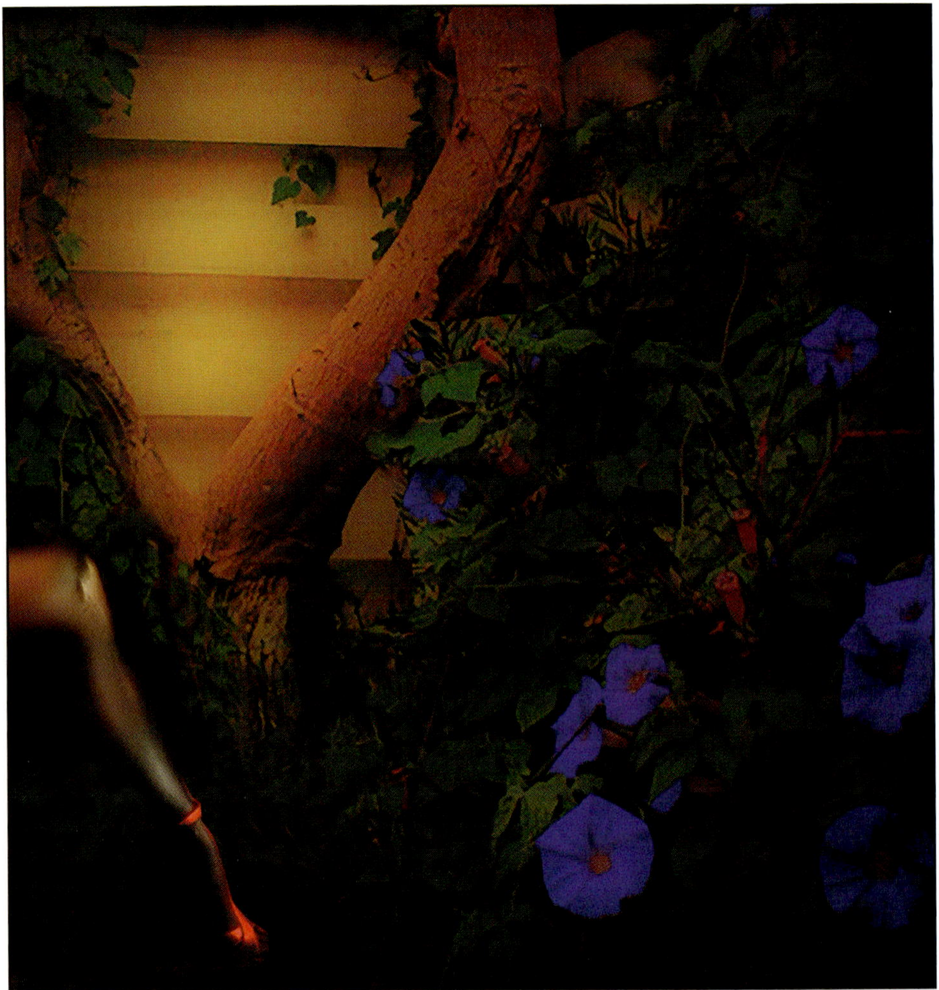

Fig. 25. Photomontage.

THERE AIN'T NOTHIN' LIKE A DAME

Don't be offended if I let out a whistle: I'm livin' in the 1940s, it's allowed. Besides, comin' from me it's a compliment because I *love* dames. Hell, I even married one. Sure, they can be dangerous, but danger's my business.

Photographing 'em requires an eye for beauty: shape, form, curves, and light. Light a dame soft as her perfume, and you're off to a good start. Catch that twinkle in the eye, the mysterious smile, the unconscious pose that can melt a statue.

Save the stark lighting and hard shadows for guys with square jaws and tattooed biceps. Reveal deep creases and flaws, and a guy's flattered about how rugged he looks. Try that with a dame and she'll pull a gun on you.

All dames are beautiful, one way or another, and it's up to the photographer to capture it, so others see it too. Add a goddess glow in post and frame it.

THE BLEMISH MASTERS

When you tamper with a photo of a dame, do it with the touch of an artist—only not a Flemish master like Rubens who, when painting nudes, included cellulite (Fig. 26). Instead, take your cue from the Blemish Masters: fashion and advertising shooters who have turned retouching in Photoshop into a genre, as well as a verb. At one extreme it's digital plastic surgery, complete with chin tucks, hip replacements, and breast implants. There may even be a "Skinny Filter" floating around the web somewhere, but I haven't seen it yet.

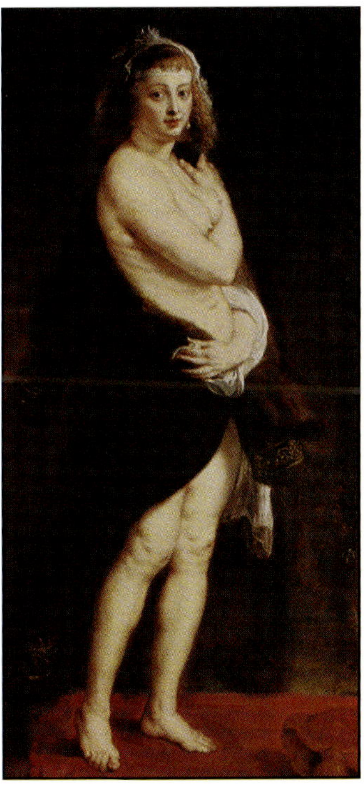

Fig. 26. Painting by Peter Paul Rubens (c. 1638).

What I have seen is a beauty-boostin' plug-in called **Portrait Professional Studio** from Anthropics in London. The retouching miracles it performs in minutes would take days to pull off using Photoshop's tools.

I'd heard rumors the software was a hit with fashion and wedding shooters. After tryin' it, I see why. You open a portrait in Photoshop, launch it from the Filters menu, and it greets you with help screens that walk you through a quick "mark-up" process where you identify the position of the subject's facial features (Fig. 27). Once done, you're ready to tamper and take human beauty to the max. (It ain't just for portraits of dames, either; you can make a sap more beautiful, too.) You can smooth the skin, whiten teeth, brighten eyes or change their color, remove blemishes, fix hair, reshape faces, and even even alter expressions. Each process is speedy, like a beauty parlor on steroids. Speaking of speed, the plug-in features a series of presets to save time (Fig. 28). For example, click the Glamour Female button and—presto—skin is beautified (Fig. 29).

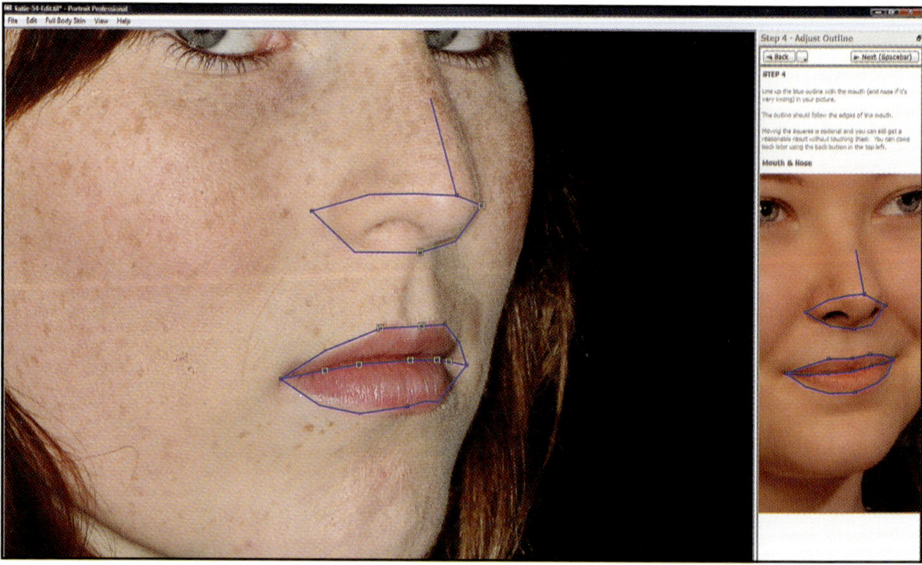

Fig. 27. Adjusting the outlines of mouth and nose in Portrait Professional Studio.

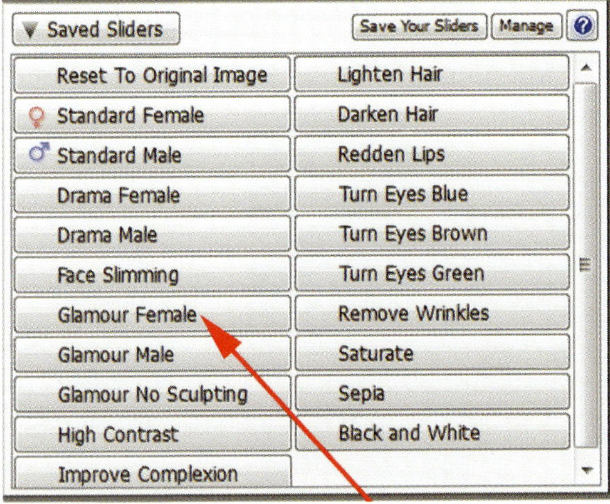

Fig. 28. The plug-in's presets offer surprisingly good results.

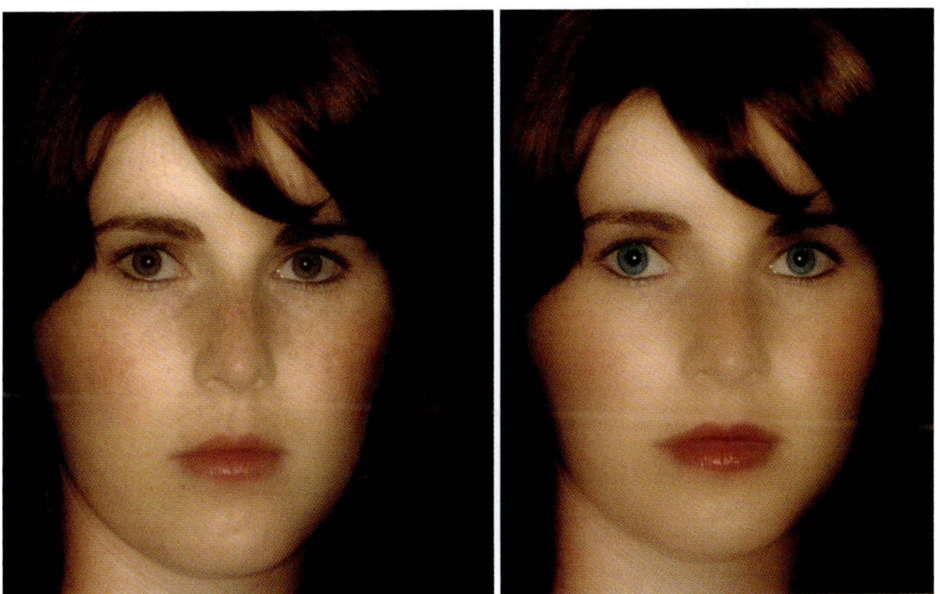

Fig. 29. Before and after using the Glamour preset. (Eye color was changed via another preset).

In addition to the Glamour preset, I changed my model's eye color to blue with the push of another button, while a slider bar enabled me to alter her expression (Fig. 29).

Eat your heart out, Mona Lisa!

If you churn out portraits, Portrait Professional is a cheap treat that gives fast, professional results (**www.portraitprofessional.com**).

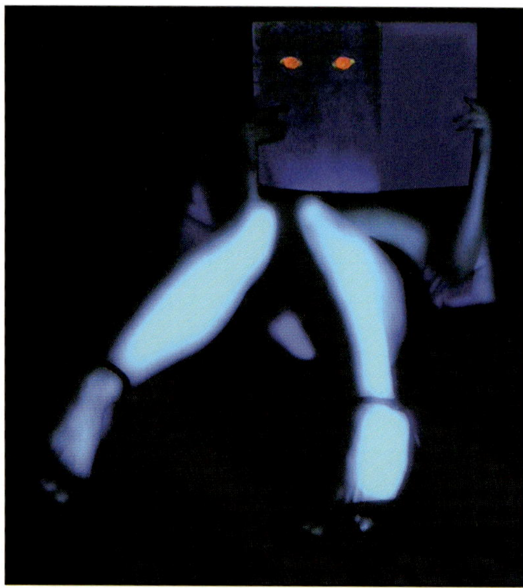

Fig. 30. Nik's Midnight Blue filter.

For more general tampering and special effects, try **Nik Color Efex Pro**. Years ago, when I stumbled upon this plug-in suite and discovered its Midnight Blue filter (Fig. 30), it was love at first sight. (For noir addicts like me, there's also a Fog filter.) For dames, I find a dose of Glamor Glow is usually all a portrait needs to amplify natural beauty. Like makeup, less is more.

Fig. 31 shows the Color Efex interface and a beautiful dame with a glow on. I threw in a Vignette Blur to add a dream-like quality to the scene.

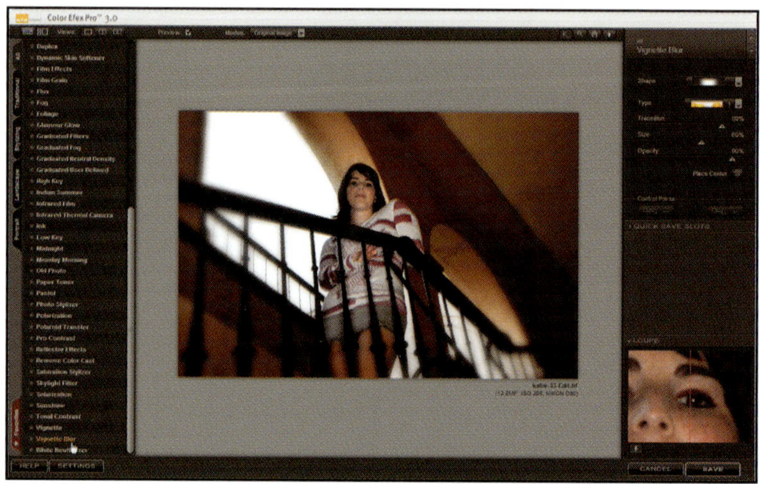

Fig. 31. The Vignette Blur filter adds a dream-like quality to this scene.

I'll close out this chapter with a gorgeous gam (Fig. 32).

No special effects filters were used. I boosted the saturation in Photoshop to intensify the purple light, desaturated the sky, and used a soft brush set to low opacity to add some fogginess along the dune's edge.

The figure in the distance wandered into the scene by accident and made my day.

Zoom Street senior editor Miggs Burroughs used this photo in his "Shop Talk" column, and his analysis digs deeper than anything I might say. I'll let the picture speak for itself here, but invite you to read his comments online: **www.zoomstreet.org/thrill/shoptalk**.

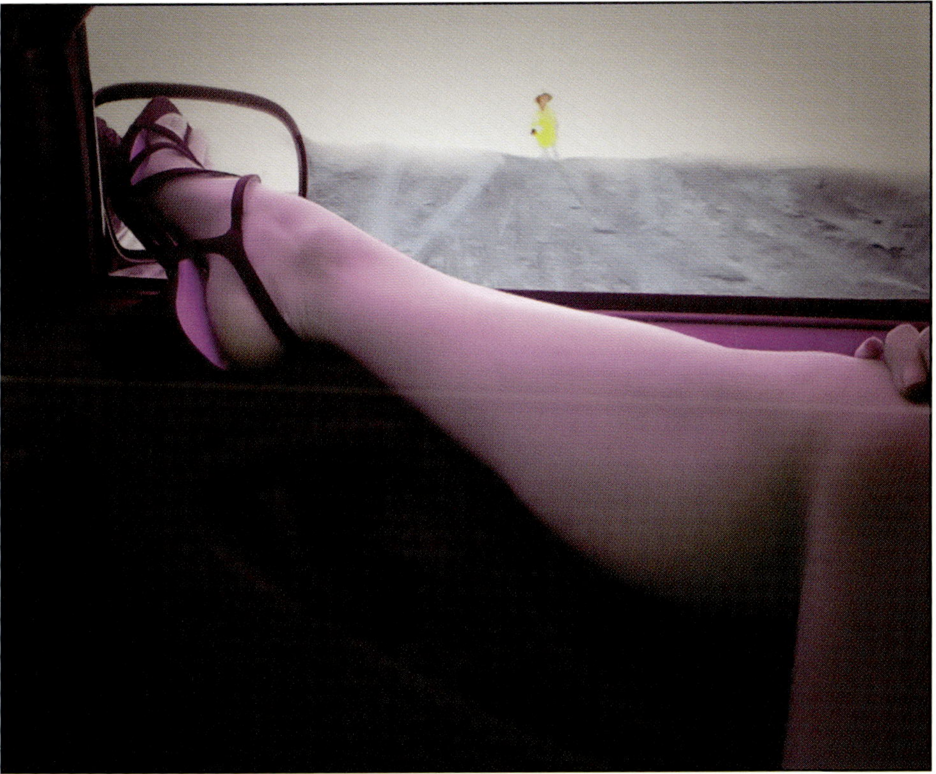

Fig. 32. La Jolla. Photo by Derek Pell.

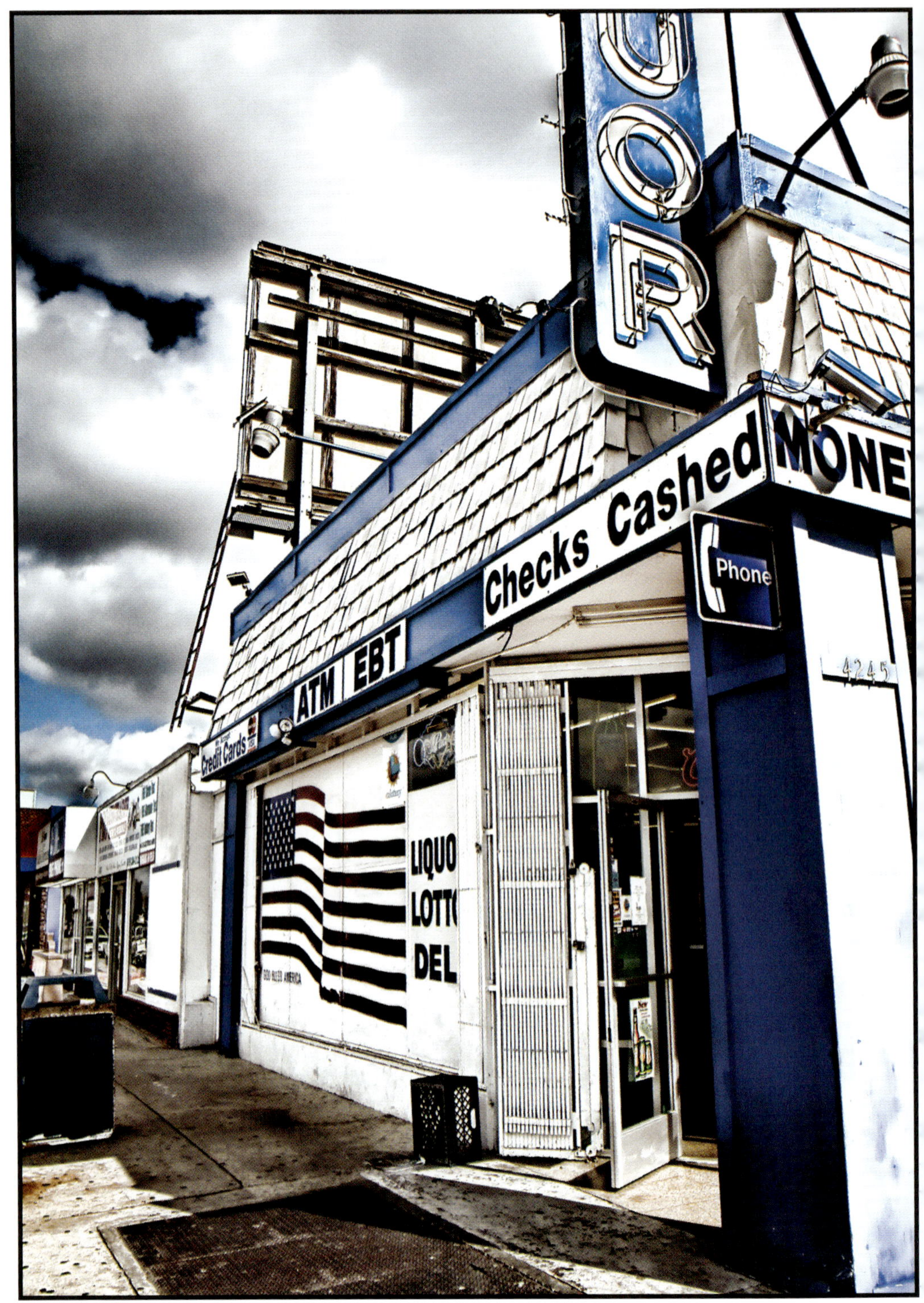

Checks Cashed (2009). Photo by Derek Pell.

8

THE DEVIL IS IN THE DETAILS

"If you want fresh air, don't look for it in this town."—The Asphalt Jungle (1950)

I was cooling my heels on El Cajon Boulevard, smoking a cigarette, waiting for Emmamarie Tran to fix the speaker in my cell phone. Across the street was a bus stop and liquor store that caught my eye. I pulled out my D90 and jaywalked to the other side for a closer look. A mural on the building of an American flag was begging me to snap it. Flanked by words advertising "Liquor" and "LOTTO," it struck me as emblematic of hard times. The clouds were cooperating, too, hanging low, adding drama to the scene. Mean streets, broken dreams.

I had some time to kill, so I did my cropping in the viewfinder. I lopped off the top of the large neon "Liquor" sign leaving three letters visible; confident viewers would fill in the blanks. I was up close

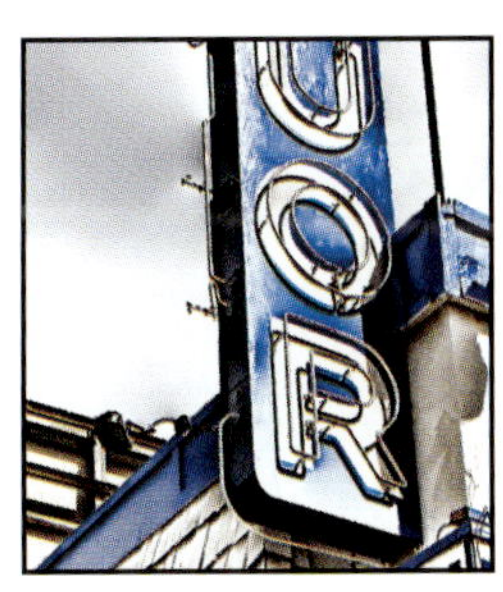

and shooting wide at 18mm to get as much of the building in the photo as I could. I underexposed by −1/3 to give the clouds some pop. The exposure was 1/250 at f/14.

I like my colors like I like my coffee—rich and saturated—so I use the camera's exposure compensation control a lot. I always err on the underside because you can't bring blown-out highlights back to life. Even a miracle worker like Photoshop has to throw up its hands when it comes to a really overexposed shot. An underexposed image has potential. White is white, but black has secrets.

When shooting in either Aperture Priority or Shutter Priority mode (see **Chapter 4, "Hand-to-Cam Combat"**) you can choose to compensate and the camera will automatically adjust the exposure and ISO to match whatever parameter you selected. And speaking of ISO, you want to keep it set to your camera's minimum. (In the case of the Nikon D90, it's 200.) A low ISO yields the best, noise-free images. Of course, if you're shooting in low light, you might be forced to boost the ISO setting, unless you're willing to whip out a tripod.

I took shots from a few different angles, but when I previewed them in the camera's LCD, it was clear that my first was the keeper. I crossed the street to my car, and as I started to slip the camera back in the gear bag, I spied another photo op (Fig. 1).

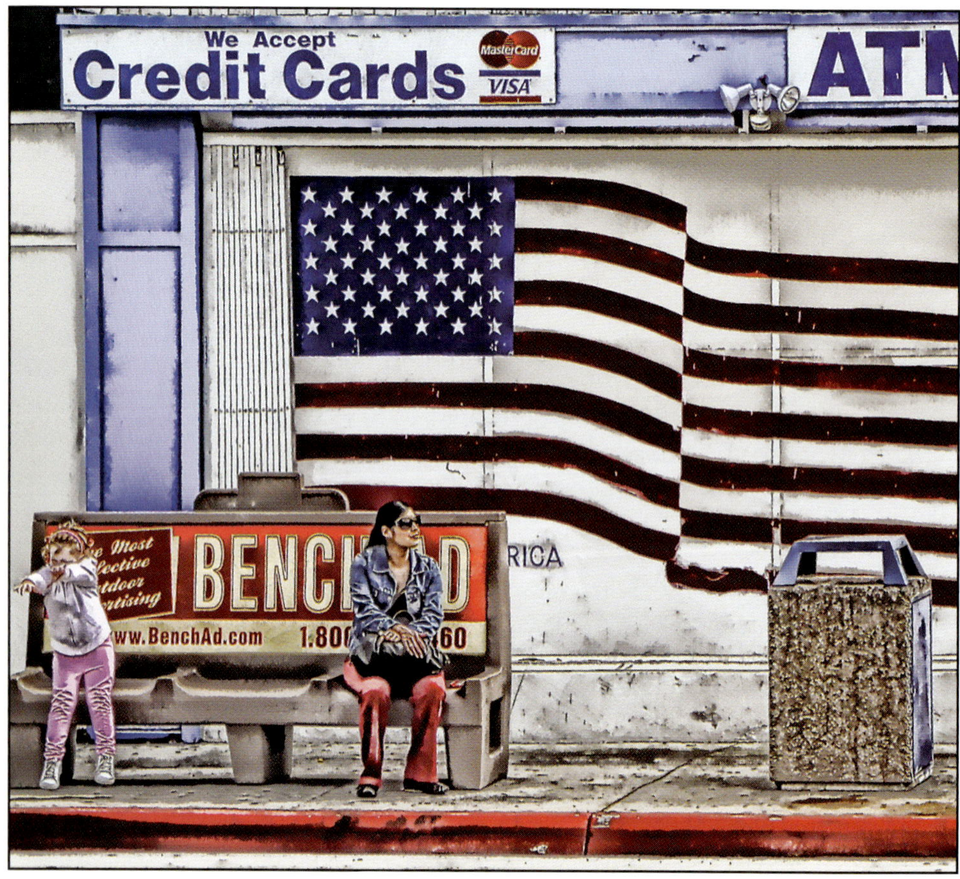

Fig. 1. Benched (2009). Photo by Derek Pell.

Sitting on a bench in front of the liquor store was a woman waiting for the bus and a little girl bouncing up and down on the seat. I pulled out my D90, zoomed in to 90mm, and started shooting. I focused on the antsy little girl and shot at 1/160 at f/14. The disassociation between woman and child was what triggered my interest.

It's a rare day when a single location yields two successful, distinctly different shots. It was good luck and timing. But since you can't count on good luck, you've got to count on your instincts. You've got to have your camera ready. (See **Chapter 1, "Packin' Heat,"** for a cool quick-draw accessory.) Only when you learn how to look can you effectively see. The distinction is an important one; think about it. There was a period in my life in New York City where I walked down the same block every day for weeks and never saw a thing. Sure, my eyes were open. I noticed buildings, shop windows, pedestrians, reflections, and shadows. But I saw nothing. Then, one day, everything changed. I began to really look. I slowed my pace down as if shadowing a suspect, and my eyes became a camera. That single block in Manhattan suddenly offered up dozens of potential photos. And every day it presented different opportunities, due to the changing natural light.

If this ain't an instinct, you better make it a habit. It's what separates the pro from the snapshooter. If you're open to every visual opportunity, you'll not only take better shots, but you'll be less likely to miss the ones that tend to get away.

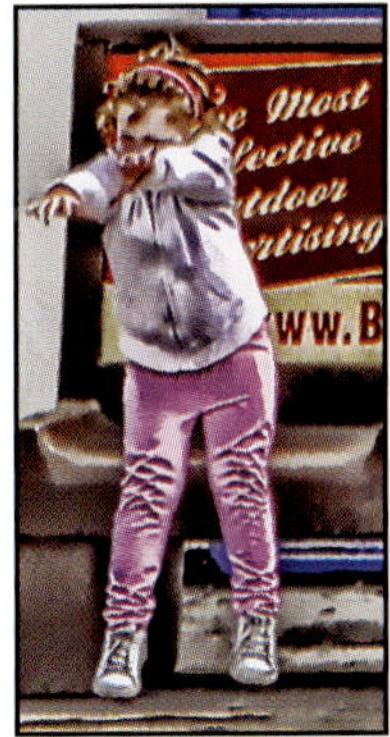

In the case of the girl on the bench, I captured her as she leapt off the seat, arms outstretched in a strange, trance-like gesture. A second later all the visual interest vanished as she walked away. It's worth emphasizing that a single gesture or movement, the look in a subject's eye, can make all the difference in the world. You just have to be watching.

HDRI ON THE STREETS OF SAN DIEGO

What makes these two images particularly striking is the heightened detail brought about by a technique known as HDRI, which stands for high dynamic range imaging. It's been around for years but it's particularly "hot" today. You often see the effect in fashion mags and print ads. There are entire books on the subject, and some photographers, such as George Fulton, have made it into a distinctive style. There is always the danger that HDRI's popularity will, like a fad, begin to fade as more and more shooters experiment with it. Then again, like everything else, it's what you do with the technique… where (and how far) you take it that matters. To put it another way and use Zoom Street's motto: *it ain't the street, it's the motion.*

At one extreme you can create gritty, graphic comic Noir-like effects, or subtle painterly results resembling the Superrealist paintings of, say, Richard Estes. I'm a fan of Estes' work, and that was what initially attracted me to the technique. I'm also a dedicated Noirist, so there was additional appeal. But I'm kind of lazy, too… always on the lookout for shortcuts to simplify complex tasks.

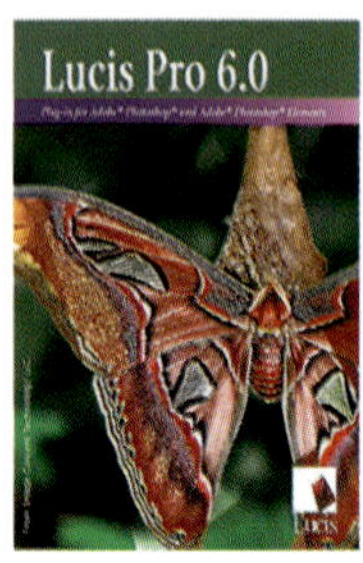

Enter **Lucis Pro 6.0** from Image Content Technology. This Photoshop plug-in, a powerful image enhancement tool aimed directly at artists and scientists, has been carefully crafted and coded over years. The software does not call itself an HDRI generator, but rather refers to Differential Hysteresis Processing (scary-sounding, ain't it?), a patented process originally developed to enhance detail in scanning electron microscope images. But, as with HDR images, Lucis brings to the surface hidden detail in the shadow, light, and mid-range areas. It's kind of like discovering buried treasure in your pixels.

Don't get me wrong; this isn't about slapping a filter onto an image. The application must be mastered to gain full control over the results. But it saves time in the field as, for example, with my photograph of the girl on the bench where there wasn't time to bracket exposures. The plug-in also saves time in the digital darkroom; it provides the necessary tools within a single panel—no time-consuming menu hopping. Had I tried to produce the same results using Photoshop and working with layers, it could have taken an hour, whereas with Lucis Pro I spent about 15 minutes.

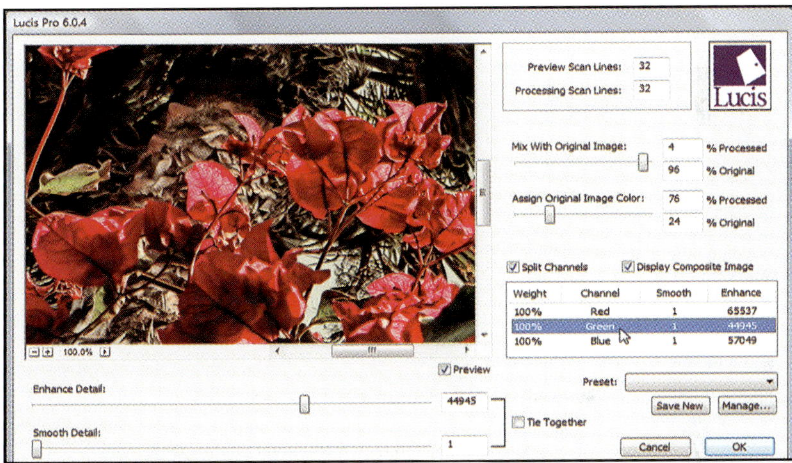

Fig. 2. Lucis Pro 6.0.4 interface.

The above screen (Fig. 2) shows the plug-in's clutter-free interface. There's plenty of room to experiment without distraction. You have a choice of working in either Single Channel mode or Split Channel mode; the latter enables you to manipulate each RGB channel separately to fine-tune based on color. You can, of course, switch between original image view and the Lucis view to gauge the effect of your custom settings. The application's main control is the Enhance Detail slider located right below the preview window.

It can work in concert with the Smooth Detail slider just below it, or it can be manipulated separately. Cranking up the Smooth Detail slider can result in some very surreal, dream-like effects.

You can input the number of scan lines, which control artifacts (the lower the number, the fewer the artifacts). You also can Mix with Original Image and assign a percentage of the original image colors to the treated version. As contrast and saturations adjustments are made, the colors shift, so here you can opt for a decidedly different look or resurrect the original image shades.

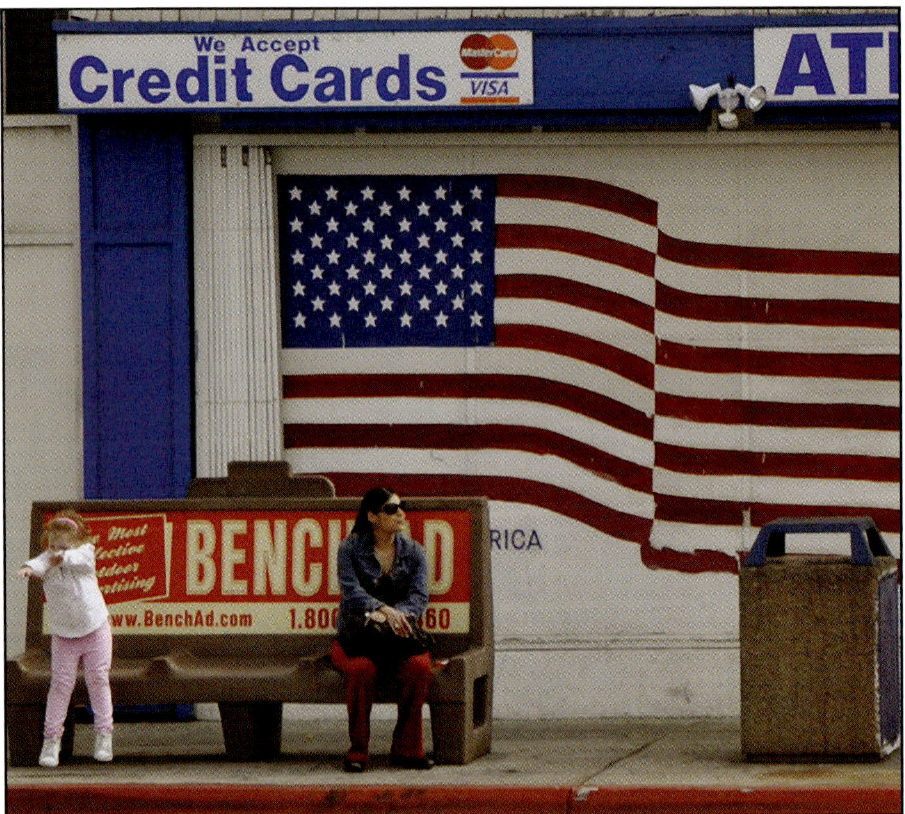

Fig. 3. The original image.

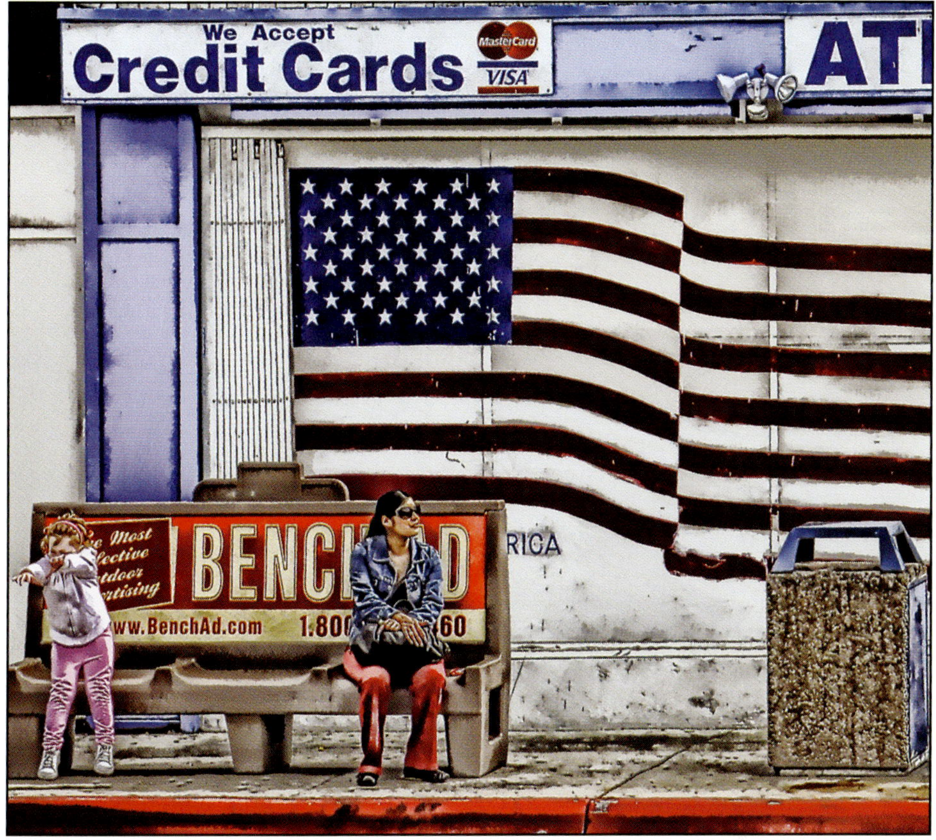

Fig. 4. The final processed HDR image.

CHEAP THRILLS CONTEST

MY ORIGINAL PHOTO "BENCHED" CONTAINED A MYSTERIOUS THIRD CHARACTER WHO HAS SINCE GONE MISSING; I.E., I CROPPED THE PERSON OUT. FIND THAT MISSING PERSON AND WIN A SIGNED COPY OF THIS BOOK. HE OR SHE APPEARS SOLO SOMEWHERE WITHIN THE PAGES OF *SHOOT TO THRILL* AND SHOULD BE CONSIDERED ARMED & DANGEROUS. THE FIRST GUMSHOE TO EMAIL ME THE CORRECT PAGE NUMBER WHERE THE MISSING PERSON APPEARS, WINS. ADDRESS YOUR EMAIL TO *DEREKPELL@GMAIL.COM* AND MAKE THE SUBJECT "CHEAP THRILLS." NOTE: MEMBERS OF MY IMMEDIATE FAMILY ARE INELIGIBLE, BUT WEALTHY DISTANT RELATIVES MAY ENTER.

The original photo has visual interest but falls short of a "wow." HDR kicks the sucker up a few notches.

Here's a portion of another photo (Fig. 5) showing a hydrant. When I increased the object's detail, the tiles in the background darkened and shifted color. Compare Figures 5 and 6 below.

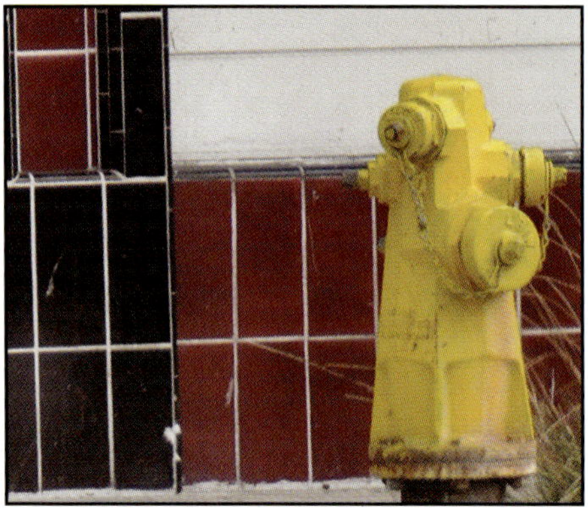

Fig. 5. Unedited image (detail).

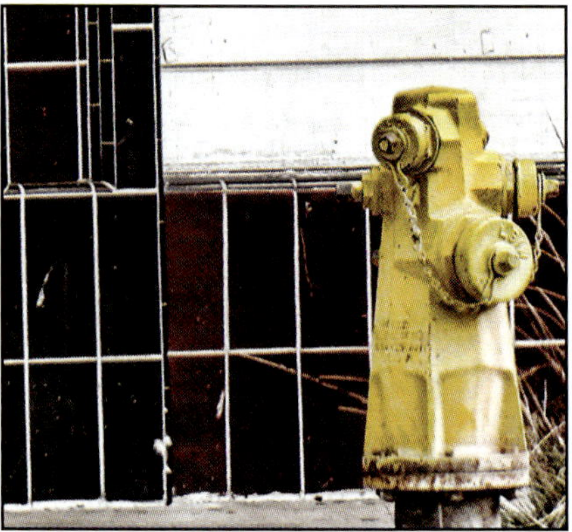

Fig. 6. Enhanced detail and contrast in the hydrant results in darkened tiles and color shift in background.

By adjusting the Mix with Original Image slider below (Fig. 7), the color of the tile returns.

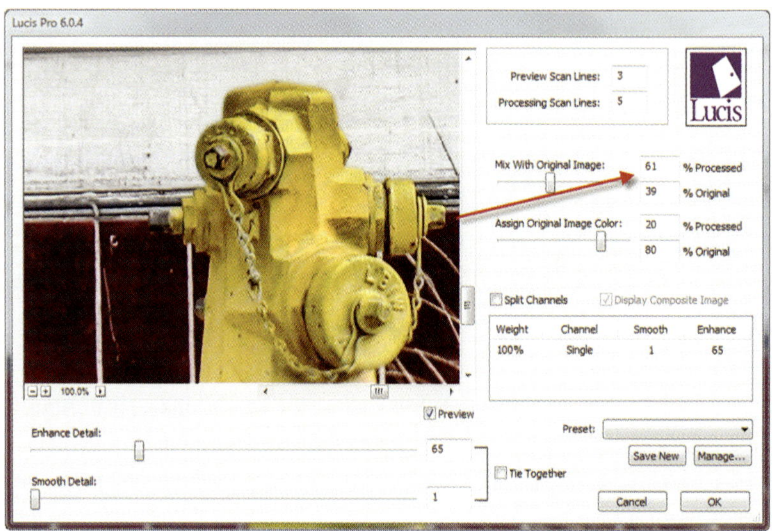

Fig. 7. Adjusting the Mix with Original Image slider.

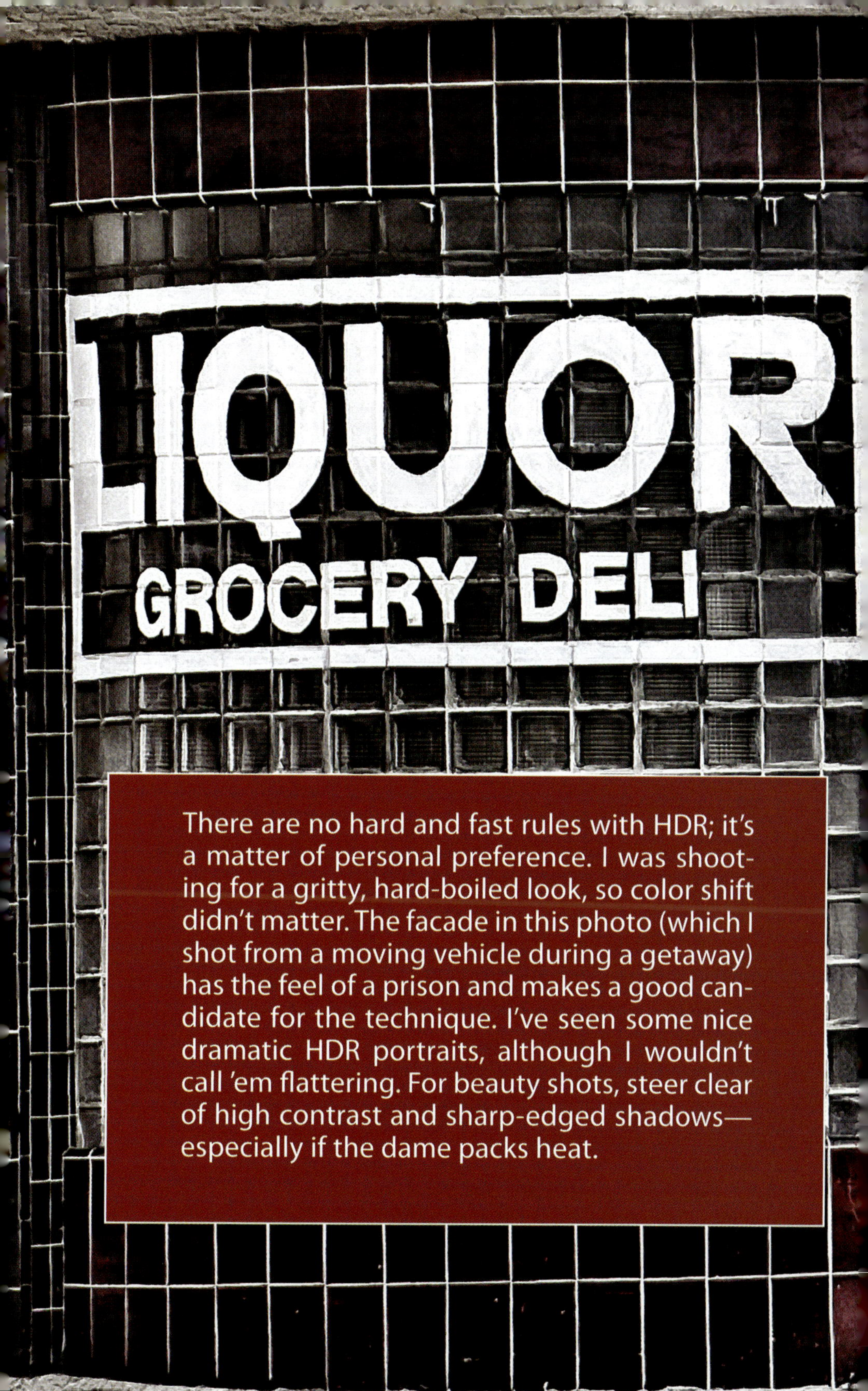

There are no hard and fast rules with HDR; it's a matter of personal preference. I was shooting for a gritty, hard-boiled look, so color shift didn't matter. The facade in this photo (which I shot from a moving vehicle during a getaway) has the feel of a prison and makes a good candidate for the technique. I've seen some nice dramatic HDR portraits, although I wouldn't call 'em flattering. For beauty shots, steer clear of high contrast and sharp-edged shadows—especially if the dame packs heat.

When you're satisfied with the results of your HDR image, you can save your custom settings as a preset and apply them to a series of photos. I've yet to use this feature because I find different images require different adjustments, but it's nice to have the option. While in theory you can turn any photo into an HDR image, be careful. Certain images lend themselves to the style; others do not. A kid's first birthday party would probably not benefit from HDR, unless you were after a menacing brat effect. A common mistake is to use HDR to mask an inferior image. Well, a crappy shot makes a crappy HDR image (for example, the sausages in Fig. 7A). Don't ask me what I was thinking when I took the picture, but I was probably starving. It sure won't win any beauty contests, with or without HDR.

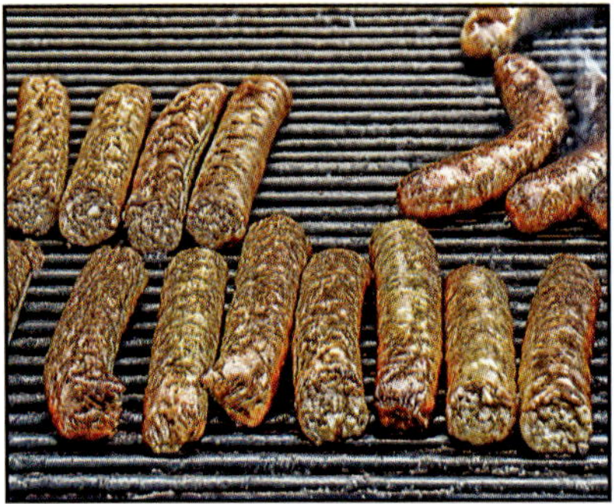

Fig. 7A. Prime candidate for the Recycle Bin.

My rule of thumbscrew is this: The original photograph should be visually interesting and stand on its own. (See **Chapter 3, "Private Eyes."**) If expanding the dynamic range adds a new dimension and helps the photo find its dramatic footing, then full speed ahead. The final result should appear as if it was born dripping detail. If it provokes a "wow" from the viewer, it's a success. Ideally, the technique will be, at first glance, invisible, supplanted by the content.

At its best HDR provides a kind of hyperrealism that haunts and echoes like a floater in the mind's eye.

Déjà voodoo.

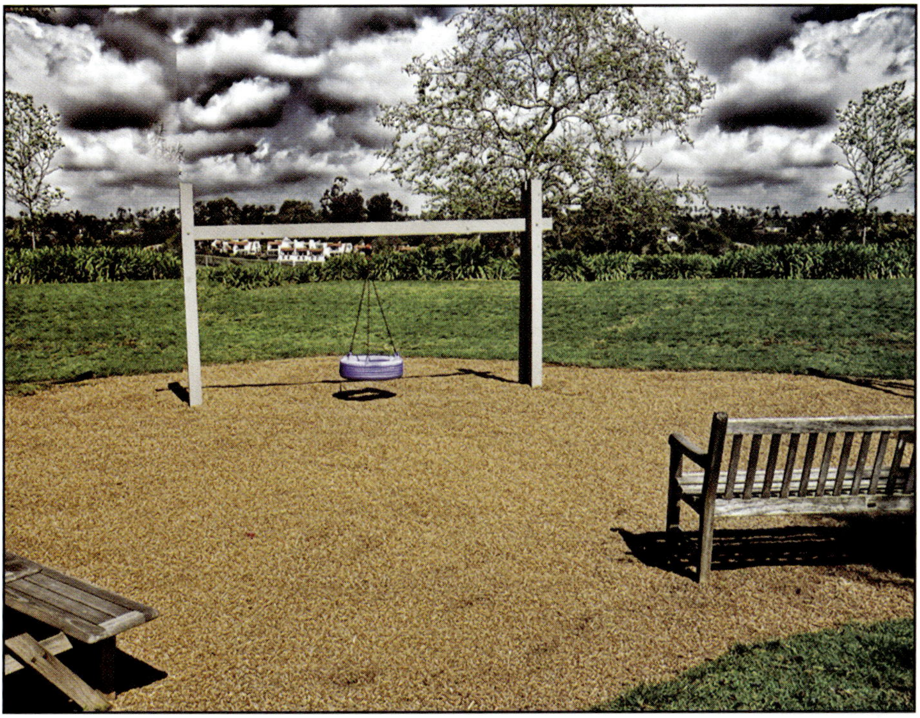

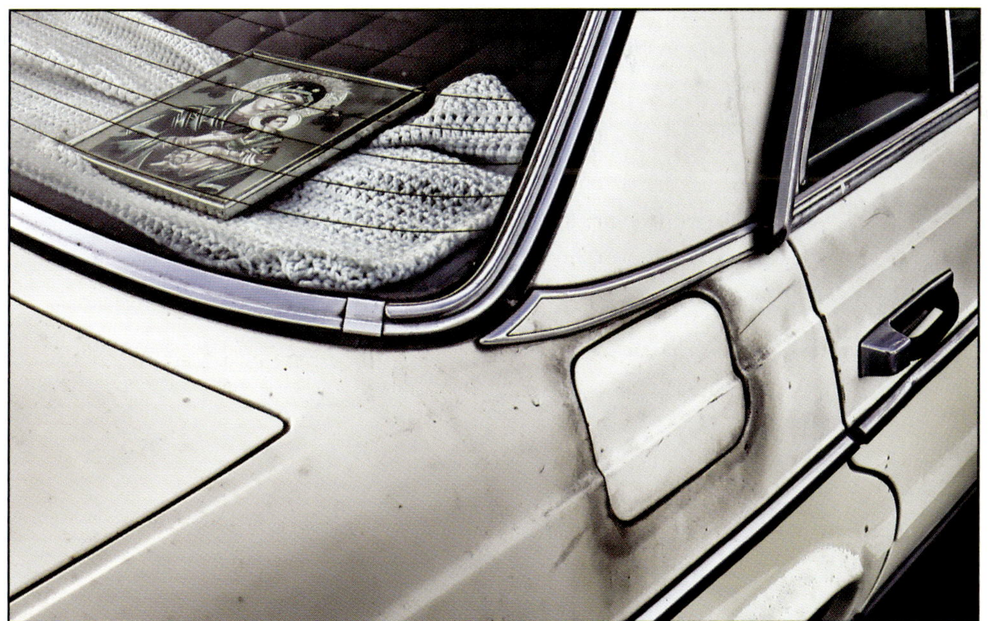

Hospice Swing (2009). Photo by Derek Pell.

Prayer Wheels (2009). Photo by Derek Pell.

BYPASS THE BLEACHED BLONDE WITH THE LUGER

Take it from me, that's good dating advice. Of course, when I see a bleached blonde, I immediately think of a popular post-production technique called Bleach Bypass. (OK, that's a lie, but you'll have to live with it.) Like HDR, the effect should be used sparingly to give a photo a little edge. It's a hot look right now and—like a blonde—is potentially dangerous.

You've seen it used in cinema a lot, and it harkens back to the days of the physical darkroom where the air was thick with pungent chemicals. Remember chemicals? The technique in film processing involves retaining silver in the negative, as opposed to removing it. It's like blending a black-and-white photo with a color image. In digital terms you're shooting for low satch and high 'trast; i.e., you're lowering the saturation in an image and boosting the contrast.

You can accomplish this in Photoshop manually, or you can use a wonder plug like Tiffen's **Dfx**, which offers multiple variations in a smorgasbord of presets (see Fig. 8). But faced with such a vast selection, I'm like a dame in a shoe shop. Which one do I choose?

By the way, Dfx is worth adding to your arsenal of third-party plug-ins for the sheer range of its filters. Tiffen put all it knows about glass filters (which is *everything*) into software that re-creates the best of what glass'll give you: HFX diffusion, gels, tints, lens and light effects, color correction, special effects such as Day for Night, polarization, infrared, and a lot more.

It's an entire film lab in a compact digital console. The biggest drawback is that once you start using it, it's hard to stop. You can easily lose a weekend trying out different variations, mixing filters, and winding up looking like a mad scientist gone wild.

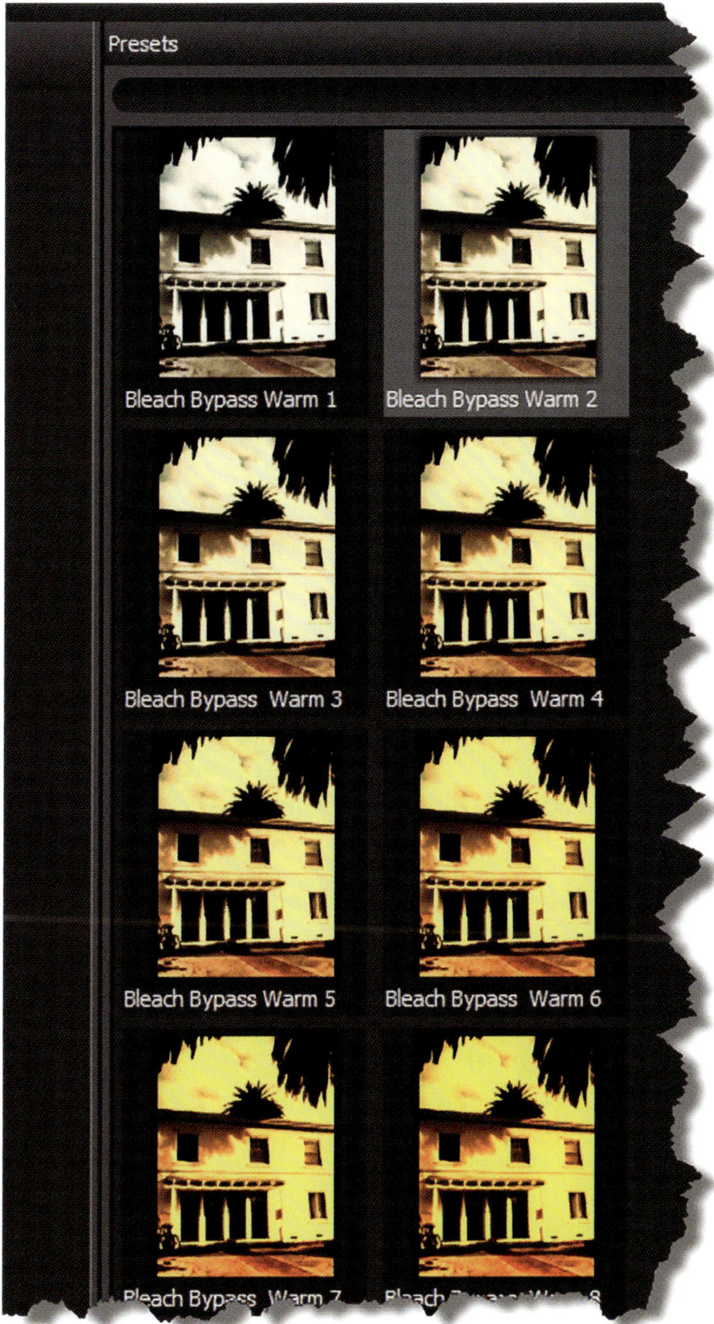

Fig. 8. Tiffen Dfx 2.0. Panel showing a few of the plug-in's Bleach Bypass presets.

My weapon of choice for focused color correction is a plug-in from Nik Software called **Viveza**. It gives you complete hands-on control. For starters, let's roll up our sleeves and apply some elbow grease using Viveza and see what the technique has to offer. Download a free 15-day trial of the software at **www.niksoftware.com**. You can tinker with my photo, *Four Doors* (Fig. 10), by downloading a low-resolution version at this link: **www.zoomstreet.org/thrill/downloads**.

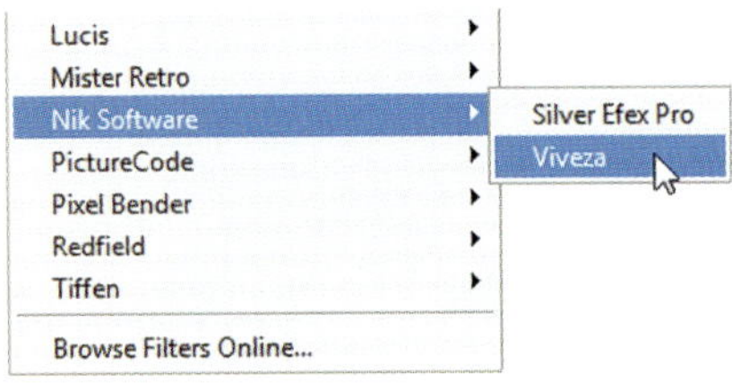

Feel free to use your own image. I'm confident that once you begin to explore Viveza you'll want to add it to your arsenal. Nothing like having a concealed weapon when you're in a jam.

Now, my original image is okay, but a little too "post cardy" for my taste. Besides, when I was on the scene, the building seemed to posses a hint of ominous nostalgia that is missing from the shot. Four doors, four windows, two bikes, you do the math. Open the image in Photoshop and launch Viveza via the filter menu.

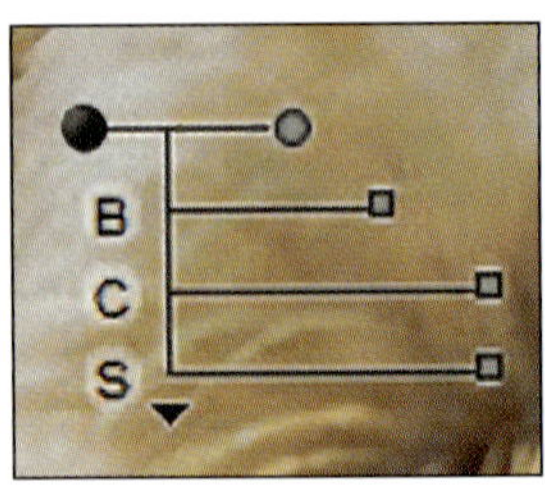

Fig. 9. Viveza's control points.

One cool thing about this plug-in is that it lets you work on selected areas of your photo, rather than making hit-or-miss global adjustments to the entire image. You use control points (Nik's patented U Point Technology) rather than selection tools. Once you click on a portion of the image, little slider bars magically appear that can be dragged to increase or decrease the photo's brightness, contrast, and saturation. A slider at the top enables you to set the diameter of the work area.

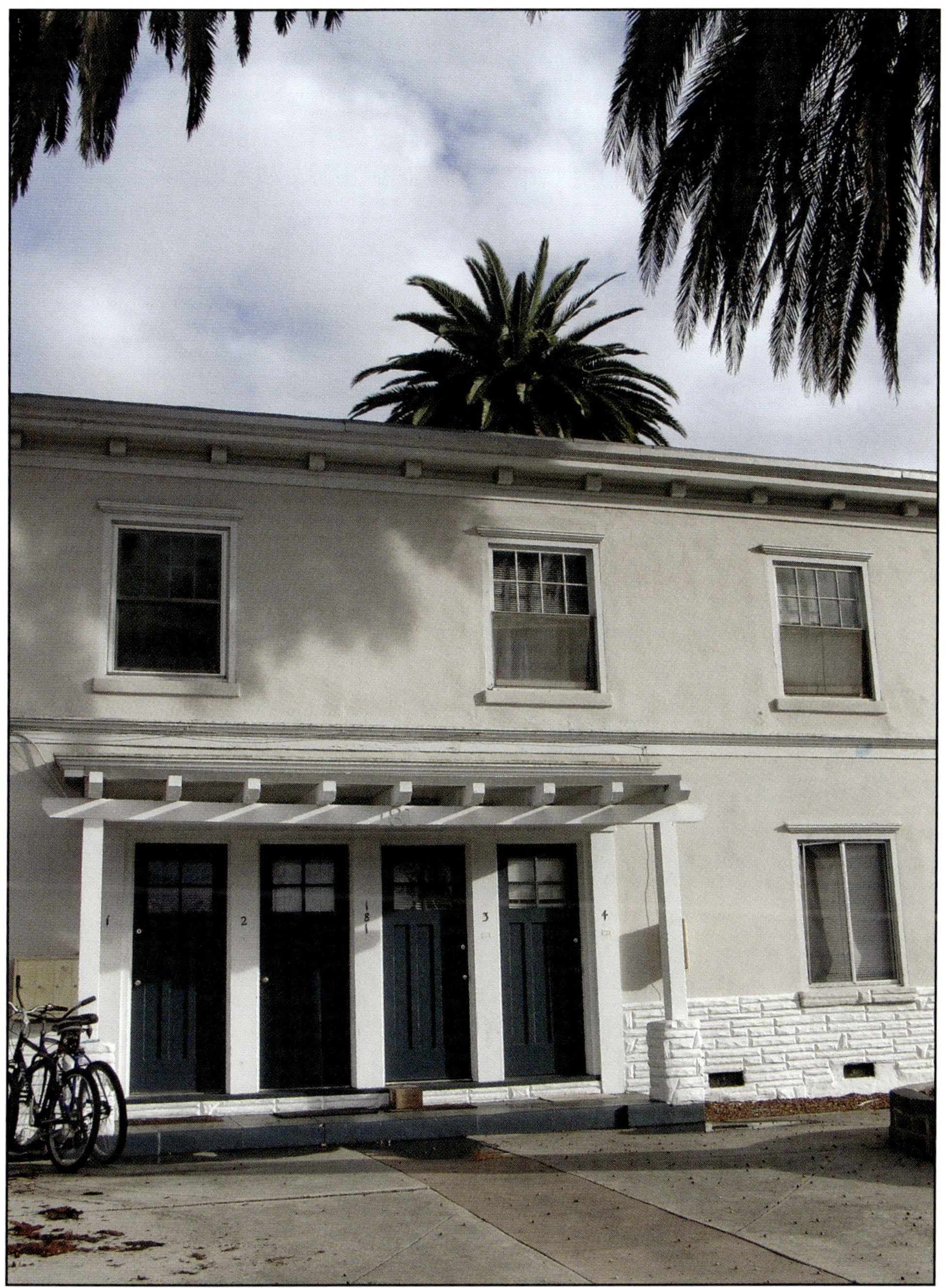

Fig. 10. Original version of Four Doors (2008). Photo by Derek Pell.

Using a split-screen view with my original on the left (Fig. 11), you can see the effect in real time. Here I placed control points above the doors, and then dragged the Contrast slider to 98%. Notice how details in the wall and window pop out. Had I lost too much detail in the shadows, I'd simply drag the slider to the left to lower the contrast.

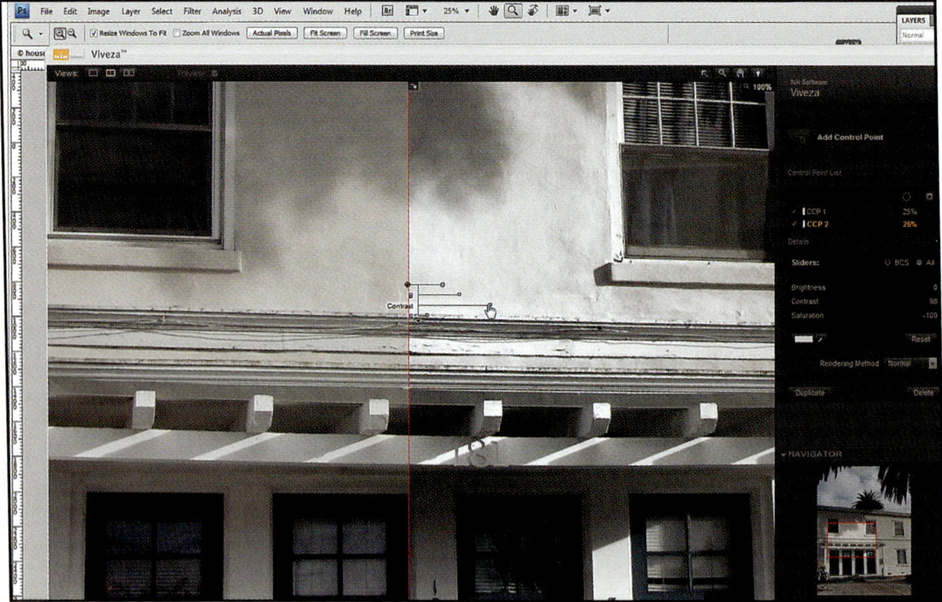

Fig. 11. Viveza's split-screen view.

Viveza has a zoom tool for changing magnification on the fly and, as with Photoshop, you zoom out by holding down the Alt key when you click the mouse. There's a thumbnail of the image in the lower right of the Viveza panel, with the magnified area highlighted by a red rectangle. You can reposition the rectangle to quickly view other areas of the image.

To remove the blue color cast (Fig. 12), I set control points in the clouds and dragged the Saturation slider to −100. I adjusted the Brightness setting to add more more definition to the clouds.

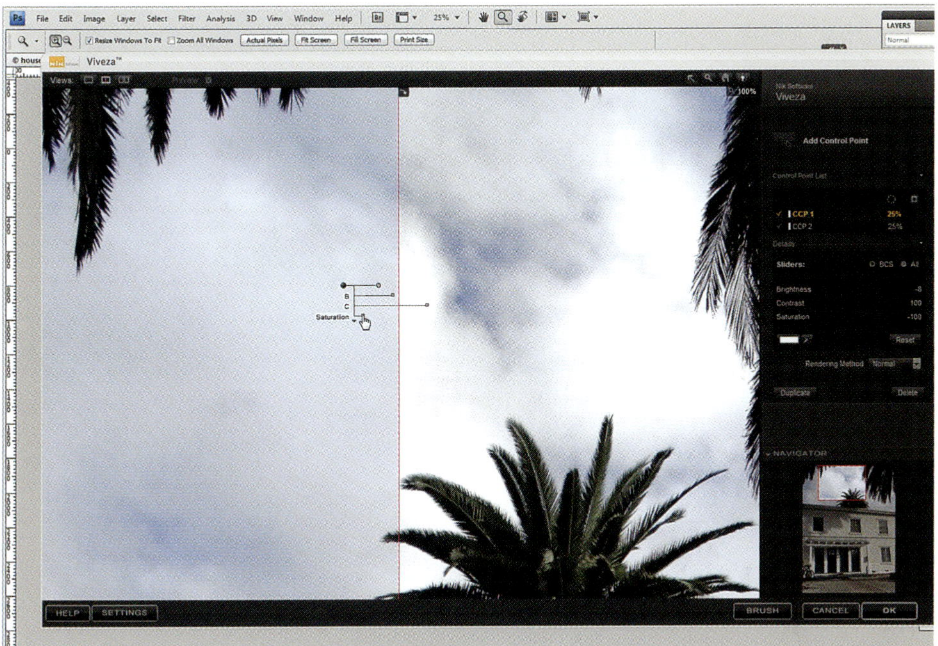

Fig. 12. Removing the color cast via the control points.

Keep in mind that these are subjective decisions, and I encourage you to experiment. The mood of the image can be radically altered by going in the opposite direction dictated by the Bleach Bypass process—that is, increasing saturation. For example, in the screen shot in Fig. 13, I boosted the saturation to 88 and lowered the brightness to −8. Presto! *The House of Usher*.

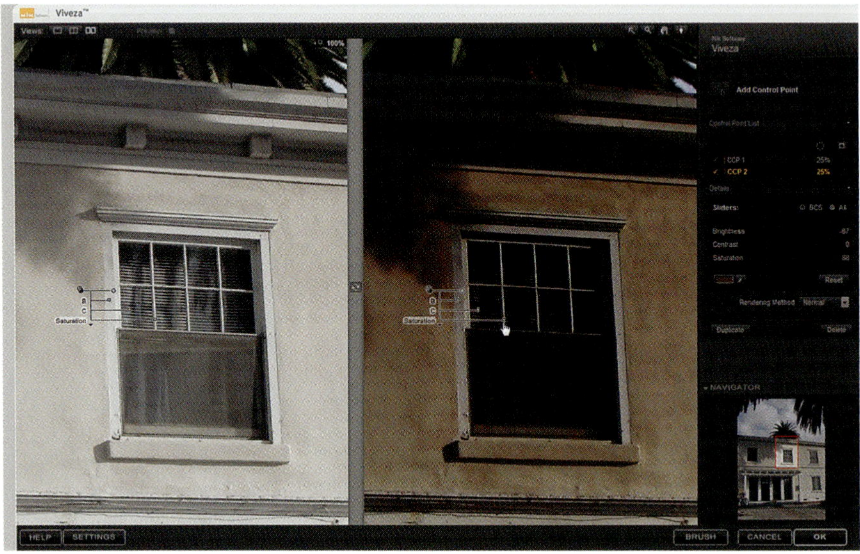

Fig. 13. The House of Usher?

When you're finished and return to Photoshop, you'll find a pleasant surprise: your processed image on its own separate layer. This is handy should you wish to do additional tweaking, because you still have your original on the bottom layer for comparison.

Viveza offers an alternative to its control points. You can make adjustments to the image, and then use Photoshop's Paintbrush tool to apply the effects. This is convenient, for example, when you want to change the color of a single object in a photo while maintaining the original color in the rest of the image.

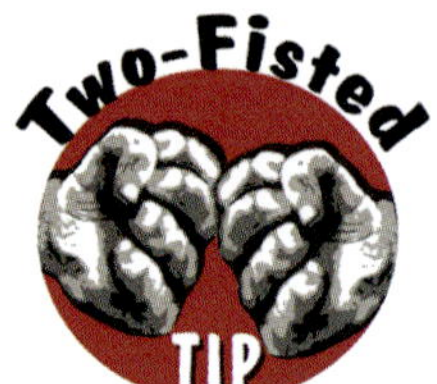

After exiting Viveza, go directly to the File menu and choose Save As. Give the file a new name and save it in Photoshop's native PSD format. That way, you have your original image and processed version in one tidy layered package, as well as the pristine original.

Looking at the results of *Four Doors*, I decided I wanted to make another change to the image using Photoshop's native Hue and Saturation controls. I took a shortcut and pressed Ctrl-U on my keyboard to bring up the panel. (If you prefer to use the menu, it's Image > Adjustments > Hue/Saturation.)

As I dragged the Hue slider (Fig. I4) into the green (–28), the building took on a soft, pinkish hue...very Hotel California. By reducing the overall saturation to –76, you strip most of the color from the sky. (What happens if you drag the saturation all the way to the left [–100]? That's right, you wind up with a black-and-white photo.) So now I had the bypass effect I wanted. Subtle, evocative.

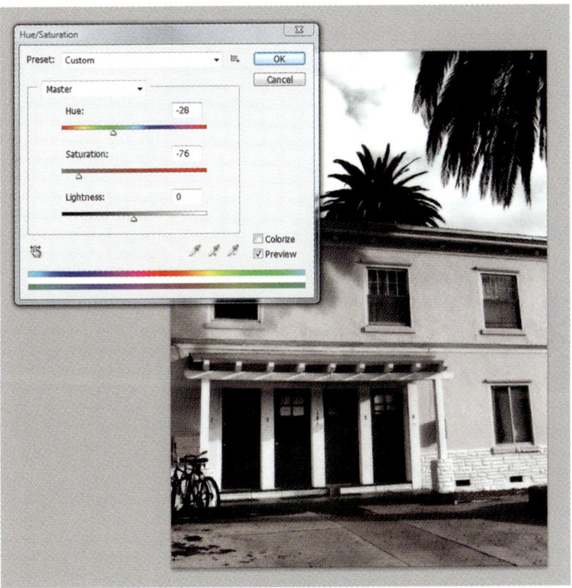

Fig. 14. Adjusting the hue and satration.

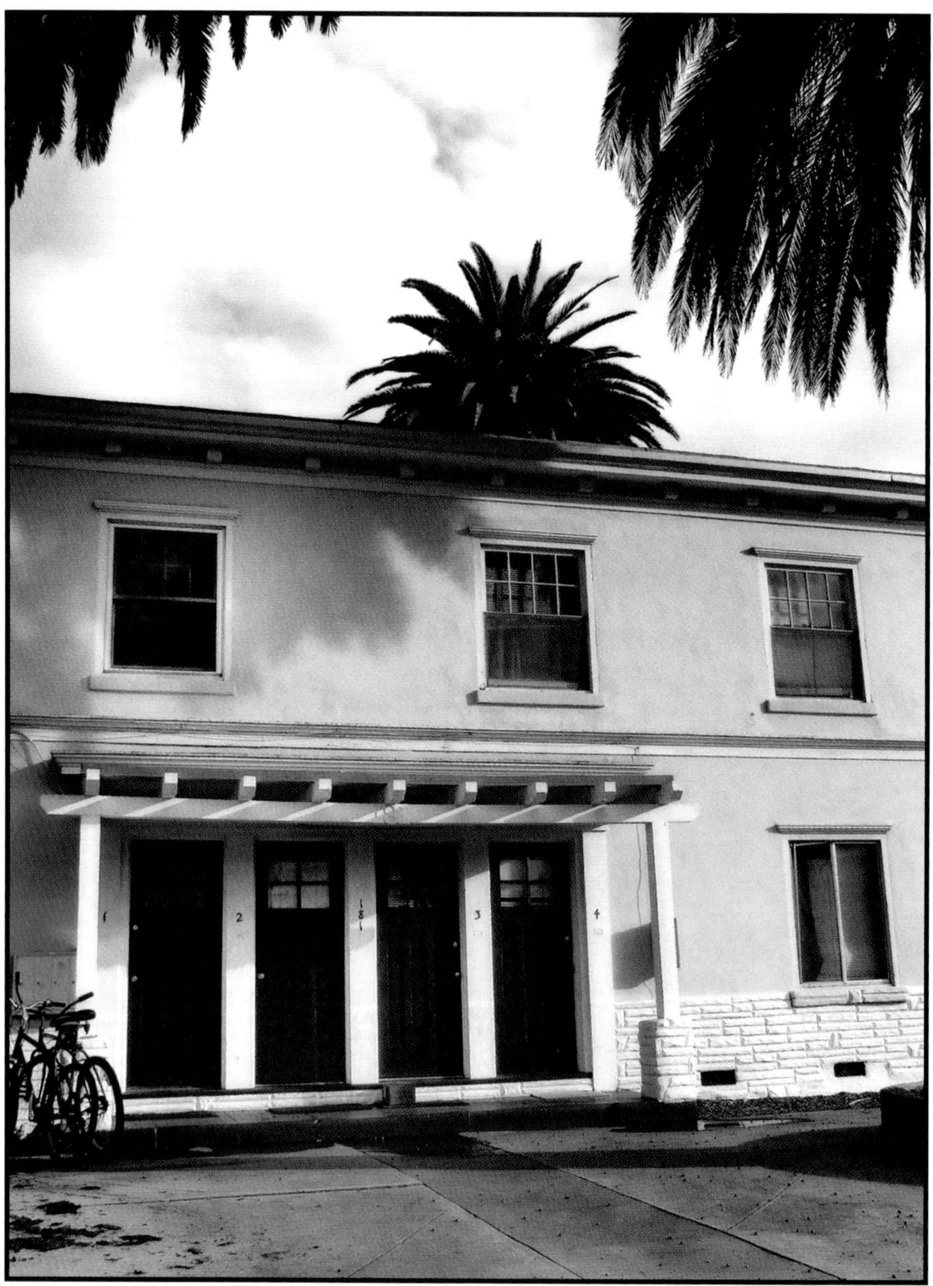

The finished photo.

The still life below was taken at a café on Coronado Island and benefits from the Bleach Bypass treatment. I was tempted to clone out those little specks of salt on the table but decided to go with the realism. After all, the devil lives in the little details we sometimes miss in the viewfinder. The camera, however, catches 'em all.

Let's grab an espresso break before moving on to Photoshop's High Pass filter.

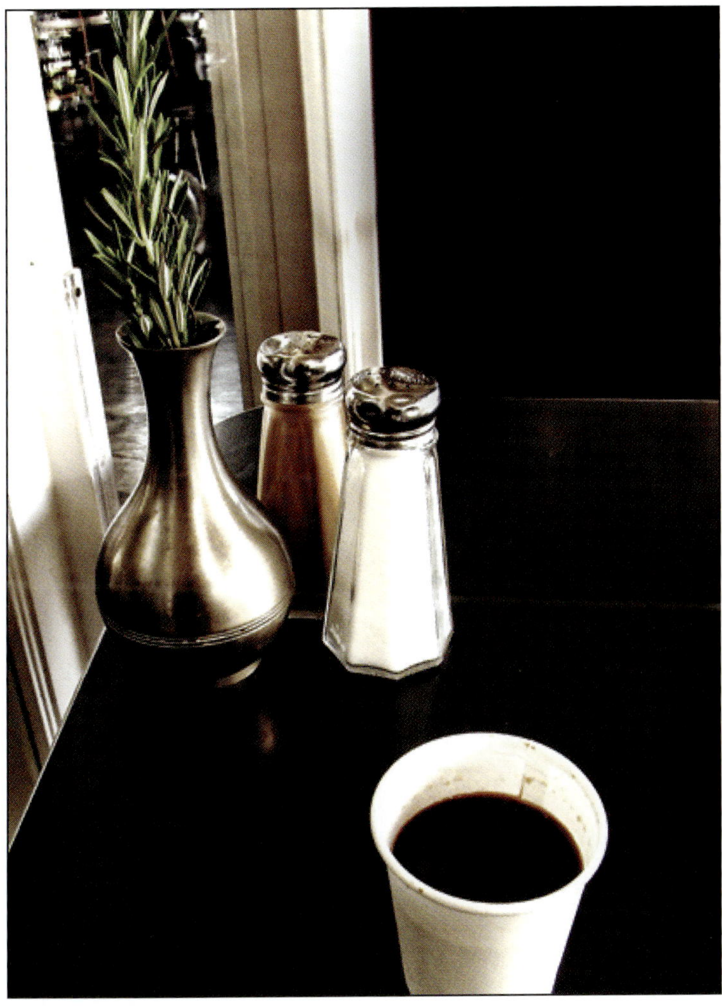

The Bleach Bypass treatment adds a hyperrealistic touch to this photo.

HIGH PASS: THE KNOCKOUT PUNCH

Like HDR imaging and Bleach Bypass, Photoshop's native High Pass filter can give a photo a unique look and take it from bland to bold. Whether the effect is hip 'n slick, strange, retro, or just plain cool depends on the subject and how you apply the technique. Experimentation is the name of the game and, remember, entire careers in photography were born by taking risks, breaking rules, and going haywire in the digital darkroom.

In essence, High Pass filtration is like a bouncer at a bar. It blocks low-wave light frequencies from getting through the door and waves in high-frequency light. The filter is primarily used in combination with other techniques to sharpen images. We'll use it to reveal and accentuate where the highest contrast lies and bring up the sharp angles and edges to add some "pop" by heightening contrast and saturation.

You can High Pass a JPEG, but you'll get the best results working with your camera's RAW format. That makes sense because a RAW file contains every "bit" of information the image has to offer. In short, you have more to work with. I set my D90 so it captures both JPEG and RAW versions simultaneously.

I like applying the High Pass filter to architectural shots. It gives flesh to a skeleton, so to speak, and adds a three-dimensional quality to what would otherwise appear dull and flat. That's why I call it the "Hail Mary Pass." When all else fails…

The photo of the parish in Fig. 15 is a good example of the High Pass treatment. The pronounced shadows of the trees are what first grabbed my attention. There was a stiff sea breeze, and I liked the way the bushes were bending. When I previewed the image later on the computer, it lacked *oomph*. I might have hit the Delete key, but all the elements I'd initially responded to were there. The photo needed a dose of HP.

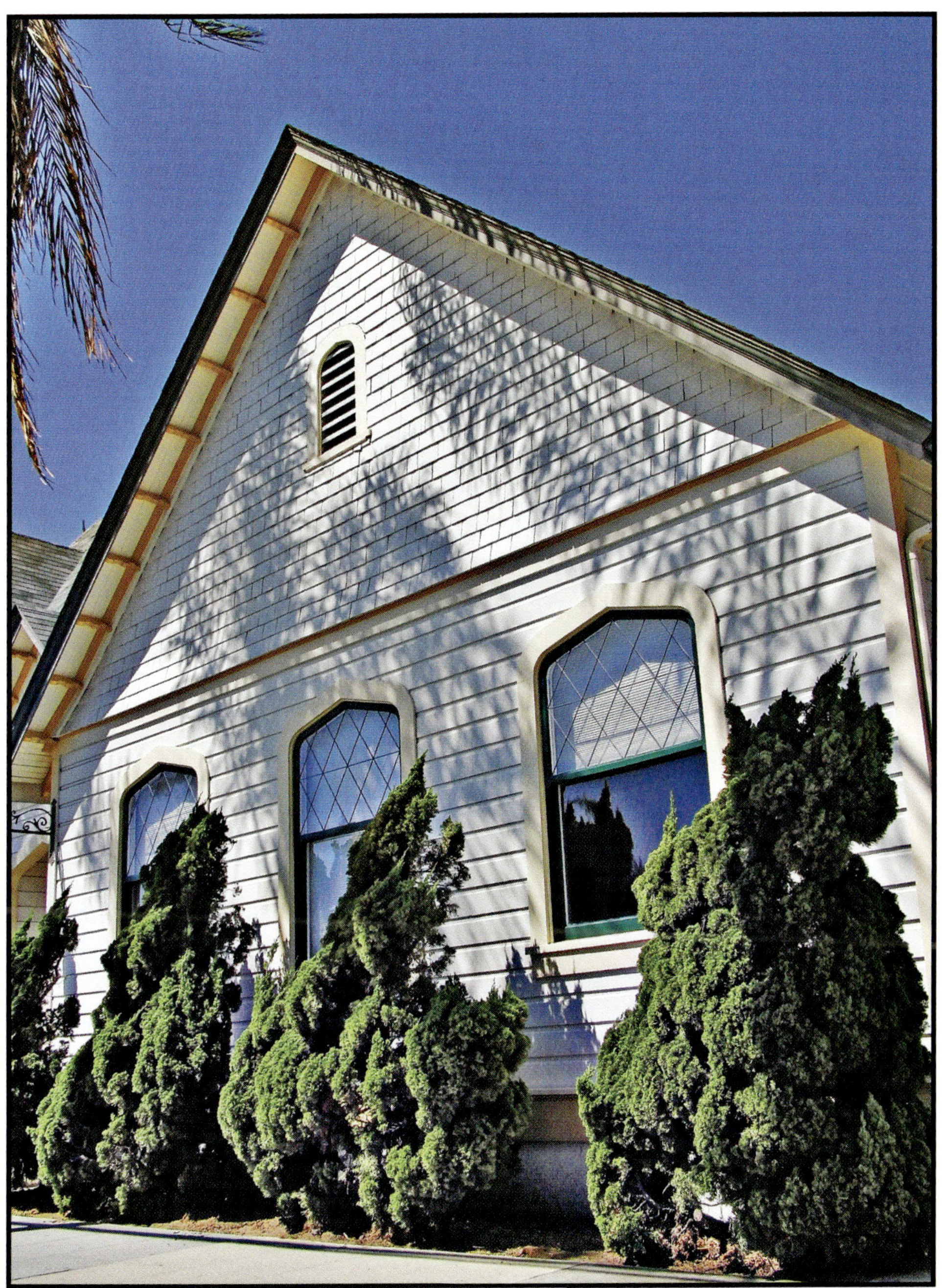

Fig.15. Image treated to High Pass filtration.

Fig. 16 shows an original photo in need of a jolt. I cropped and straightened the image in Photoshop, and then used the Clone Stamp tool to remove the annoying electrical wires. Next, I applied the High Pass filter to enrich detail and boost saturation. Notice how the clouds and windows pop out in Fig. 17. You can almost feel the facade's texture. The photo went from ho-hum to yum-yum in a few simple steps.

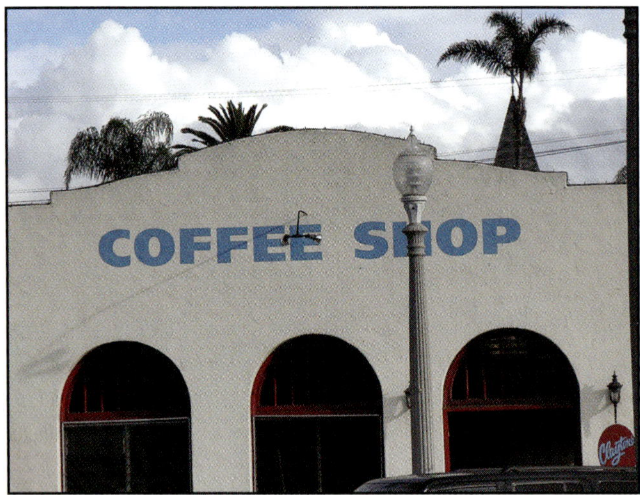

Fig. 16. The original, unfiltered image.

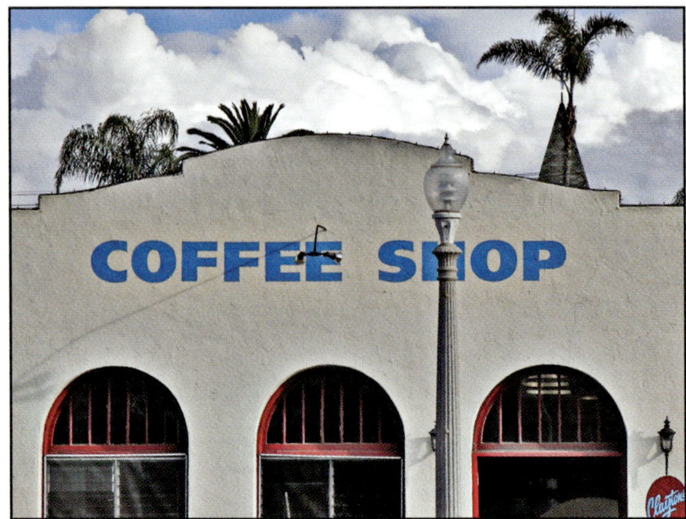

Fig. 17. The edited, filtered image.

The building in Fig. 18 comes alive thanks to the High Pass treatment. The archway above this parking garage looks like a devouring mouth with windows for eyes.

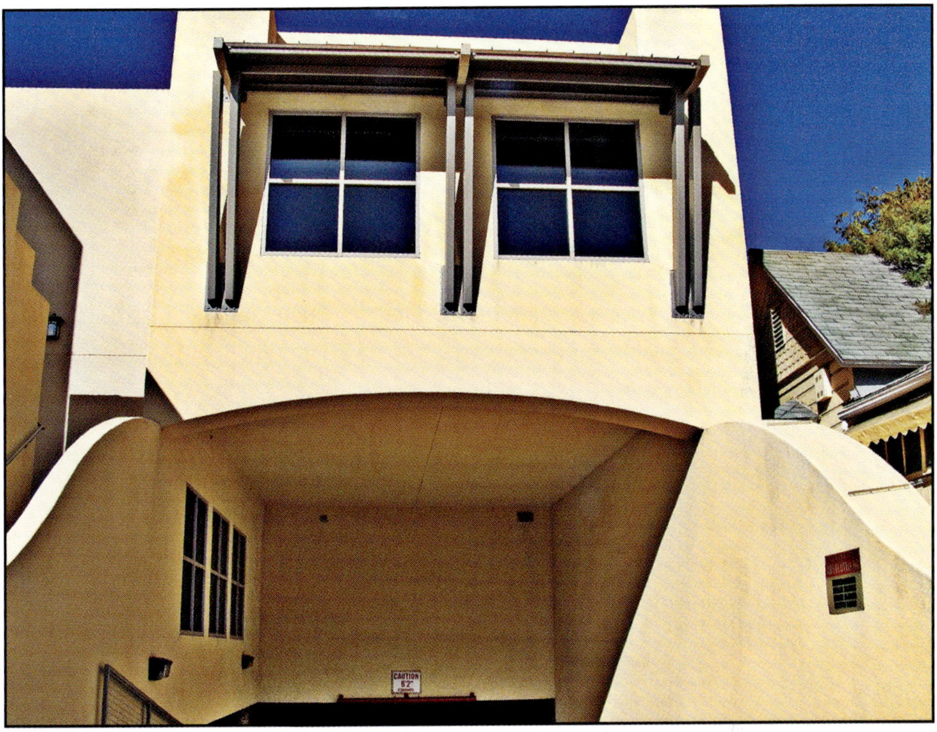

Fig. 18. High Pass filtered image.

Now let's tiptoe through a High Pass step by step. You can download the sample photo in Fig. 19 at the following URL: **www.zoomstreet.org/thrill/downloads**.

If you prefer, feel free to use your own photo.

Launch Photoshop and open the image.

Follow the steps on the next page.

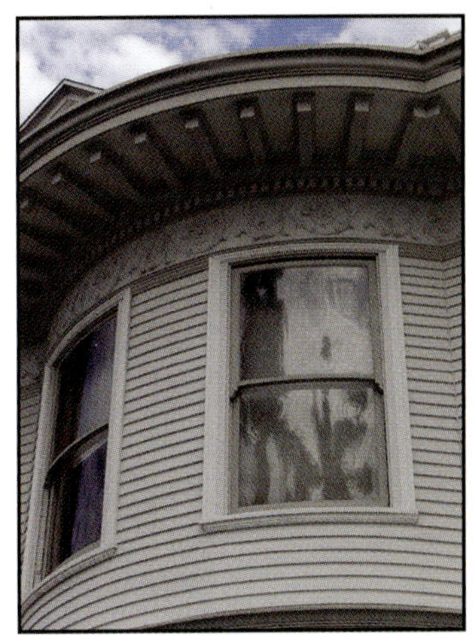

Fig. 19. Sample image to download.

HIGH PASS THRILLS AND CHILLS

1. Go to the Image menu and choose Image > Adjustments > Shadows/Highlights. Make sure Highlights is set to 0% and Shadows is set to approximately 50%. Click OK to close.

2. In the Layers palette, right-click on the Background layer and choose Duplicate Layer. This places a copy of the image ("Background copy") highlighted in blue above the Background layer. Click the Eye icon for Background copy to turn off its visibility.

3. Click on the Background layer to select it. From the Filter menu, choose Other > High Pass. Drag the slider bar, and set the Radius to 80 pixels. Click OK.

4. In the Layers panel, click the Background Copy layer to highlight it and its Eye icon to make it visible. Click on the layer mode bar and choose Overlay from the drop-down menu. Presto! The image is transformed but needs tweaking.

5. Go to the Image menu and select Adjustments > Vibrance. Drag the Vibrance slider bar to 13. Set the Saturation to −55. This desaturates the sky and removes the distracting blue color cast. Note: Vibrance is new to CS4 and alters color intensity more selectively than the Saturation control.

If you used my photo, the results should look like the image in Fig. 20. These parameters are intended as a starting point. Experiment by changing the Radius levels of High Pass, or use other filters in combination.

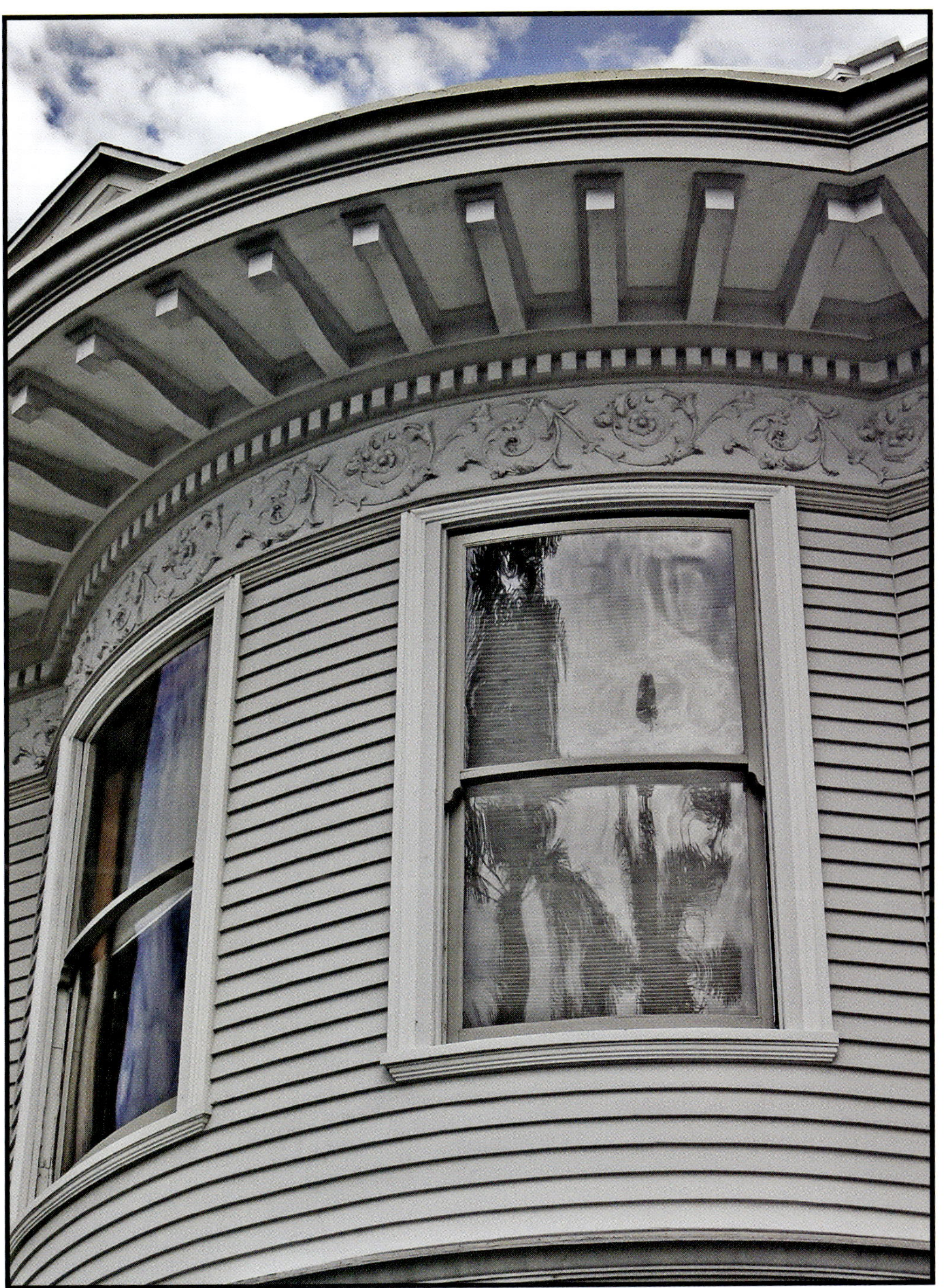

Fig. 20. A photo finish.

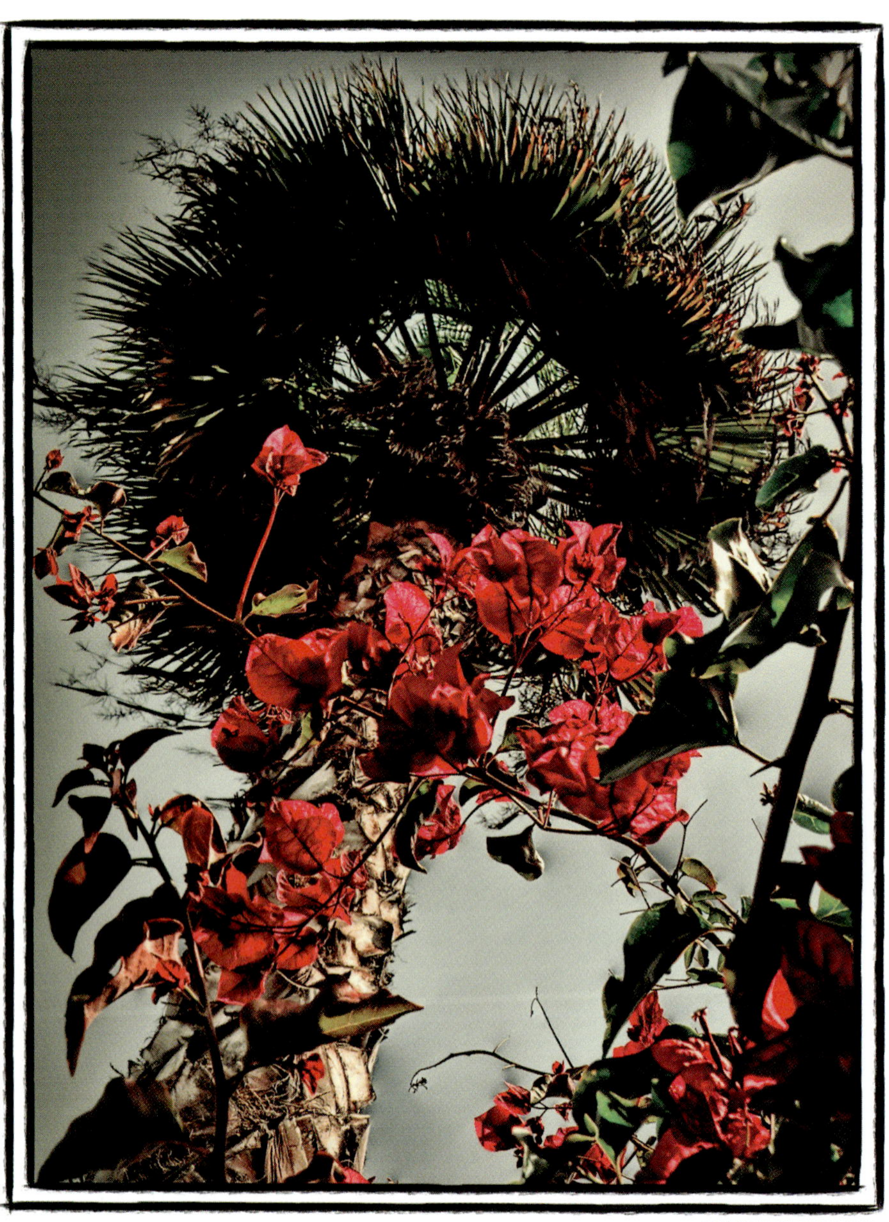

PHOTO BY DEREK PELL

9
"I'VE BEEN FRAMED!"
Showing Off in Public

"Please—one picture still worth ten thousand words."—Charlie Chan

Whodunnit? My gut tells me the butler. Maybe that's why my phone never rings. The last time a potential client came through the door was December '47. I remember it like it was 62 years ago. A blizzard hit the city with a sucker's punch—14 inches. She stepped out of a snow drift lookin' like a surfer on Redondo Beach—tan as a shoe brush. Wanda Wizner, Brooklyn, USA—so blonde I had to shade my eyes with a racing form.

"I've been framed," she said point blank.

"Doesn't surprise me—you look like a million bucks. You ought to be in pictures."

She frowned. "Somebody's trying to set me up."

"Sure, a dame like you deserves a pedestal. Lemme snap your portrai,t and I'll print you a poster on my Epson. Hang it over the mantel."

"Should've known this dump was the wrong address."

"Just temporary," I said, blowin' dust off my injet. "...while they rennovate my penthouse on Central Park West."

She gave me a look and left.

Maybe she didn't deserve a frame—not every dame does. That goes for Joes, too, and snaps of the Poconos. Frames—whether digital or solid gold—should be reserved for the best of the best.

With or without a frame, you want to present your work in the best possible light, even if it doesn't amount to a hill of beans in the grand scheme of things. Hell, they're not flesh and blood—just pixels.

HANGIN' ON THE WEB

The web is the biggest photo gallery on earth. Everything from family vacation snaps to high art—it's all up there, side by side, so to speak. Democracy in its purest form. Unfettered, uncensored, and free. The potential for attracting countless eyeballs is as seductive as a blonde in a red dress on Sunday or a lottery ticket on Saturday night.

Online photo sharing sites like flickr and Shutterfly are all the rage—a great way for snappers to show off while reeling in some feedback. Most image-editing software exports photo galleries and slide shows with a few mouse clicks, so you don't have to be a tech banana to launch them. *Zoom Street*'s monthly guest photography gallery is prepared in Lightroom using a built-in Flash-based template. It's simple to set up, elegant, and easy to navigate. Why reinvent the wheel?

Want bolder and Flash-ier? Check out the FREE **Postcard Viewer**, a third-party plug-in for Lightroom (and other apps) from **simpleviewer.net**. First time folks see it, they gasp. Click on thumbnails, and the photo zooms up at you in 3D space. You can drag a photo and flip it over to read a caption on the back. Fig. 1 shows an online sampler I made for a work in progress.

In addition to the standard portfolio of prints, today's pro has a digital version online and/or a blog, where clients can scope their latest work. If you don't have one you ain't in the game, and the name of the game is Presentation. That's what translates into assignments, sales, and mountains of moola (or in my case, molehills). Then again, just sharing your work, gaining feedback, and becoming part of a passionate community ain't bad either.

The idea for this book first smacked me in the head a couple of years ago. I banged out a proposal and fired it off to my agent and waited. And waited some more. When I got tired of waiting, I put together a visual, magazine-style presentation—complete with two-page spreads, pull-quotes, and splashly layouts. (I even made those annoying subscription cards, but I couldn't get 'em to fly off the screen into the viewer's lap. Technology has its limits.) I laid out the whole thing using **Adobe InDesign CS4**, and exported it as a Flash animation because it included a cool, page-turning feature. The viewer can click and drag a corner to turn the page—just like real life (Fig. 2). Was it worth the effort? Is that a book in your hands, or are you just glad to see me?

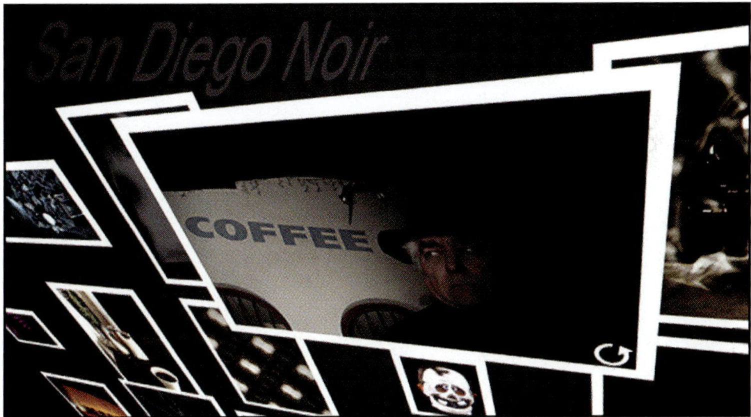

Fig. 1. Postcard Viewer in action on the web.

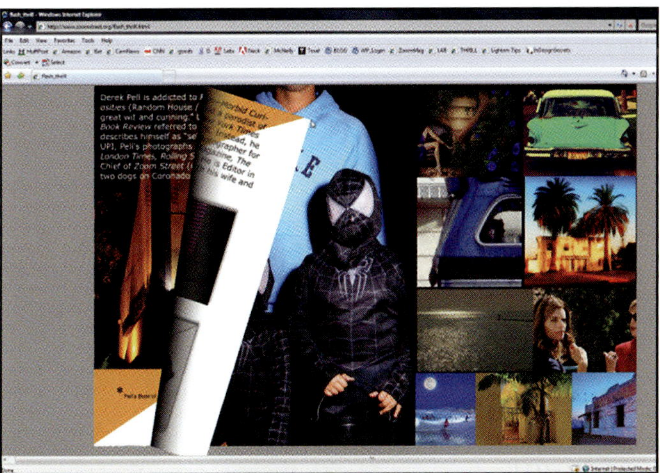

Fig. 2. *Shoot to Thrill*: The proposal, a real page-turner.

Framing ain't just for prints anymore; digital pictures can have virtual mats and frames, too. From a simple lined border to a gilded monstrosity—a frame with nooks, crannies, and gargoyles. Software makes possible every kind of frame imaginable: elegant motifs, grunge and splotches, artist and designer frames, abstract borders that explode and scatter their shards across the virtual page, trailing off into space. How about that?—a frame without borders!

Before I show a few examples, heed the words of warning below.

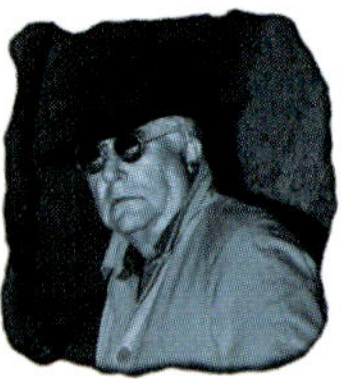

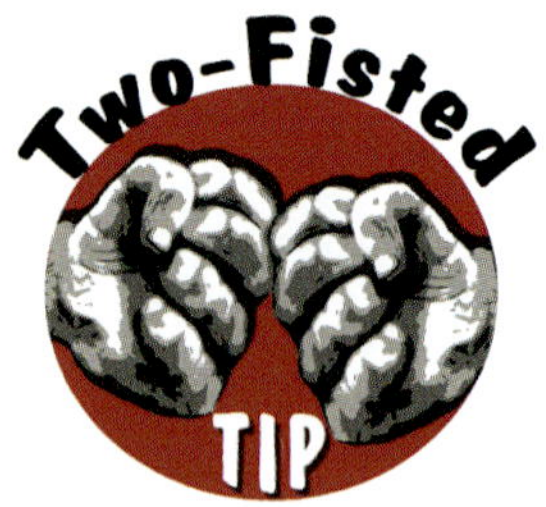

Just because you *can* frame a photo doesn't mean you *should*. Not every picture deserves or needs one. To put it another way, exotic frames can be jake as a gem, but keep 'em rare. At it's best, a frame *collaborates* with the image like a stage set for a play. At the very least, it should complement the photo rather than hog the limelight. I'm showing you possibilities here and slapping frames on photos like there's no tomorrow. But tomorrow I'll remove most of 'em.

Whatever you do, **don't frame every photo in your archive**. Unless, of course, you live in a museum.

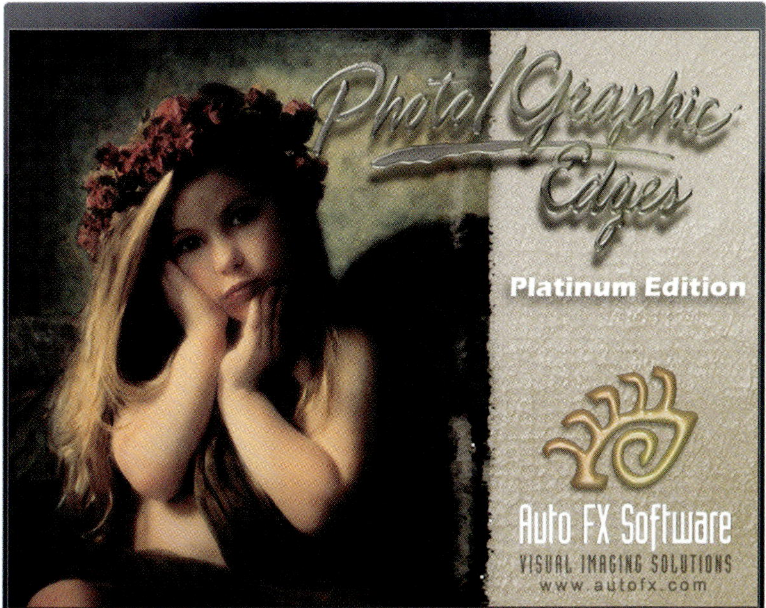

Fig. 3. The splash screen.

When I'm in the mood to get an edge on—do some serious framing—I launch the standalone version of **Photo/Graphic Edges Platinum Edition** (Fig. 3), with its boundless selection of film frames, grunge edges, natural media borders, overlays, darkroom effects, and more—more than a thousand. Just steer clear of the cheesy ones that look like rejects from a high school crafts fair.

Beware the *Curse of Kafka*, too. Edges is a dangerous place to hang. I've found myself trapped inside the app for days...customizing borders and fiddlin' with frames. I haven't found the ultimate pulp noir specimen, but I know it's in there somewhere...just a matter of time.

The interface ain't elegant, but it levels with you (Fig. 4). It has tools for resizing frames and edges, along with the photo. Mastering its Clone tool takes some practice, but with it you can extend and reshape a preset and warp it into your own creation.

In Fig. 5 I applied a border to this chapter's lead image, and it kind of cross-pollinates with the subject and animates the photo. (Anyone remember *Invasion of the Body Snatchers*?)

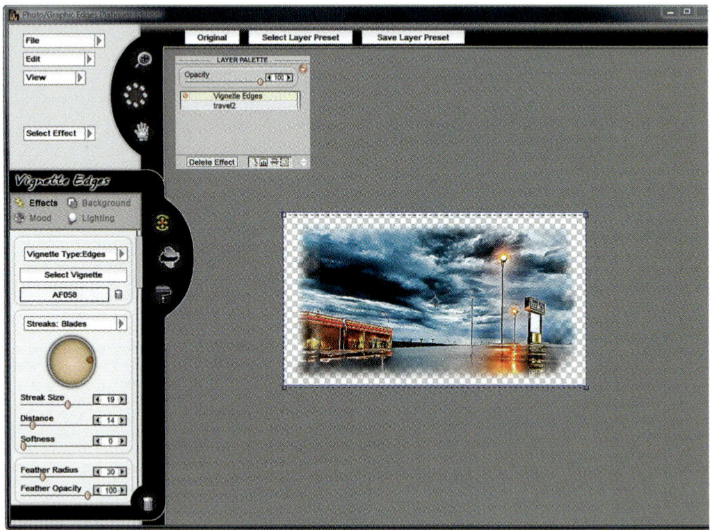

Fig. 4. The Photo/Graphics Edges interface.

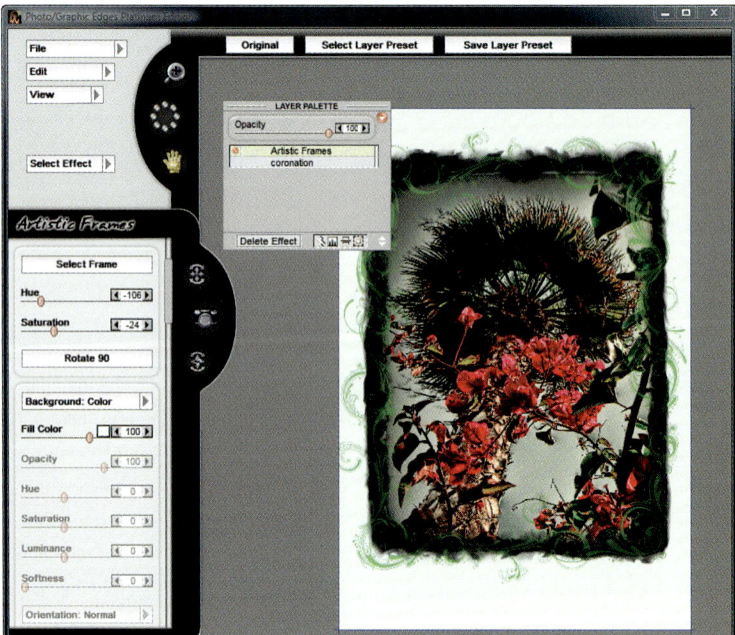

Fig. 5. One of many customizable frames.

There are presets that repeat a photo at various sizes, such as the Storyboard frame in Fig. 6, featuring a mug only my mother could love. ("I've been framed!") Later, in Photoshop, I added a splotch of grunge (see arrow) using Alien Skin's **Eye Candy** plug-in. Call it self-defacement.

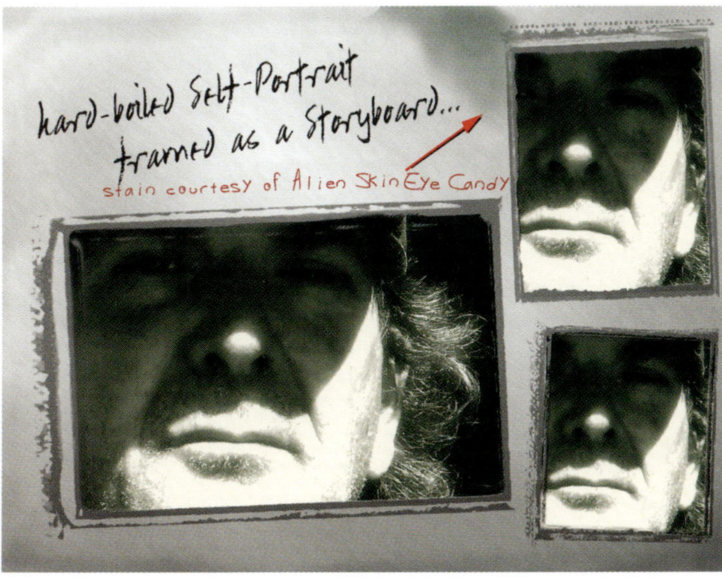

Fig. 6. Storyboard preset with third-party smudge added.

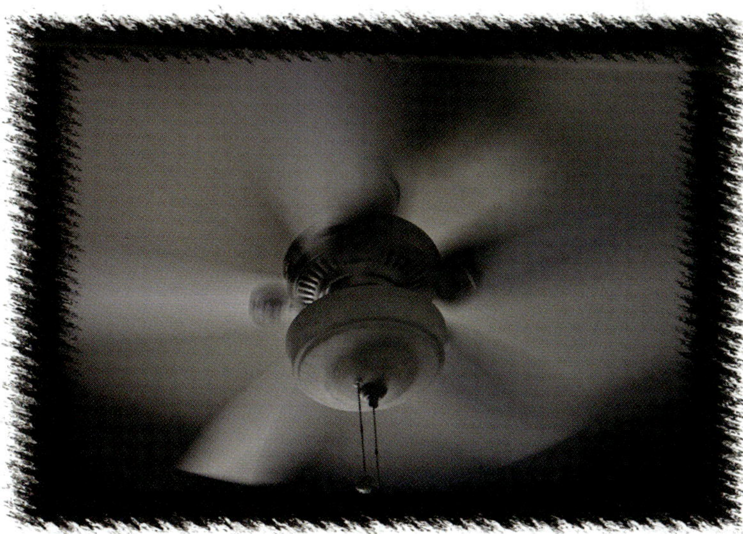

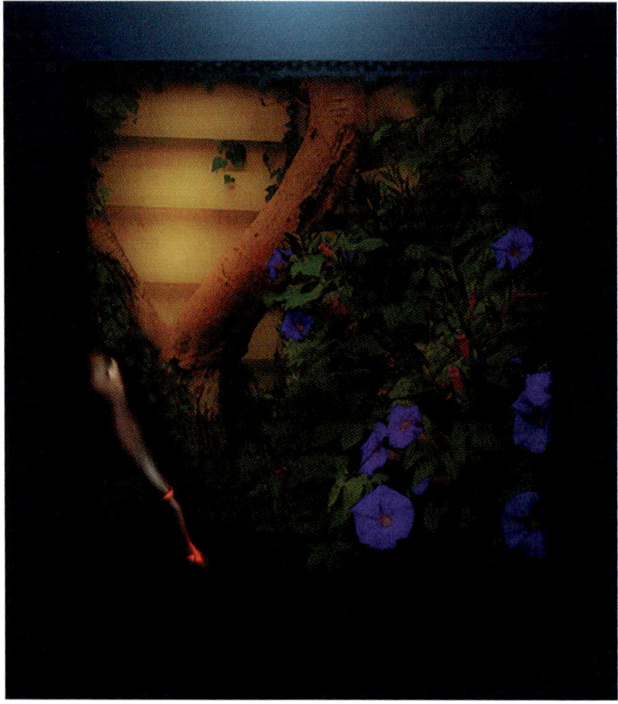

Fig. 7. This frame complements the photo's eroticism (If you recognize this shot, you've got a good memory.)

I found the perfect frame for a series of montages I was working on (Fig. 7), so I saved it as a preset. That stored a thumbnail of my framed image, making it easy to locate and apply to other photos.

A soft wet brushstroke border seemed just right for this photo (Fig. 8) of a courtyard in San Diego. It looked like Morocco to me. The only thing missing was a hookah and a snake charmer.

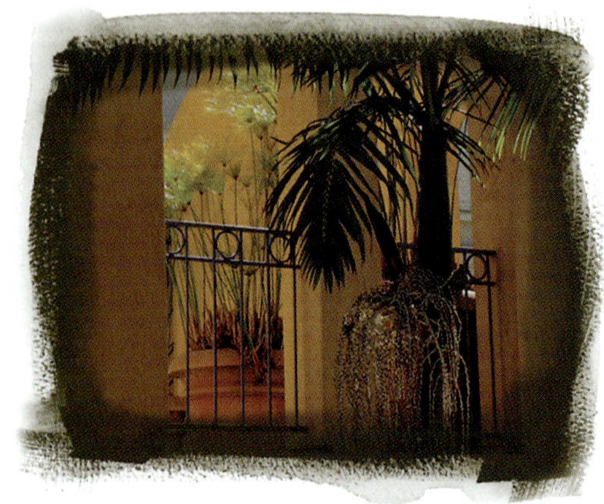

Fig. 8. Looks like Morocco, but it's San Diego, mon amour.

HANGIN' ON THE WALL

Now we come to the real deal: frames you can actually *hang*. There's no substitute for puttin' a photo under glass—instant glory. You can strut your stuff and, at the same time, cover up those bullet holes in the wall.

Every photographer needs a gallery, and that gallery can be anywhere there's wallspace—the studio, office, or home sweet Winnebago. Hell, when I'm on the road stayin' in some desolate motel—where the only action is tumbleweed—I'll hang a few photos of mine and find flaws. Still, it beats what they put on the wall.

Alternatives to a high-priced frame shop abound, and if you can cut your own matte, so much the better. Chain stores like Target usually stock a few decent-looking plain wood or plastic frames. I scour yard sales, thrift stores, and the Salvation Army for eccentric specimens. I search online, too, which is where I discovered the Wall Clock Photo Frame with noir potential (Fig. 9).

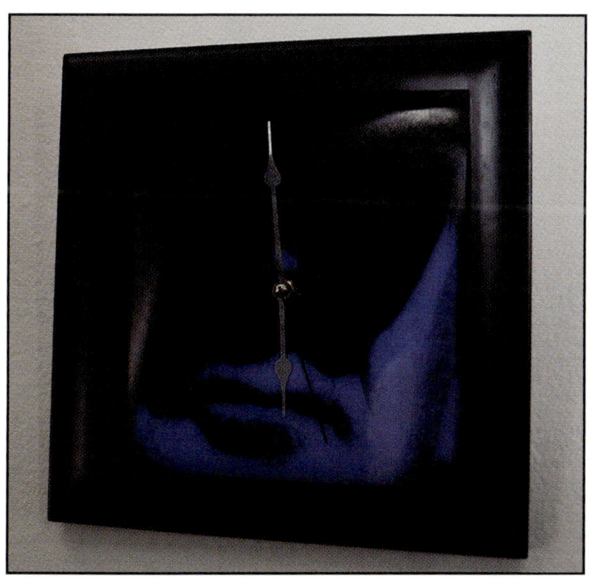

Fig. 9. Wall clock frame from Neil Enterprises, with a touch of noir.
(That's me, lookin' like Batman on a bad day.)

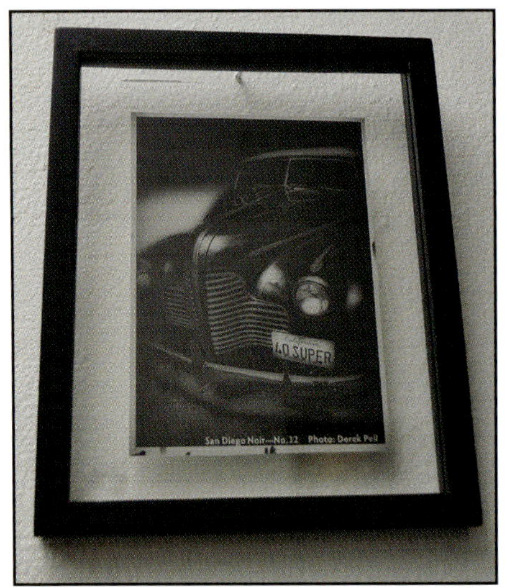

Fig. 10. Umbra's Floater Noir.

When I'm in a certain frame of mind I pay a visit to a website called Umbra, which sells designer frames you won't find anywhere else. Naturally, I had to have their black lacquered wood frame called **Floater Noir** (Fig. 10). The image floats in space and casts a shadow.

Umbra offers a panoply of frames featuring multiple openings, great for sequential shots. I used their metal **Meto** frame (Fig. 11) to display a series of 4 x 6-inch video stills showing the title sequence from a movie version of this book. (BTW, don't miss it; it has an all-star cast.) The sequence is reproduced so you can actually see it at the beginning of **Chapter 10, "Play It Again, Cam..."**)

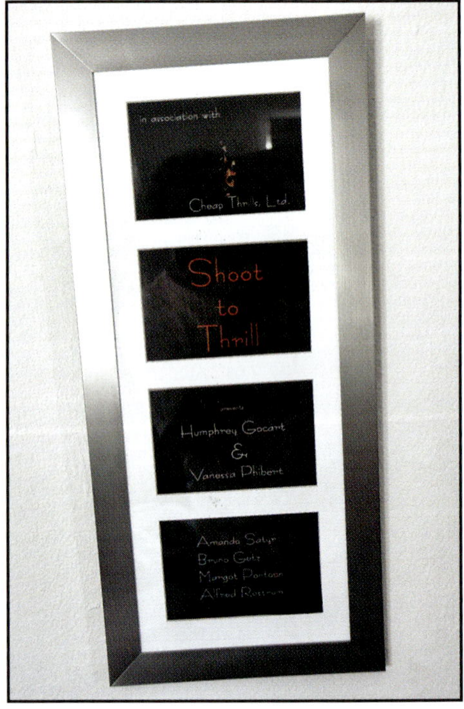

Fig.11. Umbra's Meto Wall Frame with stills from DV.

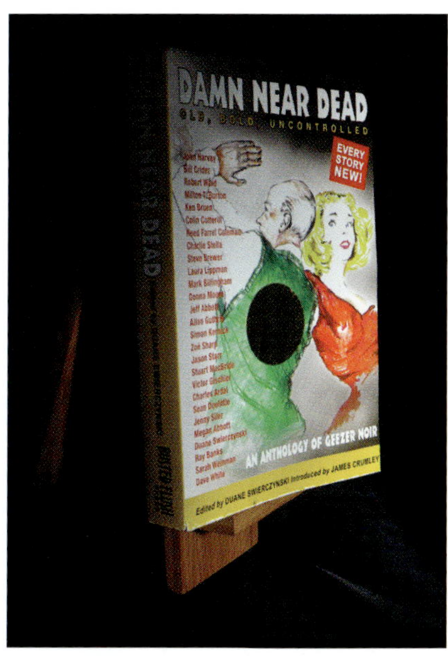

Fig.12. Bambeasel supporting "Geezer Noir."

If you run out of wall space, get yourself a bunch of **Bambeasels**. I know that sounds like something I made up (a machine-gun toting beastie?), but I didn't. Umbra did. It's their small (10 x 3 x 6-inch) wooden display stand that holds a framed photo or mounted print. Hell, I even use 'em to show off good literature (Fig. 12).

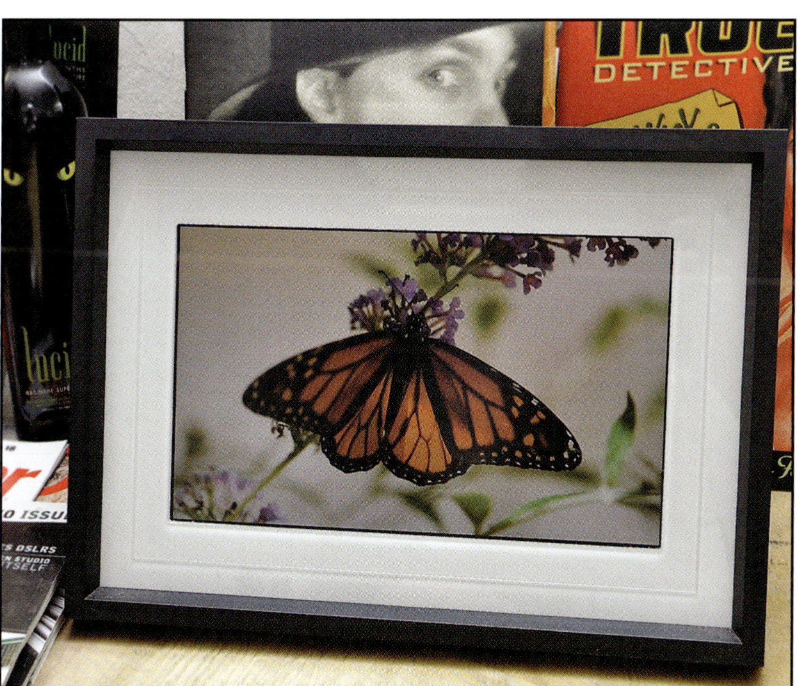

Fig. 13. This wireless digital photo frame from Kodak is an eyeball pleaser.

Don't worry; I didn't forget the omnipresent photo frame that displays digital images and videos on an LCD, yet can hang or stand upright. There are a lot of models out there to choose from, but the top one I've found is the 10-inch **Kodak EasyShare W1020** (Fig. 13). The LCD has a 16:9 HD wide-screen format and 800 x 480 resolution. The picture is crisp and bright. It can store about 4,000 photos with its 512MB of internal memory and connects wirelessly to photo-sharing sites.

A ROGUE'S GALLERY MEETS M_oMA

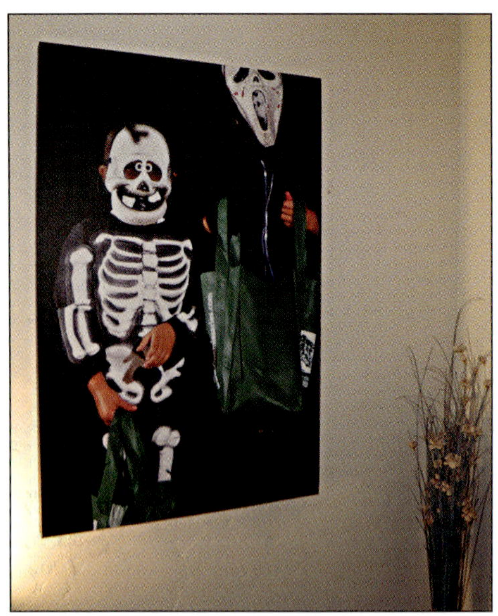

Fig. 14. Gallery Wrap (24 x 36 inches).

Want to wow visitors to your one-man show or knock out your clients? Hit 'em with a **Gallery Wrap** (Fig. 14)—a photo printed on canvas and stretched around the frame. This unique service is offered by Mpix (**www.mpix.com**), a photo lab specializing in professional enlargements. The process is streamlined thanks to a partnership between Mpix and onOne Software, makers of **Genuine Fractals**, a Photoshop plug-in for upscaling images to dimensions beyond 100% while maintaining the quality of the original. Using Genuine Fractals I blew up my Halloween shot to a monstrous 24 x 36 inches, and chose the Gallery Wrap feature, which prepared the image, exported it, and emailed it directly to Mpix. A few days later Fed-Ex showed up at my door with a wrapped wrap.

One last word on wraps: As this book goes to press, Hahnemuhle, the fine art paper maker, just released a DIY **Gallerie Wrap Kit** that looks interesting. I was gonna try it, but I'm out of shape. It requires a lot of stretching.

Roger Laudy of Image Wizards was telling me about a process he developed for printing photos on aluminum. After years of experimenting, he'd apparently struck gold with what he calls **Alumin-Arte**. He must've sensed my skepticism because he told me to send him a photo and he'd prove it. I mailed a shot of the stairs outside my office that was the inspiration for a major motion pictured based on this book. About a week later a huge wooden crate arrived. I spent half an hour with a Phillips head gettin' all the screws out, thinkin' "This better be good..." Then I opened it and had a quasi-religious experience. The photo looked radiant. I felt like I could step right into the picture and walk down those dangerous steps to an unknown fate. The reproduction in Fig. 15 doesn't do it justice. You have to stand right in front of it if you want to find god.

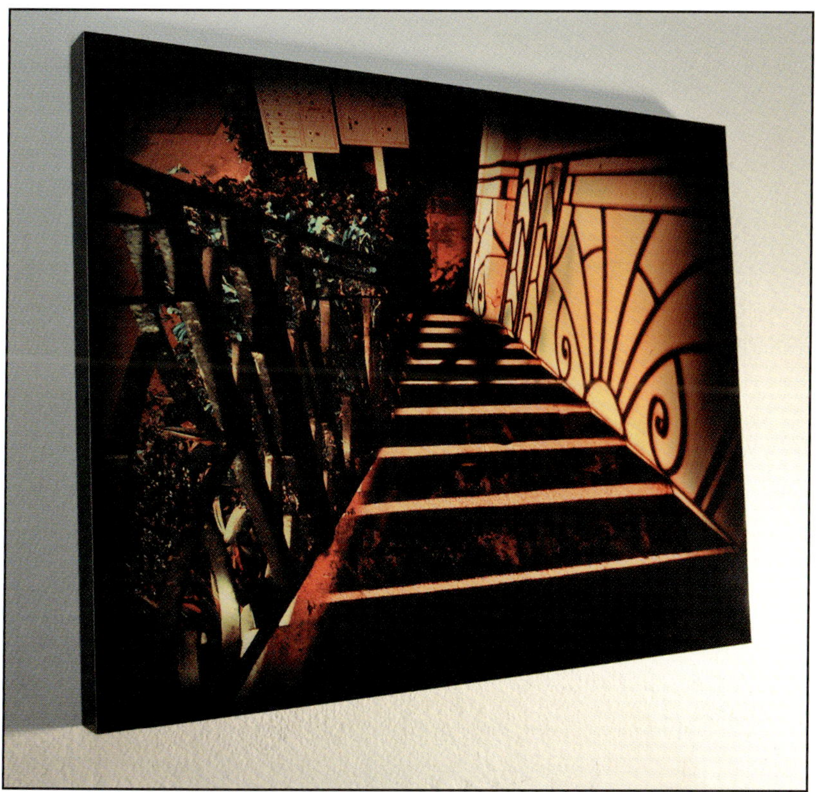

Fig. 15. This AluminArte print adds a radiant, 3-dimensional quality to the photo.

PRINT IT FOR POSTERITY

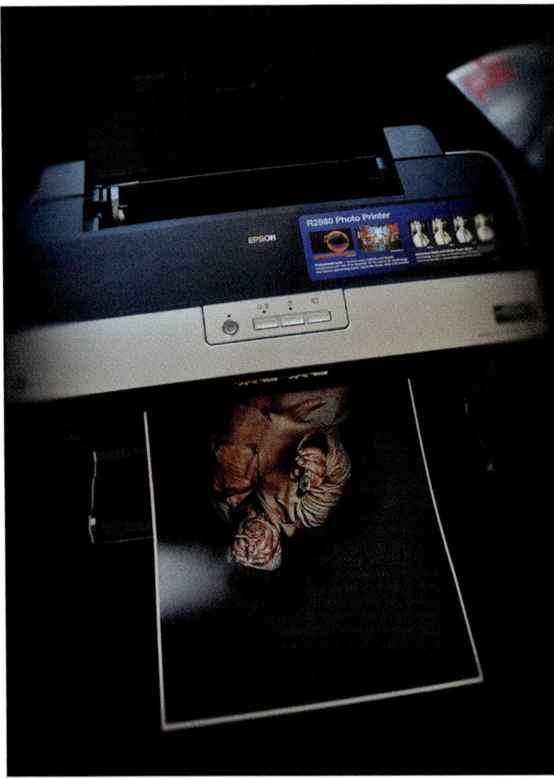

Fig. 16. The Epson Stylus R2880 spews a gorgeous, glossy 13 x 19 poster in just three minutes.

If you've been entertaining the idea that I work out of an industrial Clean Room, well...the party's over. My office is the friggin' 1930s Dust Bowl—home to all sorts of transient fuzz bunnies and malingerin' motes. Dust, as you know, is Public Enemy #1 for photo gear, so I vacuum-pack my cameras and lock 'em away. Can't do that with the big Epson printer. I wrap it in swaths of plastic till it resembles King Tut havin' a bad afterlife. And speaking of printers, get yourself a high-quality photo inkjet, and you can make your own limited edition prints and portfolio books. You can spend thousands, but you don't have to if you can settle for exhibition-quality prints up to 13 x 19 inches. In that case, grab the **Epson Stylus Photo** R2880 (Fig. 16). I've tried 'em all, and in my opinion, Epson makes the best. For under a grand, this model is gangbusters.

Now whether it's by nature or by design, we all know printers are ink-guzzlers. Hell, that's where manufacturers rake in the moo. That said, the R2880 is pretty good on ink. I say good 'cause I've yet to find the equivalent of a Porsche that gets 50 mpg. Obviously, mileage varies based on the kind of printing you do. Churn out lots of poster-sized prints at Epson's Maximum quality, and you'll get bit in the wallet. But R2880 's Fine mode is so damned good you may never take it to the max. Fast, too, at three minutes for a 13 x 19 print. The same print at Maximum quality takes about nine minutes—which ain't bad, either. Speed, however, ain't the gold ring at the carousel— it's all about quality. And the R2880 produces gallery prints that'll knock your smock off.

This model is geared toward art photographers, and it's just the cup of tea for anyone who wants to experiment with printing on the wide selection of fine art papers out there. Thick and textured, this printer can take it. Lately I've been workin' with classy papers from Canson Infinity, like their **Rag Photographique**. It has no trans fats or optical brighters, which translates into this: The paper will last longer than you and I will.

I've heard a few photogaphers griping that you have to swap out the black ink cartridge when you print on matte paper with the Epson R2880. Seems like lint picking to me since changing the cartridge is quick and easy. If you're gonna complain, complain about buyin' cartridges, not swapping 'em.

Like a lot of Epson models, this one also prints on CDs and DVDs, which is useful. Clients like getting a fancy DVD with their name and company logo. Hell, who doesn't like seein' their name in print? I mean, other than Bernie Maddoff.

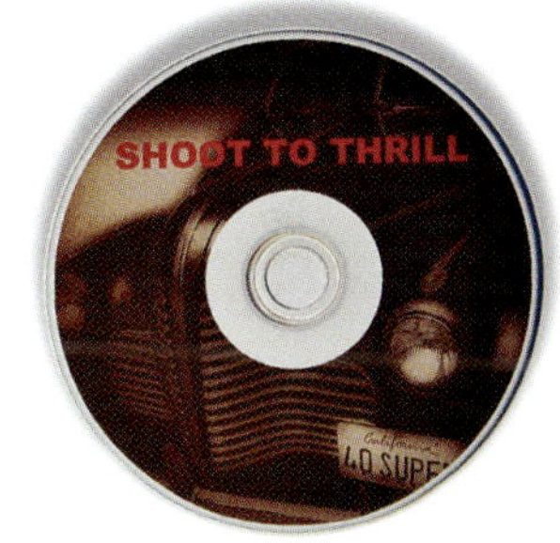

Photos always seem to look great on a monitor at 72 dpi. The real test, however, is when you print out your photos at full resolution. Holding a print in your hand that matches what you shot or created in the digital darkroom... there ain't no greater high than that.

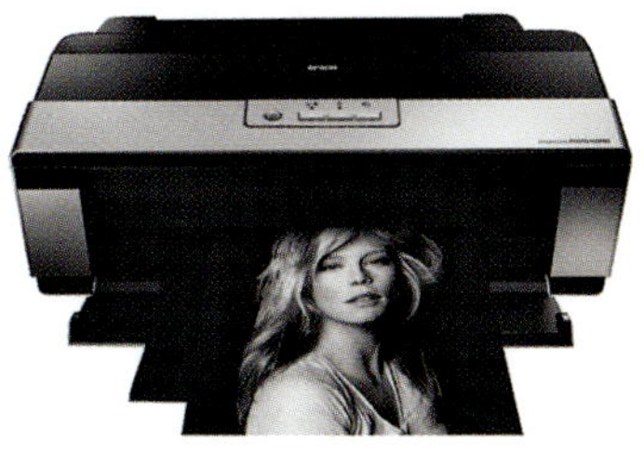

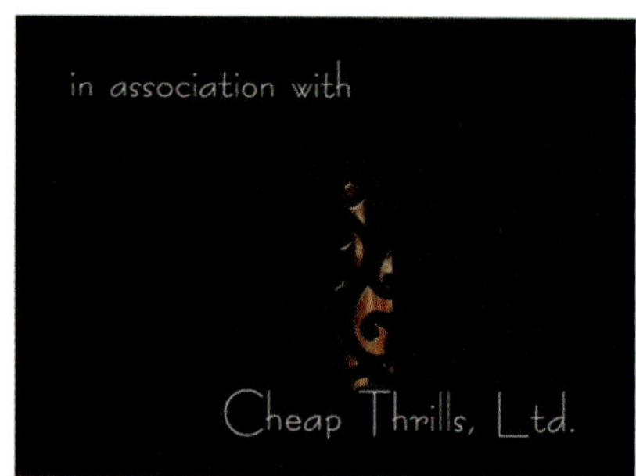

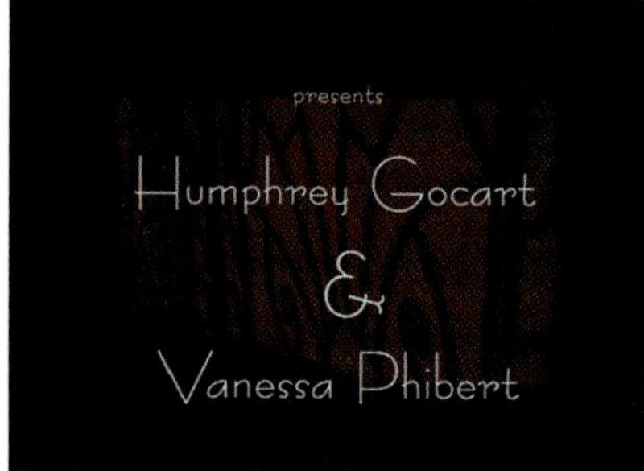

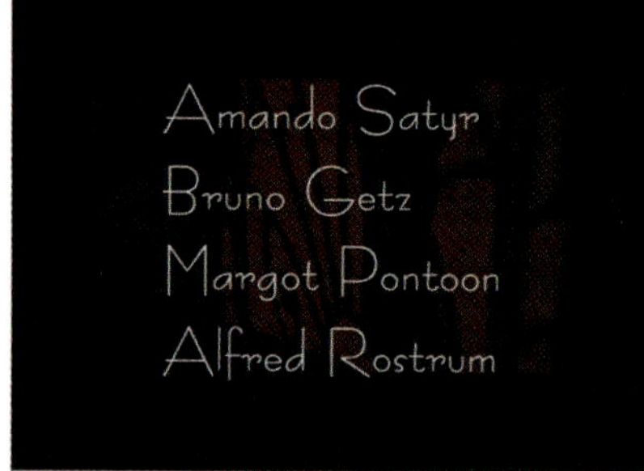

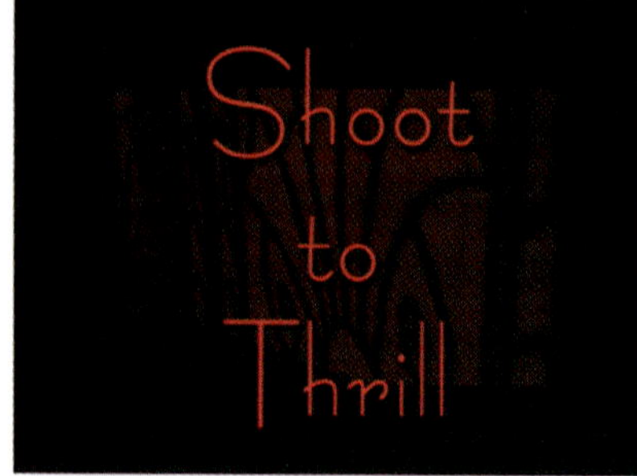

Zoom Street Productions, Ltd. © 1947-2009

Here are some thrilling stills from the credits of the 1947 film based on this book. The sequence was shot using a Nikon D90 D-SLR outside the offices of *Zoom Street Magazine* in San Diego.

10
"PLAY IT AGAIN, CAM..."
The Future Is DV

"We didn't need dialogue. We had faces." —Norma Desmond (*Sunset Boulevard*)

Convergence. Yeah, it's a dirty word, but somebody has to say it and—since it's my book—it has to be me. The word gets passed around at tea parties like sugar and echoes off the walls of conference rooms. It gets circled on yellow pads at board meetings. You read it in articles and on blogs. Wouldn't surprise me if somebody boils it down to a tweet: a one-syllable sound byte.

It's our future, the future of tech—the urge to merge, to converge, to consolidate. To put all our communication tools into a Swiss Army knife.

Well, the future is now.

Remember the day the phone became a camera? I don't, because future shock is behind us. Every day there's a revolutionary new breakthrough and a thousand salesmen hawkin' it. Every time I open my door I have to shove my way through an army of carnival barkers. *"It walks, it talks, it crawls on its belly like a wireless reptile..."*

Convergence, in the context of photography, is when the Nikon D90 snapped to attention and said, "Private D-SLR, reporting for movie duty, sir!" It was the world's first digital SLR to incorporate HD video capability. (Canon was a close second with its EOS 5D Mark II.) So what's the big deal, eh? Puny point-and-shoots have had Movie Mode for years. What's all the yak about?

In the world of freelance photography and photojournalism, DV might be a career maker, since print publications are droppin' like flies. With DV capability built in to a D-SLR...that opens doors that weren't there yesterday. Now you might get an assignment to photograph, say, a winery in Napa and—"Oh, while you're at it, gimme a nice little video I can stick on YouTube and our website."

"Yessir!" The invoice total just went up.

Suddenly, a photojournalist carries one camera instead of packing a bulky camcorder, too. Let's say you're on the streets of Peshawar when a Taliban-incited riot breaks out. You shoot a hundred stills in burst, and then switch to Movie mode and capture the action in high definition. Later, you upload the files via satellite and watch it on CNN the same day.

Hey, maybe convergence ain't so bad after all. It could even be the 21st century equivalent of FDR's New Deal for shutterbugs.

"LIGHTS...CAMERAS...LIMITATIONS!"

I'm gonna focus on the Nikon D90 because that's what I've got on hand and it's still considered a hot item—despite the fact Nikon just released another HD video-capable model, the D5000. In fact, the D90 was voted "Camera of the Year" (Advanced D-SLRs category) in the August 2009 issue of *American Photo*.

Be that as it may, as I write this, new HD-ready models have been announced by Panasonic, Olympus, Pentax, Sony, Canon, and Samsung. Everybody's in the game now, and that gives you lots of options.

Signs of a sea change are everywhere. A recent article by photographer Louis Lesko appeared in *Digital Photo Pro* with this title: "Will Video Kill the Still Photography Star?" It ain't hype, either. It reveals how top pros with no video experience have lost out on lucrative jobs to photographers packin DV. Motion and stills are shackin' up together, and it's time to start planning the shotgun wedding.

The term *video capture for stills* (VCS) is buzzin' around the ad agencies, and that means some clients are looking primarily for DV campaigns to be launched online. For print ads, they'll yank out stills from the HD video clips (Fig. 1). Almost sounds like the end of photography as we know it.

Repeat after me: *diversify, diversify, diversify...*

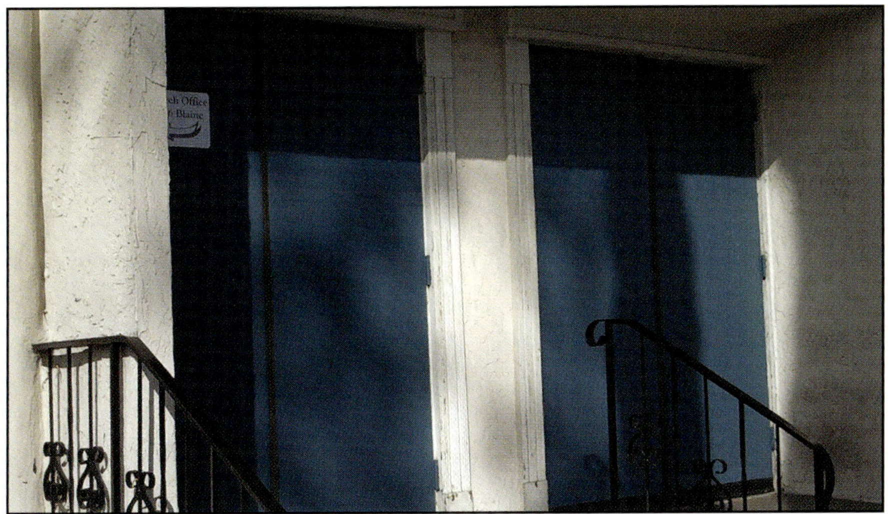

Fig. 1. Still image captured from HD video shot with a point-and-shoot.

I'm not suggesting you sell your still camera; I'm saying it's time to expand your talent and creativity. A lot of photographers are resisting digital video. For one thing, it means more stuff to learn. Suddenly you've got to consider things like sound and motion and transitions. But, hell, that's what makes life interesting. Without challenges and conflict, where's the drama that stirs the juices? More importantly, why be left behind when there's money to be made using your creative talent? You've got the eye for still images; you can train your eye to see beyond the single shot.

One other thing I forgot to mention: Shooting video is *fun*.

HYBRID ON A HOT TIN ROOF

I'll warn you up front: If your ultimate goal is to shoot movies and take an occasional still, a hybrid D-SLR doesn't replace a stand-alone camcorder—not by a long shot (sorry). If DV's your secret passion, get a camcorder and avoid the limitations.

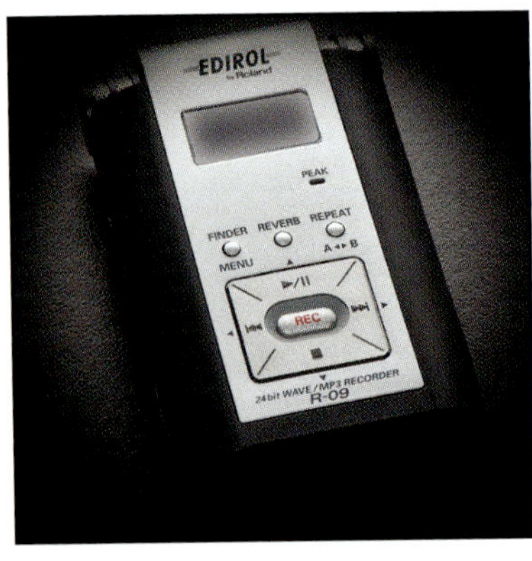

In the case of the Nikon D90, the big downer is no external microphone jack. (Naughty, naughty, Nikon.) If I want a great stereo soundtrack to accompany my video, I have to use a separate digital audio recorder, like the **Edirol R-09**. Now this doesn't mean you can't use the camera's built-in mic. It's fine for whenever top-notch audio quality isn't required— you just have to take pains to avoid picking up the sound of the camera's controls. Also, without an external shotgun mic to record someone speaking at a distance, you have to move in close to record it. Zooming the lens will bring the speaker's image closer, not his or her voice.

I've heard a lot of whiners griping about the D90's 5-minute limit per clip. But if you want to learn how to make Hollywood-type movies, that's not a limitation. It's actually a constraint that'll turn you into a hard-boiled filmmaker. No bull. Next time you go to a movie, take a stop watch with you and clock the scenes. You'll discover a 5-minute scene is about as rare as a flick that's worth its admission price. A scene will be 15 seconds, 30 seconds, 1 minute, a minute and a half. Yeah, some scenes are so rotten you'd swear they dragged on for half an hour but, in reality, they ran a few minutes.

One legitimate reason to gripe about a clip limit is if you want to plant the camera on a tripod and shoot a high school play from start to finish. In that case, use a camcorder. On the other hand, if you see yourself as a budding Orson Welles or Alfred Hitchcock, lose the weight and keep the D-SLR. Invest in Adobe's CS4 video suite, and get a workstation like the **HP Z800** (more on the latter later). If you want to dabble on the cheap, Apple's **iMovie** and **Windows Movie Maker** will do you no harm.

DV DINNERS

Before I put an edge on your appetite, here are a few basics.

Most camcorders and point-and-shoots record video at 30 frames per second. Hollywood shoots film slower, at 24 fps. 24 is the magic number. It's part of the aesthetic we associate with cinema. At 24 frames per second there's a soft, grainy quality and a blur to the motion. By contrast, digital video is razor sharp and borders on the hyperreal. We associate DV with local TV news, where the image is like looking out the window. And that's fine. That's reality (TV), life as a documentary. For make-believe stories we want the quality of film—grain and all. No grain, no gain. Of course, contributing to the look of film is the film itself, the processing. The Nikon D90 shoots video at 24 fps, which is more filmic, if not exactly the full Hollywood experience. If you want to mimic the look of cinema with video shot at 30 fps, there are post-production plug-ins for **Adobe Premiere Pro** and **Apple Final Cut Pro** (the leading professional video editing apps) that do a great job. Fig. 2 shows yours truly in a still from a digital video given the film-look treatment using a plug-in called Magic Bullet from Red Giant Software.

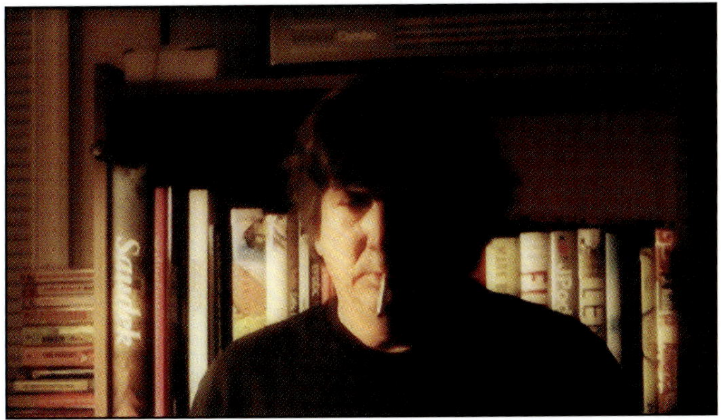

Fig. 2. This DV still featuring yours truly has the soft quality of film.

The D90's Movie mode makes use of the camera's Live View function—that is, you view the scene through the big, bright 3-inch LCD screen rather than the puny viewfinder. This, of course, makes framing your shots a pleasure. If you don't have enough space on your memory card, the camera lets you know this so you don't run into a "Gimme my gun!" moment in the middle of a great scene.

In the negative column, the camera becomes the cinematographer and takes control. You frame your shot, press the shutter halfway to set the focus, and push an OK button to start and stop recording. Nice and simple, but autofocus doesn't work in Movie mode. If an actor moves off the focal plane, you must manually refocus.

You're the boss when it comes to manual focus, zooming, white balance, and exposure compensation, but that's it.

Back on the plus side, with the D90 you can use all the great Nikon lenses. Best of all, you can open up your lens and get the shallow depth of field cinematographers eat for breakfast. How do you know when a video has been taken with a point-and-shoot? Everything's sharp. Let's say you're shooting a sequel to *The Postman Always Rings Twice II* (called *The Postman Always Rings Thrice*). You've framed a nice close shot of the deranged postal worker as he pauses on his rounds to open somebody's Social Security check. Behind him there's a cluster of mailboxes, and the audience can clearly read everyone's names. Distracting, right? It would be much more effective if he were sharp and the mailboxes were out of focus. (Not so fuzzy they become unrecognizable as mailboxes; that would destroy the subtle symbolism.)

Note how in Fig. 2 the books are slightly out of focus while the sap with the cigarette is sharp. You can't pull that off with a fixed lens.

DEAD PANS AND ZOOM GOONS

There's nothing like a nice smooth pan. Don't bother trying it hand holding the D90. The video will begin to quiver in a real annoying way. If you want your videos to have pro quality, use a good tripod with a fluid head designed specifically for pan and tilt shots.

Remember to pan slowly unless you want to take the audience on an amusement park ride.

Repeatedly zooming in and out and panning back and forth ought to be a criminal offense. Besides, panning and zooming make the editing job tougher because you get awkward intermediate frames.

A slow zoom is effective if you use it once in a blue moon. When you want to shoot a close-up, zoom with your feet.

Now for some noir...

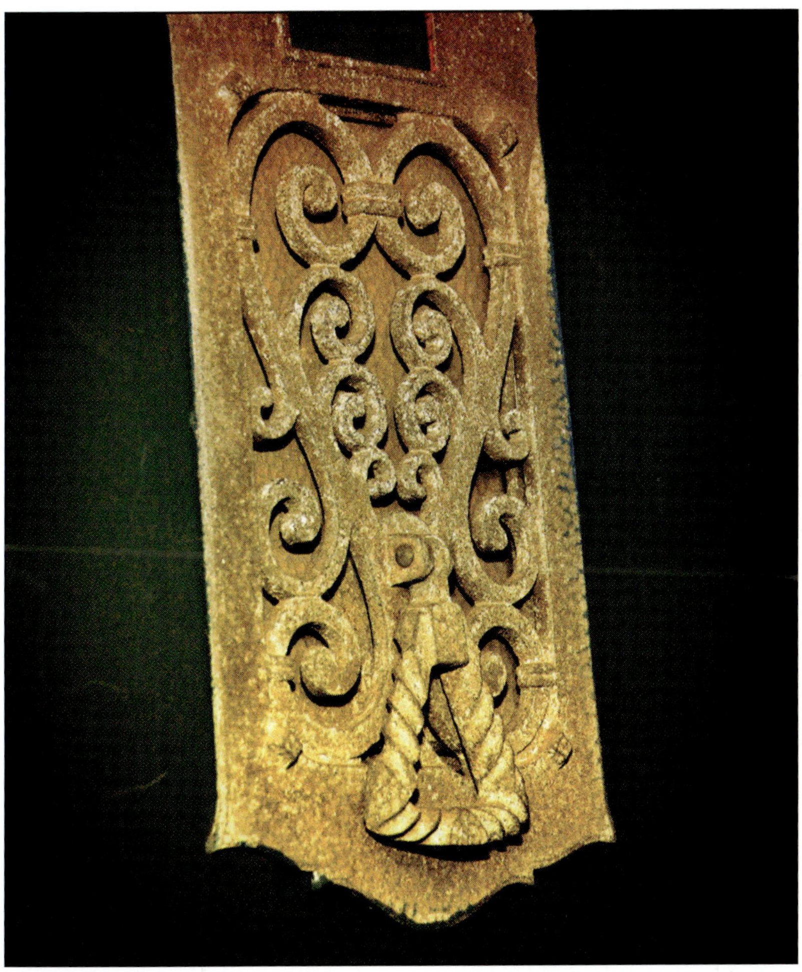

This classic "speakeasy grill" on Zoom Street's front door appears in the movie version of this book: **www.zoomstreet.org/thrill/cinema.html**.

"WE DIDN'T NEED FACES. WE HAD DIALOGUE."

But I needed a title.

One that embodied the dark spirit of film noir. I rifled through my bag of beauts and found these:

They Shoot Hearses, Don't They?

A Streetcar Named Perspire

Murder Is a Part-Time Job

Yeah, they all sucked. Then it hit me. Sheesh, what a sap I was. *Shoot to Thrill* was as noir as night and, besides, the whole point of the movie was to make its author rich.

I started jotting down ideas for opening shots. Inspiration came from the exterior stairway to my office at Zoom Street. The perfect location. Menacing shadows. A door with a speakeasy grill right out of a Raymond Chandler novel.

Just goes to show… you don't gotta travel halfway around the world to find inspiration. It can be literally right outside your door. Remember what I said in Chapter 3: Visual stories are everywhere. Whether stills or video, it's all about how you see things. There's no excuse for boredom or burn-out. Open your eyes and glom the thrills.

Possessed by the "spirit of place," the following precredit script began to write itself.

EXT. ZOOM STREET - NIGHT

Light from a street lamp casts a spidery shadow against a stucco wall.

We see a man's shoes as he climbs the stairway.

CLOSE-UP: On a door's speakeasy grill. A hand MOVES INTO FRAME and KNOCKS three times. The grill CREAKS open.

CLOSE ON EYES peering out.

VOICE FROM INSIDE: Whadaya want?

VISITOR: Frankie Sullivan, I'm here to see Lou.

VOICE FROM INSIDE: Which Lou would that be? We got five guys named Lou.

VISITOR: Lou Casarino.

VOICE FROM INSIDE: Spell it.

VISITOR (sighing): ..."C" as in caper..."A" as in assassin..."S" as in shaddup..."A"...aggravated assault..."R" for ricochet....."I"... iced..."N" your worst nightmare...*open the door before I blow your brains out.*

LONG SHOT FROM ACROSS THE STREET

Door opens, illuminating the figure on the landing.

SHOT of streetlamp. A CAT darts across the courtyard.

We HEAR three gunshots.

CLOSE on bottom of the stairs as a dead man's hand slides into view, clutching a blood-stained Webster's dictionary.

ROLL OPENING CREDITS

Now I had some credits to shoot. All I needed now was the rest of the screenplay, actors, props, and financing. No sweat.

Okay, so writing a screenplay ain't tiddlywinks—it's more like hitting yourself in the head with a blunt instrument. But I was able to knock out this killer ending. *(Note: "O.S." stands for OFF SCREEN and is interchangeable with "O.C." / OFF CAMERA), meaning a character is blabbing, or something happens, out of the camera's view.)*

EXT. DESERTED PIER - NIGHT - FOG

CLOSE on tip of a lit cigarette. It GLOWS. A stream of smoke swirls into the fog.

We pull back to reveal a FEMME FATALE in a trench coat, standing under a street lamp, smoking.

We HEAR the sound of heavy footsteps approaching.

MALE VOICE (O.S.): Come here often?

FEMME FATALE: Yeah, when I'm lookin' to meet creeps.

MALE VOICE (O.S.): Don't worry, miss, I'm here on business. That a cigarette you're smokin?

FEMME FATALE: Good eyes for a creep.

MALE VOICE (O.S.): Smokin' happens to be a felony in this state.

FEMME FATALE: (pulling a gun from her pocket; smiles) What about murder?

She FIRES two shots. We HEAR a groan and the sound of a body falling to the ground.

She takes a long drag of the cigarette, calmly slips the gun back into her pocket, turns, and walks off into the fog.

FADE OUT.

Nice tight scene. Alas, I had to cut my favorite descriptive line (*The fog was so thick you could cut it with a knife.*) to keep the pace up. As Zenny Bruce always says, "If you wanna make art, you gotta make sacrifices."

Believe it or not, these scenes (and others) are currently in production. By the time this book hits the shelves (which I guess is now if you're reading this), clips will be available for viewing on the THRILL website. Visit **www.zoom-street.org/thrill** and click on the Cinema link.

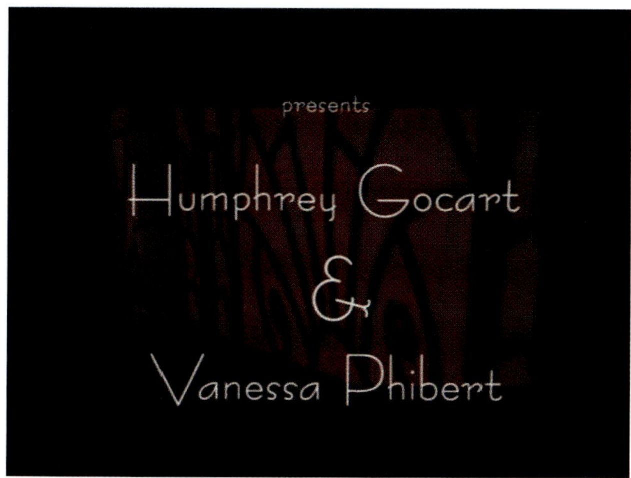

Gocart and Philbert together again! (A big screen typo.)

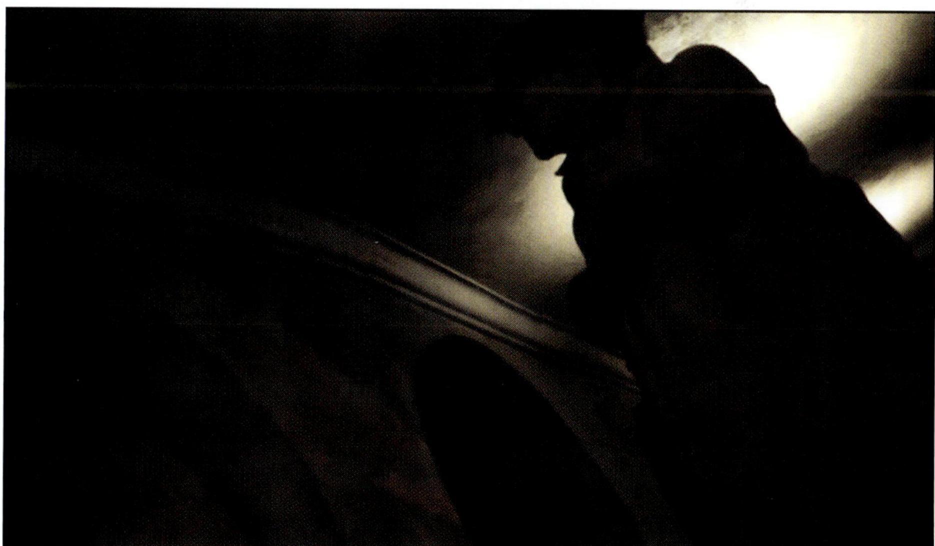

This memorable stalking scene from *Shoot to Thrill* was shot with a Nikon D90.

A DV THRILL

If you're thinking about branching out and adding video to your arsenal, a smart investment worth considering is a workstation. It'll not only save you time (and lettuce) when working with DV, but also in your day-to-day digital darkroom chores. I recently got hold of an **HP Z800** personal workstation, and I'm mad as hell

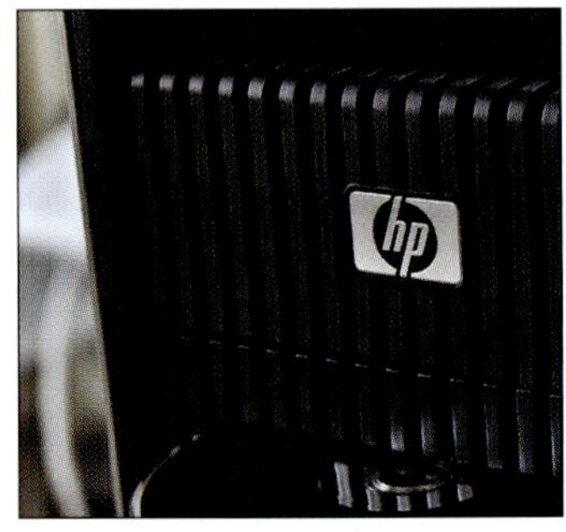

I didn't have it when I started working on this book. I'm guessing it might've shaved off a third of my hours spent processing photos.

This monster is fast. A peek at a few of the specs was enough to blow my hat into the ceiling fan. Dual Intel Xeon 3.2GHz processors, 12GB of RAM, NVIDIA Quadro FX3800 1.5GB PCIe graphics card, 1TB SATA 3GBps 7200 (Vista 64-bit OS)...on and on. If that ain't music to your ears, how about this: Working in Photoshop becomes an out-of-body experience.

I was able to open multiple CMYK images for this book (totaling a Gigabyte in size) *and work with them!* Sluggish filters suddenly rendered results in a blink. And, oh yeah, I had other apps open, too, such as Adobe Bridge and Lightroom.

I'll have more to say about how this monster handles Adobe's video software on Zoom Street.

THE HAPPY ENDING

In case you never noticed, technology books don't have endings. Not in the usual way, like a detective novel or a Hollywood movie with the words "The End" emblazoned on the silver screen. No, tech books just come to a screeching halt. One minute the author is there, the next minute he's gone. No good-byes, nothin'. The reader gets whiplash from a head-on collision with the index. BANG. Yeah, every technology book has an index. They just don't have an ending.

Here I am, a private dick in a rumpled suit and dusty fedora, lost in a fog from the 1940s. Self-employed and out of work. A loner. A flatfooted sap stumbling around the 21st century, wisecracking my way through a forest of pulp. Callin' a dame a dame, gettin' slapped but don't know why. Maybe times have changed and nobody told me.

But here's the irony. When I started out shootin', the industry was all about *specialization*. If you wanted to make a buck as a shutterbug you had to specialize. Be a food photographer, a sports photographer, a fashion photographer, a news photographer, whatever. But *specialize*. If, like me, you did a little of this and a little of that…you were dead in the water. And that's the way it's been, right up until recently, when the economy took a nose dive and the markets for photography started disappearing.

Overnight it's flipped around, and the buzzword is "diversification," as in diversify and do it all. Clients want the jack-of-all trades now, the guys and dolls who can shoot stills as well as videos—fashion one minute, architecture the next. Gotta be flexible and turn on a dime. So, by sheer accident, I find myself positioned just right for the future. I never specialized 'cause I loved snappin' all kinds of photos. Never wanted to hitch my wagon to just one.

The good old days are gone for good, and what's so bad about that? A new world needs new visions.

As for me…

If noir makes a comeback, I'm ready.

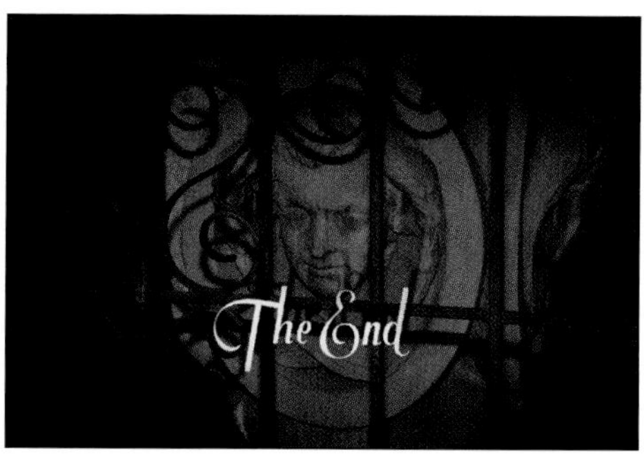

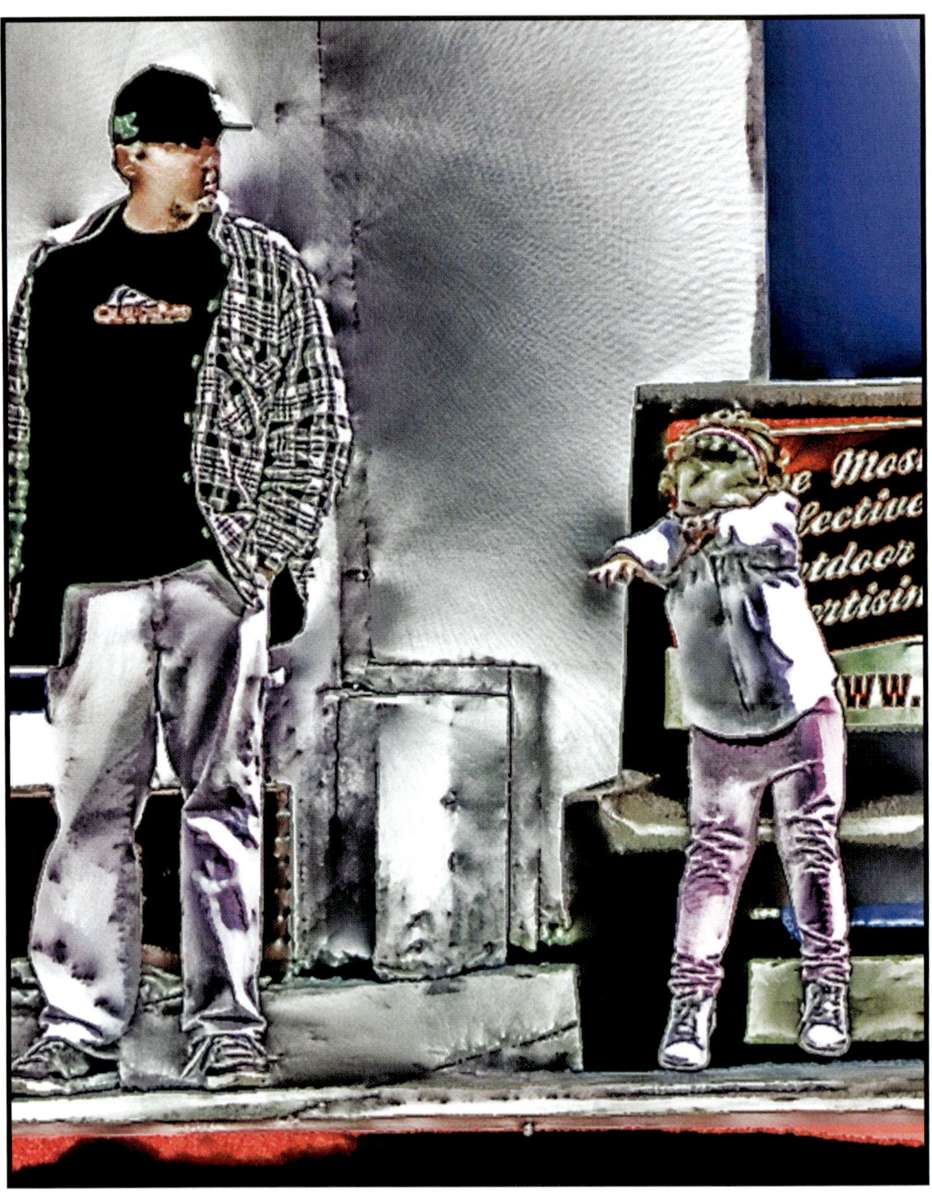

World Wide What?

A
HOT LINKS, COOL LEADS

"Anything I can do for you?"
*"Any number of things, but unfortunately
I'm here on business."*
—The Web (1947)

Here are links to sites where you can track down the hard-boiled gear I use that's mentioned in this book. Hardware, software, actions, and plug-ins. You'll also find valuable photography-related sites that I visit regularly. There's a world of free advice, tutorials, and inspiration here, so don't be a sap—start surfin'. You can also spare yourself the typing and drop by Zoom Street after hours. All these URLs (and more) are just a hop, skip, and a click away: **www.zoomstreet.org/thrill/links**.

CAMERAS/COMPUTERS/BACKUP/ PORTABLE DRIVES / PRINTERS

Nikon. The maker of great cams and glass, natch
www.nikonusa.com

HP Z800. The heavyweight champ of workstations
www.hp.com

Epson. The best inkjets in the world, period (.)
www.epson.com

RTX400-QR. RAID drive for ultimate backups
www.wiebetech.com

Western Digital. Backup drives in all shapes and sizes
www.westerndigital.com

FreeAgent Go Drive. Easily sync between laptop and PC
shop.seagate.com

MEMORY CARDS

Kingston. This king rules
www.kingston.com

SanDisk. I count on them, too
www.sandisk.com

Lexar. Ditto
www.lexar.com

TRIPODS / MONOPODS / GORILLAS

Manfrotto. Best pro pods
www.bogenimaging.com

Miller. Best tripods for DV
www.millertripods.com

Monostat RS16. Best monopod, period
www.monostat.com

Gorillapod. Attach your camera to anything
joby.com/products/gorillapod

LIGHTS / LIGHTING ACCESSORIES

Photoflex. Great lighting equipment, great prices
www.photoflex.com

Calumet. Affordable strobes and more
www.calumetphoto.com

Smith-Victor. Great lights for the pro studio
www.smithvictor.com

Honl Photo. Shapers for your speedlight
www.honlphoto.com

Ray Flash. Ring flash on the cheap
www.expoimaging.net

Tronix Explorer XT. Portable power for strobes
www.innovatronix.com

CAMERA BAGS AND STRAPS

Tenba. My favorite camera bags
www.tenba.com

Domke. My weathered video bag
www.tiffen.com

Lowepro. Great pro bags and cases
www.lowepro.com

Crumpler. Unique bags with weird names
www.crumplerbags.com

OtterBox. Indestructible cases...dare you to try
www.otterbox.com

Black Rapid. Quick-draw your D-SLR—*bang!*
www.blackrapid.com

UPstrap. Killer no-slip camera strap
www.upstrap-pro.com

ACCESSORIES

Tiffen Filters. No, not software, real glass!
www.tiffen.com

LEE Filters. More fine glass filters
www.leefilters.com

Atlas Gloves. Great gloves, long URL
www.atlasglovesconsumerproducts.com

Lally CAP. White balance with a hat!
www.lallyphotography.com/store

Opteka. Psst—getcher high-definition spy lens here
www.opteka.com

Princeton Tec. Illuminated headgear and lights
www.princetontec.com

C. Crane & Company. Get a battery checker here and more
www.ccrane.com

Koh. Industrial-strength camera cleaners
www.kohglobal.com

Magellan's Travel Supplies. Everything! I hang here.
www.magellans.com

Leatherman. Cool multi-tools and knives
www.leatherman.com

FRAMES / INKJET PAPERS

Kodak EasyShare W1020. Best digital frame
www.kodak.com

Umbra. Cool, unusual designer frames
www.umbra.com

Mpix Gallery Wraps. Large, custom 3D framing
www.mpix.com/Product.aspx/gallerywraps

Hahnemuehle Gallerie Wrap Corner Kit. D.I.Y. wraps
www.hahnemuehle.com/site/en/1909/gallerie-wraps.html

ImageWizards AluminArte. Amazing HD images on aluminum
www.imagewizards.net

Hahnemuehle. Exquisite exhibition inkjet papers
www.hahnemuehle.com

Canson. Fine art photography inkjet papers
www.canson-us.com/

HARD-BOILED SOFTWARE

Adobe. Photoshop, Lightroom, CS4, and more!
www.adobe.com

Portrait Professional. Facial retouching magic
wwww.portraitprofessional.com

Nik Software Complete Collection. Dfine, Viveza, Color Efex Pro, Silver Efex, Sharpener Pro. Plug-in stars all.
www.niksoftware.com

Genuine Fractals. Upscale photos with no distortion
www.ononesoftware.com

PhotoFrame. Digital frames galore
www.ononesoftware.com

Photo/Graphic Edges. More cutting-edge frames
www.autofx.com

Noiseware Pofessional. Kill the noise!
www.imagenomic.com/

Noise Ninja. Another great noise buster
www.picturecode.com

Lucis Pro. The star for HDR
www.lucispro.com

Mister Retro. Grunge-o-rama!
www.misterretro.com

Fractalius. Turn photos into strange art
www.redfieldplugins.com

Alien Skin. Weird wonder-plugs and effects
www.alienskin.com

Tiffen Dfx. Preset filters that mimic glass
www.tiffen.com

Panos FX. Best Photoshop actions on the planet
www.panosfx.com

SlideShowPro. Cool pan and zoom effects for Lightroom
www.slideshowpro.net

INSPIRATION

Diana Scheunemann
www.dianascheunemann.com

Ellen Von Unwerth
www.home.frognet.net/~mcfadden/evu/Ellen_
von_Unwerth.htm

Erwin Olaf
www.erwinolaf.com

James Christopher
www.moderncitizen.com/#/client/
template.ml?aaa=home&bbb=

Julie Blackmon
www.julieblackmon.com

Kim Joon
www.kimjoon.co.kr

Loretta Lux
www.lorettalux.de

Vincent Laforet
http://blog.vincentlaforet.com

Stephen Perry
www.stephenperry.com

Joe McNally
www.joemcnally.com

Steve Thornton
www.stevethornton.com

Mary Ellen Hendricks
www.maryellenhendricks.com

Ken Rockwell
www.kenrockwell.com

Miggs Burroughs
www.miggsb.com/mbpages/lenticular.html

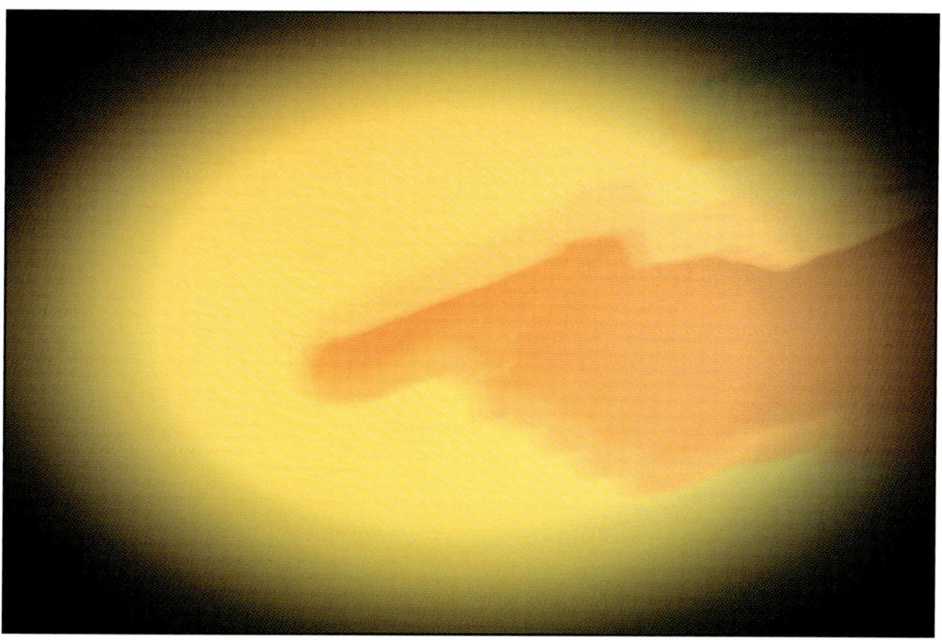

This Squirt Gun For Hire (2009). Photo by Derek Pell.

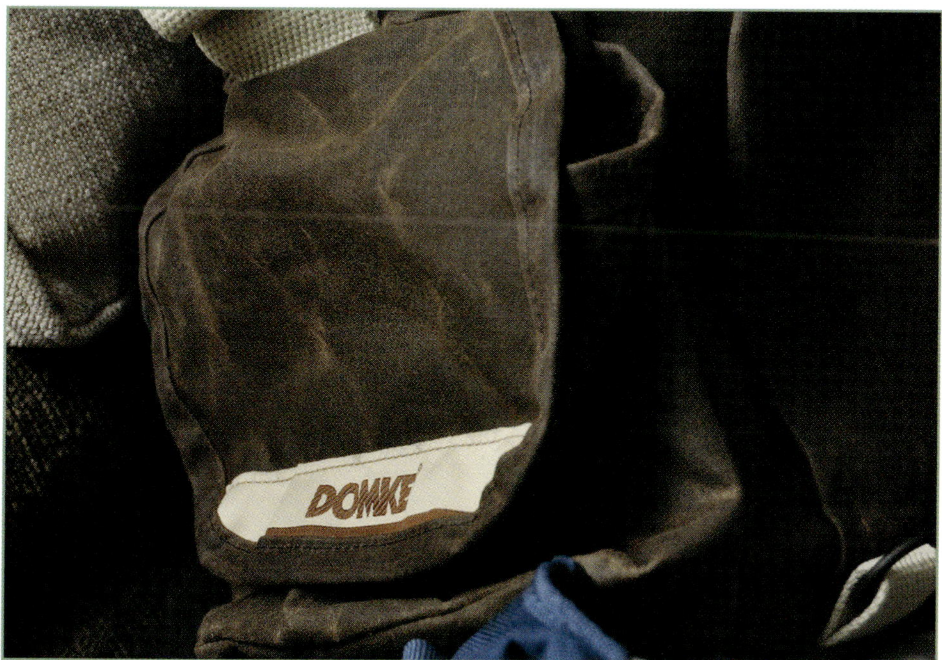

Author's hard-boiled video bag.

ONLINE PUBS, BLOGS, AND REFERENCE

Aperture
www.aperture.org

PDN
www.pdnonline.com

PHOTO
www.photo.fr

Shutterbug
www.shutterbug.com

Zoom Street
www.zoomstreet.org

Digital Photo Pro
www.digitalphotopro.com

The Strobist
www.strobist.blogspot.com

Digital Outback Photo
www.outbackphoto.com

Lens Culture
www.lensculture.com

Nikon Rumors
www.nikonrumors.com

D-Town TV
www.dtowntv.com

Pixsylated
www.pixsylated.com

John Nack on Adobe
http://blogs.adobe.com/jnack

Joe McNally's Blog
www.joemcnally.com/blog

Lightroom Killer Tips
www.lightroomkillertips.com

Shorpy
www.shorpy.com

Pinhole Pips

www.pinholepip.com

Road to Dreamland (nudes)

blog.voissa.com/bodyspirit

Trend de la creme

www.trenddelacreme.com

Last but not least...my noirish lair:

The Editor's Blog

www.zoomstreet.wordpress.com

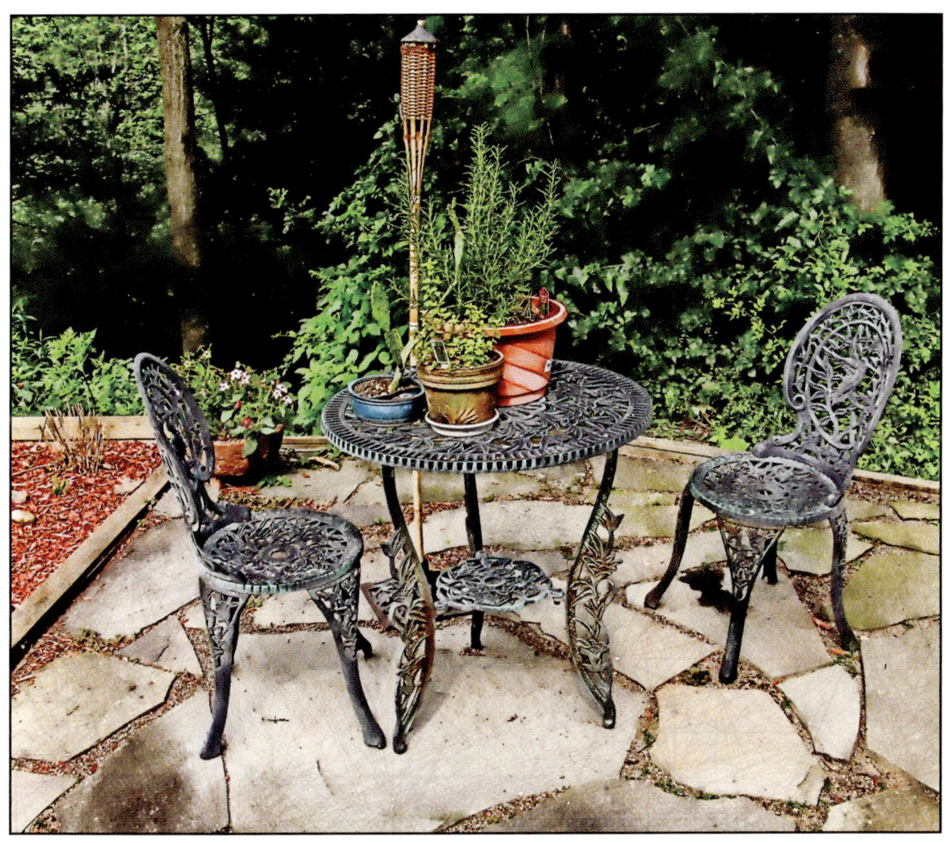

Gone Missing in Horseheads (for Linda, 2008). Photo by Derek Pell.

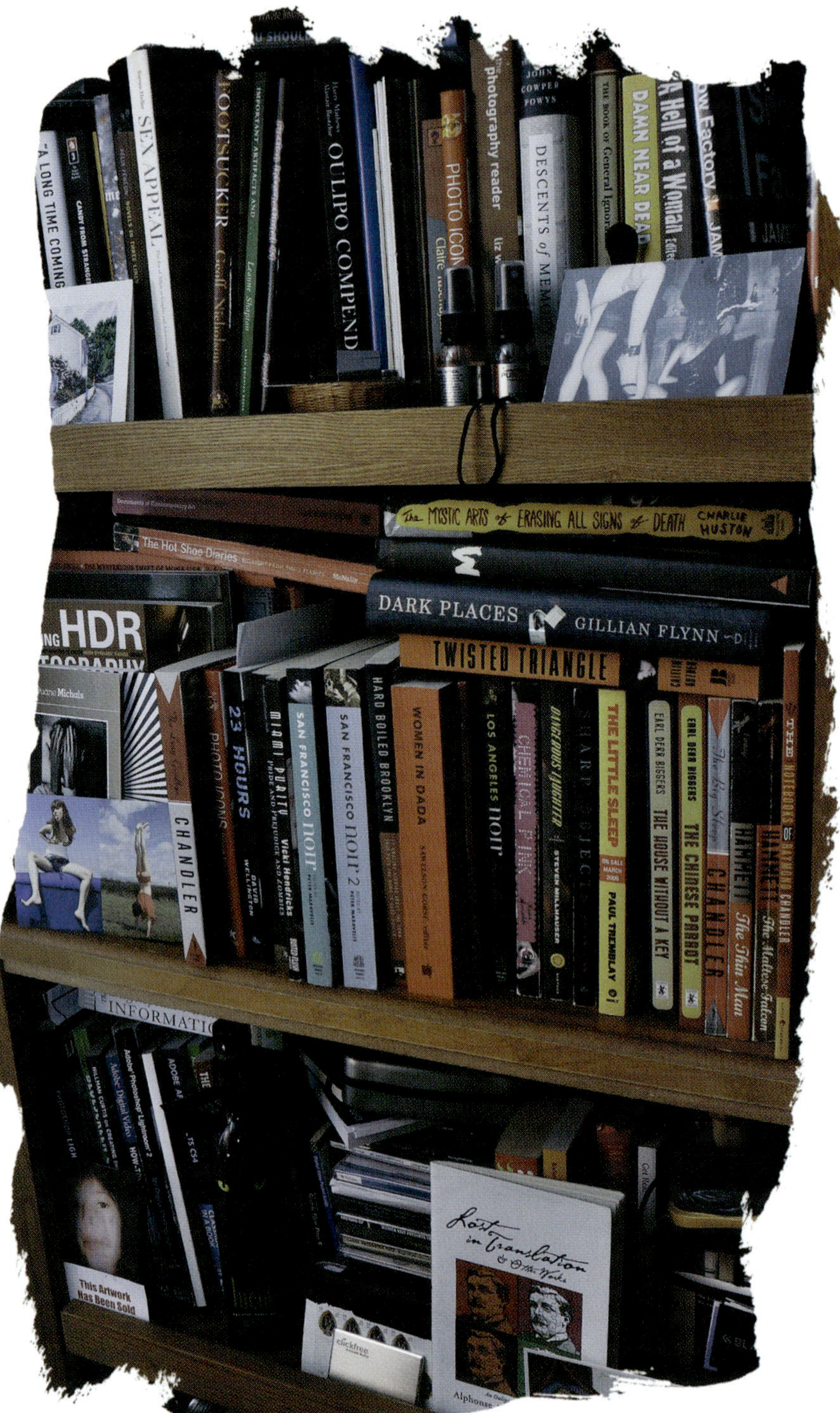

B
A HARD-BOILED LIBRARY

"Mind like parachute, only function when open."
—Charlie Chan

I've been collecting books for as long as I can remember. Someday I hope to read them all again. That would be like living forever, and we all know how long that is.

I've bought, lent, borrowed, and stolen books. Sold them to stay alive, and then bought 'em back again. I've traded books, written books, published books, and donated 'em. I've lost 'em. I've slept with 'em. I've dreamed of books that never existed and invented others that should have (like my coin-operated novel). I've sculpted 'em and painted 'em. I've made objects out of books and books out of objects. I've collaged and massaged 'em. Fetishized 'em. Worshipped 'em. I've driven spikes through their spines and bled on 'em. I've sniffed 'em, kissed 'em, cursed 'em, too. I've signed 'em, inscribed 'em, annotated 'em. I've missed some and mourned others. They are all flesh to me. This list focuses on photography: how-to, art photography, criticism, and reference. And some books that fuel my passion for noir.

Despite hard times, publishers are still presenting work by talented shutterbugs—classic names and newcomers. It ain't just museums and big houses like Abrams, Rizzoli, Phaidon, and Taschen that are stoking the visual fire, either. Investigate small independent publishers like Twin Palms, Aperture, Nazraeli, FOIL, Steidl, Radius, Hatje Cantz, and powerHouse Books. The greatest source for photography books on the planet is D.A.P. (Distributed Art Publishers, Inc.). They have everything. Download the D.A.P. catalog for a blast of inspiration: **www.artbook.com**.

You'll find "live" links to all the books listed here at **www.zoomstreet.org/thrill/library**.

NUTS 'N BOLTS

The Nikon Creative Lighting System
Mike Hagen
(Rocky Nook)

Nikon D90
Magic Lantern Guides
Simon Stafford
(Lark Books)

Mastering HDR Photography
Michael Freeman
(Amphoto Books)

Practical HDRI
Jack Howard
(Rocky Nook)

The Moment It Clicks
Joe McNally
(New Riders)

The Adobe Photoshop Lightroom 2 Book for Digital Photographers
Scott Kelby
(New Riders)

Adobe Photoshop CS4 One-On-One
Deke McClelland
(O'Reilly)

Within the Frame
David duChemin
(New Riders)

Spirit of Place: The Art of the Traveling Photographer
Bob Krist
(Amphoto Books)

Light & Exposure for Digital Photographers
Harold Davis
(O'Reilly)

ART PHOTOGRAPHY/CRITICAL WORKS

The Photography Reader
Edited by Liz Wells
(Routledge)

Erwin Olaf
Erwin Olaf
(Aperture)

5 x 7
William Eggleston
(Twin Palms Publishers)

Duane Michals
Duane Michals
(Thames & Hudson)

Freedom in Flashes
Diana Scheunemann
Koepfli & Partners Limited

Domestic Vacations
Julie Blackmon
(Radius Books)

Nudes: The World's Top Photographers and the Stories Behind Their Greatest Images
Anthony LaSala
(RotoVision)

***Nude Photography:
The Art & the Craft***
Pascal Baetens
(DK Books)

L'amour Fou: Photography and Surrealism
Rosalind Krauss and Jane Livingston
(Abbeville Press)

The New Erotic Photography
Edited by Dian Hanson and Eric Kroll
(Taschen)

The Stamp of Fantasy:
The Visual Inventiveness of Photographic Postcards
Clement Cheroux and Ute Eskildsen
(Steidl)

NOIR REFERENCE

Dark City: The Lost World of Film Noir
Eddie Muller
(St. Martin's Griffin)

Encyclopedia of Film Noir
Edited by Geoff Mayer and Brian McDonnell
(Greenwood Press)

True Crime Detective Magazines 1924–1969
Eric Godtland
(Taschen)

The Notebooks of Raymond Chandler
Edited by Frank MacShane
(Harper)

The Long Embrace:
Raymond Chandler and the Woman He Loved
Judith Freeman
(Vintage)

Hard-Boiled: Great Lines from Classic Noir Films
Peggy Thompson and Saeko Usukawa
(Chronicle Books)

FICTION

The Maltese Falcon
Dashiell Hammett
(Vintage)

The Big Sleep
Raymond Chandler
(Vintage)

The Little Sleep
Paul Tremblay
(Holt)

The House Without a Key
Earl Derr Biggers
(Academy Chicago)

M: A Graphic Novel Based on the Film by Fritz Lang
Jon J. Muth
(Abrams)

The Mystic Arts of Erasing All Signs of Death
Charlie Huston
(Ballantine)

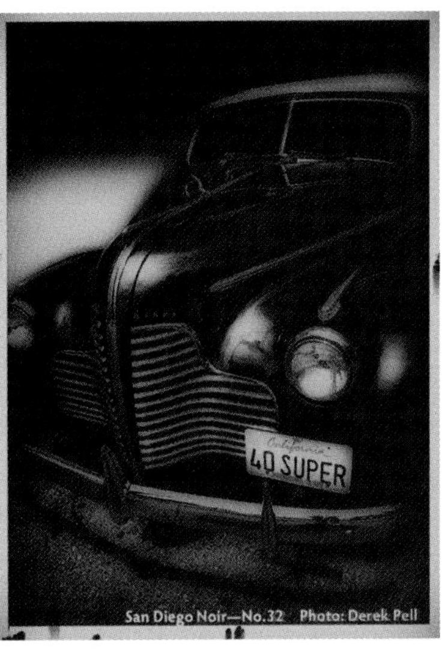

Criminal Paradise
Steven M. Thomas
(Ballantine Books)

Los Angeles Noir
Edited by Denise Hamilton
(Akashic Books)

San Francisco Noir
Edited by Peter Maravelis
(Akashic Books)

Hard-Boiled Brooklyn
Edited by Reed Farrel Coleman
(Bleak House Books)

A Hell of a Woman: An Anthology of Female Noir
Edited by Megan Abbott
(Busted Flush Press)

Damn Near Dead: An Anthology of Geezer Noir
Edited by Duane Swierczynski
(Busted Flush Press)

It's All Too Too Divine
Jim McMenamin
(Editions Le Scat Noir)

The Penultimate Truth
Philip K. Dick
(Vintage)

Miami Purity
Vicki Hendricks
(Busted Flush Press)

DV

Placing Shadows: Lighting Techniques for Video Production
Chuck Gloman and Tom Letourneau
(Focal Press)

Hillman Curtis on Creating Short Films for the Web
(New Riders)

Adobe Digital Video How-Tos
Jan Ozer
(Adobe Press)

Digital Video Pocket Guide
Derrick Story
(O'Reilly)

The DV Rebel's Guide
Stu Maschwitz
(Peachpit Press)

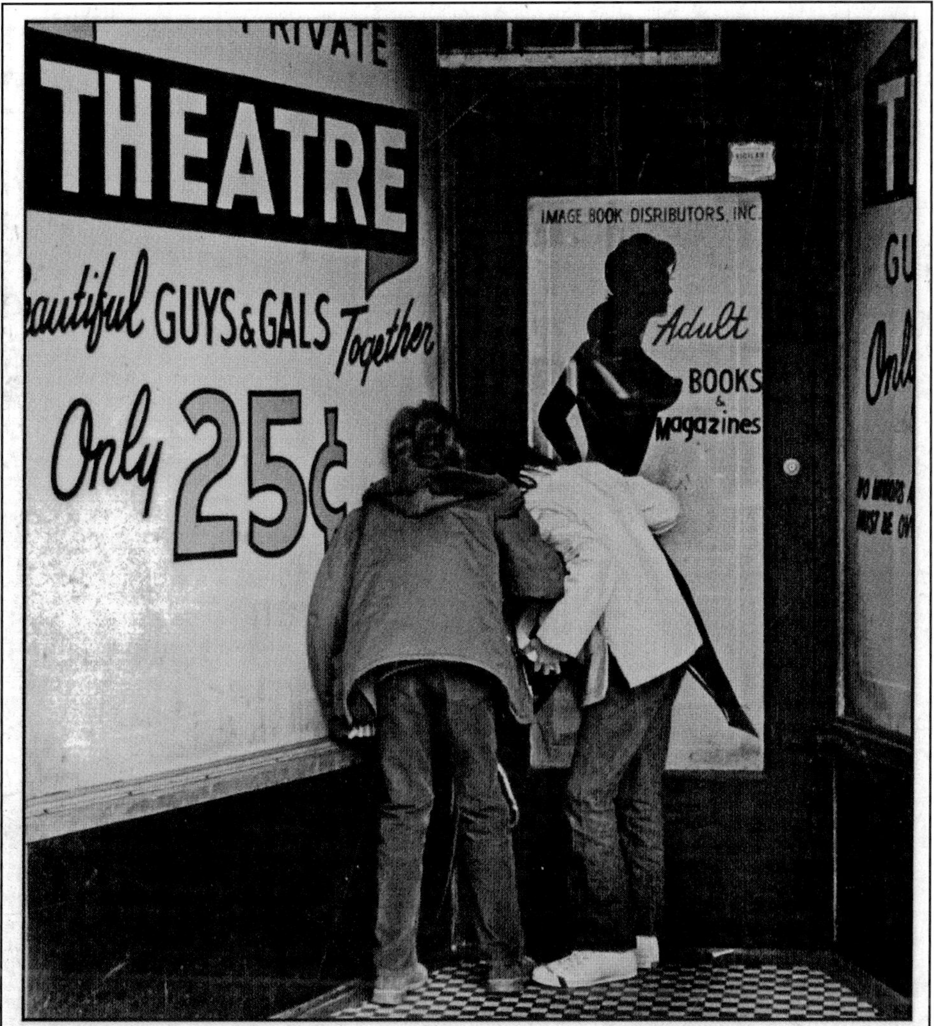

Photo by Derek Pell.

INDEX

3D Tracking, 122
370 Atlas Nitrile gloves, 28

A

acting (method) and photography, 50–53
action photography, 119–120
    3D Tracking, 122
    fast-focusing, 121
    flashes, 132
    freezing action, 133–134
    incremental movement, 135
    LCD auto preview function, turning off, 121
    looking for unique shots, 136–137
    parades, 122–124
    roller derby, 130–132
    skate parks, 125–129
    taking breaks during shooting, 136–137
Add Noise filter, 102
Adobe, 47
    Bridge
        assigning keywords to photos, 40–41
        Batch Rename window, 42–43
        Camera Raw feature, 46–47
        Comparison view, 44
        drag/drop operation, 46
        organizing photos, 35, 39
        renaming photos, 42
        reviewing thumbnails in, 39
        stacking thumbnails, 41
        web resources, 232
    InDesign CS4, 201
    Lightroom
        adding customized data to photos, 33
        Crop Overlay feature, 141
        custom presets, 38
        importing photos to, 37
        organizing photos, 35
        Postcard Viewer (Lightroom), 200–201
        Preview area, 33
        reviewing thumbnails in, 33
        web resources, 232
    Photoshop
        altering photos, 36
        Content-Aware Scale, 150–151
        Crop tool, 149
        Genuine Fractals plug-in, 210
        High Pass filter, 192–197
        Lucis Pro 6.0 (Image Content Technology), 174–181
        organizing photos, 35
        Rectangular Marquee tool, 150
        Unsharp Mask, 139–140, 152
        web resources, 232
Advanced Exposure Modes
    Aperture Priority, 77–81
    Manual exposure mode, 77, 83
    Shutter Priority, 77, 82–83
air blowers, 26, 232
altering photos, Photoshop (Adobe), 36
aluminum, printing photos on, 211
ambient light, 65, 90–92, 95–96, 105
American Photo magazine, shooting video, 216
A.N.G.E.L. acronym, 53
    Anomaly, 54–57
    Expression, 63–64
    Gesture, 58–62, 173
    Light, 65
    Nuance, 65
animation (Flash), Bridge (Adobe), 39
Anthropics in London, Portrait Professional Studio, 166–168
Aperture Priority, 77–81, 171
approach to photography, developing, 49–50
artifacts (noise), 68–70
    low ISO speeds, 172
    Noisewear interface, 156–157
Asphalt Jungle, The, 170
audio recorders, 218

auto backup DVDs, 34
auto preview function (LCD), turning off, 121

B

backpacks, 23
backups, 31
    auto backup DVDs, 34
    cameras, 18
    DVDs, 33
    Epson P-4000 Multimedia Storage View, 33
    eXtreme portable backup drives (Nexto), 32–33
    FreeAgent (Seagate), 33
    memory cards, 33
    multiple backups, importance of, 32–34
    web resources, 229
Bambeasels (Umbra), 209
Batch Rename window (Bridge), 42, 43
batteries
    Battery Caddy, 19
    Battery Checker, 19
    battery packs, 19
    D-SLR usage, 18
Big Combo, The, 67
Big Sleep, The, 15, 89
Blair, Linda, 63
Bleach Bypass, 182–191
blemishes, removing (portrait photography), 165–168
blogs, web resources, 236
Born to Kill, 6
bracketing (exposures), 84–85
Bridge (Adobe)
    assigning keywords to photos, 40–41
    Batch Rename window, 42–43
    Camera Raw feature (Bridge), 46–47
    Comparison view, 44
    drag/drop operation, 46
    organizing photos, 35, 39
    renaming photos, 42
    reviewing thumbnails in, 39
    stacking thumbnails, 41
    web resources, 232
brushtstroke frames, 206
Burroughs, Miggs, 169
burst mode, 119–120

C

C. Crane Company, Battery Checker, 19
camera bags
    backpacks, 23
    ProDigital Messenger Satchel, 23
    Shootout Medium Shoulder Bag, 22–23
    web resources, 231
Camera Raw feature (Bridge), 46–47
canvas, printing photos on, 210
Carey, Hugh, 61
caution tape, 27
Center-Weighted metering, 76
Chandler, Raymond, 139
chizzling (light-shaping), 106
Churchill, Winston, 58
cleaning kits
    air blowers, 26
    web resources, 232
clip limits (video), 218
CLS (Creative Lighting Systems), 24–25
color correction, 191
    Dfx (Tiffen), 182–183
    Viveza (Nik Software), 184–190
Color Efex Pro (Nik Software), 168
color shifts, ISO speeds, 69
Comparison view (Bridge), 44
Content-Aware Scale (Photoshop), 150–151
Continuous mode, 120
Crawdaddy magazine, 8, 12–13
creativity, developing, 49–50
credits (video), 222–224
cropping, 140, 142–145, 171
    Crop Overlay feature (Lightroom), 141
    extending photos, 148–150
    extreme cropping, 146–147
    portrait-oriented photos, 150
custom presets, Lightroom (Adobe), 38

D

D-90 (Nikon), 17
    3D Tracking, 122
    Continuous mode, 120
    EV (Exposure Compensation), 86
    metering patterns, 75
    pop-up flashes, 111
    shooting video, 218–220
    Shutter Priority, 82
D-300 (Nikon), Continuous mode, 120
darkness, noir lighting, 96
Daylight White Balance setting, 74
Dean, John, 8, 59
Dean, Maureen (Mo), 59
designer frames, 208–209
details, enhancing, 171–173
    Bleach Bypass, 182–191
    Dfx (Tiffen), 182–183
    Differential Hysteresis Processing, 174
    HDRI, 174–181
    High Pass filter (Photoshop), 192–197
    Lucis Pro 6.0 (Image Content Technology), 174–181
    Viveza (Nik Software), 184–190
Dfx (Tiffen), 182–183
Differential Hysteresis Processing, 174
digital frames, 90, 209–210, 232
Digital Photo Pro magazine, shooting video, 216
digital photos, noise (artifacts), 68–70
doctoring photos, Photoshop (Adobe), 36
DOF (depth of field)
    Aperture Priority, 78
    Shutter Priority, 83
drag/drop operation, Bridge (Adobe), 46
D-SLR (Nikon), 16–17
    battery usage, 18
    bracketing, 85
    hybrid D-SLR, shooting video, 218
    metering patterns, 75
    white balance, 71
Durrell, Lawrence, 89

dust particles, removing
    air blowers, 26
    web resources, 232
Dutch angles, 91, 105
DV (digital video), 219
DVDs
    auto backup DVDs, 34
    backups, 33

E

Edirol audio recorders, 218
editing photos, 169
    Color Efex Pro (Nik Software), 168
    cropping, 140, 142–145, 171
        Crop Overlay feature (Lightroom), 141
        extending photos, 148–150
        extreme cropping, 146–147
    ethics and, 160–162
    HDR (High Dynamic Range), 160–162
    noise (artifacts), Noisewear interface, 156–157
    photomontages, 162–164
    portrait-oriented photos, 150
    sharpness, Sharpener Pro (Nik Software), 152–155
effects software, web resources, 233
Ehrlichman, John, 63
electrician's (gaffer's) tape, 26
enhancing details, 171–173
    Bleach Bypass, 182–191
    Dfx (Tiffen), 182–183
    Differential Hysteresis Processing, 174
    HDRI, 174–181
    High Pass filter (Photoshop), 192–197
    Lucis Pro 6.0 (Image Content Technology), 174–181
    Viveza (Nik Software), 184–190
Epson
    P-4000 Multimedia Storage Viewer, 33
    Stylus Photo R228 printers, 212–213
    web resources, 229
Estes, Richard, 174
ethics and edited photos, 157–159
EV (Exposure Compensation), 86

Exorcist, The, 63
Explorer XT powerpacks (Tronix), 116
exposure
    Advanced Exposure Modes
        Aperture Priority, 77–81, 171
        Manual exposure mode, 77, 83
        Shutter Priority, 77, 82–83, 171
    bracketing, 84–85
    EV (Exposure Compensation), 86
    Programmed-Auto exposure mode, 84
    underexposure, 86–87
Expression (A.N.G.E.L. acronym), 63–64
extending photos by cropping, 148–150

F

Farewell My Lovely, 139
fast-focusing, 121
feel of a camera, adjusting to, 16
film speeds, changing
    color shifts, 69
    ISO speeds, 68
    lighting, 96
    noise (artifacts), 68–70
filters
    Add Noise filter, 102
    High Pass filter (Photoshop), 192–197
    Midnight Blue filter (Color Efex Pro), 168
    noise (artifacts), 69
    UV (ultraviolet) filters, 18
    Vignette Blur filter (Color Efex Pro), 168
    web resources, 231
flags (gobos), 106–107
Flash animation
    Bridge (Adobe), 39
    sharing photos, 201
flashes
    action photography, 132
    CLS (Creative Lighting Systems), 25
    Hobby, David, 25
    pop-up flashes, 111
    portable drives, 97–102
    ring flashes, 108–110
    small flashes, 25
    Speedlights, 25, 99–101, 105
    web resources, 230–231
Flashes, CLS (Creative Lighting Systems), 24
Flashlight FL110K Kit (Smith-Victor), 115
flashlights, Serac S2 LED Flashlight
    (Leatherman), 27
flickr, 200
Flow-Mo (incremental movement), 135
focusing, fast-focusing, 121
footwear, Slip-Ons (Magellan), 29
formatting, memory cards, 21, 34
fps (frames per second), 219
framing photos, 202
    brushstroke frames, 206
    designer frames, 208
    digital frames, 90, 209–210
    Gallery Wraps, 210
    montages, 206
    Photo/Graphic Edges Platinum Edition,
      203–204
    stock frames, 207
    storyboard frames, 205
    web resources, 232
FreeAgent (Seagate), 33, 229
freezing action (action photography), 133
Fulton, George, 174

G

gaffer's (electrician's) tape, 26
Galella, Ron, 54
Gallery Wraps, 210
gear bags
    backpacks, 23
    ProDigital Messenger Satchel, 23
    Shootout Medium Shoulder Bag, 22–23
    web resources, 231
Genuine Fractals plug-in, 210
Gesture (A.N.G.E.L. acronym), 58–62, 173
glamour photography, 165–168
gloves
    370 Atlas Nitrile gloves, 28
    web resources, 231
gobos (flags), 106–107
grids (light-shaping tools), 106–107

H

HD2 High Definition Conversion Lenses
(Opteka), 28
HDR (High Dynamic Range), 157–159
HDRI, 174–181
headlamps
Matrix 2 headlamps (Princeton Tec), 28
web resources, 232
Henry, Ron, RapidStrap shoulder straps, 20
Henry Miller on Writing, 50
HEPA Jet Air Blower (Koh), 26
High Pass filter (Photoshop), 192–197
Hilton, Paris, 60
Hitchcock, Alfred, 55
Hobby, David, 25
Honl
Speed Grids, 106–107
Speed Snoots, 107
Hopper, Edward, noir lighting, 95
HP Z800 (Hewlett Packard)
editing video, 226
web resources, 229

I

I Cover the Waterfront, 13
Image Content Technology, Lucis Pro 6.0,
174
imagination, developing, 49–50
imagining lighting, 93–94
Impact, 119
importing photos, Lightroom (Adobe), 37
incremental movement, capturing, 135
InDesign CS4 (Adobe), 201
inkjet printers
Epson Stylus Photo R228 printers,
212–213
paper, web resources, 232
inspirational websites, 234–235
Invasion of the Body Snatchers, 6
ISO speeds, changing
color shifts, 69
lighting, 96
noise (artifacts), 68–70, 172

J

Jolson, Al, 49

K

Kelby, Scott, 150
Key Largo, 31
keywords, assigning to photos, 40–41
Kingston
SDHC (memory) cards, 20
web resources, 230
Koch, Ed, 61
Koh HEPA Jet Air Blower, 26

L

landscape-oriented photos, creating by
cropping, 148–150
Laudy, Roger, printing photos on aluminum,
211
LCD auto preview function, turning off, 121
Leatherman, Serac S2 LED Flashlight, 27
Lennon, John, 12
lenses
Opteka HD2 High Definition Conversion
Lenses, 28
UV (ultraviolet) filters, 18
zoom lenses, 17
Lesko, Louis, shooting video, 216
Lewis, Martin, Watergate, 13
Lexar, web resources, 230
libraries, developing, 239–244
Light (A.N.G.E.L. acronym), 65
lighting
ambient light, 65, 90–92, 95–96, 105
flashes
CLS (Creative Lighting Systems), 24–25
pop-up flashes, 111
portable flashes, 97–102
ring flashes, 108–110
small flashes, 25
Speedlights, 25, 99–101, 105
flashlights, 27
headlamps, 28
Hobby, David, 25
imagining lighting, 93–94

improvising, 96
ISO speeds, changing, 96
light-shaping tools, 106–107
metering patterns, 75
natural lighting, 92
noir lighting, 91–92, 95–96
reflectors, 102–105
studio strobes, 112–116
web resources, 230–231
white balance, 96
Lightroom (Adobe)
Crop Overlay feature, 141
custom presets, 38
customized data, adding to photos, 33
importing photos to, 37
organizing photos, 35
Postcard Viewer, 200–201
Preview area, 33
thumbnails, reviewing, 33
web resources, 232
Lite Panel Kit (Photoflex), 103
Lucis Pro 6.0 (Image Content Technology), 174–181

M

Mailer, Norman, 12, 60
Maltese Falcon, The, 104–105
Manual exposure mode, 77, 83
manuals, reading, 67
Matrix 2 headlamps (Princeton Tec), 28
Matrix metering, 75
Matthews, Chris, 63
McNamee, Wally, Watergate, 8
memory cards, 20
backups, 33
formatting, 21, 34
web resources, 230
metering patterns
Center-Weighted metering, 76
Matrix metering, 75
Spot metering, 76
method acting and photography, 50–53
Midnight Blue filter (Color Efex Pro), 168
Miller, Henry, 50

Miller, Max, 13
mirror angle scopes, 28, 231
Mitchell, John, 6–7, 11–13
Mitchell, Martha, 6
monopods, 24, 230
montages, 162–164, 206
motivations, finding, 53
movement, capturing, 119–120
3D Tracking, 122
fast-focusing, 121
flashes, 132
freezing action, 133–134
incremental movement, 135
LCD auto preview function, turning off, 121
looking for unique shots, 136–137
parades, 122–124
roller derby, 130–132
skate parks, 125–129
taking breaks during shooting, 136–137
Multidisk Kit (Photoflex), 103
multiple backups, importance of, 32–34

N

Nanucci, 12
natural lighting, 92
New York Times, The, 8
Newsweek magazine, 8
Nexto eXtreme portable backup drives, 32–33
Nighthawks at the Diner, 95
Nik Software
Color Efex Pro, 168
Sharpener Pro, 152–155
Viveza, 184–190
Nikon
CLS (Creative Lighting Systems), 24, 25
Continuous mode, 120
D-90, 17
3D Tracking, 122
Continuous mode, 120
EV (Exposure Compensation), 86
pop-up flashes, 111

shooting video, 218, 220
    Shutter Priority, 82
  D300, Continuous mode, 120
  D-SLR, 16
    bracketing, 85
    hybrid D-SLR, 218
    shooting video, 218
    white balance, 71
  SB-900 Speedlight, 25, 99–101, 105
  web resources, 229
  zoom lenses, 17
Nixon, Pres. Richard M., 6, 7
noir lighting, 91–92, 95–96
noise (artifacts), 68–70
  low ISO speeds, 172
  Noisewear interface, 156–157
Nuance (A.N.G.E.L. acronym), 65

O

O'Keeffe, Georgia, 53
Onassis, Jackie, 54
online publications, web resources, 232
Opteka HD2 High Definition Conversion Lenses, 28
organizing photos
  Bridge (Adobe), 35, 39
  Lightroom (Adobe), 35
  Photoshop (Adobe), 35

P

P-4000 Multimedia Storage Viewer (Epson), 33
PackSeat stools, 27
pan shots (video), 220–221
parades (action photography), 122–124
PCs, formatting memory cards, 21
people, photographing, 165–168
Photoflex
  Lite Panel Kit, 103
  Multidisk Kit, 103
  reflectors, 102–103
Photo/Graphic Edges Platinum Edition, framing photos, 203–204

photomontages, 162–164
Photoshop (Adobe)
  altering photos, 36
  Content-Aware Scale, 150–151
  Crop tool, 149
  Genuine Fractals plug-in, 210
  High Pass filter, 192–197
  Lucis Pro 6.0 (Image Content Technology), 174–181
  organizing photos, 35
  Rectangular Marquee tool, 150
  Unsharp Mask, 139–140, 152
  web resources, 232
Plan 9 From Outer Space, 26
Plan 9B From Outer Space, 63
pocket flashlights, 27
political rallies, 61–62
pop-up flashes, 111
portable drives, web resources, 229
portable flashes, 97–102
portrait photography, 165–168
portrait-oriented photos, creating by cropping, 150
Postcard Viewer (Lightroom), 200–201
power supplies
  batteries
    Battery Caddy, 19
    Battery Checker, 19
    battery packs, 19
    D-SLR usage, 18
  Explorer XT powerpacks (Tronix), 116
presets (custom), Lightroom (Adobe), 38
Preview area (Adobe Lightroom), 33
Princeton Tec, Matrix 2 headlamps, 28
printing photos
  aluminum, 211
  canvas, 210
  Epson Stylus Photo R228 printers, 212–213
  web resources, 229
ProDigital Messenger Satchel, 23
Programmed-Auto exposure mode, 84
Psycho, 55

R

rallies (political), 61–62
RapidStrap shoulder straps, 20
RAW format, shooting in
High Pass filter (Photoshop), 192–197
white balance, 72–73
Ray Flash: The Ring Flash Adapter, 108–110
recording audio, 218
Rectangular Marquee tool (Photoshop), 150
reference websites, 236
reflectors, 102–105
renaming photos, Bridge (Adobe), 42
Rice, Condoleezza, 63
ring flashes, 108
roller derbies (action photography), 130–132
roping off areas, 27
Rubens, Peter Paul, 165

S

San Diego Noir, 51
SanDisk, web resources, 230
SB-900 Speedlight, 99–101, 105
scopes (mirror angle), 28
SDHC (memory) cards, 20
backups, 33
formatting, 21, 34
web resources, 230
Seagate FreeAgent, 33
secondary (backup) cameras, 18
Serac S2 LED Flashlight (Leatherman), 27
shadows, noir lighting, 91–92, 95
sharing photos
Flash animation, 201
flickr, 200
Postcard Viewer (Lightroom), 200
Shutterfly, 200
sharpness, Sharpener Pro (Nik Software), 152–155
shoes, Slip-Ons (Magellan), 29
Shootout Medium Shoulder Bag, 22–23
shoulder straps
RapidStrap, 20
UpStrap, 19–20
web resources, 231

Shriver, Maria, 64
Shutter Priority, 77, 82–83, 171
Shutterfly, 200
skate parks (action photography), 125–129
Slip-Ons (Magellan), 29
Smith-Victor Flashlight FL110K Kit, 115
snoots (light-shaping tools), 106–107
sound, recording, 218
Speed Grids, 106–107
Speed Snoots, 107
Speedlights, 25, 99–101, 105
Spirit of Place, 89
Spot metering, 76
stacking thumbnails, 41
Stafford, Simon, 17
stepladders, 27
Stieglitz, Alfred, 53
stools, 27
storyboard frames, 205
storytelling techniques, developing, 50–53
straps (shoulder)
RapidStrap, 20
UpStrap, 19–20
web resources, 231
stretching photos by cropping, 148–150
strobist blog, 25
studio strobes, 112–116
Sunset Boulevard, 215
Sweda, Wendell, 116–117

T

tampering with photos (editing), 169
Color Efex Pro (Nik Software), 168
cropping, 140, 142–145, 171
Crop Overlay feature (Lightroom), 141
extending photos, 148–150
extreme cropping, 146–147
ethics and, 160–162
HDR (High Dynamic Range), 160–162
noise (artifacts), Noisewear interface, 156–157
photomontages, 162–164
portrait-oriented photos, 150
sharpness, Sharpener Pro (Nik Software), 152–155

Temperature slider, white balance adjustments, 72
Tenba ProDigital Messenger Satchel, 23
Thames, George, 8
thumbnails
reviewing, 33, 39
stacking, 41
Tiffen Dfx, 182–183
Tint slider, white balance adjustments, 72
tripods, 24, 230
Tronix, Explorer XT powerpacks, 116
TTL (Through the Lens) metering patterns
Center-Weighted metering, 76
Matrix metering, 75
Spot metering, 76

U

Umbra photo frames, 208
underexposure, 86–87
Unsharp Mask (Photoshop), 139–140, 152
UpStrap shoulder straps, 19–20
UV (ultraviolet) filters, 18

V

VCS (video capture for stills), 217
video, 216, 225–227
Bridge (Adobe), 39
clip limits, 218
credits (video), 222–224
D-90 (Nikon), 218–220
DV (digital video), 219
fps (frames per second), 219
HP Z800 (Hewlett Packard), 226
hybrid D-SLR, 218
pan shots, 220–221
VCS (video capture for stills), 217
zooming in/out, 221
Vignette Blur filter (Color Efex Pro), 168
Village Voice, The, 12, 60
Vista Voyager FZ10 tripods, 24
Viveza (Nik Software), 184–190

W

Watergate, 6–13
waterproof shoes, Slip-Ons (Magellan), 29
web resources
backups, 229
blogs, 236
camera bags, 231
cameras, 229
cleaning kits, 232
computers, 229
effects software, 233
flashes, 230–231
frames, 232
gloves, 231
inkjet papers, 232
inspirational websites, 234–235
lighting, 230–231
memory cards, 230
mirror angle scopes, 231
monopods, 230
online publications, 236
portable drives, 229
printers, 229
reference websites, 236
shoulder straps, 231
tripods, 230
white balance, 231
Western Digital, web resources, 229
white balance, 70–71
Daylight setting, 74
lighting, 96
RAW format, shooting in, 72–73
Temperature slider adjustments, 72
Tint slider adjustments, 72
web resources, 231
World Affairs Center, Watergate, 9
World Affairs magazine, 9

Z

zoom lenses, 17
Zoom Street Magazine, 98, 148, 151, 169
zooming in/out, video, 221